CANADA AND
THE CANADIANS

CANADA AND
THE CANADIANS

by

George Woodcock

with photographs by Ingeborg Woodcock

FABER & FABER
LONDON

First published in 1970
by Faber and Faber Limited
24 Russell Square London WC1
Printed in Great Britain
by Ebenezer Baylis & Son Ltd
The Trinity Press, Worcester, and London
All rights reserved

ISBN: 0 571 08267 X

To the memory of my Father
who never came back

CONTENTS

ILLUSTRATIONS

Plates

*Except when specified in the captions, all the photographs have been taken by
Ingeborg Woodcock.*

Maps

PREFACE

This is a book on Canada. It is also, like all books on one's own land, a personal testament. Canada is the place where I was born. It was also the enormous myth of my English childhood. My father had gone there in 1907 from the Shropshire town that was his birthplace. He had worked as a hired man on ranches and homesteads, ploughing the matted, immemorial skin of vegetation that clothed the virgin prairie, watching the great migrations of birds towards the Arctic, hearing the melancholy singing of the coyotes, knowing the dusty heat and the cold that sealed a man's skin to metal. A faded photograph shows him, youthful and sunburnt as I never knew him, in a long-legged, wasp-striped bathing suit, standing in the shallows of some distant water, with the dark line of an immeasurable forest on the shore behind him. A few months after I was born in Winnipeg, he and my mother, who had joined him via Boston and the frantic house of Amy Lowell, returned to England; the extremes of climate had broken his health, and he went back to face a dozen years of failure until death.

But for a dull life in a Thameside town, as small as that in which he had been born, he compensated with nostalgic elegies on his young manhood in the West. He described the scenes of that fluid frontier with a practised evocativeness—the farm days in Manitoba, the great pink-bellied hawks settling at evening over the prairie, the sweet shadows of cottonwoods in the coulées, Saturday night in the weekend towns, fishing camps on the pristine shores of Lake Winnipeg, Cobalt in the silver boom, and the great winter fires of the cities when burnt-out buildings became palaces of ice. Among such scenes their necessary characters came and went. Lefty Louis and Zip the Blood—refugees from Chicago—fought to the death with the Canadian police from a Winnipeg streetcar abandoned by its panic-stricken passengers; Charlie Chaplin toured the one-elevator hamlets along the CPR with Fred Karno's troupe; Victor McLaglen, then a young bruiser, set off with my father on a prospecting trip that brought no pay dirt; Blackfoot and Crees sauntered on the wooden sidewalks; Chinese in blue gowns and pigtails scurried along Portage Avenue with bundles of washing; strange Russian sectarians came in winter to shovel snow from the streets and were given, when the religious fit struck them, to stripping in public.

Always, like a mirage above the Shropshire and Chiltern landscapes in which my childhood passed, there floated this memory country which my parents' talk constructed, until the land I had left when I was less than a year old seemed to have become a part of my own memory, its scenes imagined vividly and imprinted on my mind with an accuracy which I found astonishing when I later travelled over the actual soil of the Canadian prairies. As a boy I asserted my Canadianness, and this was from no desire to shine above my companions, since in the English schools which I endured colonials were regarded as a lesser breed, slightly above Frogs and Dagos. It was rather from an identification with my father's nostalgia, from a blind, intuitive understanding of his ambitions and his failure.

There are always tempting simplicities to explain one's life, and I have often wondered how far mine was shaped to give a different ending to my father's. He was a musician and a scholar *manqué*; the desire and the will to succeed as a writer and a scholar have largely dominated my own life. It was he who longed to return and resume his life in Canada; it is I who have done it. When I was ten years old, we made plans for that return. We would go to the Peace River, far over the prairies, where the great white mountains would lie on the horizon; build ourselves a house of poplar logs and walk in autumn through our fields of wheat billowing in the wind; make beehives to catch the sweet honey of the prairie flowers and grow melons in cold frames according to the pamphlets distributed by the Canadian immigration agent who one day in the twenties appeared with a van full of propaganda in the square of our little town.

My father died. The Depression closed down over my youth, and the immigration agent did not return. The War filled my young manhood, but through the years when return was impossible I retained as my own my father's memories. At last, late in my thirties, I returned to Canada. I went beyond the prairies, beyond even the Peace River, and settled far to the west, in the remotenesses of Vancouver Island, within hearing of the Pacific tides.

For twenty years Canada has been my home. I have, indeed, spent long periods away, in Asia and South America, in Europe and the United States, but these absent times, rich as they have been in experience and pleasure, have encouraged rather than diminishing my sense of identity with Canada. By nature I am averse to nationalism in any political shape, yet I feel a swell of emotion, coasting in by plane over the great muddy fan of the Fraser estuary from Japan, with the mountains rimming the horizons, or sailing slowly up the St. Lawrence with the aurora borealis pulsating over the starboard sky and the first small settlements of Gaspé glittering to port. I feel a sense of liberating space under the vast skies of the prairies and the Barren Land such as I have felt elsewhere only on the high plateau of Mexico. I know of no city, among the hundreds I have passed through or lived in over the map of the world, that I would sooner make my place of constant return than Vancouver, which has been my home for sixteen out of my twenty years in Canada; its combination of sea, mountain and pearly light still seems to me inimitable. I have found, even intellectually and politically, more freedom, more space to move my mind, in Canada than in most of the other places I have known.

The local patriotism with which I write will be evident. I am glad to be a birthright Canadian; I also find pleasure in being an adoptive British Columbian. I believe intensely that small local loyalties are the necessary complement to global loyalty, and I think that in the next stage of world history we shall see the *patrias chicas* rising into prominence in the twilight of the great states which are already the dying gods of our present era. But I hope and believe that my attachment to the particular *patria chica* in which I am writing these words, on a day when the burning leaves of the vine maple are beginning to fall and the geese are crying southward over the mountains sugared with first snow, will not lessen the objectivity with which I shall write of Canada or of this south-western corner of it in which I live.

Nineteen years ago, on our first winter in the country, my wife and I undertook an exploratory journey along the Pacific seacoast as far as the southern heel of Alaska, and then over the Rockies and through the ranges and valleys between the Great Divide and the ocean. We looked with the sharp, observant eyes of first travellers; we judged with the critical view of Europeans encountering a magnificent land populated by people of many racial origins who were still collectively struggling out of a colonial era. From that experience I wrote the first of all my travel books—*Ravens and Prophets* (1952). It was a book less good than I would now like it to have been, but it expressed honestly my perceptions and reactions, and it earned me an unpopularity among many Canadians so well remembered that only last autumn, fifteen years after the publication of *Ravens and Prophets*, the *Oxford Book of Canadian History and Literature* could still record: 'The book aroused resentment among some British Columbians who felt that several of the author's observations were patronizing.' My observations were not patronizing, but they were critical, and I have lived here long enough to see the causes of most of them disappearing as Canada has moved socially and culturally into a phase of life more sophisticated, more cosmopolitan, and more conscious of its own identity.

There are only two really satisfactory ways to write about a country. One may see it as a stranger, travelling quickly, and recording the fresh impressions of the innocent eye; this at its best can produce a sharp-edged, luminous view such as no native can achieve because his impressions will always, in one way or another, be misted by emotion and blurred by familiarity. Or one can live in a country for a long period, several years at least, so that one has formed habitual associations, lived into the society, immersed oneself in the land. Then one's view will inevitably be different from that of the traveller with his predatory eye. Many things that strike the stranger because they are like nothing in his own life, lose their exotic curiosity when one stays among them, and become merged into the background of customary existence. But there are other features of a country's life which the stranger would never perceive, or whose working he could never understand, and these become evident and comprehensible when one has lived in a country day in and day out, repeated beyond counting. Innocence has been replaced by experience, and experience sees through different eyes.

Only twice in recent years have I looked at parts of Canada with the innocent eye: last year, when I first saw the pastoral world of Prince Edward Island, the most humanized and cultivated province of all Canada, and this summer when I went for the first time to that last frontier, half as big as Europe and empty of people, of the Canadian

North—Hudson's Bay, the Barren Land of Keewatin, the environs of Great Slave Lake and the wide valleys of the Yukon.

Canada outside these remotenesses I cannot view with any other eye than that of experience. Inevitably, its life has become my life. I have enjoyed prosperity there and a modicum of success, and have known also the edge of near-starvation. I have worked, like many Canadians, with my hands as well as my brain: as labourer for builders and farmers, as carpenter's mate and master ditch-digger, as broadcaster, journalist and professor. For a year my wife and I tilled an infertile market garden, and with our hands we built two houses of Canadian wood, one on a clifftop looking out over the Juan da Fuca Strait to the white pinnacles of the American Olympics, at a place where the eagles rested, and the seals slapped the water in echoing play, and the little red orchids grew in the shadow of the Douglas firs, a place so beautiful that we could not resist its first attraction and so lonely that we could not endure it for more than two winters. Four years in the Canadian countryside have been followed by sixteen in a western metropolis so close to the wilds that the bears come from the mountainside into the gardens of its remoter houses, and in the cherry tree outside my study window the raccoons forage when the fruit are ripe. For ten years I have edited a magazine devoted to the writing of the country, *Canadian Literature*, and many of Canada's best artists and intellectuals, and of its fameless ordinary people, are now my old friends. By hand and eye and mind I have come to know the country; whether I like them or not, its politics are mine to accept or criticize; I view the exploitation of its land with the jealous eye of one who lives there; I am involved in the fates of all its people and its peoples.

Though my immediate attachment is to British Columbia, I have travelled backwards and forwards over Canada's mountains and forests, its plains and lakes, all abundant enough for a dozen normal lands, until, though every detail of those inexpressible distances obviously is not remembered, the shapes and moods of every region are. My wife and I have crossed the country many times by rail, occasionally by air, and four times, more questingly, by road. We have travelled in all Canada's ten provinces and its two territories. We have been in every Canadian city from Victoria on Vancouver Island to St. John's in Newfoundland, and in hundreds of towns and of villages and of embryo settlements on the edge of civilization. In preparation for this book alone, between May 1967 and September 1968, we travelled approximately twenty-five thousand miles, by car and bus, by regular air services and chartered bush plane, and by sea-going ferries. Before that, between 1949 and 1967, we travelled about twice that distance in our restless wanderings over the country. Yet the land is so great that there are still places and regions that I have not seen, such as Labrador and Baffin Island and the dense mountain core of Northwestern British Columbia.

But this is not meant to be a book of exhaustive detail. It is a picture of the country where I was born and to which I have returned; it is shaped by the limitations of my experience and by idiosyncrasies which no discipline can suppress. Seventeen years ago, in the first book I wrote on Canada, I could be detached and critical; now I cannot be other than involved, but for that very reason the criticism will perhaps be even more direct.

The time at which I write has, in many Canadian eyes, a special aura that may be historic. 1967 was the centennial of Confederation, when Canada celebrated a life of evolving independence longer than that of many European countries. At this very time it seemed racked with dissension, as separatist emotion rose in Quebec to one of its periodical crescendi. Yet French and English Canadians, and the quarter of the population who belong to neither of the founding peoples, collaborated in an event which was not entirely surprising to those who had studied Canadian cultural trends over the past decade, but which displayed Canada to the world in an unexpected and totally original way: the international exhibition known as Expo '67. Even Canadians were astonished at the ease with which they had shed the familiar grey image of caution and compromise; as showmen they gained a place in the world's attention which other and perhaps more solid aspects of their country and their life could not command; for a season Canada moved on to the front page of American and Canadian newspapers and became a focus for admiring visitors from all parts of the world.

How far Expo, by bringing together existing cultural trends, may have set going a wave which swept on into the social and the political world is a subject I shall reach later in this book. But, causative or coincidental, it preceded an extraordinary shift in the appearance of Canadian politics, precipitated when the Liberal Party chose for its leader an eccentric and attractive French-Canadian intellectual, and so placed itself at the head of a movement that united the alienated young and those of all ages discontented with restrictive and puritanical outlooks. In the election that followed, in June 1968, Pierre Elliott Trudeau was swept to power by a majority not only in Ontario and Western Canada, but also among those French Canadians whose loyalty to Confederation had so shortly before seemed in the extremest doubt. Whatever its political consequences—and these may not be so revolutionary as first appearances suggested—the election of 1968 did express urges towards change and renewal which have made Canada an interesting corner of the world to live in during the past decade. The great post-war immigrations from Europe, the erosion of puritanical and Jansenist inhibitions, the re-opening of Quebec to France and the opening of Western Canada to the influences of the orient, and the inevitable and incessant play of influences—to be accepted or resisted—from the United States, have all combined to create a society which is astonishingly different from that I entered, not without consternation at its provincialism and narrowness, when I returned to Canada in 1949.

The plan of this book is simple. It sets out to portray this Canada in transformation against the background out of which it has emerged. The first part will present the land and its peoples, and show how men and the land came together, in terms of exploration and exploitation. It will introduce the institutions which were created in response to the special circumstances arising from that encounter and which, even today, largely dictate the functioning of the Canadian economy and the Canadian polis. The second part will deal with change, its roots and flowers; it will be a portrait of Canada in becoming, the land which in the eye of the world has at last replaced that vision of a country of priest-ridden *habitants*, prairie farmers and romantic frontiersmen which was never more than part of the reality. It will show the startling disparities in standards of living, not only between classes, but also between regions and races, that lies at the base of much of the present ferment. It will show how Canada, possessing so much land, has paradoxically let its spaces grow even emptier and has become one of the most urban nations in the world, with dramatic effects on the character of its society. It will demonstrate the difficulties which the geography of a land more than four thousand miles wide, compounded by differences of tradition and language, imposes on a political system borrowed from a tight little island and adapted to a federalist necessity. It will portray the upsurge which has taken place in every Canadian art and which over the past decade has been wisely fostered by successive Canadian governments. And it will show Canada looking outward, across the oceans and the southern border to the rest of the world, and across the northern woodlands to its own last frontier, the North which, in comparison with Russia's Arctic and sub-Arctic regions, has hardly been developed. At the end Canadian Everyman will take the stage—the portrait of a generation.

In writing such a book I have inevitably incurred debts of gratitude which extend over all the years of my experience of Canada. The individuals, all over Canada, who have given time and information and often hospitality during those two decades of learning to know the country are too innumerable to mention, but I offer them my gratitude in the hope that they will regard the enlightenment they have brought me sufficient reward. Specifically, to the Canada Council which partly subsidized my travels in 1968, and to the Hudson's Bay Company which most generously provided transport to the Hudson's Bay and the Barren Land; to my publishers who saw that I should not want on my travels in 1967; to the Canadian Broadcasting Corporation which many times over the years enabled me to gather information by commissioning talks and documentaries; and to the University of British Columbia, which has graciously accepted long absences from the editorial chair of *Canadian Literature*; to all these I express my deepest thanks. I express my gratitude also to Mrs. Catherine Easto, who has collaborated so patiently and understandingly in preparing the final typescript of this, as of so many of my other books. I express it above all to my wife, who has shared the endurance and enjoyment of those long wanderings, has driven many thousands of miles of Canadian roads and with her camera has provided the necessary visual accompaniment to this narrative.

PART ONE

The Shaping of the Land

Chapter I

THE PRODIGAL LAND

~~~~~~

I

Canada is one of the largest and one of the least populated countries of the world. Only Russia excels it in size; yet few countries outside the classic desert lands contain such a proportion of uninhabitable or uncultivable or generally unprofitable land. Voltaire's jibe about 'a few acres of snow' may have been an imaginative exaggeration, yet it is surprising to those who think of Canada as a land of natural riches to realize that less than 8 per cent of its area is at present used for farming, that only one man in thirteen works on the land and that even when all the potentially usable soil has been occupied, it will still be no more than 12 per cent of the total area. 88 per cent of Canada is economically useless for any purpose other than growing trees or providing minerals. When one compares this situation with that of a country like Denmark, where 75 per cent of the land is under cultivation, it makes Canada seem a poor land, but only because in one country the land is used intensively and in the other it is used extensively.

For even in this context Canada is a prodigal land. It is, after all, a country of 3,850,000 square miles, and the 8 per cent now occupied by farms amounts to approximately 270,000 square miles, or rather more than the total combined areas of France, Belgium, Holland, Luxembourg, Switzerland and Denmark. Everything in Canada is gigantic, every natural feature magnified on a prodigious scale. Across the open prairies from the foothills of the Rockies to the edge of the forest east of Winnipeg one travels a thousand miles. In the opposite direction, from the end of the prairies west of Calgary to the seacoast at Vancouver, lie seven hundred miles of mountain ranges and valleys. As for the forests of Canada, they are so immense that no single man can possibly have seen them all; the latest figures, based on copious aerial surveys, place their extent at approximately 1,700,000 square miles, more than the combined area of India, Pakistan and Nepal. Canada is also the world's most watery land. Its lakes and rivers extend over more than 290,000 square miles, half the fresh water of the world and just a little less than the combined area of Norway and Sweden. There are, in addition, tens of thousands of square miles of dusty and infertile semi-desert growing cactus and sagebrush in the south-western prairies and the interior of British Columbia, and to crown all, beyond the tree line in the North-west Territories, a million square miles of tundra and of far northern land under the perpetual captivity of ice.

The size and emptiness of the land are two facts that are ever present in Canadian minds. Men are few and the solitudes are vast; Canadian life is lived mainly in a long strip of land four thousand miles long and rarely more than three hundred miles deep, where all the larger towns are situated, and all industries and most farming are carried on; to the south of that narrow strip is the world's most culturally aggressive nation, and to the north the forests and the cold barrens press downward from the pole.

Even to say that the 22,000,000 people of Canada, spread over their 3,850,000 square miles, make a population density of less than six per square mile, does not give a true idea of the country's emptiness, since they are by no means spread over the country in an even ratio. During the century since the first Canadian census in 1871, the population pattern has shifted radically, so that the country which a hundred years ago was dominated by a rural population has become urban-oriented. In 1871 four Canadians out of five were countrymen, directly or in-directly dependent on agriculture. Today only one Canadian in three lives a rural existence. Outside the sheltering confines of the towns, there are less than two Canadians to every square mile of open country. In many regions the land is even less populated than it was a hundred years ago, and travelling over the modern roads through the great forests of Ontario, New Brunswick and British Columbia, one can go many miles without seeing a sign of habitation or a human being other than the motorists who share the road. A hundred years ago Sir William Butler called it 'The Great Lone Land', and a great lone land most of it remains. As for the North, the million and a half square miles above the 60th parallel are populated by about 50,000 people, including Eskimos, Indians and resident whites. This vast emptiness, with all its undeveloped resources, may hold the promise of Canada's future, and of that there will be more to say. But for the present it is enough to note that the theme of human communities and beings defending themselves against a great solitude is with justification a recurrent and almost obsessive one among Canadian novelists and poets, and represents a feeling of vulnerability that has settled deep into the Canadian psyche. There are, of course, other aspects to such an environment. Every time I return from Asia or Europe I feel a liberation within boundless space that is exhilarating, and I believe that the unobtrusive cultivation of concrete freedoms (as distinct from abstract liberties) which characterizes the Canadian is partly a response to his environment, as, undoubtedly, is the nomadic rootlessness which characterizes so many Canadians in youth. But even the exhilaration that comes out of Canada's vastness has its complementary opposite, when exaltation has given way to a sense of oppression by so much space, and finally to an overbearing boredom that makes one long to reach the next dusty little prairie town. Ennui, like loneliness, is another Canadian theme and another Canadian reality, and if such recent phenomena as Expo and Trudeaumania have shown the capacity for exaltation among Canadians, there have been whole periods, like the era of Mackenzie King, when their capacity for accepting a dull existence has been extraordinary.

Canada, I have implied, possesses a psychological identity which surpasses its cultural divisions between English and French, and between the founding races and the European late-comers who are often rather slightingly described as 'the ethnic groups'. They share the battle against the land and its loneliness; they share the mental fight against another common peril. The war of 1812 between Britain and the United States, which plays a small part in histories written outside the North American continent, still has an intense symbolic significance for Canadians; it was the point when their land first began to stir in embryonic self-awareness. From 1812 until the days of Theodore Roosevelt the fear of American military invasion was never absent from Canadian minds; that fear has been replaced in our day by fear of American economic and cultural domination. But if history has made the United States the dearest enemy of Canadians, geography has made it also Canada's closest associate, and has produced a present-day relationship that oscillates between guarded friendliness and muted hostility. Canadians make up for their physical weakness by assuming an air of moral superiority towards Americans, not unlike that which Scots assume towards English.

The special relationship between Canada and the United States emphasizes the fact that, even if one can isolate a political identity for Canada and the makings of a psychological and cultural identity for Canadians, geographically the country has no natural *raison d'être*. Its motto, *A mari usque ad mare*, can be translated as 'from ocean even unto ocean', and it is true that the Atlantic and the Pacific provide natural eastern and western boundaries, as, to the north, do Davis Strait and the Arctic Ocean. But though there are fragments of natural boundary to the south, particularly along the Great Lakes, the long frontier that follows the 49th parallel from Lake Superior across the prairies and mountains to the Pacific has no justification except in politics and history. Geographically the only region that is peculiarly Canadian is that vast and ancient battlefield of glaciers known—because of its shape on the map—as the Pre-Cambrian Shield, whose combination of rock outcrops, low forests, marshland, and tundra, reminiscent of Finland, stretches over all of Ontario except the fertile alluvial regions close to the Lakes and the St. Lawrence, and swings upward on the western shore of Hudson's Bay to include the northern forests of Manitoba and Saskatchewan and the treeless barren lands as far west as Great Slave Lake and as far north as the Arctic Ocean. The Shield was once rich in fur and still is rich in minerals and pulpwood, but no country could feed itself on such infertile terrain, and the lands that give Canada life are those she shares with the United States. The Rocky Mountains and their sister ranges run from north-west to north-east, ultimately linking the cordilleras of Alaska and Mexico; the Appalachian plateaus and lowlands which form the Canadian maritime provinces of Nova Scotia, New Brunswick, Newfoundland and Prince Edward Island continue into New England and beyond, while the great central plains of North America flow downward from the Mackenzie valley into the Canadian prairies and the American middlewest, with no natural barrier of any kind to divide them.

A frontier based on nature would have placed the American states of Maine in the east and Washington and Oregon in the west within Canada's territory, while the boundary line across the prairies would most appropriately have followed the line of the Missouri and thence leapt over the mountains to the Columbia. The 49th parallel was a compromise boundary reached in negotiations dominated by acquisitiveness in Washington and a desire in Westminster for North American peace at almost any price. The Canadians have always felt themselves betrayed by the various territorial agreements reached during the nineteenth century between Britain and the United States, and on grounds of history and geography alike they were justified.

Yet the southern boundary of Canada, agreed by politicians and laid out by surveyors, but ignored by the buffalo herds and the wild Indian bands until the former had been destroyed and the latter starved into tameness, has stood solid in spite of its unnaturalness, and in spite of the pressures of midwestern American politicians with a lust for land and Fenian warriors with a chronic hatred for anything remotely British. It was sustained by tenuous lines of communication whose binding force still seems a historical miracle. When Confederation took place in 1867, Canada petered out in trackless forest and muskeg to the north of Lake Superior, and no regular communication existed to the isolated settlements of the Red River. Even when the region between the Red River and the Rockies had been transferred from the Hudson's Bay Company in 1870, it was a great, almost empty plain—populated only by wandering Indians and métis hunters—that Canada received. If a distant anchor had not been made secure with the accession of the crown colony of British Columbia in 1871, Canada would never have had a West.

One of the conditions for the entry of British Columbia into Confederation was the building of the Canadian Pacific Railway. The railway was not completed until 1885, after great engineering difficulties, and equally great political storms in which the British Columbians were several times on the brink of secession. But once it was established, the immigrants began to flood into the prairies; the surveyors laid out their chessboard patterns, and square by square the land was taken up, with the network of railways spreading between. The work of unification which canals had performed in the smaller Canada of the early nineteenth century was continued here by the iron tracks, and by the end of the century Canada as a transcontinental nation was at last a reality; its boundary, so absurd geographically, developed a political rationale. Since emigration southward was in those days an easy path taken by many people, it was clear that those who remained in Canada had elected to accept the combination of a harsher climate and a British political tradition.

There is a temptation to simplify the history of Canada by finding explanations in terms of trading patterns; a whole school of native historians has studied Canada's record as a series of economic empires, dominated by fur, wheat, minerals, etc. Undoubtedly those historians of staples have their share of the truth; when fur, and the timber of eastern Canada, and the clipper ships of Nova Scotia, had ceased to be important items of export, the opening of the prairies and the development of British Columbia provided primary industries whose products —wheat and gold and base metals, lumber and fish—tided over the years until Canada began to develop its own industries and to gain a measure of self-sufficiency in production.

For this economic success, Canada has paid a curious price. Its standard of living now fluctuates between the second and the third highest in the world, lower always than that of the United States, and sometimes, but not always, higher than that of Sweden. Compared with the peoples of southern Asia, the most depressed Canadian paupers are men of riches. But such a standard has been achieved only by accepting enormous amounts of foreign capital to develop mines, oilfields and factories. Two-thirds of the large industrial and mining corporations operating in Canada are now under foreign (mainly American) control, and there are many—not only among the extreme Canadian nationalists—who regard this as a sign that Canada has thrown off in vain its colonial dependence upon Britain.

I shall be discussing later the implications of this situation in terms of Canada as it has developed during the 1960s, but, serious as it may be, it does not detract from Canada's political and psychological separateness, or from the curious unity that over the past century has survived strains at least as great as those which in recent years have been created by the separatist movement in Quebec; one has only to remember the extreme nationalism that swept Quebec after the execution of Louis Riel in 1886, or the bitterness between French and English over the conscription issue in both world wars, to look with some wonder at a land so vast, so unpopulous, so divided, that has lived to be older than united Italy or united Germany.

Perhaps it is the very looseness of its links that has enabled Canada to remain whole, and, as recently as 1949, to round off its completeness by drawing into its federal pattern the island country of Newfoundland whose people for generations had sung with gusto:

> *Men, hurrah, for our own native isle, Newfoundland,*
> *Not a stranger shall hold one inch of her strand;*
> *Her face turns to Britain, her back to the Gulf.*
> *Come near at your peril, Canadian Wolf.*

Newfoundland has stayed with Canada. So has Quebec—at least up to the present—and so has British Columbia, though one of its leading politicians declared as recently as 1967: 'This province is capable of growing more rapidly, separate from Canada, than as part of it; we are not dependent on the rest of Canada for our well-being.' All these independent-minded regions have remained in Canada because the burdens of unity in a federal system are less frightening than the other possibilities that might face them: absorption as new states into the American colossus, or division into a group of relatively small and vulnerable independent countries, most of which would sink rapidly into the economic and political condition of South American republics.

II

This brings us back to the map of Canada, and geography interpreted in political terms. That map is divided into a dozen sections, some minute and some enormous, and each of these sections is a political entity, one of the ten provinces and two territories that comprise the federation known as Canada. The smallest province, Prince Edward Island, is 2,184 square miles in extent, just a little larger than the county of Norfolk. But into the 594,860 square miles of Quebec, one could cram all the countries of the European Common Market and still have room for Britain. West of Quebec the smallest province, Manitoba, is still somewhat larger than France, and India could be absorbed into the vastness of the Northwest Territories with room to spare.

The provinces of Canada can best be defined as semi-autonomous commonwealths. They do not possess the degree of independence which Swiss cantons have in theory and which American states have in practice, but they enjoy a far greater degree of self-government than French provinces or English counties. Each of them has its own miniature parliamentary system with a Premier, a Cabinet, a Legislative Assembly, and, in Quebec's case, an upper house, called the Legislative Council, while the Queen, by virtue of her title as Queen of Canada, has direct representation in each provincial capital through a Lieutenant-Governor. Under the British North America Act of 1867, which still serves Canada as a Constitution, the provincial governments have wide powers over matters of local concern, including the profitable mineral and forest rights and other natural resources, while the federal government in Ottawa deals with matters of national and international importance. During the last twenty years the influence of the provincial governments has increased considerably, and the annual conference at which local Premiers meet each other and the federal Prime Minister, and bargain over spheres of power, has become an unconstitutional but important element in the structure of Canadian politics. The tendency of the Ottawa politicians is towards centralism, that of the provincial politicians towards an ever more decentralized federalism, and the balance and tension between centripetal and centrifugal political forces have always been vital elements in Canada's growth as a nation.

One has only to glance at the map and learn a little history to realize that, far from being fragments of a uniform country, inhabited by people who look and behave alike, the Canadian provinces are regions with their own physical identities, their own needs, their own ways of life, regions which culturally and economically are widely different. Their inhabitants are all, indeed, Canadians, but perhaps the best definition of a Canadian is a North American who does not owe allegiance to the United States or Mexico. Francophone and Anglophone Canadians nowhere look or behave alike. English-speaking Canadians may seem a uniform breed when one meets them abroad, but at home the Newfoundlander is extremely conscious of his difference from the Nova Scotian Bluenose, the Albertan sets great store by the characteristic expansiveness of his prairie way of life, and the British Columbian will accord to nobody who lives east of the Great Divide of the Rockies the special grace of being a Westerner. These differences between provinces and their peoples are the more striking because most of the provincial boundaries are creations not of nature, but of legislators and of surveyors obsessed with the quadrilateral patterns that mark out American plains and cities.

The only provinces with completely natural boundaries are the islands of Newfoundland and Prince Edward Island and the peninsula of Nova Scotia. The rest show in their shapes, as much as in their traditions, the marks of historical events and compromises. New Brunswick was carved out of old Acadia as a province for the United Empire Loyalists at the end of the American War of Independence, and it is the one part of Canada in which French and English traditions have lived together in relative harmony for almost two centuries. Quebec, despite its vast hinterland, still centres on the St. Lawrence valley which the French began to settle three and a half centuries ago, and its western boundary is the frontier which the Bourbon kings established between the settled land of the *habitants*, and the *pays d'en haut*, the forests where the *coureurs de bois* would go to meet and trade with the Indians for the furs which formed the commercial basis of New France.

The French traded and hunted in the *pays d'en haut*, but the English-speaking races settled there. South of the Great Lakes, the *pays d'en haut* was absorbed into the United States. North of the lakes, another contingent of United Empire Loyalists began to clear the forest and establish their farms; they were joined by British officers and soldiers who had served in the wars, by mutually antagonistic Orangemen and southern Irish, and by Scots, particularly from the depopulated Highlands. Their land became known as Upper Canada, to distinguish it from the Lower Canada of Quebec, and the people of these two provinces, divided by language and traditions, acted and reacted vigorously upon each other during the eighty years between the arrival of the Loyalists and the establishment of Confederation in 1867.

Both provinces contained rebels who were attracted by the republicanism of the United States, but the armed insurrections led by William Lyon Mackenzie in Upper Canada and Jean Louis Papineau in Lower Canada in 1837-8, while they revealed a widespread discontent with an undemocratic system of government, did not gain the kind of support which suggested that either French or English Canadians were disposed to welcome a breach with Britain that implied a marriage with the United States. Instead, after Lord Durham—the Radical Jack of English politics—had reported on the state of Canada, Upper and Lower Canada were brought together in a united Canada (without, of course, the Atlantic provinces, which remained separate crown colonies). In this union the differences between the two groups were accentuated and, as the English-speaking population grew larger than the French, the latter for the first time began to realize the need for a province of their own, which they could govern according to their own customs and in their own language. Out of the need to break the legislative union, combined with an equally urgent need to unite all British North America in a closer and more viable bond as a protection against the American threat, Confederation emerged. Lower Canada and Upper Canada became respectively the provinces of Quebec and Ontario. In size and population they were the largest provinces in the original Confederation of 1867, dwarfing the little colonies of New Brunswick and Nova Scotia which were their first partners, and they have retained their lead ever since; even now they send twice as many members to the Canadian House of Commons as the eight other provinces and the two territories put together. They are, also, the main industrial centre of Canada, and their two great cities, Montreal and Toronto, share the roles of business and financial capitals. It has been in their traditional rivalry that the division between the Québecois and other Canadians, a division deeper than any geographical frontier, has been most sharply maintained.

Of the second file of provinces, which entered Confederation in the 1870s, Prince Edward Island's sea-marked frontiers emphasized the withdrawn insularity of its people, a quality they have sustained to this day; the Island was brought into Confederation, like Newfoundland eighty years later, by a combination of financial and geographical circumstances; a small island commonwealth inhabited by a few thousand people who lived by farming and fishing was not economically viable in the vastnesses of North America, particularly if, as the Islanders did, its people wanted such luxuries as a railway and a regular ferry to the mainland where its produce was sold.

Before Prince Edward Island had joined Canada in 1873, Manitoba and British Columbia were already within the confederation. British Columbia was in some degree a natural region, since its western boundary was the watershed of the Rocky Mountains. Its first European settlements had been the fur-trading posts scattered through the wilderness—then called New Caledonia—in the early decades of the nineteenth century by fur traders like Simon Fraser and David Thompson. New Caledonia became part of the vast empty empire of the Hudson's Bay Company, but gained a special destiny when gold was discovered on the Fraser River in the 1850s and the miners from the exhausted diggings of California pushed northward to pan the Fraser sandbars and spread into the rich minefields of the Cariboo. As the mountain shacktown of Barkerville grew to be the next largest western city to San Francisco, and declined to a village with the waning of the rush, the lands west of the Rockies were hurriedly taken out of the Company's shaky jurisdiction. The 49th parallel, which bounded the new colony to the south, was a reminder of what had happened in the past when British rule was not firmly stated. The north shore of the Columbia down to the Pacific had been Hudson's Bay Company territory until American settlers moved in during the 1830s and the United States laid threatening claims which the British were not in 1849 willing to resist. The bargain they made in the face of American demands for the whole

1. Ancient Man. Prehistoric Indian petroglyphs at Sproat Lake, Vancouver Island.

2. Arts out of Time. Indian sculptures and modern hoarding paintings at the Provincial Museum, Victoria.

Pacific coast up to Alaska lost Canada the rich lands of Oregon and Washington. When American miners came northward in 1858, the threat of a repetition of the Oregon Boundary Question was evident, and a crown colony was hastily established which generated enough sense of separateness from the American states to the south to reject the annexationists and join Canada in 1871.

If British Columbia was born in a gold rush, Manitoba, which lies in the very heart of modern Canada, was bred of a rebellion. By the 1860s Upper Canada had already become a land-hungry region, where the younger sons of the original settlers developed a longing for new frontiers to exploit. In 1869, the Hudson's Bay Company sold to the new Dominion the vast region known as Rupert's Land, which stretched from the rocky woodlands above Lake Superior as far north as the Arctic Ocean, and as far west as the Rockies. The Upper Canadians regarded this as their special preserve, and in particular they eyed with anticipatory greed the rich prairie lands beside the Red River. But here there lived already a mixed population of Scottish settlers, whose ancestors had been planted there by Lord Selkirk in 1812, and of métis, descended from Cree Indian women and French Canadian voyageurs employed by the fur traders. The métis considered themselves a separate people, blending the civilization of their French ancestors with the prairie skills and aboriginal land rights of their Indian forebears. They possessed a quasi-military organization which governed their annual buffalo hunts, and when it became evident that the Northwest had been sold to Canada without any provision for defending the land rights of its existing inhabitants, they were the one group on the Red River with sufficient discipline to organize resistance, under the leadership of one of the great Canadian folk heroes or folk villains (according to one's place in the racial-political spectrum), Louis Riel. Riel established a provisional government, and, though he was branded a rebel and chased from the country with a price on his head, he gained an ironic victory by forcing the Dominion government to turn the Red River into a minute province with a degree of self-government equal to that of Ontario and Quebec; it was called Manitoba—the land of the Indian Great Spirit, Manitou. Its boundaries were drawn in a perfect square, and this geometrical pattern was continued when it was later expanded to reach the 60th parallel and Hudson's Bay. As the plains beyond Manitoba were settled, and communities took shape on the remote prairies, the last lands south of the 60th parallel in 1905 were divided

3

by the surveyor's straight lines, running at right angles to the American border, into the eighth and ninth Canadian provinces, Saskatchewan and Alberta. Thus, except for the tiny original nucleus of Manitoba, the prairie provinces were arbitrary divisions created in the early twentieth century to bring manageable administration into the vast plains of the Northwest. They were inhabited by a mixture of peoples quite different from those of the original provinces, for in the 1890s the promise of free land brought in men and women, not only from Britain and the United States, but from every poor and persecuted land of Europe, with the result that in the prairies both of the founding peoples of Canada now are outnumbered by the late-coming peoples of the Slav and Germanic worlds.

Yet, though they were settled at the same time, marked out in the same arbitrary manner, and inhabited by the same mixture of peoples, the three prairie provinces have come to differ profoundly in their styles of life. It is partly a matter of economic differences. In Manitoba, Winnipeg, which was the first metropolis of the west, formed a nucleus attracting industry and business which the other provinces did not until much later possess. The Canadian Shield cut deeply into the north-eastern corner of the province, providing the great lakes of Winnipeg, Manitoba and Winnipegosis, the rich mines at Flin Flon, Lynn Lake and Thompson, and even the one seaport of central Canada, Churchill on Hudson's Bay, where for three months of the year the ships from Europe come in to load with prairie wheat. Alberta to the west was saved from the perils of a wheat economy by cattle ranches in the foot-hills of the Rockies, tourism in the high mountains, and, in the last twenty years, by the opening and exploitation of great oil and natural gas fields. Saskatchewan was for many years cursed by its subjection to the hazards of world markets, to short seasons and long droughts like those which in the 1930s sent the farmers' fields blowing away, season after season, in clouds of dust. Even in the Depression, it was the poorest of the prairie provinces, and only in the last decade, with advanced irrigation and the discovery of small oilfields and of extensive potash beds, has it begun to move towards greater security. Even social and political styles differ profoundly in the three prairie provinces.

The stereotype of the Albertan is a loud, large, breezy man, who wears a broad-brimmed Stetson, drives his oil-bought Cadillac as if it were a quarter horse, and combines hard business with a hot line in the Gospels: the stereotype is surprisingly often true to life, and it goes with a local form of free-enterprise populism which, in all the world, Alberta shares only with its neighbour, British Columbia. Both provinces are ruled by Social Credit governments, though the fulfilment of Major Douglas's monetary utopia is still—even for western Canada —in the remote and nebulous future.

About the Saskatchewanian there is nothing flamboyant. His stereotype is a man tied to the geometrical monotony of his farm; a man in cap and dungarees, with leathered face and sober manner, driving his crimson tractors and combines across the solitude of his great unhedged fields and watching anxiously the caprices of a climate that may bring him money in the bank and a winter in Florida, or a season of indebtedness and anxiety. Such an existence produces its own radicalism; the farmers of Saskatchewan turned to the left, and provided the driving force in the formation of the Commonwealth Co-operative Federation, which for many years ruled the province as the only socialist government to hold power north of Mexican territory.

The Manitoban is another type again; there is an even chance that he will be a city dweller, from the multi-racial and multi-lingual jungle of Winnipeg, and that he will combine political conventionality with a good deal of intellectual independence. The local politics of Manitoba have been, until the recent and surprising electoral victory of the left-of-centre New Democratic Party, the most conservative of the west, but its cultural life is the most vigorous to be found in the prairies.

So, within Canada's artificial boundaries, one encounters a spectrum of life-styles as variant as the land itself; Canada is a world of little commonwealths in more than political terms. But what I have been saying about them is a matter of maps and history. It does not convey the actual feeling of living in Canada, the look and the sensations of that earth on which, scattered over their immense distances, Canadians live.

Chapter II

FROM SEA EVEN UNTO SEA

I

To know what it means to a dweller in any country, the character of the land must be experienced, by direct travel if possible, and by vicarious travel if not. For this reason, the most convenient framework for transmitting something of the world in which Canadians live is to adopt the framework of the journey. The obvious route for such an imaginary journey is that of the Trans-Canada Highway, which was finally completed in 1962 and for the first time linked the country by road, with a beginning at Victoria on Vancouver Island in the far west, and an ending at St. John's, Newfoundland, in the far east, a total distance of 4,361 miles. It is a journey I have taken twice, and parts of it I have covered many times, so that I describe from nature.

Road travel in Canada is very much a seasonal activity. The blizzards of the Rockies and of the shores of Lake Superior are notoriously severe and unpredictable, and it is mainly trucks and buses that brave the sub-zero weather to traverse the country in winter. And, apart from perils and discomforts, winter is no good time to get the real sense of Canada's variety, for the monotonies of the country are infinitely increased by the uniform carpet of snow that drifts in great smooth dunes over the plains and the Barren Land, turns the stumps of the forests into grotesque mushrooms and the trees into white ghosts, and in the mountains builds strange architectures of jade and silver ice. The only refuge from this long tyranny of snow is the Pacific coast, where the Japanese Current preserves great rain forests all winter long in damp and steaming greenness.

So we must imagine the traveller starting on his exploratory journey in May, when the prairies are liberated from winter and migration is in

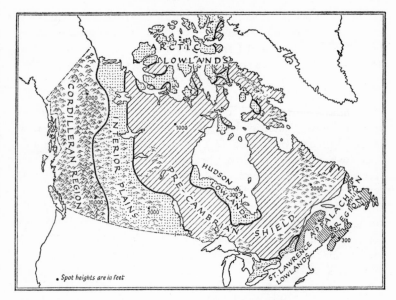

1. Physiographic regions of Canada

the air. The great flocks of geese and swans have passed over on their way to the Arctic, and the bluebirds and American robins have flown up from the south into Canadian gardens. In the north the caribou are beginning to move out of the northern forests as the snow softens on the Barren Land beyond the tree line, and in the valleys of British Columbia shimmering green humming birds are coming to hover on the red-flowered shrubs and trees of early summer. In keeping with the spirit of the season, young Canadians—always a nomad generation— are beginning their hitch-hiking pilgrimages from city to city and job to job.

II

The road and the journey begin at Victoria. Victoria is the capital of British Columbia, though not its principal city, and Vancouver Island, on which it lies, is part of the long line of half-submerged mountains, ending in the Queen Charlotte Islands to the north, which shield the mainland of British Columbia from the storms and surfs of the Pacific Ocean. Vancouver Island consists mainly of a hilly core, rising to mountainous plateaus, and peaks more than 7,000 feet high, with a few small fertile plains on its sheltered south-eastern side where Victoria lies, the mildest corner of Canada. From a Hudson's Bay port of the 1840s Victoria grew to a remote colonial capital in the 1860s, and then to a centre of exiled English manners in a developing Canada. The influence of the Victorian age is still evident in its public buildings and in the houses of its wealthier quarters; along its coastline of little rocky capes and coves, tufted with woods of oak and arbutus, are the most beautiful gardens of Canada, lush, brilliant and nostalgically English, with roses blooming in November and daffodils in February. Prairie farmers rich enough to escape from their bitter winters are inclined to retire there, and so are the Old India Hands and Old China Hands who find alarming the prospect of returning to a diminished England. But the remittance men, wastrel sons of good English families, who once set the tone of Victoria's social life, are now a dying race, and Victoria has become much less English in tone and much less a city of the aged than it was even twenty years ago. Like all Canadian cities, it has gained from the post-war migration, has become more cosmopolitan, and its new University shelters some of the best scholars who have found their way in recent years to Canada from other parts of the Commonwealth.

From Victoria the Trans-Canada Highway runs northward up the eastern shore of Vancouver Island, leaping in a high corniche over the Malahat mountain, from which one sees panoramically the slopes of giant fir and cedar plunging to miniature fjords, and the silvery expanse of the Gulf of Georgia bounded by the blue horizon of the distant mainland. Between are scattered the Gulf Islands, sunny domains of rocks, woodland and driftwood-piled beaches, once inhabited by eccentric exiles, but now part of the resort area through which the people of Vancouver range at weekends in their pleasure boats. All through the islands, when the salmon run, the fishing boats float in great white shoals.

The car ferry at the little coal-mining and logging town of Nanaimo links the end of the highway on the island with the mainland section of the Trans-Canada Highway, which begins at the village of Horseshoe Bay, where Howe Sound and Burrard Inlet, the southernmost of the fjords of British Columbia, come together. Northward up Howe Sound, outline fading beyond outline into softer blues, rear the tusked peaks and knife-edged ridges of the mountain wilderness of Garibaldi Park; beyond them stretch the wilderness and the North. Eastward along Burrard Inlet lies the most beautifully sited of Canada's three metropolises. On the northern shore the wooded mountains come down almost to the water's edge, and every year the suburban streets of West Vancouver climb higher up the slopes; by now they have reached the 1,100-foot level. On the peaks are hotels and chalets and skiing grounds. The inlet tightens and the road leaps the narrows at the entrance to Vancouver Harbour by the Lion's Gate Bridge, a suspended structure of airy steel below which the tallest ships make their way to the wharves and grain elevators of the city and the oil refineries higher up the Inlet. The bridge comes to earth in Stanley Park, a peninsula of woodland and lakes and gardens, seven miles in perimeter, which the fathers of Vancouver set aside from the greed of the speculator at the city's founding eighty years ago. It was, in words unusually enlightened for the North American 1880s, dedicated to people of 'all creeds and colours'; British Columbians of that day were proud that among them were former slaves who had found freedom there in the years of the American Civil War.

Until recently, Vancouver shamed its setting. A low, ragged roof-line of nondescript buildings characterized its main streets; there were no public buildings of architectural distinction; and, while the wealthier districts had some reasonable houses and better gardens, the western Canadian passion for every man to own his own house by grace of mortgage (70 per cent do in Vancouver) had led to an undisciplined urban sprawl as Vancouver filled the low range of hills between Burrard Inlet and the Fraser delta, and then burst outward to invade with its suburbs the rich farmlands of the Fraser valley. Only Stanley Park and the woodlands around the University on Point Grey remained inviolate from this invasion, though the geography of the area was such that no inhabitant was very far from mountains or salt water, and Vancouverites made full use of their long beaches, of the sheltered waters which in summer are always gay with white and coloured sails, and of the looming peaks and ridges. During the past decade the centre of Vancouver has at last begun to grow upward, and the shores of its harbour and of the West End, a thickly populated isthmus which joins Stanley Park to the city centre, have grown a forest of high-rise apartments and office blocks; from the water these present a splendid vista, the white buildings against their background of blue mountains varying subtly in tone as the atmosphere shifts constantly from sharp-edged brilliance to golden mistiness to sombre greyness. Around the feet of the skyscrapers the good and the bad of old Vancouver remain. Some of the few remaining wooden mansions from the 1880s are still splendid pieces of Victorian colonial architecture, but the brick and concrete age between then and now has left many monstrosities, and the East End of Vancouver has its slums and near-slums. In the skid-row of the old Gastown waterfront there are more heroin-addicts, drug-peddlers and police spies per acre than anywhere else in the western world; here the Indian girls slip hopelessly into prostitution, and derelict drunkards die unnoticed on the sheetless dollar beds of cheap hotels. But others among the older and poorer areas of Vancouver have a less morbid interest, such as the Chinatown around Pender Street, the largest community of its kind in Canada, the Japanese community on Powell Street, and the East End area where Italian cinemas, shops and restaurants cater for a population of Calabrians and Sicilians to whom even the least affluent quarter of a Canadian city seems, by comparison, a paradise.

Vancouver is of course neither a paradise nor, as Eastern Canadians are often prone to assume, a lotus land of easy living. Western prosperity, and expansiveness, are not reared on idleness. Vancouver is the industrial and commercial centre of the whole region west of the Rockies; more than that, it is Canada's leading grain port and its main gateway to Asia, where the prairie wheat leaves for China and the cheap merchandise comes in from Japan and Hong Kong.

From Vancouver the Trans-Canada Highway follows the broad Fraser Valley, one of the richest farming areas of Canada, where in the mild, damp climate the deep meadows grow several crops of grass a year, and the dairy farms and berry gardens are often polders separated by diked and heron-guarded sloughs where the bullfrogs sing like choruses of Tibetan trumpets. Here there are prosperous white and green riverside towns, and Indian villages, each with its miniature wooden mission church, jealously guarding their exclusive native right to fish for salmon as soon as it has passed the mouth of the river. From the high, conical waste-burners of sawmills the smoke plumes drift over the murky, clay-coloured river, and one is often aware of the sharp smell of cut fir and cedar felled from the mountains which narrow in as one advances towards the head of the valley at Hope, where the tall peaks of the Cascade Mountains cast shadows that bring early twilight. Through these coastal ranges the road now penetrates, turning northward up the great canyon named after Simon Fraser who with his men perilously descended it in 1808, climbing over the sheer cliffs by the shaky, slippery ladders which the Indians had suspended from them. Later, during the 1860s, a wagon trail was hacked and blasted out of the cliffsides by the Royal Engineers to take the traffic to the Cariboo gold-fields. Even in 1950, when I first followed the road, it was still a rather frightening experience, since the highway in many places consisted merely of a platform of thick worn planks, exceedingly slippery in rain or snow, braced outward from the cliffside on wooden brackets. Now a modern highway, with tunnels and spectacular bridges, has taken its place, a symbol of the new order which came to British Columbia when the Social Credit Party gained power in 1952 and decided to make a grandiose programme of road-building its main way of appealing to the rural voters on whom it depended. British Columbia now has the finest road system in Canada, and Social Credit has enjoyed seventeen years of virtually unchallenged power.

On the cliffs overlooking the rapids and narrows through which the constricted volume of the Fraser pushes its way towards the coast, there are still rough platforms on which the Indians dry the salmon they catch in the canyon. The few villages that nestle here are mainly inhabited by railway workers, since the two main lines, Canadian Pacific and Canadian National, share with the Trans-Canada Highway this narrow corridor from the rest of Canada to the Coast. The mountains are still clothed with the dense rain forest that spreads over the coastal slopes from Alaska to Oregon. Except on the most difficult crags one sees the logging roads serpentining upwards, and the woodland is mostly second-growth; the vast old firs and cedars, fifteen feet in diameter and seeded in the days of Alfred the Great, which Vancouver and Fraser saw a century and a half ago have long been felled.

At the northern end of the canyon the landscape changes. The firs and cedars are replaced by dark jack pines scattered on slopes grey with sagebrush. It is the far side of the mountains, the dry belt of British Columbia, which continues for many miles east and north in a semi-desert where the summers are hot, cactus grows freely, and rattlesnakes are probably more common than anywhere else in Canada. It is cattle country; herds of white-faced Herefords wander over the open ranges, tended by Indian and half-breed cowboys, and the horse is still master of the landscape. Just within the dry belt, at Lytton, a half-white, half-Indian town perched on a bench high above the river, two of the great Canadian rivers come together, and the clear, malachite-green glacial waters of the Thompson push into the clay-coloured flow of the Fraser and keep their colour and purity for a few hundred yards along the eastern shore of the united river until eventually the murk and mire of the Fraser overwhelm them.

A side road goes along the Fraser, through scattered pinewoods blue in summer with wild larkspur, to Lillooet and the gold mines at Goldbridge and Bralorne. But the main road follows the Thompson, another canyon, this time through hard, arid mountains, their strata slanted and twisted by ancient convulsions and coloured purple and pink by the tints of ores. At Ashcroft the highway climbs onto open ranges of burnt grass and sagebrush, and at Cache Creek it turns east towards the great mountain ranges of the interior.

North from Cache Creek the Cariboo highway continues, and that is another and a splendid journey, overlooking the great open vistas of poplar and spruce forest in the upper Fraser valley, passing the ranch lands of Chilcotin and the old mining country of Quesnel and Barkerville, and at Prince George, the lumber and paper centre of the north, dividing into a northerly road that crosses the Rockies at Pine Pass to join the Alaska Highway among the wheatlands of the Peace River, and a westerly road running past splendid and almost unknown mountains—the Hudson Bay Range, the great Rocher du Boule—and through the Indian villages of the Skeena, where the last totem poles decay among the fretwork houses of the mission era, to the fishing port of Prince Rupert.

But our way is eastward along the Thompson, past bench farms where the white arcs of sprayers irrigate the dark green fields of alfalfa, between dry, smooth-folded hills dotted with pine, and through country towns like Kamloops and Salmon Arm. Southward run the cobalt lakes and the vast orchards and vineyards of the Okanagan, a desert valley turned into a gigantic oasis. Ahead lies the intricate maze of channels pushing into mountain valleys which forms Shuswap Lake, its beaches a necklace of bright cottages which are the summer refuges of people from Vancouver and Calgary. Here the rain forests begin again in the shade of the inland mountains, and the ranges follow in relentless succession. First the sombre Monashee, out of which one emerges to see the white aluminium roofs of Revelstoke gleaming across the southward-flowing reaches of the Columbia. Next the ancient Gothic pinnacles of the Selkirks, ten and eleven thousand feet high; it is dangerous country, where blue icefields hang in the saddles between saw-edged ridges and the Canadian army takes its howitzers every year to shake down the avalanches that threaten the highway. Out of the Selkirks one emerges again into the valley of the Columbia, this time running northward, through great marshes inhabited by beaver and muskrat, towards the Big Bend where it turns direction for Revelstoke and the south. The valley here is part of the great Rocky Mountain Trench, running for hundreds of miles north-west to south-east between the ranges, and harbouring the remnants of a pioneer sub-sistence agriculture in its log-cabined farms with old decaying orchards and pastures dotted with fire-blackened treestumps. There is a southern route to the Rocky Mountain Trench from Vancouver that goes through the lower mountains and more intimate valleys of the Kettle River and the Kootenays, which contain the most beautiful lakes of Canada (Christina and Arrow and Kootenay), harbour dissenting minorities like the Doukhobors of Krestova and the Quaker communi-tarians of Argenta, and hold within their volcanic strata a wealth of minerals which at the century's turn led to the foundation of a whole series of mining cities, some, like Rossland and Greenwood, still surviv-ing as country towns, and others, like Phoenix, rotted down to cellar holes among the encroaching forest. Still, in the smelting centre of Trail, and in a series of coal towns that mark the line of the Crow's Nest Pass into southern Alberta, mining remains one of the chief industries of this southern region.

III

Three hundred miles to the north, the Trans-Canada Highway con-tinues on its way high over the Kicking Horse Pass, where the Canadian Pacific ascends through spiral tunnels cut in the faces of solid cubist mountains which, if the Selkirks remind one of Gothic cathedrals, call to mind the worn blockish outlines of Egyptian step pyramids. At the Great Divide, where the waters begin to run towards the Arctic Ocean instead of the Pacific, British Columbia ends, but the forest continues into the foothills beyond Banff; it is a great game preserve, where, without effort, one can see wapiti and moose, mountain sheep and black bears and, a little farther on the higher slopes, the great white mountain goat which as summer continues follows the receding snow line into the highest and most inaccessible mountain pastures where the grass is starred with flowers as varied and intensely coloured as those of the Swiss alpine pastures. On Banff and the resorts around it tourists from the whole of North America converge; in one afternoon there I saw cars from sixteen American states and six Canadian provinces. They ski in winter and spring, and in summer fish in the lakes, ride the trails into the high meadows, and very occasionally indulge in a little mountaineering. But most of the best climbers are Europeans. Among Canadians, as among Americans, the pioneer virtues of initiative and endurance have long been abandoned; they are to be found now, as no doubt they always were, among the immigrants.

Beyond Banff the road begins its long run down the steady slope of the prairies that will not end until the Red River valley nine hundred miles away. First, the foothills, tufted with copses of stunted poplar and grazed by the horses of the Stony Indians; then the city of Calgary, climbing with rectangular monotony out of the valley of the Bow River on to the wide, flat prairie that runs, windy and hardly broken by a hill, 180 miles northward to Calgary's rival, the provincial capital of Edmonton. Edmonton and Calgary have both grown in a couple of decades from market towns to cities next in rank to the metropolises of Montreal, Toronto and Vancouver. In ten years of oil and cattle prosperity, each has doubled in size, but it is Edmonton that has moved farthest ahead, taking advantage of the deep and curving valley of the North Saskatchewan which introduces the third dimension into the flatness of the surrounding prairie. Visually, Calgary remains, in comparison, a raw and unsympathetic city.

A similar rivalry, farther across the prairies, exists in Saskatchewan. The highway from Edmonton joins the Trans-Canada Highway at Regina, the legislative capital of Saskatchewan, and on the way it goes through Saskatoon, the academic capital. Regina, set in a dead-flat prairie, is uncouth and unformed, its centre marred by waste areas and used car lots so that one feels its original name of Pile o'Bones might have been changed more appropriately to Pile o'Junk than to the queenly epithet of Regina. Its modern architecture is so unimaginative that its most distinguished architecture is still the Scottish baronial pastiche of the Hotel Saskatchewan. Saskatoon, on the other hand, while aspiring to no great modernity, has nevertheless, like Edmonton, taken advantage of a wide river, this time the South Saskatchewan, and incorporated the restrained Gothic of its academic and public buildings into a green and attractive pattern of parks and parkways centring on a fluid spine.

The differing characters of these cities, and of lesser towns like Lethbridge, Medicine Hat and Moose Jaw, is only one manifestation of a physical variety in the prairies which the stranger rarely expects. The billiard-table plains of legend are in fact the exception; such flatnesses do exist, mainly to the north and south of the stretch of highway between Moose Jaw and Winnipeg, in the south-eastern quarter of Saskatchewan and the south-western quarter of Manitoba. Elsewhere, and particularly near the Rockies, the prairie undulates in long super-Atlantic swells; the depressions contain lakes and sloughs, peopled with ducks or white-scurfed with alkali deposits.

The most appealing part of the prairies is the region between Medicine Hat and Moose Jaw, where the undulations develop into ranges of little hills, covered with sagebrush and olive-green grasses, with shadowy folds like groins where dark low bushes grow, and many emerald ponds. This is the famous infertile Palliser Triangle where wheat cannot be grown successfully. The farms are difficult, all slopes and dips, with weather-worn, unpainted clapboard houses, small herds of beef cattle, and fields of oats which are stooked in the old-fashioned way because the farmers here cannot afford modern reapers.

Because it has not been worth cultivating extensively, this land among the little hills is nearer than any other to the wild prairie the first white travellers saw. The buffalo have gone, their fifteen thousand survivors confined in game preserves, but every time I have travelled the Trans-Canada Highway east of Medicine Hat I have seen small herds of pronghorn antelope grazing in the folds of the hills, or standing alert on the skyline.

The home of the antelope is the strange region known as the Cypress Hills, a kind of plateau oasis lying between the Trans-Canada Highway and the American frontier and spanning the border between Alberta and Saskatchewan. From time immemorial the Cypress Hills have been a refuge for men and animals. Rising to a height of 4,800 feet, they were surrounded by the glaciers of the ice age without being submerged, and today they combine a fauna and flora belonging to the Rockies three hundred miles away with species native to the hot dry desert lands of Arizona and New Mexico, such as scorpions and hog-nosed vipers, kangaroo rats and the odd, dumpy lizards known as horned toads. Woodland mingles with meadows on their slopes, and here one finds that millefiori carpeting of flowers which must have characterized the great buffalo pastures before they were disciplined into wheatlands. Standing for five minutes among the tall grasshopper-ringing grass on a day in September I saw close around me a variety of intensely hued species which included wild gaillardias, blue flax, sunflowers, carmine wild pinks, yellow sweet clover, dwarf amethyst blue asters, and various purple and carmine labiates. The last buffalo of the plains took refuge in the Cypress Hills and so did Sitting Bull and his Sioux braves when they were hunted down in revenge for the defeat of Custer at the battle of Little Big Horn, and Gabriel Dumont and other leaders of the Northwest Rebellion after the defeat of Louis Riel in 1885. Today the Cypress Hills are being tidied up into a park where holiday-makers can satisfy their nostalgia for a vanished pioneer past, and their haunting wildness is quickly being tamed.

Where the prairie is flat and fertile, its monotony of appearance is intensified by the regular pattern of the roads which run at right angles to each other, forming squares within which the fields are lesser squares as regular as a chess table. The pattern is repeated in the typical farmyard, squared off by the windbreaks of willow and poplar surrounding the house and buildings, thickest to the north-west where protection is needed against snowdrifts as well as wind. Yet even this flat land, seen in detail, is not without its peculiar beauty. Spring, just after the thaw, is the deadest time, when the ploughed soil is sodden and the stubble left as summer fallow is grey from submergence under the snow. But then comes the green of the springing wheat, and afterwards the golden seas of grain in high summer under the vast skies in which sudden storms may appear, with clouds sweeping low like veils over the country. In the autumn, when ploughing has taken place, there is the striking pattern of black soil and golden stubble alternating in long, wide strips, and on undulating land, where contour ploughing is necessary, curved patterns of an extraordinary beauty are created which, like much of the prairies, are best seen from a low-flying aeroplane. Even in winter there are touches of colour, for then, on the endless carpet of the snow, the orange-yellow branches of the willows acquire a luminous intensity of tone; so do the crimson barns and farm buildings which seem—as indeed they are intended—to be beacons of colour in the white desert which the land has become. The prairie also resembles the desert in its mirages, so that often one seems to be driving into great lakes on which the distant cars float like snub-nosed boats, and the settlements stand like Venetian islands in the sea, with grain elevators in the place of campaniles.

The wheatlands are crisscrossed not only with roads but also with branch railways linking up with the two main lines that go from east to west, and at intervals of roughly five miles there are hamlets with names that set incongruous associations working in one's mind— Balzac and Granada—or have their own evocativeness, like Seven Persons and Manyberries, like Indian Head, and, most haunting of all, Qu'Appelle. Most of them are tiny places with a church, an abandoned wooden schoolhouse, a few houses sheltered by willows, and perhaps two hundred inhabitants, counting in the outlying farmsteads. But every twenty miles or so there will be a larger settlement. One turns off the main road into a single dusty street going down to the railway tracks; there are a couple of stores with jumbled windows, a weather-beaten brick hotel, a restaurant run by a lonely Chinese, a barber's shop with a faded pole and ornate Edwardian chairs, and a decayed and forbidding building near the railway depot announcing on a faded card 'Rooms for Single Men'. If by some chance the street is populated by a shambling retired farmer too poor to make it to the Coast, or by a lounging and sardonic Indian, he will certainly ignore your presence, though there will be faces at windows, and a notice at the entrance to the town saying 'Welcome, 5 m.p.h.' and another at the exit saying, equally inexplicably, 'Come again.' But all these places, whether small or large, will have their towering grain elevators, painted white or brilliant red or orange, and few types of building are more satisfying in their tall and functional massiveness, or more welcome when, rising like cubist fingers in the distance, they record the completion of another segment of the long prairie journey.

Even the flattest prairie is saved from complete monotony by the action of its streams and rivers, which over the millennia have cut deep channels into its smooth surface. These valleys, or coulées, are usually far wider than the existing streams seem to justify; their sloping sides are folded into mounds and gulleys which give shelter to small copses of poplar, and on each side of the shallow river, which runs around sandbanks and between wide borders of gravel, there are long and shady groves. The coulées are the haunts of birds and of the few deer which have survived the massacre of the larger animals that once were so numerous on the prairies.

Age is acquired quickly in Canada; west of Quebec a building a hundred and fifty years old is rare and one a century old is likely to be guarded jealously by the local organizations which are the Canadian equivalent of the Society for the Preservation of Ancient Buildings. As

I write, indeed, an agitation is being raised in Vancouver to preserve the 'historic' buildings that survive in the city's original waterfront, none of which is more than seventy-five years old. It is this kind of time spectrum that gives an air of positive antiquity to the towns one approaches as the Trans-Canada Highway nears the flat centre of Manitoba. The Red River Settlement which Lord Selkirk founded in 1812 was the first organized attempt at forming an agrarian society west of Upper Canada; by the late 1860s, when the new Dominion of Canada began to negotiate for the acquisition of Rupert's Land, villages had been well established along the river both north and south of the Hudson's Bay Company's prairie headquarters of Fort Garry, and forty miles west on the prairie, where the buffalo hunters used to camp, settlers from Ontario had already founded Portage la Prairie, which for a brief interlude during the troubled 1860s declared itself a republic separate even from Louis Riel's insurrectionary commune. The political fires of a century ago have burnt low in Manitoba, and Portage la Prairie, and Winnipeg even more, have shed that restless, temporary feeling which still characterizes Calgary and Regina and Edmonton despite their great modern buildings. Main Street, Winnipeg, is no longer the muddy highway with wooden sidewalks which my parents remembered; the city has long been a place of spreading railway yards, of the bleak, massive building that houses the Canadian headquarters of the Hudson's Bay Company, of great mail-order houses which serve the scattered farmhouses of the prairies, and in recent years it has begun to rival the large eastern cities and Vancouver as a centre of light industry. But it has been slow to change its low prairie skyline, and only now, at the windy corner of Portage Avenue and Main Street, are the first Winnipeg skyscrapers rising up to create even taller landmarks for the traveller than the grain elevators.

IV

Winnipeg is almost the far edge of the prairies. Less than an hour's drive eastward the landscape is already changing, scrubby copses appearing among the grassland, and then dank marshes dotted with stunted moss-covered spruce, the most dismal of all Canadian woodlands, until finally the humpbacked rock outcrops begin to emerge and one is at last entering the great wilderness of the Shield.

Like that of the prairies, the unique character of the Shield can best

3. The old Chinese quarter at Duncan, Vancouver Island.

4. The great trees. Loggers felling a Douglas fir born with Magna Carta, Vancouver Island.
(BRITISH COLUMBIA GOVERNMENT TRAVEL BUREAU)

5. Fur trade fortress. The surviving bastion of the Hudson's Bay Company's Fort at Nanaimo, Vancouver Island. (BRITISH COLUMBIA GOVERNMENT TRAVEL BUREAU)

be appreciated from the air, since the ancient mountains that once dominated this vast region have been worn down to such a flatness by time and ice, that one rarely reaches an elevation high enough to get a good view of the landscape or to appreciate the extraordinary loneliness of the land. Along the road one passes a succession of low ridges and bits of woodland, of dank marshes so deep that whole locomotives vanished into them when the railway was being built here ninety years ago, and of multitudinous lakes, from mere ponds to freshwater seas. But this is a linear view, episodes strung along the road on which the trees close in the vistas; from the air one sees the pattern, the coloured rocks lapped by sickly green bogs, the thin pelt of woodland, and the lakes scattered like the pieces of mirror on a Rajasthani garment. In one area of six thousand miles in northern Ontario no less than three thousand lakes have been counted; many of them are unnamed and most unvisited, though they are all well populated with fish and wildfowl. Communities are few and scattered, and means of communication in these hundreds of thousands of square miles of agriculturally barren land are scanty. A hundred years ago the voyageurs travelled this way to the west by following the rivers and lakes and carrying their light birchbark canoes over portages where the waterways failed. In the 1880s the engineers of the Canadian Pacific Railway had finally made their difficult way through the tortuous terrain near Lake Superior, and twenty years later the Canadian Northern—later the Canadian National —followed a different way, through Cobalt and the mining settlements to the north. Until less than a decade ago the only road communication between Ontario and western Canada was an interminable dirt road which followed this northern route, but finally in 1962 the Trans-Canada Highway was completed through the most attractive regions of the Shield, skirting the many-armed Lake of the Woods and the cliffs and beaches of Lake Superior.

In summer Lake Superior often reminds one of the Mediterranean, but in winter it is gripped hard in ice, and at all seasons it is subject to the extremities of weather, from the blinding blizzards which often persist into April to the violent thunderstorms that in July and August shake the humid air over Port Arthur and Fort William. These towns, the largest along the Canadian shores of Lake Superior, owe their existence to the great water transport system of which the lake is the centre. Fort William was originally the depot from which the Northwesters, fur-trading rivals of the Hudson's Bay Company, would send their brigades

4

of canoes towards the prairies and the mountains. Today, like its neighbouring city of Port Arthur, it is a great inland port; through the St.
Lawrence Seaway freighters from Europe can now sail into the very
heart of the North American continent, and at Fort William and Port
Arthur they load prairie grain from the massive batteries of the cylind-
rical concrete elevators which stand like groups of gigantic organ pipes
along the lakeshore. Sault Ste. Marie, to the south-east, where the
Highway leaves the Lake to follow the northern shore of Lake Huron,
owes its existence originally to the canal and the locks by which ships
are raised from one lake to the other; now it is the westernmost of
Ontario's important manufacturing towns.

Along the shores of Lake Huron, Canadian art came of age, for it was
here, in Georgian Bay and in the Algoma region, that the Group of
Seven abstracted the twisted forms of the Shield's landscapes, the
peculiar atmospheric conditions of this land of lakes and roads, and the
vivid autumn colours of the eastern forests, and transformed them into
paintings that were nothing else than Canadian. This is mining country
that has been exploited since the early nineteenth century, but most of
the veins along the lakeshore have long been worked out, and the communities that arose when the mines were prospering have declined into
somnolent villages with the air as well as the look of poverty. It is one
of those regions of abandoned marginal farms, and collapsing houses
among ruined orchards, that one encounters so often in Canada, regions
where inexperienced pioneers exhausted the land, and a new generation
was disinclined to work for the mere subsistence that had contented
their fathers.

It is not until one reaches the hell of Sudbury that one realizes with
very mixed feelings what wealth of minerals lies hidden beneath the
surface of the Shield. From the beginning of the present century the rich
veins of nickel ore at Sudbury have been mined steadily and their end is
still not in sight. It is not the mining, but the smelting of the ore that
has given Sudbury its special and Satanic appearance, for the fumes
killed off trees, bushes and even grass for many miles around the town,
and only now, with the pollution of the air somewhat controlled, are
a few hardy plants beginning to spring out of the ruined soil. There are
places around Sudbury which still look as though they had been burnt
up by an atomic blast, so total and lasting is the devastation. Of its
effect, physical and mental, on the hundred thousand people who populate this man-made desert, no study has yet been made.

At Sudbury one is almost at the edge of the Shield. Both the easterly road into Ottawa and the southerly road to Toronto lead one through a country that grows steadily more cultivated and more inhabited. To Toronto one goes through pastoral and orchard country, where the white farmhouses are prosperous, the cattle fat in the deep grass, and the small towns have all the solidity of Victorian brickwork.

Toronto is the epitome of the North American metropolis in its Canadian form. Montreal is bigger but also more cosmopolitan. In Toronto one encounters a peculiar combination of Scottish, English and American elements which affect not only the appearance of the town but also its life and its very atmosphere. Not many years ago Toronto was more British in sentiment even than Victoria, largely through the now diminished influence of the Orange Order and of White Anglo-Saxon Protestantism in general. That age has passed. The cultural links between Toronto and New York have strengthened, so that in many ways it is now the most 'American' of all Canadian cities. At the same time, post-World War II immigration has completely changed its view of Europe; an eighth of its people are now Italian by race.

Toronto is the most hated city in Canada. Its rivalry with Montreal is traditional, and Montrealers resent the fact that the balance of prosperity has shifted to the slightly smaller city; Bay Street, Toronto, is indisputably the financial capital of Canada. Business men in the Prairies, in Vancouver, in the Maritimes, bring the same accusations of attempted centralism against Toronto as are brought in by local politicians against Ottawa, and radicals see the city in the image which Stephen Leacock satirically presented when he portrayed the Torontonian élite in *Arcadian Adventures of the Idle Rich*, the other face of 'Toronto the Good'. The Augustan smugness of Toronto's academics arouses resentment in lesser Canadian universities, which often have better scholars, and the smart theatrical, artistic and literary journalists maintain an exasperating air of condescension toward other centres which are not lacking in genuine cultural life. The feeling between Vancouver and Toronto in this field is particularly sharp.

It is true that Toronto offers opportunities which attract many people of talent; it almost monopolizes the English-language publishing industry, and is the main centre of radio and television production. Much of its financial power comes from the fact that, apart from controlling through its Stock Exchange most of the mining investments in Canada's north, it lies in the heart of Canada's great industrial belt which runs along Lakes Erie and Ontario and down the St. Lawrence as far as Quebec, and includes such important centres as the automobile town of Windsor and the great steel complex of Hamilton.

If Toronto were another Paris, or even another London, one might forgive its size and power. But it is, physically, an unattractive city; its centre was built fifty years ago in an unimaginative era of non-architecture, and has been little improved; its admirable lakefront has been wasted by bad planning; its sprawling suburbs lack the lush charm of Vancouver's, and, apart from a few Olympian districts of gardened mansions and some fashionable shopping streets where Victorian brick has been tastefully restored, there is little that attracts the eye, outside the Royal Ontario Museum, which houses one of the world's noblest collections of ancient Chinese artifacts. It is a city wholly dependent for its attraction on the life that its inhabitants inject into it, and here at least Toronto has become much more vivacious during the past decade, rather like one of those ugly girls who find themselves suddenly drifted off the shelf of neglect by the oddities of modern fashion.

The immediate attractiveness that Toronto (which was once called Hogtown) can never have possessed is evident in many of the small towns through which one passes as the road follows the shore of Lake Ontario to the east. This is the long-established farming country of Upper Canada, with white windmills that have lost their sails, old barns with massive stone foundations, and brick and wood houses in harmonious Georgian proportions which were built by the Loyalists and the early German settlers. Some of these places, like Fort Hope, remind one of Kentish towns, while Brockville, with its dour, stone houses, might have been transferred from Scotland, and Cobourg has a more French look than many a town in Quebec. Kingston has the best architecture of all, but for setting and atmosphere the most pleasant town is Ganonoque, a little Georgian settlement which lies where Lake Ontario narrows and flows through the Thousand Islands into the St. Lawrence. Seen on a misty autumn morning, with the fishing boats sailing out of the reedbeds among the small islets that carry summer houses like scenes in formalized miniatures, the river has the peculiar melancholy idyllicism which one senses in Chinese landscape paintings. Farther on, drawing near to Montreal, the banks of the St. Lawrence are industrialized, and the towns no longer have the green and white Upper Canadian charm.

The Trans-Canada highway runs a few miles north of this lakeshore highway in order to pass through Ottawa, the federal capital, before it reaches Montreal. Government is a booming business in Canada as in other modern countries, and Ottawa is rapidly losing the flavour of a backwoods capital which once characterized it. Originally a lumbering settlement called Bytown, to which the great timber rafts floated down the Ottawa River from the north Ontario forests, it was chosen by Queen Victoria as the compromise capital that would end the rivalry on this issue between Toronto and Montreal. In this raw setting, on a cliff overlooking the great river, rose the Victorian Gothic pinnacles of the Canadian parliament buildings, which were still uncompleted when the first Confederation parliament met. For years the contrast between these august edifices and the wretched town around them was astonishing to every visitor, but it was not until the status of Canada began to change from a dominion into that of an independent nation during the 1940s that much was done to improve Ottawa. Then, a National Capital Plan was evolved, and during the past twenty years much has been done in turning the banks of the Rideau River into a park several miles long, and in furnishing the centre of the city with buildings in keeping with the capital's pretensions. Ottawa is now a pleasant city to the eye, but still needs the proximity of Toronto and Montreal to raise its life above dullness. Some of the dullness is due to the heavy weight of British tradition that still hangs over the city, symbolized in the Gothic buildings and the bearskinned and scarlet-coated Canadian Grenadiers who perform their stiffly ceremonial drills upon its close-cropped lawns. Perhaps these symbols are useful to impress upon American visitors that Canada is not a mere extension of the United States, but to many Canadians, particularly in Quebec, they seem the annoying vestiges of an imperial past which has little relation to the aspirations of the modern generation of Canadians.

V

Two hours' drive down the Ottawa River lies Montreal on its island, Canada's largest city, with more French-speaking people than any city except Paris, more Jews than any other city in Canada, several hundred thousand English Canadians and a strong contingent of recently arrived Italians. It is an explosive mixture, and Montreal has always been Canada's most turbulent city, given to linguistic and political rioting, and to gang-wars which at times come near to emulating those of Chicago in its grandest days (in 1968 more than thirty people died in such criminal conflicts). But the same mixture is also immensely fertile, and Montreal is not only the most cosmopolitan Canadian city in its style of life, the only city that could have conceived and carried out Expo, but also the most exciting visually. The decaying Victorian areas at its heart are being cleared and replaced by great building complexes that not only go upward in stark, magnificent towers but also probe into the earth to make underground networks of pedestrian streets filled with shops and cafés and offering complete protection from Montreal's harsh winter climate; one can spend whole fascinating days wandering in these urban warrens.

As a port Montreal is declining with the passing of the ocean liners, and with the opening of the St. Lawrence Seaway which now takes freighters to the Great Lakes and the centre of Canada. But, as a manufacturing town, it is second only to Toronto; it is the home of great corporations like the CPR and the CNR, it is the centre of fashion for all Canada and in everything but politics it is the capital of Quebec. On the slopes of Mount Royal and in the Anglophone suburb of Westmount life is, unostentatiously, more affluent than anywhere else in Canada; but the east end of the city contains some of the worst slums of Canada, and they are mostly inhabited by French Canadians. Neither the discreet affluence nor the poverty is evident to the average visitor to Montreal, who seeks out the exotica of the city, and is likely to be found observing the Jewish life of the St. Urbain quarter, which is rapidly losing its rich East European flavour, or wandering in the little hilly streets at the base of Mount Royal in search of the bistros and clubs which are the haunt of Montreal's bohemians. If Western Canadians may almost universally hate Toronto, Montreal is foreign enough to be attractive to them, and I have noticed that those young people who leave Vancouver for excitement rather than money are inclined to go there as a substitute for going abroad, or a prelude to it. Perhaps the main reason why I would regret the secession of Quebec is that it would mean the loss of Montreal, without which Canada would be a far, far duller place.

Quebec City, the other pivot of French Canada, lies 170 miles down the St. Lawrence from Montreal. The Trans-Canada Highway between the two cities is one of those autostradas on which one avoids towns and misses everything characteristic of the country, and the wise traveller follows the ancient roads along the St. Lawrence, going one way by the southern bank and returning by the northern. New France was a country of riparian settlements; the farms were long and narrow, so that each should have a frontage on the river, and this traditional pattern is still followed, the farms stand close together, and the riverside roads have the look of loose and immensely extended villages. Every few miles the line of houses thickens and clusters around a church with shining aluminium roof, a few larger houses and a street of shops. Some of the towns, like Trois Rivières and Sorel, have been subjugated by industry, but the villages, with their iron-balconied houses, still have a look of somnolent nineteenth-century well-being. Farther inland, where younger sons went to farm a century ago when the old lands became crowded, there is no look of well-being. The fields are divided by long loose piles of stones which had to be removed by hand before the land could be cultivated, and even now the soil is poor and barren, the houses stark and forbidding, the people poorly dressed and uncouth in manner.

Quebec City is ancient in North American terms. Founded in 1608, it is older than any other city north of Mexico. Twenty years ago its antiquity was still overpoweringly impressive as one climbed from the lower town and through the old walls into an upper city that seemed inhabited by priests and nuns, tourists and fiacre drivers. All this is still there, and, in spite of the Quiet Revolution which here expresses itself overtly in long-haired young men and mini-skirted girls, the old Jansenist gloom has not entirely vanished. But much more formidable now is the industrial gloom of the ring of factories in which Quebec is encysted. Even this citadel of the past has been taken up in the stream of change that has affected all French Canada during the past decade. In places the old Quebec still survives; one gets the flavour of it by going out from Quebec City to the pilgrimage centre of Ste. Anne de Beaupré, where men and women still climb on their knees up the sacred staircase. But such scenes are vestiges rather than signs. The Quebec people who now live in the past are those in the infertile back lands and in the remote eastern regions of Gaspé, and they are kept there by poverty.

VI

From Quebec the Trans-Canada highway follows the south-east shore of the St. Lawrence to Rivière du Loup, and then turns southward over the Appalachians into New Brunswick. These hills, on whose forests the great New Brunswick timber industry of the past was based, reveal the eastern Canadian woodland in its most splendid form. The trees are small compared with the giants of British Columbia, but the woods are largely deciduous, and the autumn colouring is of an extraordinary vividness, so that whole hillsides burn with the most brilliant reds and vermilions. Before I went to New Brunswick in the autumn, I imagined the photographs I had seen exaggerated the colouring; afterwards I realized that the reverse was true, since the leaves acquired a translucency which, in the sunlight, gave a peculiar vibrancy to the colours of that incandescent landscape.

All scales are smaller in the Maritimes—the trees, the hills, the rivers, the bays and capes of the seashore, the towns and even the houses and farms. The immensities of the western mountains, of the prairies and the Shield are left behind. One is getting close to Europe—Fredericton, New Brunswick, is nearer to London than to Vancouver—and the proportions are European, as the names of the towns often are. Perth and Bristol, Woodstock and Keswick, all are beside the Saint John River as it leads the road down to Fredericton, the capital, where Cobbett soldiered and the garrison buildings he knew still stand in the main street of that transplanted English market town.

The standard and style of living also diminish with the scale of the land. There is nothing resembling western expansiveness, or Torontonian high smugness or Montreal extravagance. Incomes on the Maritime Provinces run on the average from half—in Newfoundland—to two-thirds the western level, and the lack of affluence is evident in every phase of living, from the sober, unfashionable clothing of people in Maritime towns, to the scarcity of large cars and the smallness of houses. In the low hills that pass for mountains in Nova Scotia one sees poor white families living in the kind of two-room shacks which in other parts of Canada are beginning to be considered insufficient for Indians. Farms are too small and rocky for modern equipment, and many fishermen still use primitive methods. One has the impression, often, of a region that has not merely failed to progress, but has actually retreated since the age of the clipper ships when the Maritime ports were busy with shipbuilding, and when seaborne trade combined with an active lumber industry to make Nova Scotia and New Brunswick the most prosperous of the colonies that entered Confederation in 1867. The advent of the steamship and the steady exhaustion of the forests completely changed the relationships between the Maritimes and the rest of Canada. There was not much to fall back on, once shipbuilding and timber began to fail. Except for the coal mines of Cape Breton, there was little mineral wealth; tiny Prince Edward Island, where 75 per cent of the surface is cultivated, was the only Maritime province that could live well by agriculture. Fishing consequently took on a special importance, particularly in Nova Scotia.

As a port used by ocean shipping and by the British and later the Canadian navy, Halifax belonged to a special category, and continued until very recently to look nostalgically across the Atlantic towards Britain, as did St. John's in Newfoundland; St. John's, in fact, remained the centre of opposition to union with Canada as late as the 1940s, since its merchants preferred to joining Confederation the semi-colonial association with Britain which has existed in the past. In the long run, however, though all the Atlantic provinces doubted the benefits of joining Canada, and both Prince Edward Island and Newfoundland remained aloof in 1867, the union undoubtedly turned out to be beneficial, most notably in the tax adjustments and cash subsidies which have favoured these depressed provinces and have offered industrial development to halt the steady descent into regional poverty accentuated by the exhaustion of natural resources. During the Depression, as an independent colony, Newfoundland actually went bankrupt; in 1934 it had to appeal to Britain for financial aid, and gave up its constitutional government to be ruled by a commission which was little more than a committee of receivers. When I landed on the island in 1949, just after it had joined Canada, the chronic poverty of St. John's was striking even after my experience of working in the Whitechapel Road during the 1940s; St. John's, however, was prosperous compared with the outports. A great deal has changed since 1949. Newfoundland, with increased mineral and paper production, had climbed a long way out of the pit of the thirties, though its people are still poor in comparison with Canadians in British Columbia, a theme of inequality to which I shall be returning.

Yet when one sums up the Maritimes, the verdict is by no means a negative one. It is true that people are shabbier and work longer hours and longer years than western Canadians. It is true that whole regions have died to human habitation, so that often in Nova Scotia one comes on a sign announcing a settlement where there is nothing but the same scrub woodland one has already been driving through for the past hour.

It is true that towns like St. John's and Halifax and Saint John (New Brunswick) are still in great part decrepit survivals from the high days of the clipper ships, and that formerly prosperous shipbuilding centres like St. Andrews are almost ghost towns. It is true that the railways run antique trains such as no-one has seen elsewhere in Canada for half a generation, and that the car ferry from Saint John across the Bay of Fundy to Digby, Nova Scotia, is probably the most dirty and decrepit in the country. It is true that the bitter religious factionalism which dominated the region in the past has left communities divided into a multitude of sects so that often one sees three or four churches on the hillside overlooking a village with a hundred houses.

But when all this is granted, one still must insist that the Maritimes have provided a setting which has encouraged the local differences and the personal individualities that did not flourish so well in the rest of Canada. In part this has been due to the terrain, to the fact that until recently communication by land was not easy, and people lived in small communities, most of them in the numerous sheltered bays and inlets. Some of these communities are two centuries old and more, and have preserved, and adapted to the local conditions, the ways of working and recreation, of speech and thought, which their ancestors brought from the Old World. Until very recently the people of Lunenburg observed half-magical German peasant customs, connected with farming and fishing, whose origins lay far back in the middle ages, and in many villages of Nova Scotia, Prince Edward Island and of Newfoundland, there linger accents and dialects that are extinct in the parts of Britain from which they derived. The whole region has proved a treasure house of folk song—both European songs transplanted and adapted, and, in Newfoundland, the songs of a living tradition which still comment, like Trinidadian calypso, on the ordinary and extraordinary events of the fisherman's life.

In fact, the Atlantic provinces have nurtured a peasant culture, in which occupations like logging and fishing are seasonal and usually tied to small farms which provide both food and cash. In some of the older towns, such as Fredericton and Lunenburg, there are characteristic and strongly Europeanized styles of building, and the small coastal villages, with their jetties and old warehouses, still have the atmosphere of a pre-mechanical age. Nowhere is this atmosphere so strong as in the outport villages of Newfoundland, beyond the end of the Trans-Canada Highway, where the inhabitants still live in the wooden houses built by their great-grandfathers on rocky shores, and patiently dry on wooden flakes or racks the cod which is sold in the markets of the West Indies. These are places whose very names on such a poor and fog-ridden island suggest the humour and courage that inspired their founders, for it needs as much of both to give these bleak little outposts names like Hearts Content and Hearts Desire as it does to call them by openly derisory names like Mosquito or Lushes Bight.

The individuality of the Maritime villages, and the similar character of those—mingled French and English—along the remote Gaspé coast of eastern Quebec, is a quality which cannot long continue. Like all such poor and stagnant communities, they contain few young people, and those who remain are affected by the universalizing influences of education and of the mass media, particularly television. The paved highways have reached many of the most attractive places in Nova Scotia and Prince Edward Island, and already they are being incorporated into the tourist culture, which means that while their physical appearance may be preserved more securely, the process that makes for uniformity will work more rapidly on their ways of life. As for the Newfoundland outports, the more remote of them are likely to become extinct very shortly owing to an official policy of concentrating the population in larger centres; even villages that are saved will be modernized and changed beyond recognition. All this is an inevitable process, and in terms of comfort and security it is probably desirable, but it will mean the rapid loss of regional traditions that emphasized vanishing qualities of courage and initiative.

Much the same might be said of vast areas of the country which a journey by the Trans-Canada Highway leaves out of account. These are the less inhabited parts of Canada, for apart from Edmonton and Saskatoon there are no large cities that lie away from the Highway. The métis region around Batoche in Saskatchewan, where Louis Riel fought his last rebellion in 1885 and was defeated, once had a prairie culture of its own, but now one can go there and find very little distinctive except—again—poverty. The characteristic way of life of the remote mining communities is virtually extinct; all the raw boom towns of the northern woodland, from Flin Flon in Manitoba over to Yellowknife on Great Slave Lake and Whitehorse on the Yukon River, try to reproduce life lived in the south as far as their climate will allow, and it is only a passionate intensity in the search for profit that really distinguishes them. Farther north one follows the intermittent plane routes to the settlements built on the Arctic coasts and on the inland tundra. Until little more than a decade ago, this was the home of the highly specialized culture of the Eskimos, so well adapted over the centuries to life in a frozen country that the first white men were forced to imitate them in order to survive. Now that culture is dying a rapid death, and the great spaces of the North are emptier than they have been for thousands of years, since the Eskimos, like the Newfoundlanders, are being drawn into a few scattered modern communities like Rankin Inlet, Baker Lake and Frobisher Bay.

This does not change the look of the North. The vast skies and the great sweeps of the open tundra still evoke an extraordinary feeling of a pristine world, unhumanized but, by the same token, unspoilt. In winter, like the prairies, it is a white desert, a desert where day surrenders to night, and such it continues for more than half the year. But the season of sunlight and warmth, where spring, summer and autumn pass in three months like a speeded-up film, has the same purity as summer in the high mountains, and the abundant, miniature but singularly brilliant flora of the Arctic emphasizes the resemblance.

The North is still a difficult place to reach and to live in. Transport and accommodation are scarce and expensive, and no amount of conveniences imported from the south can protect men from the mental effects of the long darkness of winter. It is therefore still a far emptier land than even the rest of Canada, though the near elimination of the great caribou herds, which indiscriminate hunting reduced from three million to less than half a million, is an example of the kind of destruction from which even a solitary and relatively inaccessible region is not, in our day, immune.

The present situation in the north in fact emphasizes the paradox which haunts any new and potentially rich land and which has haunted Canada throughout its history. To realize such a land's possibilities, to humanize it, means also, in the beginning, to violate it, though the end of the process of humanization, as the best of Europe's cultivated landscapes show, may well be a new flowering.

Chapter III

THE COMING OF THE PEOPLES

I

Man was not aboriginal to the Americas. There are no signs of human evolution there before the emergence of Homo sapiens, and he came, as all the archaeologists agree, at a late period over the land bridge where the Bering Sea now flows, continuing through Alaska and Canada into the double continent of the New World. Fifteen or twenty thousand years ago those whose descendants created the great civilizations of Mexico and Peru followed this route as primitive neolithic hunters; they must have been originally people of temperate lands, for they left the barren tundra of the North unoccupied, and it was here, perhaps five thousand years ago, that another people settled, the ancestors of the Eskimos. They too came over the land bridge or, if it was already submerged, crossed the straits in their primitive skin-covered boats; some of their race they left behind, and today a little group of 1,500 Eskimos in Soviet Russia proclaim the Siberian origin of their brethren who live scattered over Alaska, the Canadian North and Greenland.

In the descriptions of Canadian peoples favoured by politicians and academics there are some rather curious distinctions. Debate swirls around the question of federation and the status of Quebec and one hears constantly the phrases 'founding races' and 'founding peoples'. To the stranger's surprise, these are not Indians and Eskimos, but French and English. The people who laid the real foundations of human existence on the North American continent are referred to as 'native peoples'. The implications of this distinction are that the Indians and the Eskimos merely occupied the land, as the buffalo and the cariboo did. The building of a civilization and of a nation was the achievement of those who came afterwards.

Yet one only admires the ingenuity with which both Indians and Eskimos confronted their environment and devised a variety of ways of living suited to its differing conditions, which ranged from the harshness and scarcity of the barren tundra inhabited by the inland Eskimos to the temperate climate and natural abundance of the Pacific Coast. It was only by imitating the Indians and the Eskimos, by borrowing and adapting their inventions, that white men succeeded in dominating the wilderness which was Canada when they first came a thousand years ago in the long ships of the Vikings.

Of the original Indian peoples we know little. Whole peoples must have passed on through Canada in their migration towards Central and South America, leaving no visible trace. Those who remained in Canada formed at least nine linguistic groups, speaking tongues as distinct from each other as French and Hebrew. These differences are the more astonishing when one remembers that when the white men came the total Indian population of Canada was probably no more than it is today—about a quarter of a million people, scattered very thinly over the regions where hunting and fishing were the only ways of life, and somewhat more densely in areas where primitive agriculture or abundant fishing allowed settlement. Some of the languages were spoken over a great area. The Algonkian dialects and the related Siouan tongues extended from Newfoundland, home of the extinct Beothuks, across forests and prairies to the lands of the Blackfoot Confederacy in the foothills of the Rockies. The Athapaskan languages were spoken in a great sweep of northern forest country from Alaska to the southern end of Hudson's Bay. The Iroquians, on the other hand, inhabited a relatively small area along the St. Lawrence and around the eastern Great Lakes, while in British Columbia there were not only some isolated Athapaskan tribes in the northern interior, but also no less than six distinct groups of languages—Salish, Waskashan, Haida, Tsimshian, Tlingit and Kootenayan—peculiar to the Pacific region and completely unrelated to each other and to other American Indian tongues; some of which were spoken by only a few thousand people. Only one of the Canadian language groups appeared to be related to Old World tongues; the Athapaskans speak tonal dialects which may be distantly linked to early Chinese and to Tibetan. Whether the nine language groups were brought to North America, or whether they evolved during the millennia since the Indians first reached the continent, is undetermined. Isolation may have been one of the conditions affecting their

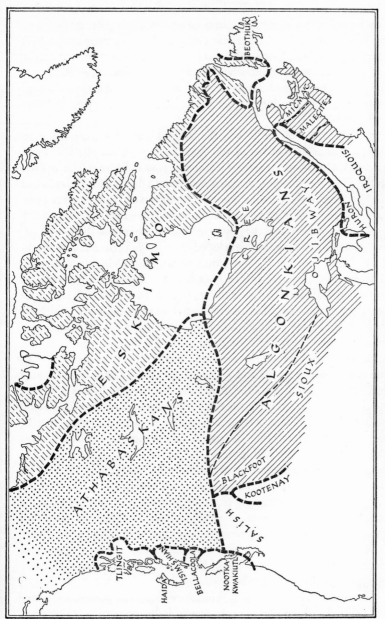

2. Native Canadian groups when Cartier came in the sixteenth century

development, but against this supposition one must pose the fact that, by war, trade and even phratric relationships, five peoples speaking mutually unrelated languages lived beside the coastal waters of British Columbia in close contact when the first white men appeared among them in the early eighteenth century, and, if they did not exchange languages, they certainly exchanged trade goods, and even art forms and ceremonials.

In their ways of life it was the Algonkians who were the most varied. The eastern tribes of this great family—Micmacs, Ojibways, Ottawas, Crees—had perfected a nomadic way of life suited for hunters in the great forest region that stretched from what is now Nova Scotia to the margins of Manitoba. For the tortuous waterways and the portages where boats must be carried they developed the light birchbark canoe; for winter travel they invented the toboggan and the snowshoe; as a portable dwelling they developed the wigwam covered with birchbark. These were the Indians who first taught travelling and hunting skills to the white men; if it had not been for their superbly functional canoes, it is doubtful whether the traders of the seventeenth and eighteenth centuries would have carried out their explorations so effectively or have established such efficient transport systems for a fur trade that eventually extended from Montreal to the Pacific.

Algonkians of the prairies developed a distinct way of life adapted to the great treeless plains and followed by many tribes over an area reaching far down into the American Southwest. It was a highly specialized life, resembling the single-crop agriculture that followed it on the prairies, in that it depended mainly on a single animal species, the North American bison, or buffalo, whose vast herds wandered over the prairies from the Red River to the Rockies, and whose migrations were followed by the Indians as faithfully as they were by the wolves. To the plains Indians the buffalo gave almost everything they needed for existence: rawhide to cover the tipis which they adapted from the eastern wigwams and to make garments; robes for warmth; sinews for thread; fresh meat and pemmican; bone and horn for a hundred uses. The magic and the ceremonial patterns of the prairie peoples were determined by the needs of the buffalo hunt; their year was divided by the movements of the herds.

Originally they followed the buffalo on foot, their possessions carried on the backs of women or on frames of lodge poles dragged by dogs. After the Spaniards conquered Mexico the horse, which they intro-

6. Sea, mountain and city. Vancouver from the air. (VANCOUVER VISITOR'S BUREAU)

7. The fishing fleet. Salmon trollers at False Creek, Vancouver.

8. The Chinese apothecary, Pender Street, Vancouver.

9. Pacific Lotus Land.

duced into the Americas, appeared in the prairies, and passed northward from tribe to tribe, reaching Canada early in the eighteenth century. Then a great change took place in the prairie culture; the mounted hunt replaced pursuit on foot, and horses became prized possessions, more valuable than wives, to be stolen and fought over. The internecine warfare of the prairies reached a more murderous level when the white men introduced firearms, with which the Indians not only slaughtered each other, but also took an enthusiastic part in the wasteful massacres which in the generation between 1850 and 1880 reduced the vast buffalo herds almost to extinction.

The prairie Indians were traditionally divided into mutually hostile groups. There were the Assiniboines, who occupied southern Manitoba and Saskatchewan, spreading over the border into the United States, the Crees who occupied the northern parts of the same provinces, and the formidable Blackfoot Confederacy, which occupied southern Alberta and extended southward across the frontier. The Sioux also raided over the border, and some of them eventually settled in Canada after the defeat of Sitting Bull's doomed war against the American army in the 1870s. As a result of the continual warfare produced by the introduction of the horse and the musket, the tribes developed political organizations, each band having its own chief, and the whole tribe meeting for several weeks once a year, when a paramount chief was chosen, and ruled with the active assistance of a council consisting of band chiefs, famous warriors and leaders of ritual fraternities. The Blackfoot Confederacy was an even more ambitious organization; its three original tribes, the Blackfoot, the Piegans and the Bloods, were linguistically related, but the tribes later adopted into the confederation, the Sarcees and the Gros Ventres, belonged to other groups. The Confederacy had positive as well as negative virtues; not only was it a military alliance against the other tribes of the plains, but it was also a guarantee of internal peace and fraternity over a considerable area. One prairie tribe unrelated to any of the others, the Kootenay, was driven over the Rockies by the Blackfoot Confederacy, and occupied the British Columbian valley which now bears its name.

When Cartier reached Canada in 1534, the people he encountered in Stadacona and Hochelaga, the villages which later became Quebec City and Montreal, were not the hunting Algonkian tribes that later occupied this region. They were people of Iroquois stock. Later, when Champlain established the first settlements on the St. Lawrence in the

5

early seventeenth century, the Iroquois peoples were divided into two groups: the Hurons, Tobaccos and Neutrals, who occupied the triangle of land between Lakes Huron, Erie and Ontario; and, now living south of the great river, the tribes more commonly called the Iroquois, who formed the League of the Five Nations (to become Six Nations in the early eighteenth century when the Tuscaroras came north from Carolina to join them). The Iroquois peoples lived a primitive agrarian life. They had no domestic animals, but they cleared the forest by burning, and in their gardens they grew a variety of foods—corn, squash, beans and sunflowers from which they pressed oil—that preserved them from the feast-and-famine cycle familiar among more primitive tribes; yet hunting and war still remained the honourable occupations of men, most of the cultivation being done by the women. The Iroquois lived in communal houses built of poles covered with bark; these were often sixty yards long and provided a dwelling for a dozen families. They had a rich ceremonial life, carved ritual masks, and developed a Manichean religion in which the universe was moved by the eternal conflict of two Great Spirits, one good, one evil.

An equally developed and even more original culture existed among the Indian tribes of the Pacific Coast. These peoples lived in the most abundant of Canadian environments and famine was virtually unknown among them. Each year the salmon came up the rivers, and were caught, and smoked or dried for the winter; the greasy oolachon fish were pressed for their oil, and the woods provided an abundance of berries and vegetable foods. The great cedar trees of the Pacific Coast could be split with antler wedges into wide, smooth planks, from which the Indians built their massive communal houses; the trunks could be worked with stone and later iron tools into elaborate sculptures representing the crests and legendary histories of the chieftains' families; from the shredded bark were woven garments to supplement the robes of sea-otter skin or mountain-goat wool worn on ceremonial occasions. Carved chests were made of cedar wood to hold the wealth which these Indians accumulated, and also great dugout canoes, some of them holding fifty men, in which they raided or traded with their neighbours, and even hunted whales with nothing more than harpoons, skill and courage.

These were the only Canadian Indians who could develop an affluent society with the surplus of goods on which an elaborate class system must be built. Politically, they were much less sophisticated than the Blackfoot and the Iroquois; their largest unit was the village, dominated by two or three powerful clan chiefs, and it was rarely that one village entered into more than a fleeting alliance with another, though occasionally a chief of commanding personality and skill in warfare might temporarily extend his influence over a considerable area, like the celebrated Maquina, who ruled at Nootka Sound when the first Europeans began to trade for furs along the Pacific Coast. The social pattern, on the other hand, was elaborate. There was nothing resembling the rough democracy which among the prairie tribes forced a chief to take account of the views of his warriors. Each great house belonged to a nobleman, and the commoners lived under his roof and his protection. Lowest of all were the slaves, captives in war; they were mere chattels, often sold, and sometimes sacrificed when a new house was consecrated or a great carved pole was raised to validate a chief's titles.

The surpluses of fish and oil, of cedar blankets and carved wooden objects which the chiefs accumulated, encouraged the development of a special kind of feast, the potlatch, where chiefs distributed presents to enhance their prestige. A nobleman could use the names and crests, the songs and dances that belonged to his lineage only after validating them with a potlatch, and the chiefs vied with each other in what to a cursory observer might pass for generosity; in fact, each gift conferred a debt, since the receiver must make an even costlier gift at his own potlatch, and the potlatches finally reached the point of extravagance at which chiefs would compete not merely in the giving but also in the destruction of goods, accompanied by speeches boasting of the donor's lavishness and the inferiority of his rivals, who happened also to be his guests. Parallel with these elaborate family feasts were the winter ceremonials of the quasi-religious secret societies. The most prestigious was the Hamatsa Society, whose members practised ritual cannibalism, eating at their initiations the flesh of corpses. An elaborate regalia of masks and illusionist devices were needed for these ceremonials, in which supernatural happenings were simulated for the edification of the credulous, and it was on these occasions that men and sometimes women (who were admitted to certain societies and could even act as chiefs among the Tsimshian) performed their personal dances.

Thus the half of the year not taken up by fishing and food-gathering was devoted to celebrations and the preparations for them, and it was out of this rich ceremonial life, with its accompanying corpus of songs and myths, that the high artistic tradition of the Coast tribes developed. They were magnificent carvers of wood and argillite (a black slate found in the Queen Charlotte Islands); their great heraldic poles—erroneously called 'totem poles'—were often works of art of a high order, and shared with the stone and bone carvings of the Eskimos the distinction of being the finest works of sculpture ever performed in Canada, by native peoples or Europeans.

The culture of the Pacific Coast Indians survives only in the world's art museums, and the way of life of the prairie Indians vanished with the buffalo; it is only among the Athapaskans who inhabited the cold northern forests far from the areas of white settlement that the traditional Indian life continued into the present century. Even they, in more recent decades, have been taken up in the slow process by which the Indian becomes dependent on the white culture of Canada without being part of it.

The destruction of the native way of life went on by an inexorable process of invasion and acculturation. At first the white men did not want the Indians' lands; they merely wanted furs, and used the Indians as hunters, in the process making them dependent on metal tools, muskets and other trade goods. The Indians not only collected furs for British traders at Hudson's Bay and French traders in the *pays d'en haut*; they also served as auxiliary soldiers when the British and the French went to war; in the process the Iroquois Confederation, who then lived mostly in New York State, destroyed the Hurons in a series of savage massacres. Ironically, the Iroquois fought on the British side in the American War of Independence, and later trekked into Canada and were given land in Ontario and Quebec, where they endeavoured to adapt themselves to the ways of the white men.

The destruction of the prairie Indian culture by the extermination of the buffalo coincided with the initiation of a paternalistic policy on the part of the newly established Dominion of Canada. By the time of Confederation, the Indians had already given up their aboriginal rights in Ontario and the Atlantic provinces, and had accepted treaties restricting them to small areas of land which made the old hunting life impossible. In the west, it was obvious, the advance of settlement would lead to demands by white farmers for access to the rich lands of the prairies. The problem of dealing with the Indians became urgent. In comparison with the Americans, the Canadians kept their hands clean of the crueller oppressions. There were no major Indian wars in Canada, and the opinion that 'the only good Indian is a dead Indian' was imported only by a few American whisky-runners and wolf-hunters who came over the border and illegally set up their forts in the Cypress Hills. In 1873 the Hills were the site of the cowardly massacre of a band of Assiniboines by a gang of Montana wolf-hunters, an incident whose very notoriety emphasizes the infrequency of such episodes on the Canadian side of the border.

The instrument of Canadian paternalism, as well as the symbolic manifestation of the British presence in the prairies, was the semimilitary force, the Northwest Mounted Police, which was founded in the same year as the Cypress Hills massacres. Dressed in their red jackets, which reminded Indians of the good old days when their fathers were subsidized by British officers to make trouble for the Americans, the Mounted Police negotiated the treaties that ensured both the physical survival of the Indians and the death of their way of life. The appearance of white settlers had aroused resentment among the Indian tribes, and the arrival of Sitting Bull and his Sioux tribesmen in 1877 aggravated the situation. But Crowfoot, the head of the Blackfoot Confederacy, realized that with the diminution of the buffalo the Indians' only alternatives were to make terms with the new Dominion, or to starve to death. Accordingly, in a series of treaties completed between 1871 and 1877, the tribes from Lake Superior to the Rockies signed over their rights to the prairies in return for small reserves of land, food rations, and agricultural training and equipment. They were also allowed to hunt over unsettled land, but this was a pointless privilege, since the game was already exhausted. Treaties were later made, some as late as the early 1920s, with the Athapaskan Indians of the northern woodlands. No treaties were ever signed in British Columbia; there, when the province entered Confederation, parcels of land—some very small indeed—were set aside as reserves, and the rest of the province was regarded as Crown property, with the result that to this day Coast Indians present periodical claims for compensation for the land which, they claim with justice, was taken from them without their consent.

The paternalistic policy of the Canadians saved the Indians from famine, and from the exploitation of the American whisky-runners, whom the Mounted Police deported with exemplary rapidity. But it did not save them from the white men's diseases, from smallpox, measles and tuberculosis, which made such ravages that by the end of the nineteenth century barely a hundred thousand Indians survived, and the lament for 'the vanishing Indian' seemed all too tragically justified. Those who survived sank into apathy in the isolation of their reserves, irremediably cut off from their stone-age pasts, but slow to adapt to the life of twentieth-century white men. Canada's first inhabitants, they became wards of the state without rights of their own. Today their situation has changed somewhat. They have won their battle against disease, have more than doubled in numbers, and are now increasing more rapidly than any other group in Canada except the Eskimos. A few have achieved prosperity as fishermen on the Pacific coast or, among the Iroquois of Caughnawaga Reserve, as workers on the high steel frames of skyscrapers. But, though they are all now Canadian citizens, most of them are, in every sense but the political, second-class citizens, their standards of living and education both far below the general Canadian level.

II

The racial affiliations of the Eskimos are not easy to determine; they are obviously a Mongoloid people and they do not resemble any tribe of Indians in either North or South America, though they do resemble quite closely certain groups of Tibetan nomads, and this fact, combined with the similarity of their Shamanism to the primitive Bon religion of Tibet, suggests that they started their long pilgrimage, thousands of years ago, from somewhere in the heart of Central Asia. Because the North has never been disturbed by agriculture, and because of the imperishable materials which Eskimos so often used, it is possible to conjecture their prehistoric life with more accuracy than that of most Indian groups. A proto-Eskimo culture of about 1000 B.C.—the Dorset culture—appears to have lasted for two thousand years. The later Thule culture developed at the time of the Icelandic penetration into Arctic waters about A.D. 1000; it has left many interesting bone carvings, as well as the remains of houses built of whalebone, and, in general, evidence of a highly developed Arctic culture from which that of the present Eskimos probably derived. Some archaeologists have attributed the sudden technological upsurge at the beginning of the Thule culture to the influence of the Icelanders, but they have established no more than an interesting possibility.

The modern Eskimos are divided into several dialect groups, and formed two regional groups divided by their ways of life; the inland Eskimos of Keewatin depended almost entirely on the caribou and on fish caught in the lakes and rivers, and the rest of the Eskimos on marine mammals and sea fish. Otherwise, their customs and practices did not differ greatly. They lived in skin tents in the summer and igloos made of snow-blocks in the winter; they used the dog as a domestic animal to draw their one form of land transport, the sleigh; they had two types of skin boat, the kayak for hunting caribou at river crossings and marine mammals, and the umiak, which was used by families for travelling with their possessions. Their well-tailored and often highly embroidered skin clothing, their ingenious tools and weapons of stone and bone, and later of metal, all witnessed to a considerable technical ingenuity, while their carvings, in stone and bone, and their haunting oral poetry were the products of a fertile imagination kept in a state of perpetual activity by the starkness of the land, which imposed so many tests on the men who inhabited it. The Eskimos lived a very simple social life and developed no politics at all. They had no clans, bands or tribes, and, indeed, no collective organization other than the extended family. A few families might gather casually at certain seasons when their hunting brought them together, but the need to be constantly on the move in search of food made their existence inevitably nomadic, so that people never stayed together in large groups long enough to create elaborate social or political patterns. It was a hard but a surprisingly joyful existence. Girl babies might be killed and old people left to die, but the ordinary relationships between Eskimos were peaceful and good-natured, the women were held in much higher regard than among the Indians, and, where possible, the children were indulged. Theft, war and sexual jealousy were virtually unknown. The virtues of the Eskimo may at times have been exaggerated, yet in his traditional setting, which has now vanished, he faced utopians and social reformers with a curious paradox: that the nearest approximation to collective human goodness existed in one of the most appalling environments that man has elected to inhabit.

After the connections with the Icelanders nearly a thousand years ago, the contacts between Eskimos and Europeans were sporadic until the beginning of the present century. Martin Frobisher received an Eskimo arrow in his rump at Frobisher Bay in 1576; Franklin made contact with the northern people, and during the series of expeditions which went in search of him in the 1860s most Eskimos of the central

Arctic must have seen white men. In the more open waters on the eastern and western sides of the Arctic Archipelago, the whalers were in somewhat demoralizing contact with the Eskimos throughout the mid-nineteenth century, until their trade came to an end. Not until the early twentieth century did the missionaries and the Mounted Police begin to show the Bible and the flag in Eskimo country, and, surprisingly enough, the Hudson's Bay Company showed little interest in this region until the first posts were opened in the Arctic at about the same period, when fur supplies in the northern forests were beginning to diminish. Even these contacts were limited to a few white men, and the mass acculturation of the Eskimos did not really begin until the Second World War, when thousands of Canadians and Americans came into the North as soldiers, airmen, meteorologists and construction workers and many Eskimos were taken into their employment.

Like the Indians, the Eskimos were decimated by white men's diseases, particularly tuberculosis, while famine grew to be more of a danger with the spread of modern weapons. During the early 1950s, it seemed as though extinction faced the inland Eskimos. Many of the caribou-hunters starved to death in the Barren Land, and a census in 1950 estimated the number of Eskimos in Canada at less than four thousand. Since, today, less than twenty years afterwards, there are more than thirteen thousand Eskimos in the North, the 1950 figure was obviously inaccurate; the Eskimos are now increasing rapidly, but not rapidly enough to more than triple their numbers in eighteen years. The Eskimo, like the Indians before him, has now been taken under the paternal wing of the Canadian government and has saved his life by losing his traditional culture. To that development I shall return.

III

It is customary in Canada to contrast the national attitude towards minorities with that of the United States, and against the American concept of the 'melting pot' is put the Canadian concept of the 'mosaic'. Like most neat-looking distinctions, it is only partially true. There are ethnic groups which for various reasons have sustained a high degree of separateness within Canadian society; the French Canadians of Quebec, for example, and religious sects like the Russian Doukhobors. Other groups have become more or less absorbed into English-speaking society. The cases of Pierre Elliott Trudeau and John Diefenbaker typify the two extremes. Trudeau remains French in culture and everyone is aware of it; the fact that Diefenbaker was the first Canadian prime minister of German ancestry is rarely remembered. In Canada, then, the mosaic and the melting pot exist side by side.

The Indians and the Eskimos belong to the mosaic rather than the melting pot. During the present century racial prejudice on the part of other Canadians, and later their own racial pride, have tended to keep them apart. In earlier days, however, there was considerable mingling between native peoples and Europeans. The fur traders and their Scottish and French Canadian employees would enter into temporary common law marriages according to 'the custom of the country' with Indian women, and out of such connections grew the halfbreed 'nation' —as they called themselves—of the métis, who were left, as the dominion of the fur traders came to an end, as a separate group, rather like the cholos of Peru, intermarrying with neither whites nor Indians, and forming their own little society first on the Red River and later on the Saskatchewan. Many of the métis have since been absorbed into the cities and live as other Canadians do, but in Saskatchewan there are still about eighty thousand of them, ill educated, impoverished and lacking even the minute privileges which most Indians enjoy by virtue of their treaty status.

On the Pacific coast, during the later nineteenth century, there was a great deal of interbreeding between the women of the local tribes and transient white men—miners, fishermen and whalers—while the whalers in the North took advantage of the permissive mores of the Eskimos. The children of these unions usually remained with the mother's band and were brought up as Indians or Eskimos, so that, in some remote Indian village at the head of a British Columbian inlet, one occasionally encounters a tall man with fair hair and blue eyes who counts as an Indian, or somewhere around the Beaufort Sea one meets a red-haired Eskimo. In such areas the completely pure-blooded Indian or Eskimo must now be very rare. In all, even counting those who are still regarded as métis, the identifiable native peoples number little more than 300,000, or about one Canadian in seventy-five. How much they have contributed in hidden strains to the Canadian nation it is difficult to estimate; Wyndham Lewis believed that almost every French Canadian had Indian blood in his viens, but, though the early French settlers regarded religion as more important than race and were less discriminatory than their descendants, it is unlikely that enough converted seventeenth-century Indians were absorbed into the society of New France to leave such a universal mark on the people of Quebec.

IV

Did other Europeans before the French leave a lasting heritage among the Canadian people? Despite the agonized protests of Italo-Americans, history and archaeology have now established that the Icelanders appeared in Canadian waters and on Canadian land a good five centuries before Columbus. Blown off course on his way from Iceland to Greenland in A.D. 986, Bjarni Herjolfsson was the first European to sight the North American coast, and about 1000 Leif Ericsson voyaged to regions which he called Helluland, Markland and Vinland, creating at the last point a short-lived colony. It has been established that Helluland was Baffin Island and Markland was Labrador, while the recent discovery by Helge Ingstad of the remains of Viking houses at L'Anse au Meadow in Newfoundland leaves little doubt of the locality of Vinland. It is now proved beyond any reasonable doubt that the Vikings were the first Europeans to create a settlement on Canadian soil, and some historians, like Tryggvi Oleson, have suggested that they made their contribution to the Canadian mosaic by interbreeding with the Thule people on Baffin Island and so making a racial as well as a technological contribution to the culture of the Eskimos.

In the centuries that followed, the Viking settlements on the western shores of Greenland declined; their people either died or were absorbed into the native population. But the knowledge of the lands beyond the ocean persisted in Scandinavia and elsewhere in Europe, and recent investigations which have been upsetting many Victorian notions about the links between the Old and the New Worlds suggest that at least as great a part in exploring the approaches to Canada was played by humble and forgotten Breton, Basque and Portuguese fishermen as by famous explorers like Cabot and Cartier. It is now by no means certain that Cabot was the first western European mariner to reach Newfoundland, and even if he was, by 1506 the Portuguese had already established a commercial fishery on the Grand Banks where in those days, as early voyagers remarked, one had only to lower a bucket over the side of the ship to draw in the cod, so numerous they were. Even if Cabot did not have his predecessors in these waters, Cartier certainly did. Breton fishermen went before him into the Strait of Belle Isle and the Gulf of the St. Lawrence, and when he set sail on his historic voyage in 1534 his crew was largely made up of such men. Yet it was certainly Cartier who first sailed into the St. Lawrence itself, landing on the shore of Gaspé to plant a great cross, bearing a shield decorated with fleurs-de-lis, and afterwards continuing up 'the river of Canada' to Stadacona and Hochelaga. He did not find the passage to China he was seeking, and the glittering stones he took home merely added to the French vocabulary a new name for things that are not what they seem—'diamants du Canada'.

These first approaches resulted in no settlement, but soon the Basques set up at Tadoussac, where the Saguenay enters the St. Lawrence, a base from which they could fish, hunt whale and trade with the Indians for fur. The wealth of furs that flowed into Tadoussac stirred in the minds of French speculators and of the French king's advisers the desirability of laying effective claim to the new land by permanent settlements, and in 1598 the Marquis de la Roche established a colony on the somewhat inappropriate Isle des Sables, a desolate Atlantic island about a hundred miles east of Nova Scotia. It was a pointless enterprise; five years later the eleven survivors of the original fifty settlers were evacuated to France. The first French settlement that has any claims to permanence was established in 1605 by the Sieur de Monts at Port Royal on the Annapolis Basin in Acadia—the present Nova Scotia. Later, thirty-two French farming families, experienced in the construction of dikes, established their polders on the shores of the Bay of Fundy. With brief interruptions, the colony continued until Acadia was ceded to Britain in 1713; then the Acadian French numbered about 1,600. They prospered for a generation and in 1755, when they were expelled from Nova Scotia, they numbered approximately twelve thousand. Some retreated into the woods of Western Acadia (later New Brunswick) or to Prince Edward Island, and later on others returned to these regions; the continuity of settlement was preserved, so that the Acadian community in Canada is older by a few years than the French community of Quebec, for the *habitation* at Quebec was not founded until 1608. Separated by several hundred miles of difficult forest country from the St. Lawrence, and subjected to quite different experiences from the settlers there, the Acadians developed a colonial culture of their own, and even today consider themselves distinct from the Québecois. Today, in the Atlantic provinces of Canada, there are 350,000 people of French descent, and most of these are Acadians, though in recent years there has been a considerable influx from eastern Quebec into western New Brunswick. Three-quarters of the Acadians still speak French as their mother tongue.

Yet it was the basin of the St. Lawrence which became the real heartland of New France, and today it remains the centre of French-speaking Canada. Quebec City began as a fur-trading centre, and, as was usual in such circumstances, permanent settlers were not at first very welcome. Not until 1627, under Richelieu, did the French government seriously turn its attention to settlement and, though colonization was interrupted by an invasion of British privateers in 1629, it was resumed in 1633 when Champlain returned to Canada; Trois Rivières was founded in 1634 and Montreal in 1642, while the first seigneurs or estate-holders were established at this period along the St. Lawrence, and colonized the lands granted them with families from France, many of whose descendants still live in Quebec. Most of them came from Normandy and Brittany, and all of them were Catholics. Huguenots had played a considerable part in the early fur trade at Tadoussac, but with the coming of the religious orders, the Recollets in 1615 and the Jesuits in 1625, the missionary character of New France was established, and a strict religious domination was established by the clergy over the people; in 1628 Richelieu decreed the exclusion of Huguenots, and foreigners also were vigorously excluded from New France.

In 1666 the first census was taken; there were 3,215 French people in the colony; by 1698 the population had risen to more than 15,000. At first, the increase was limited by a shortage of women. The deficiency was eventually made up by the recruitment of 1,100 robust French peasant girls, the *filles du roi*, who were shipped over to marry the surplus bachelors, veteran soldiers and former indentured servants who had decided to remain permanently in the freer environment of New France rather than return home. It is estimated that in all no more than 10,000 French people actually emigrated during the century and a half between the foundation of Quebec City and its surrender to the British in 1760, but the rate of reproduction after the arrival of the French women was so healthy that by this time the population had reached 65,000.

It was a miniature society that had already attained a strong sense of its own identity. The farmers—or *habitants*—were spread along the banks of the St. Lawrence and some of its tributaries; they cleared the forest and established the long strip farms which survive to this day.

While certain corvées were expected of them, the burden of feudalism weighed much more lightly here than in the France they had left and, if they had no voice in the government of the colony, they had much more freedom in their personal lives than those who had remained at home. Many of them in fact became *coureurs de bois*, fur traders and trappers who went into the *pays d'en haut* of the great western forests and lived like the Indians. Quebec, Montreal and Trois Rivières were small towns with merchants, artisans, soldiers and many priests and *religieuses*. There was even a miniature court which revolved around the governor, and a native aristocracy appeared; by the early eighteenth century the French born in Canada had already adopted a creole attitude, regarding themselves as *canadiens*—the first self-conscious Canadians—and resenting the pretensions of the metropolitan French who sought to monopolize the administrative posts. It was this sense of belonging to Canada, and nowhere else, that made the French Canadians cling to their land even after it had fallen into British hands; their loyalties had already become local ones.

During the two centuries between 1760 and today, the French Canadians have performed a unique feat of reproductiveness. Since 1760 new immigrants from France have been few and the increase in people of French origin has been almost entirely a natural one; yet in 1961 Canada contained no less than five and a half million people of French ethnic origin (not counting a million people in New England descended from French Canadians who migrated during the nineteenth century). Thus, in two centuries, the French Canadians have multiplied about a hundredfold. They form approximately 30 per cent of the Canadian population, and they are the largest single group, since those of English descent, as distinct from English speech, comprise only 23 per cent.

The French are tenacious of their traditions. Few have abandoned their gloomy, Jansenist form of Catholicism, and more than 90 per cent of them still regard French as their mother tongue. Nearly three and a half million of them speak only French, and in Quebec outside Montreal the proportion of unilingualism rises to five out of six persons. In this the French resemble the English Canadians, whose proportion of unilingualism is even higher (in British Columbia as high as 95 per cent), and both of these 'founding peoples' contrast with Canadians of other ethnic origins, almost all of whom speak English or French in addition to their mother tongue; only 232,000 Canadians speak neither French nor English, and many of these are Indians or Eskimos living in remote places.

V

The British quickly followed the French lead to Canada. The first English colony in present Canadian territory was Newfoundland, where in 1610, two years after Champlain founded Quebec City, a settlement was set up under the auspices of a group of Bristol merchants. Other attempts at colonization were made during the next twenty years, the most ambitious being that of Sir George Calvert in 1622. In 1629 Calvert departed for Virginia, and eventually—as Lord Baltimore—colonized Maryland. His departure meant the end of pioneering by chartered companies, and for nearly two centuries government policy discouraged settlement in the interests of the west-of-England merchants who profited by the dried cod industry. Nevertheless, permanent settlements were founded in the 1630s and augmented by deserting mariners; they followed, and their descendants have continued to follow for three centuries, a precarious existence based on fishing and very primitive agriculture. By 1753, Newfoundland had in this haphazard way acquired 13,000 inhabitants, a third of them Irish, and it was developing a poor man's culture of considerable vigour, based on a combination of traditions imported from Devon and the south of Ireland.

Later in the reign of James I came the first tentative British settlement on the mainland of Canada, when the king ignored French claims to Acadia, and granted it to his friend, Sir William Alexander. Alexander named it Nova Scotia, and in 1629 settled a group of Scots on Cape Breton Island and occupied Port Royal, but he and his followers were soon expelled, and, though Nova Scotia changed hands several times until it finally became a British possession in 1713, both the British and the New Englanders were at first reluctant to settle there. There were government officials and a garrison in Annapolis Royal, and a few families wintered in the fishing station of Canso. Halifax was established in 1749, as a counterpoise to the fortress which the French still held at Louisbourg on the tip of Cape Breton, and attracted a largely British population who lived on the needs of the garrison, the navy, and the government, which was transferred from Annapolis. By 1753 it had 3,000 inhabitants, of whom 1,000 were Irish. But real settlement on the peninsula of Nova Scotia did not begin until after

Louisburg had been captured in 1758 and Quebec in 1760. Then the New Englanders, who previously had regarded the region as too vulnerable to French attack, began to move northward. While Halifax developed into a British town overseas, its merchants linked closely by financial interest to the imperial capital, the dissenting tradition of Massachusetts was established in the country areas. When the American War of Independence broke out, Yankees comprised at least two-thirds of the population of Nova Scotia; if they did not become Loyalists in the sense of rendering active support to the British, they also refused aid to the rebellious colonists, with the result that Acadia remained British, and the westerly half—shortly to become New Brunswick—was settled in 1783 by United Empire Loyalists who lost their land and their livings in the success of the American Revolution. There had been small settlements of Yorkshiremen and Irishmen during the 1770s, but by 1790 the bulk of the English-speaking population in Nova Scotia and New Brunswick alike was in one way or another American in origin.

After the conquest of New France in 1760 a few British officials went to Quebec City, and a few merchants—mostly Scottish in origin—settled there and in Montreal, where they quickly gained control of the fur trade. But it was not until 1783 that agrarian settlers arrived. Then some 6,000 Loyalists migrated to the Eastern Townships of Quebec, and west of Montreal to the northern shores of the St. Lawrence and Lake Ontario. Before the century was over they were outnumbered by a great influx of immigrants from New York, Pennsylvania and Vermont who had no Loyalist affiliations, so that when war broke out between Britain and the United States in 1812, Upper Canada, like Nova Scotia in the War of Independence, was mainly populated by people of American origin. Once again, only a few individuals made common cause with the invading American armies; most of the former Yankees proved acquiescent Canadians.

It was not until after the battle of Waterloo that the great immigrations from the United Kingdom began. Crop failures in Ireland, the dispossession of the Scottish crofters, and poor economic conditions in England were among the basic causes of this movement of peoples which aroused the anger of William Cobbett, who believed that if English rural society were properly organized there would be no need for the labourer to cross the Atlantic in the cramped and often disease-ridden holds of returning timber-vessels. Many such immigrants died of cholera, but those who survived the crossing materially shifted the balance of Canadian population. The Irish were the most numerous. In the 1820s and the 1830s they came in large numbers to the settlements of Upper Canada. Twenty thousand Catholic Irish settled new country around Lake Erie, and others established themselves in yet unbroken regions inland from the lake shores. Protestant Orangemen from Ulster settled in Kingston, Toronto, London and other Upper Canadian towns. By Confederation, the Irish were next to the French the largest racial group in Canada. The 1871 census listed 846,000, as against 1,083,000 French and 706,000 English, but the Irish never formed a homogenous national group, and during the nineteenth century most of the serious Canadian riots were set off by Orangemen interfering with Catholic Irish parades, or vice versa. Many of the Irish who migrated to Canada at this time eventually settled in the United States, so that their relative strength in the Canadian population diminished steadily.

The English and Scottish immigrants of the mid nineteenth century were less numerous than the Irish, but more inclined to remain and prosper. At Confederation the Scots numbered only 500,000, a seventh of the population of Canada, but for the first twenty-four years of Canada's life as a Dominion its Prime Ministers were Scots by birth, as were many of its leading politicians and merchants. A surge of Highlanders had begun to reach Cape Breton in Nova Scotia in 1814, and continued into the 1840s; by which time some 50,000 of them had settled in the coal-mining area of Cape Breton and along the fertile shores of the Gulf of St. Lawrence. They preserved their Gaelic speech (there is still a Gaelic college on Cape Breton), and gave Nova Scotia the Scottish flavour its name demanded. They provided not only miners and farmers, but also, for a century ahead, a high proportion of Canada's directing intelligences, such as university presidents, civil servants and high business executives. Other Scots made their settlements in Upper Canada, and the district of Glengarry, near the border of Quebec, was famous for its rugged Gaelic-speaking lumbermen whose life was celebrated by Canada's earliest best-seller novelist, Ralph Connor. In the Northwest, which only joined Canada in 1870, the Scots had arrived even before they began to emigrate to the Maritimes and Upper Canada. Since the eighteenth century the Hudson's Bay Company had employed Orcadians in the factories and posts of Rupert's Land, and some of these joined the Highland settlers who were

10. MacMillan Bloedel Building, Vancouver. (ARCHITECTS: ERICKSON, MASSEY. PHOTOGRAPH: JENNINGS LTD.)

11. Simon Fraser University, Burnaby, B.C. (ARCHITECTS: ERICKSON, MASSEY)

brought in 1812 to the Red River settlement by Lord Selkirk; when Manitoba was founded in 1870 their descendants formed an important element in the population of the villages along the Red River. Many Scots, particularly from the Hebrides, were also employed by the rival Northwest Company, and played a great part in establishing the geography of western Canada and marking out the lines that settlement would eventually follow.

Though there were more people of English than of Scots descent in Canada at the time of Confederation, the majority of them were children or grandchildren of settlers who had come from the United States, and immigrants direct from England were comparatively few until the later 1870s, when the opening of the prairies coincided with economic distress in England, so that many people were brought out by aided emigration schemes. British Columbia became in the 1870s, after the Cariboo gold rush had declined, a predominantly English outpost and to an extent it still remains so; in the immigrations which have taken place since the Second World War, most of the English have found their way either to the Pacific Coast or to Ontario. Over the century since Confederation the originally sharp distinctions between those of Irish and Scottish, of English and American descent, have almost smoothed away, so that they are seen collectively by the French Canadians as 'les anglais', and are now even shown under a single undifferentiated heading in the census, where together they make up 44 per cent of the population.

VI

The 'founding peoples'—French and British—thus form approximately 74 per cent of the Canadian population. Indians and Eskimos account for a little over 1 per cent, and the remaining quarter consists of an extraordinary variety of peoples drawn from every corner of the world. The largest group among them is of German descent. The Germans almost qualify for the title of a 'founding people', for when they began to arrive there were still few people of British descent in the colonies that became Canada. The first came to Nova Scotia as early as 1750; and in 1753 a group of Hanoverians founded the town of Lunenburg which became the most famous of the Maritime shipbuilding centres. After the American Revolution, German Loyalists settled in Upper Canada, where the town of Berlin (its name was changed to Kitchener during the First World War) became the centre of a predominantly German area; many of these settlers were strict Mennonites who to this day have kept their community organization and who retain the antique and sombre garb which their ancestors brought from Europe in the eighteenth century. During the 1870s other German-speaking Mennonites fled to Canada to avoid religious persecution in Russia. Between 1874 and 1889, 6,000 of them settled in Manitoba, and later they planted their colonies in other parts of the prairies. The Mennonites of the Fraser valley in British Columbia came in the 1920s, fleeing from another Russian persecution, that of the Bolsheviks. During the same period several communities of Hutterites, a German-speaking sect related to the Mennonites, migrated from Dakota in the United States, where they claimed their Christian communism had earned them persecution. They found Canadians no more tolerant than Americans; their successful farming aroused jealousy among their neighbours and laws were passed in the prairie provinces to prevent religious communities acquiring more than limited areas of land. More recently the Hutterites have found themselves in opposition to Canadian methods of education, to which they object on religious grounds, and many of them have already migrated to South America in search of greater freedom.

During the 1920s, after the emotions generated by the First World War quietened down, many German artisans and technicians migrated to Canada, where they found employment in the growing industrial towns of Ontario. The Depression virtually ended all immigration until after the Second World War. But in the 1950s a quarter of a million Germans entered Canada; again, the greater proportion of them were technicians and skilled workers who tended, unlike the earlier German immigrants, to establish themselves in the cities. In Vancouver, Toronto and the prairie cities, there are quarters where German influence is evident in shops and restaurants, but most recent immigrants are inclined to blend quickly into the Canadian background, and once established they rarely create sharply defined racial enclaves as some other groups do. In this they differ from the descendants of the pre-1914 immigration, who for the most part still favour farming as an occupation, and tend to live in predominantly German districts.

Dutch and Scandinavians, Negroes and Chinese, were also among the early immigrant groups. The first Dutch settlers reached Upper

Canada in the 1780s among the Loyalists from New York State and Pennsylvania, but it was not until the 1890s that they emigrated to the prairies in large enough numbers to become a significant element in the population. Since the Second World War the Dutch government, acutely aware of the problem of a growing population in a small country, has encouraged and subsidized emigration to Commonwealth nations, and there were years in the 1950s when the Dutch were the most numerous immigrants into Canada. Now they number about 450,000.

Swedes were among the first settlers whom Lord Selkirk brought to the Red River Colony as early as 1812. But it was not until the 1870s that the first large Scandinavian migrations began. Most of the Swedes at this period came through the United States and settled in the prairies, though later some found their way to British Columbia, and played an important part in the development of the logging industry. British Columbia also attracted many of the Norwegians who began to arrive during the 1890s; in the coastal inlets which reminded them of their native fjords, they became fishermen, and even founded settlements of their own, some of which, like Bella Coola, are still mainly inhabited by Norwegians. At about the same period, arrived the first contingent of Finns fleeing from Czarist Russian oppression; they worked mainly as railway navvies, as miners and loggers. One of their early settlements —Sointula on Malcolm Island in the Gulf of Georgia—was also one of the last Utopian Socialist communities to be founded in North America. The very name of the settlement—Sointula or Harmony—indicated its spiritual descent from the experiments of Robert Owen almost a century before, and, though 2,000 people arrived and departed during its active years from 1901 to 1905, it proved as unsuccessful as Owen's New Harmony. But most of the Finns settled in Ontario, particularly during the 1920s, when 30,000 of them reached Canada as part of the movement of Europeans which followed the First World War.

The most internally cohesive of all the Scandinavian groups has been the Icelanders. They fled, not from persecution, but, like their ancestors in the days of the settlement of Greenland so many centuries before, from a harsh and infertile country where land was becoming scarce. Their departure was unclouded by bitter feelings, and they have retained a strong sense of identity with Iceland and its traditions. The first groups arrived in the 1870s and found their way from eastern Canada to the lake and scrub country of northern Manitoba, which seemed like a mirror reflection of their own country. There, in 1875, they founded the town of Gimli—'the great hall of Heaven'—and combined farming with commercial fishing for the goldeye and whitefish of Lake Winnipeg which are bought as delicacies by the Jews of Chicago. Eventually, as other settlements sprang up along the lake shore, the area became known as New Iceland. Not only has the Icelandic community retained much of its original cohesiveness, but it is one of the few smaller ethnic groups in Canada which still produces a considerable body of literature in its native language.

The Chinese came first as miners, arriving in British Columbia from the exhausted California goldfields when the rush to the Fraser River began in 1858. Names like China Bar and China Creek, repeated throughout the mining areas of the west, celebrate their industry. They would pan bars where the gold was thin, or bars abandoned when they ceased to pay highly, and they looked out for the jade which white miners despised. By endurance and economy they prospered, setting up little Chinatowns on the edges of the mushroom mining settlements. Many took their gains back to China; those who remained to work as laundrymen, market gardeners and house servants were joined in the 1880s by thousands of coolies recruited in Kwangtung to build the Canadian Pacific railway through the Rockies. Enough stayed in Canada to establish the Chinese districts which are a distinctive feature of Vancouver and Victoria. Despite anti-Oriental feeling, immigrants continued to arrive from Canton and Hong Kong until after the First World War. In 1923, in response to the pressure of trade unions whose members feared the competition of cheap labour, a Chinese Immigration Act was passed which so limited the eligible categories that during the eighteen years from 1923 to 1941 only fifteen Chinese were admitted. During the 1960s, however, there have been progressive relaxations of the discriminatory provisions against Asian immigrants, so that now the Chinese are at least theoretically on an equal footing with other races, and many are reaching Canada from the Overseas Chinese settlements in Hong Kong, Malaya and Singapore. They are no longer the coolies and servants of the Victorian age; they tend rather to be doctors, nurses, university teachers, and other professionals and semi-professionals. The occupational pattern of the Canadian-born Chinese has also changed considerably in recent years. The Chinese laundry has become scarce, the once numerous Chinese houseboys of Victoria and Vancouver are almost a vanished breed, and it is now only middle-aged women and older men who toil under their wide sunhats in the vegetable fields of the Fraser Valley and Vancouver Island. On the other hand, the Chinese are powerful in small commerce; they have a virtual monopoly of greengrocers' shops and small general stores on the Pacific Coast, and as restaurant proprietors they have spread over Canada, so that one will encounter them in three-elevator prairie villages and in small Quebec towns where only French is spoken; many young Chinese become doctors and lawyers, or work in banks.

The Japanese came later than the Chinese, beginning to reach British Columbia in the 1890s They concentrated mostly on the Pacific Coast, establishing their own mercantile quarter in Vancouver, and forming a considerable fishing community at Steveston on the Fraser Delta. Like the Chinese they incurred the hostility of the strongly racialist trade unions, but they suffered most during the Second World War, when fears of a Japanese invasion led to plans for their wholesale deportation from Canada. In the event, they were not expelled, but the treatment they received is a matter of shame and regret for Canadians today. Their houses and businesses were confiscated and sold for derisory sums to white purchasers, and they themselves were expelled to half-deserted mining towns in the interior of British Columbia, or to communities in the prairies. They made the best of their fate, created occupations for themselves, and earned the grudging respect of the local people, so that today many of them are honoured and prosperous citizens of the little mountain towns like Greenwood and Nakusp and Revelstoke which were their Siberia. In the prairie town of Lethbridge there are now 4,000 Japanese Canadians, descendants of the wartime diaspora, and the traveller is astonished to discover there a park laid out in Japanese gardens as classic as those of Kyoto.

Another Asian people who added their colourful fragment to the Canadian mosaic of populations were the Sikhs, who reached British Columbia in the early years of the present century, some of them expelled from Seattle by the American immigration officers, and others arriving by sea via Hong Kong. Their arrival in 1907 sparked an anti-Asian riot in Vancouver, the most spectacular episode in which was a spirited counter-attack by the Japanese population, armed with sticks and knives, which completely routed the Anglo-Saxon Protestant hooligans. The Sikhs presented a special problem. They were Asians and would work for any wages they could get to establish themselves in the little businesses they liked to conduct and enlarge; this made them doubly unwelcome. But they were still British subjects. In the end, by

Orders in Council, their entry was restricted, and in 1914 there was a famous and shameful incident, when a Japanese steamer, the *Komagatu Maru*, arrived with 376 Sikhs aboard and was refused permission to land its passengers. For weeks the ship lay in Vancouver harbour as the deportation orders were fought individually through the courts. The incident reached epic intensity when 175 police and immigration officers attempted to board the *Komagatu Maru* to transfer its passengers on to a liner leaving for Hong Kong. The Sikhs, many of them black-turbaned Akali fanatics, repelled the invasion with well-directed volleys of coal, and eventually a cruiser was called from the naval base at Esquimalt to force the embattled *Komagatu Maru* out to sea. There was never a more convincing demonstration that the welcome accorded in Canada to a British subject depended on the colour of his skin. Those Sikhs who had reached Canada before the immigration ban was imposed remained mostly in British Columbia, and entered the timber industry, selling firewood, running small logging operations and saw-mills, and often parlaying them into large businesses and considerable fortunes. The modern Canadian Sikh tends to shed the external marks of his religion; today it is chiefly the older men who retain their long hair, beards and turbans, though the gurudwara or temple is still the centre of local Sikh social life.

Other Asians, especially from the Levant, have reached Canada in small numbers. I have encountered Pathan shopkeepers in small Nova Scotian towns, and a Pakistani nurse in the High Arctic, and a Lebanese trader who had spent fifty years of his life on the shores of Great Slave Lake. But in all, there were still only 130,000 Asians in Canada at the 1961 census, a fair indication of the needle's eye through which Oriental immigrants passed for most of the present century. Recently, however, as a result of liberalized regulations, Hong Kong and India stand high on the list of countries sending immigrants to Canada.

The experience of Negroes has been similar to that of Asians. They had an early and unique place among immigrants, for—except for a few domestic servants—the first of them to arrive were fugitive slaves who, during the years before the outbreak of the American Civil War, were transported to Ontario by means of the celebrated abolitionist 'Underground Railway'. Many of them remained and formed communities in Montreal, Toronto and Halifax. By 1871 there were already more than 20,000 of them. Another group left California during the Fraser River gold rush, and for long they and their descendants farmed on Salt Spring Island in the Gulf of Georgia. Though Canadian sympathies for political reasons tended to be with the southern states, the Negroes were welcomed, and in the early period little discrimination was shown against them. The more adventurous of them wandered into remote places and often became, like Moses, the barber of Barkerville, or John Ware, the Negro rancher of Alberta, celebrated frontier characters. Their most typical occupations, however, were those of entertainers and railway porters, and to this day most sleeping-car attendants and most porters at Canadian stations and airports are still Negroes, though of recent years there has been a tendency for the employers to break up this racial preserve by introducing German immigrants. Negroes arriving in the present century have not found the same open welcome as the ex-slaves of a past era with their romantic aura of escape. Most of them were West Indians, and the conditions under which they could enter were onerous and restricted. Women were admitted on condition that they became domestic servants, while the academic world seemed the only refuge which—as teachers or students—West Indian men could find in Canada. However, during the past two years the restrictions on West Indians, like those on Asians, have been relaxed, and Negroes no longer find themselves faced with the same wall of illogical discrimination.

It is this history of discrimination which explains why Negroes, also, are few in Canada. This means that at least in the sense in which it is understood by Americans there is not a 'Negro problem' in Canada. Few Canadians have Negroes or Asians for neighbours, and the rather self-righteous attitude they are inclined to show towards their southern neighbours over colour prejudice is due in part to the fact that they have never been put to the test; the few occasions on which Asians have threatened the wage standards of white workers have created resentments which reproduced in miniature the kind of racial situations that flourish below the border.

Nor have Asians and Negroes been the only victims of prejudice in Canada, shown overtly or translated into the discreet obstructionism of government departments. When the Ku Klux Klan operated on the prairies during the 1920s, its hatred was not directed towards Negroes, who were rare in that part of the country, but towards Catholics, Jews and non-Germanic peoples in general. The Klan was merely manifesting with more extremity the antagonisms which the Orange Order had brought with it from Ulster a century before. For a long time there was a marked tendency for Canadians to regard with disfavour immigrants who were not of British, Scandinavian or German stock, and this view was reflected in the attitudes of governments who framed immigration policies. Only urgent political and economic necessities opened the doors of Canada wide to the Slavs and then to the Mediterranean peoples.

As Canada moved into the old Northwest, following the lengthening railway beyond the narrow bounds of the Red River settlement, the impetus of the surplus farming population of Ontario was quickly spent, while it soon became evident that the immigrants arriving from Britain and the United States were neither numerous, enterprising, nor —in most cases—hardy enough to populate the arable lands and ensure them against American ambitions. In 1896, Clifford Sifton, the Minister of the Interior in Sir Wilfred Laurier's Liberal Government, instituted a radical new policy of recruiting farmers for the prairies wherever in Europe there were peasants willing to leave their homelands and settle the great Canadian spaces. Poles, Czechs and Hungarians were brought in. Seven thousand pacifist Doukhobors came with Tolstoy's blessing, in flight from religious persecution in the Caucasus. But the greatest influx consisted of Ukrainians or 'Galicians'. These 'men in sheepskin coats', as they were called in the journalese of the day, were hardy landhungry peasants, used to wheat-growing and to the extremes of a continental climate; the conformation of the prairies resembled that of their own steppes, and the huts they originally built, of sods or—where there were trees—of poplar poles roofed with sods, were little worse than the homes they had lived in under the Czars. (A few such huts survive to this day on old Ukrainian farms, used by the animals, and give an idea of the primitive conditions in which prairie pioneers lived.) By 1910, 75,000 Ukrainians had arrived. They had not come without opposition, for the many conservatively minded people who wished to keep all Canada outside Quebec solidly British were vocally hostile for many years to Sifton's policy of allowing large areas of the prairies to be occupied by Eastern European peasants. The situation was not improved when the Russian Doukhobors—whom ordinary Canadians found it hard to distinguish from the Ukrainians—became embroiled with the government over the oath of allegiance required to gain title to their lands, and introduced an original form of protest by holding nude marches across the prairies. With Laurier's support, Sifton stood firm in his policy and it was continued during the 1920s, and again immediately after the Second World War, when further generations of Ukrainians sent their exiles to Canada, fleeing this time from Communist imperialism.

The Ukrainians have retained an exceptionally strong sense of national identity, and next to the French Canadians are the most aggressive group in asserting their ethnic separateness. There are signs among the younger generation of a willingness to become absorbed into the general stream of Canadian life, and intermarriages with people of other racial groups are becoming more frequent, but the ethnic organizations founded by the older generation are still extremely strong, maintaining daily and weekly Ukrainian newspapers, fostering the music, dances, literature and other arts of their homeland, and showing a prodigious activity in lobbying parliament, packing the meetings of Royal Commissions and in all other possible ways asserting their claim to a place in the sun. There are less than half as many Ukrainians as Germans— about half a million of them at present—but in some rural areas and in the city of Winnipeg they are the largest single ethnic group, and it is they and not the Germans who have always formed the spearhead of the movement to give official status to languages and cultures other than English and French; they would like to see the Canadian mosaic clearly defined, with no blurring of the edges, and the rich pattern of European cultural variation perpetuated in almost unchanged form in the New World. There are other substantial groups of Slavic peoples in Canada, notably the 320,000 Poles (who are largely found in the mining areas), the 75,000 Czechs and Slovaks, and the 70,000 Serbo-Croatians, but none of them rival the Ukrainians in asserting their national identities.

However, people who are politically articulate are inclined to be culturally conservative, and the Ukrainian contribution to Canadian intellectual and artistic life has been traditional rather than original. Even the leading translator of their literature for the benefit of other Canadians has been, not a Ukrainian, but a Nova Scotian Scot, Watson Kirkconnell. In this they contrast strikingly with another group who came at the same period and from the same places—the empires of the Habsburgs and the Romanovs. These are the Jews, whose arrival in Canada has been a slow penetration over a long period. In the years immediately after the conquest, a few Jews were among the merchants who settled in the cities along the St. Lawrence, and one of them,

Ezekial Hart, gave the French Canadians a chance to prove that religious prejudice is not peculiar to Anglo-Saxon Protestants. He was elected in 1808 by the people of Trois Rivières to the Legislative Assembly of Lower Canada, and was twice voted ineligible because of his religion by the French-Canadian majority; the English-speaking members voted in his favour. Fortunately the experience of Ezekial Hart did not set a precedent. Anti-Semitism has not been absent in Canada, but it has rarely taken an aggressive form. As early as the 1880s destitute Jews fleeing from the pogroms of Eastern Europe were admitted into the country. Many of them went to the prairies, and some founded families which are farming in Manitoba to this day. But most of them settled in the towns, particularly Montreal and Winnipeg, where the younger generation are now moving out of the voluntary ghettoes established at the beginning of the century. Still, in spite of the arrival of fugitives from Nazi terror in the late 1930s, there are only about 200,000 Canadians who declare themselves of Jewish ethnic origin. Their contribution to the country's life has been out of all proportion to these small numbers, not only in business, but even more in education and science, in literature and in the performing arts.

In terms of numbers, the heyday of Canadian immigration was the decade before the First World War, when approximately two and a half million people arrived. But so many people left Canada at this period that the net gain was very much less than half the number of entries. Nevertheless, those who remained changed the nature of Canadian life by populating the prairies and by providing labour for the transition from a mainly agrarian to a mainly industrial economy which began during the First World War.

The immigration since the Second World War has been as large—more than two and a half million people from 1946 to 1965—but the net gain has been numerically higher, since only a million people left Canada during this period, and in quality it has been immeasurably greater. The universities, the medical and engineering professions, and above all architecture, have been greatly strengthened by this influx, as have the creative and the performing arts. Skilled technicians and industrial workers have also formed an extremely high proportion of the new arrivals, and have largely made up for the Canadian lag in higher education. This has been an immigration to the towns rather than to rural areas; only the Dutch have still shown a marked inclination to go in for farming.

In its racial composition also the new immigration differs from the old. It began, immediately after the war, with the arrival of the so-called 'displaced persons', mainly Poles, Ukrainians and people of the Baltic states, who contributed a very high proportion of professional men, educators and scientists. Later, in 1956, the Hungarian uprising brought in one year 35,000 refugees, and as I write, the first groups of refugees from the Czech incident of 1968 are entering the country at the same time as a steady stream of political fugitives from the United States, largely young men intent on avoiding participation in the Vietnam war. Since the McCarthy period, in fact, the influx of Americans attracted to the freer and less megalomaniac life of Canada has been steady, and it has included many academics.* A lingering prejudice against Orientals has kept out another important and tragic group of refugees; in spite of the example of Switzerland, and in spite of the efforts of many Canadians, not a single Tibetan has yet been given asylum in Canada.

Of the recent immigrants who came for opportunity and adventure rather than as fugitives, the British have perhaps naturally been the most numerous. In the years immediately following the war, the Dutch followed them closely, and then, after 1951, it was the turn of the Germans to take second place. It was still a matter of deliberate policy to encourage principally people of Germanic race, but midway through the 1950s the need for construction and transport maintenance workers led to an opening of the frontiers to large numbers of Italians, particularly from Sicily and Calabria. Relatively small groups of Italians had arrived in the past—including railway construction workers in the 1880s—and the town of Trail in interior British Columbia had been colonized in the 1920s by Italians who worked in the great smelting plant. But the large immigrations were reserved for the present period. More than 300,000 Italians have come since 1950, bringing with them skills like terrazzo, mosaic and Venetian glass blowing, and encouraging the spread of vineyards in Ontario and British Columbia and the growth of a Canadian wine industry. In numbers the Italians—half a million of them—are now on the verge of replacing the Ukrainians as the fourth largest ethnic group in Canada.

---

* The Canadian mosaic is nowhere more in evidence than on the university campus. A faculty in which born Canadians form the majority is rare indeed; most will include not only British and Americans, but also continental Europeans of many origins and very often, as well, Chinese, Japanese and Indians.

Thus recent Canadian immigration policy has tended towards eliminating progressively the racial barriers that in the past determined the composition of Canada's population. As the years after the Napoleonic Wars saw the great influx of Irish and Scots, so the 1890s established the Slavic element, and the 1950s finally opened the country to the Mediterranean influx.

In the 1960s the last of the overt discriminations against Asians, Africans and West Indians have finally been dissolved. However, this is unlikely to lead to any further change in the balance of peoples, since the new immigration pattern, based on usable skills rather than race or nationality, still militates against people from underdeveloped countries, who are less likely than Europeans to have the required technical or professional qualifications, and in practice the Asians and Negroes who do succeed in entering Canada are few in number and belong almost exclusively to the western-educated classes. The game of robbing Peter to pay Paul is here enacted on a global scale. Canada loses many of its best young academics and professionals to the United States, where salaries are higher and opportunities greater; in turn, it shows no scruples about welcoming doctors and engineers and university teachers who are badly needed in their own countries. The importation of coolies from Bengal to supplement the labourers who arrived from Calabria a decade ago, is another matter. Canada may have benefited by easing the population and employment problems of European countries. Faced with the surplus millions of India or Pakistan, it is unwilling, and indeed unable, to accept the challenge.

The consequence is that, with the exception of Australia and New Zealand, Canada is still the most European country outside Europe; it even has a proportionately smaller non-European population than the United Kingdom, and it is the consciences of Canadians rather than the peace of the country that are disturbed by the demands for equality of its more exotic minorities.

VII

But if Canada does not suffer disunity to the point of such violence and hatred as have been engendered between blacks and whites in the United States, it does have a cleavage among its peoples which is potentially as dangerous. The confrontation between Quebec and the rest of Canada arises partly from the political circumstances of Confederation, which I shall discuss later. But it is also the result of tension between a large group which has tenaciously clung to its French language and its Gallic traditions, and an even larger group whose members uphold the English language and Anglo-Saxon traditions or are willing to accept them as part of the working compromise a country expects of its immigrants. The French Canadians are too numerous to be counted as a minority in the ordinary sense; as we have seen, they are the largest single ethnic group in Canada. But the ethnic is complicated by the cultural. If the medium-sized national groups, like the Germans, Ukrainians, Dutch and Italians, had kept their native languages and cultures as obstinately as the French Canadians, a real mosaic would have existed, and a third force which would have mediated between Francophones and Anglophones. If this had happened, the situation of the French would actually have improved over the past eighty years. Their proportion of the population has remained surprisingly constant, while that of the British has declined steadily. In 1881 the French stood at 30·8 per cent, and in 1961 at 30·4 per cent; by a phenomenally high birth-rate they had neutralized the achievements of an immigration which was almost entirely non-French. The British—including in this case Scots, Irish and Welsh—have declined over the same period from 58·9 per cent to 43·8 per cent. However, immigrants and their children almost invariably learn English in preference to French, since it assures them greater mobility, and the same thing happens among French Canadians when they live outside Quebec and Acadia.

Thus, when one considers mother tongues, the situation is drastically different from what it is when one considers ethnic origins. Only 28 per cent of the population regard French as their mother tongue, as against 58·5 per cent who so regard English. Now that the birth-rate in French Canada is falling quickly, and the immigrants still tend to make English rather than French their adoptive language, the proportion of French-speakers in Canada is likely to fall with increasing momentum. The realization of this important demographic fact is one of the most dramatic factors in the rise of separatist sentiment in Quebec (to which I shall later return in detail), and it is creating havoc with the neat image of the Canadian mosaic of peoples. For it seems clear that in nine provinces of Canada, despite the self-dramatization of the Ukrainians, despite the clannishness of Chinese and Jews and first-generation Italians, despite the slow climb of Indians and Eskimos, the edges of the mosaic are, culturally at least, beginning to blur and soften, and even to bubble a little, so that it looks surprisingly like an American melting pot after all; around the tenth province, on the other hand, the neat little cracks of the mosaic are widening into a dark fissure.

Perhaps the fissure may cease to widen and be recognized as part of the landscape, as similar fissures are in Switzerland, which is a real mosaic of peoples and places. That possibility also will be the subject of later discussion. But before leaving this survey of the peoples of Canada, one should at least consider the entity they have become. Can one call it a nation? A sixth of its members were born outside Canada, while more articulate French Canadians assert that the rest constitute 'two nations' in a single land. On the other hand, there are many English-speaking Canadians, such as the novelist Mordecai Richler, who consider themselves and their countrymen as just another kind of American, with cultural roots not at home but south of the border; in other words, not a nation at all. This view is held mainly by Canadians in that southern tongue of Ontario, surrounded on two sides by American territory, where the influence of at least three great American cities, New York, Detroit and Chicago, is strongly felt. Western Canadians who surrender to the attractions of San Francisco, are less inclined to think in continental terms; they see themselves as part of a common Pacific Coast culture, looking, paradoxically, westward to the Orient.

The view of Canadians as Americans divided from others by a merely political barrier, is given a plausibility by first appearances. Canadians and Americans mingle freely, since they share a highly permeable 3,000-mile frontier. Canadians spend a great deal of their time listening to American radio, watching American television shows, reading American magazines and books, particularly paperbacks. If one goes north over the border from Seattle to Vancouver, or from Buffalo to Toronto, it is not easy to distinguish Canadian from American towns; they have the same supermarkets and shopping plazas, the same suburban housing developments, the same styles of advertising, the same fashions in clothes, the same juvenile fads, and this applies even in Quebec, where only the language is different. Trade unions and fraternal organizations ignore the frontiers, as do hippies and student rebels.

Yet there are differences, and profound ones, between Canadians and Americans, and even between the kinds of life they live. To begin with, many Canadians have a clearly marked regional identity like nothing else in North America; no-one would take a Quebecker or even a

Newfoundlander for an American. His look, his speech, his manners, distinguish him clearly. Then there are the multiple ties of a mixed ancestry. French Canadians harbour an attachment to France which in recent years has increased rather than diminished, and many British Columbians, Ontarians and Maritimers still preserve an attachment to Britain which one rarely finds among Americans, so that they sometimes choose to cultivate English accents and manners and to live for long periods in England, as many Canadian writers do (including, strangely enough, the Americanophile Richler).

Moreover, the political division between the two countries is emotionally as well as historically strong. The Canadian is concerned about his identity. As the lucky citizen of a middle power which has never started a war of its own accord, has never oppressed another people, and has won its independence at the cost of three tiny rebellions, he has few glorious events around which to build his sense of nationhood. What he does have is precisely his collective sense of difference from the Americans. Canada came into existence because a group of British colonies did not wish to be subjected to the Caesarism that is endemic in the American political system. The people of these colonies were not impressed by the megalomania of the United States, they contrived—though hopelessly outnumbered—to avoid being swallowed up by the American colossus, and their attitude had the curious effect of converting the Yankees who settled among them into loyal if not enthusiastic British subjects. As a political being, the Canadian has remained markedly different from the American, experimenting with socialism and social credit, favouring a parliamentary style of government which avoids the dangers of disguised dictatorship implicit in the American institution of the presidency, and developing an individual form of confederation which is even now in the process of evolution. Canadians are less inclined to the emotional and cruel extremes of politics than Americans; on the other hand, they sustain more consistent trends of radicalism. Such comparisons between Canada and the United States are inevitable, and Canadians spend much of their time making them, for they are daily conscious of living between a powerful and politically dangerous neighbour to the south and a bleak wilderness to the north. They draw a satisfaction which sometimes verges on smugness from being somewhat more tolerant and more independent than Americans.

Outside the American context, they sometimes astonish themselves with their capacity for original creation, and in many ways they have recently grown more permissive and flamboyant in their private and public lives. Yet still their position in the world evokes a certain modesty of approach, a habit of looking at themselves and their pretensions rather ironically. They are a sane people whom the gods visit, not very often, with moments of creative madness, of which the greatest was undoubtedly that in which the leaders of a handful of colonies on the Atlantic coastline and the St. Lawrence valley decided to found with three million people a realm that stretched across millions of square miles from ocean to ocean. In four short years between 1867 and 1871 they brought it into being as a nation that would weather into a second century of existence the dangers of external greed and the threats of internal disintegration. The Fathers of Confederation, as Canadians call them today, were of both the founding races, but they and their supporters saw astonishingly alike in the emergency that united them, as their ancestors had done in 1812 and their descendants were to do in 1968 when Quebec joined the rest of Canada in sending an obscure academic, Pierre Elliott Trudeau, into power with an unmistakable mandate to find the means of preserving Canadian unity. Outwardly, English and French Canadians may appear to differ greatly; inwardly they are far more closely linked to each other than either is to the Americans, and at times of crisis this curious symbiosis of different peoples speaking different tongues and upholding different traditions has always amazingly shown its strength.

Chapter IV

THE EXPLOITATION OF THE LAND

〜〜〜〜〜〜〜〜〜〜〜〜〜〜〜〜〜〜〜〜〜〜〜〜〜〜〜〜〜〜

I

The foreign stereotype of Canada is still most often that of a pioneer land devoted to the immediate exploitation of the gifts of nature. The wheat waves over the prairies, the gold lies in the rock, the salmon crowd in the rivers, the underground lakes of petroleum lie silent under the prairies, and the forests shadow half the land; and this is what the passing visitor actually sees, if he once leaves the shelter of the cities. Then the towns dwindle in his mind in comparison with the visible presence of those endless acres where a thousand million bushels of grain are grown every year, making Canada the world's second largest exporter of wheat; of those woodlands which each year add nearly three thousand million dollars to the gross national product; of the even richer mines and oil wells. It is little wonder that in his mind the typical Canadians are still such figures as the wheat farmer and the logger, the trapper, the prospector and the fisherman.

Such people indeed still exist in Canada, and the wealth they extract in one way and another from the land and water of Canada is still the basis of Canada's economy. But their relative position has changed during the past century. One might make the comparison between Canada a hundred or even fifty years ago and Canada today by imagining two of those allegorical cartoons to which nineteenth-century Canadians were as partial as their contemporaries elsewhere. The first would show the farmer striding over the land with little above him but the cloudless sky; the second would show him still on his field, but bearing up on his shoulders, like Atlas, the weight of a globe many times his size. A hundred years ago Canada depended almost entirely on what man could gain by directly exploiting the products of the soil;

its industries were few and primitive, and it relied on the export of farm, forest and mine products for most of the manufactured goods its people used. Today Canada has come a long way out of such a colonial economy, and primary products account for only a relatively small proportion of the gross national product.

This change is linked with the steady urbanization of Canada, which since Confederation has completely transformed the character of the country's life. Four out of five Canadians lived in the country in 1871; even in 1931 one of every two Canadians was a rural man, and 29 per cent of the people made their living by farming. By the 1961 census seven Canadians out of every ten were town dwellers and one in every ten earned his living by agriculture; by 1966 the proportion of farm workers had shrunk to one in thirteen of the population, and the value of wheat exported was less than that of factory products.

The implications of this process for the immediate present will be discussed in the second part of this book. Here I am concerned with the way man's relationship to the land of Canada changed from the simple one of a society of primary exploiters to the technologically more sophisticated one of a society which has acquired a complex super-structure of manufacturing and service industries, activities which determine the affluence of a people but which—as in recent years we have been taught rather emphatically—do not guarantee either its happiness or its internal harmony.

The Europeans who first reached Canada came from a society whose development of machines and industries was still at a primitive level. Intellectually and spiritually they may have been more developed than the Indians and Eskimos they encountered, though this is highly debat-able, but technically their civilization differed in degree rather than in kind from that of the native peoples of Canada, and they depended mainly on the simple activities of hunting, fishing and farming which the Indians were already in some degree practising. The manufacturing processes introduced into New France, and even into Upper Canada at the time of the Loyalist influx, can mainly be classified as handcrafts, with some use of water and wind power in the early sawmills and flaxmills, and on this level the native peoples could often compete in ingenuity and efficiency, for the kayak and the birchbark canoe were almost perfectly adapted to the purposes for which they were intended, while the Pacific Coast Indians developed elaborate fish traps and weirs, built well-constructed wooden houses and showed a considerable mechanical aptitude in the construction of theatrical devices for use during their winter festivals. Both Indians and Eskimos had domesticated at least one animal, the dog; and they had already made the first step out of the stone age by using virgin copper for metal tools. The Iroquois practised a form of agriculture which doubtless had its origins in Mexico, and cultivated a number of plants which were later to be incorporated into the crop pattern of Canadian agriculture, particularly maize (Indian corn), squash and various kinds of beans. They had even reached the stage of food manufacture, since they produced a kind of flour by pounding their corn in a wooden mortar, and made oil out of sunflower seeds. A similar advance in processing had been achieved by prairie Indians, who invented the long-keeping food known as pemmican, made by pouring tallow into skin bags of dried and shredded buffalo meat.

The first Europeans were near enough to the Indian way of life to adopt its techniques with relative ease. Conditions in the homes of seventeenth-century French peasants were often little better than those prevailing in the long houses of the Iroquois, and European standards of behaviour, in that age of the Inquisition and the Thirty Years' War, were not so greatly superior to those of the Iroquois as to justify the tones of moralistic horror in which some of the French condemned Indian conditions and cruelties. Indeed, many of the immigrants of that early period found the life of the *coureur de bois*, with its trading and hunting, its immersion in Indian customs and sometimes in Indian warfare, so much more interesting than the cultivation of Laurentian strip farms that the French authorities had at times to issue strict edicts forbidding the young men of the colony to take to the woods.

II

In fact the first relationship between European men and the land of Canada, in the sixteenth century, was on the most primitive level, that of the hunter and fisherman. It is true that the Europeans did not hunt and fish for their own immediate needs; they came first to catch cod to be dried and sold in Europe, and later they left the seas for the woods to collect furs which were also intended for the European market. But even this commercial aspect had been anticipated by many Indian tribes, particularly on the Pacific Coast, where the trade in preserved foods (dried salmon and oolachon grease) and even in sea-otter furs was already highly developed when the early English and Spanish explorers arrived in the eighteenth century.

The Europeans contributed to this primitive exploitation of the environment a few revolutionary inventions—such as firearms and metal tools—which increased the destructiveness of Indian hunting techniques and swelled the crop of furs. They also contributed the organizational skills which were developed by the merchant guilds of the mediaeval European cities and inherited by the chartered companies of merchants who set out in the sixteenth and seventeenth centuries to exploit newly discovered foreign lands in the Orient and the Americas. While the East India Company traded for the products of exotic Asian civilizations, the Hudson's Bay Company, which was chartered in 1670, and the earlier Company of New France (1627) traded with hunting peoples for all they had to offer that might interest Europeans of the time—the furs of wild animals and particularly of the beaver, whose hairs were admirably suited for felting. To this day the beaver appears on the Hudson's Bay Company's coat of arms and on the Canadian five-cent piece; the tribute is merited, for it was on the pursuit of the beaver into ever-retreating fastnesses that the European penetration into Canada was based. Ideas of conservation were slow to develop in such a country, where everything seemed to exist in abundance. In their greed for trade goods, the Indians would kill every fur-bearing animal they could track down; and the competition of rival fur traders for the increasingly scarce beaver led them to explore Canada and open up the cross-country trade routes which anticipated the railways and highroads of a later era. The competition appeared first in the regions west and south of Montreal, where the French *coureurs de bois* clashed with Dutch and later British traders who came up the Hudson from New York; and more seriously, with the Iroquois, who sought to monopolize the position of middlemen between distant tribes and European merchants. This struggle over the fur trade was the main cause of the Indian wars which plagued New France for most of the century and a half between the foundation of Quebec and its surrender in 1760. To establish closer connections with actual hunting tribes as beaver became more difficult to obtain, the French thrust out to the westernmost of the Great Lakes, Superior and Michigan, continued into the valleys of the Ohio and Mississippi, and eventually, under the Sieur de la Verendrye and his sons in the 1730s, traded in the

12. Promise of Summer. Eagle Harbour, West Vancouver.

13. Veterans of the Coolie Ships, Vancouver.

14 House of Gordon Smith, the painter, West Vancouver. (ARCHITECTS: ERICKSON, MASSEY, PHOTOGRAPH: JOHN FULKER)

prairies, particularly around Lake Winnipeg and the lower reaches of the Saskatchewan River.

After the early attempts at settling in Newfoundland and Nova Scotia had failed, the first effective British beach-heads on the mainland of Canada were also established as a result of the fur trade. In the 1650s two enterprising *coureurs de bois*, Radisson and Groseilliers, had explored far up the Ottawa River and, having observed the complex network of waterways in the Shield country, had conceived the idea that practicable water links must exist between the Great Lakes and Hudson's Bay. Having been fined by the Governor of New France for travelling without his permission in the *pays d'en haut*, they left the colony in anger and offered their services to the British, convincing merchants in London of the wealth of furs in the Canadian North, and leading in 1668 the exploratory voyage whose successful outcome resulted in the foundation of the Hudson's Bay Company, which established forts on the bay whose name it bears, and which, except for a few years when its posts were put out of action by seventeenth-century French competitors, has dominated the fur trade of the Canadian north for three hundred years.

At first the Hudson's Bay traders found it enough merely to occupy their forts on the Bay and wait until the Indians came to trade. However, by the mid-eighteenth century the competition of French traders in the prairies made it necessary for the English to establish their own inland posts and trade routes, and after 1760, when the French traders of Montreal were replaced by the aggressive Scots of the Northwest Company, they had to probe even deeper into the interior in order to maintain competitively their supplies of fur. The Hudson's Bay Company's charter gave it exclusive trading rights over the whole area between Hudson's Bay and the Rockies, but this legality was ignored by the Montreal merchants, and it was they who pushed most aggressively into the west, led by a group of men in whose characters courage and ruthlessness mingled. The Northwesters became the pioneer explorers and geographers of the far Canadian West: Peter Pond certainly reached Lake Athapaska and probably reached the Great Slave Lake; Alexander Mackenzie explored to the Arctic Ocean the river that bears his name and afterwards made the first land crossing of Canada to the Pacific Ocean; Simon Fraser established the first trading posts beyond the Rockies and reached the ocean by way of the Fraser River; David Thompson followed the long course of the Columbia River, to reach its mouth three months after John Jacob Astor's agents had established there a post for the American Fur Company.

In this long process of penetration into the great northern half of the sub-continent, the knowledge of the native hunting population was used to the greatest possible extent, but it was combined with the European's quicker inventiveness and his wider grasp of geographical realities. The fur traders adapted the Indian birchbark canoe, eventually producing the great *canot de maître*, forty feet long, capable of carrying four tons of goods, and operated by a crew of eight to ten voyageurs. Even with these superbly functional craft, the voyages were arduous; between Montreal and Lake Superior there were no less than thirty-six portages. In exploring the routes which the *canots de maître* would follow into the west, the Northwesters lived off the land like the Indians, hunting and fishing for fresh food where possible and otherwise eating pemmican prepared on the prairies. They also availed themselves of the knowledge of the terrain which the Indians possessed in great local detail but rarely over considerable distances, and by piecing together such fragments of knowledge, conveyed in conversation and sometimes in rough maps drawn on pieces of bark, and by using whatever guides they encountered, the exploring fur traders formed their own general but at first vague conception of Canadian geography. Once their routes were established and the first trading posts built, the great task of transportation across a continent could be organized. Each spring the 'brigades' of canoes would set out from Lachine near Montreal, laden with trade goods, and at Fort William on Lake Superior they would meet the inland brigades which the wintering partners had brought with furs from the prairies, the Mackenzie Basin and the Pacific slopes. The exchange would take place, and the eastern brigade would return with its furs to Montreal, while the wintering partners went back with their trade goods in time for the cold season when the furs were at their prime. Later, after the Hudson's Bay Company and the Northwest Company amalgamated in 1821, the much shorter route via Hudson's Bay was used, and sturdier and heavier craft, the York boats which were modelled on whale boats, replaced birchbark canoes on the wide rivers of the prairies.

I have devoted attention to the mechanics of the fur trade because they show how the primitive exploitation of the land developed by a native hunting society could be adapted and used to further the financial aims of the Europeans who began the exploitation of Canadian resources. Agriculture followed, but even though the St. Lawrence valley was settled territory by the time of the British conquest, the fur trade still played an extremely important part in its economy, and it was the foundation on which Montreal's prosperity was built. As for the rest of Canada, until the middle of the nineteenth century, domination by the fur trade was unchallenged, and even in the 1850s it was threatened only in the Red River valley and in the mining areas of British Columbia. After 1870, however, a variety of circumstances made its decline inevitable. The passing of the Indian way of life in the prairies, owing to the destruction of the buffalo herds and the gradual spread of agriculture wherever there was fertile soil, resulted in the rapid retreat of the fur trade into the northern forests and the tundra, where it remained dominant in the regional economy until the end of the thirties, by which time the trade in wild furs was being threatened by the increase in fur farming. Today, even in the Arctic, trapping is sharply declining in importance; the Hudson's Bay Company, which adroitly changed with the times to become a chain of department stores, now estimates that no more than a twelfth of the trade in its Northern Stores division is in furs. Even the Indians and Eskimos have other means of survival, and the trade which for more than two centuries helped to shape the history of Canada has now sunk into insignificance.

III

Other forms of primary exploitation—farming, logging, mining—have survived to become more important in terms of productivity than they ever were, though their growing mechanization has reduced drastically not only the quantity of human participation in them, but also the extent to which they involve man in the kind of elemental struggle with the land that one associates with the pioneer stages of any society.

All these activities developed after fur trading and fishing. In this way the progress of Canada recapitulated the evolution of human society in general from the primitive hunting and fishing stage, through an agrarian society to a highly industrialized and urbanized world. The rapidity of this development can be seen in the history of a city like Edmonton. Until the 1870s, as Fort Edmonton, it was still a fur-trading post whose life had been only lightly troubled by the passage of miners on their way to the British Columbian goldfields. In the 1880s, as settlement spread into the northern prairies, Edmonton became the centre of a cattle-ranching and later a wheat-farming area. In the 1940s the discovery of great petroleum and natural gas deposits gave an additional dimension to its reliance on the primary exploitation of the land's resources. Only in the 1960s has it started on a significant industrial development. Even so, four different economic phases have been telescoped into about eighty years of rapid change.

For a century and a half Canada has been dependent on the export of farming products to preserve the balance of its economy, but it was not until the turn of the century that it became one of the world's great granaries, while the earliest Canadian farming was strictly subsistent. If we can trust the evidence of the sagas, it began almost a thousand years ago, when Leif Ericsson's successor, Karlsefni, with a group of followers which the sagas variously describe as 65 and 160 in number, set out for Vinland with cattle on board their longships. Having reached Newfoundland, they established a settlement whose remains have been found at L'Anse au Meadow, and there found excellent grazing, so that their cattle prospered. They wintered on Vinland, but, having obtained a rich supply of furs by trading with the local Indians, Karlsefni returned to Greenland, and this early pastoral settlement was abandoned.

The first actual cultivation of Canadian soil by a European took place more than five centuries later, when Jacques Cartier, sent in 1541 with Sieur de Roberval to establish a colony, cultivated a small patch of land at an encampment on the St. Lawrence which he called Charlesbourg-Royal and grew a few catch crops. Like Karlsefni, he stayed only one winter and abandoned his pioneer vegetable plot. Only two generations afterwards did the true pioneer of Canadian farming appear, a Parisian apothecary named Louis Hébert, who arrived at Port Royal in 1606, and immediately began to cultivate the first Acadian garden. Shortly afterwards he returned to Paris, but the idea of farming in the New World haunted him, and in 1617 he obtained an appointment as apothecary to Champlain's settlement of Quebec, and sailed there with his family. He was given a piece of land, and in the face of positive discouragement by the fur traders who then dominated New France he set out to cultivate it. Already what was to become a traditional antagonism between fur traders and farmers had developed, the former realizing that if settlement were encouraged it would destroy the cover for wild animals and make their trade more difficult.

Hébert persisted, and eventually, through a sympathetic viceroy, he was granted his lands 'en fief noble', and thus became the first seigneur of New France. He had pastures, grain fields, vegetable patches and even an orchard of apple trees that had been brought from Normandy. By the end of his life, in 1626, he was able to keep himself and his family with the produce of his land. He did so in a hard and primitive way, for all his fields were dug with the spade, and it was not until 1628, when Richelieu began to encourage agrarian settlement, that the first ox team drew the first plough through the earth beside the St. Lawrence.

The opposition between the cultivator and the man who lived from the products of the hunt persisted for more than two hundred years. The traders resented every stage by which, with a slow inevitability, the farmers pushed forward, occupying the St. Lawrence valley, and then, with the arrival of the Loyalists, felling the forests of the traditional *pays d'en haut* and establishing the wheat farms and pastures of Upper Canada. The farmers, in their turn, resented the attraction which the forests wielded over their more wayward sons and looked with the settled man's customary mixture of contempt and fear on the Ishmaelite existence of the voyageurs. Yet in the beginning there was little to distinguish between the two ways of life so far as sophisticated comforts were concerned. The original *habitants* were little more advanced in their ways of farming than their Iroquois neighbours. They ploughed shallowly, knew nothing about crop rotation, and rarely fertilized. They grew enough for a rather monotonous subsistence diet, supplemented often by game and fish; in many ways, they continued to live on the edge of a hunting society, and there were times when food was critically short in New France, though most of the *habitants* had more to eat and all of them more freedom than they would have enjoyed if they had stayed in France.

It was the arrival of the British—and particularly of gentlemen farmers from England—that introduced the more scientific forms of cultivation which had been developed in England under Dutch influence in the earlier part of the eighteenth century and had stimulated the agricultural revolution, with its rotation system and its development of root crops as part of a balanced system of mixed farming. Not every farmer who broke new land in Upper Canada followed these methods; there was still enough fertile land to allow many to practise a wasteful kind of farming in which they would clear and burn the forest, grow crops among the stumps until the land was exhausted, and then move on to new ground. The early farming society of Upper Canada still consisted of primitive pioneering communities, which sold their scanty surpluses locally to the garrisons and townspeople. It was not until after the Napoleonic Wars had come to an end that the export of wheat in large quantities brought the prosperity which justified the building of the attractive colonial towns along the shores of the Great Lakes. At this point the pioneer's struggle against the natural environment turned into the settled farmer's domination of that environment. The primeval forest steadily fled before the axemen, the difficulties of land tenure were gradually settled, and where the *coureurs de bois* had roamed and the French had warred against the Iroquois, the neat Ontario farms came into existence, conducted as skilfully as any English farms of that Victorian heyday. This triumphant progress was facilitated by the local development of agricultural machinery, in which the inventiveness of two famous Canadian families, the Masseys and the Harrises, played a leading part. It was appropriate, considering the importance of farm machines in the development of Canada, that a member of one family, Vincent Massey, became the first native Governor General of Canada, and that a member of the other, Lawren Harris, belonged to the Group of Seven who created the native tradition in Canadian painting.

But it was in the prairies that domination over the environment was most dramatically and rapidly achieved. The first farming in the Northwest had been carried on by fur traders at distant forts, anxious to grow a few simple crops, particularly turnips and potatoes, to relieve the monotony of a diet dominated by pemmican. It was they who first tested the possibilities of successful cultivation in the northern prairies, where Fort Edmonton grew considerable quantities of root crops; in British Columbia, where the Hudson's Bay Company started a farm near Fort Victoria in the 1840s; and on the edge of the Arctic Circle, where the fur traders in 1826 established a vegetable garden at Fort Good Hope on the Mackenzie. This was for long the most northerly of all outdoor cultivation, but today there is a vegetable garden at Tuktoyaktuk, on the Arctic Ocean and within the Arctic Circle.

Arctic farming was too difficult ever to become a commercially feasible operation, and it represents a defiance rather than a conquest of the environment. But the activities of the pioneers who had first broken the alluvial soil beside the Red River, and by the 1860s were already farming the open plains around Portage la Prairie, led eventually to the radical transformation of Canadian agriculture.

In New France the enemies that had to be fought to establish an agrarian economy were twofold—the Indians and the forest. By the time Upper Canada was settled, the focus of Indian power had shifted westward to the plains, and it was mainly the dense, largely deciduous forest of southern Ontario that had to be conquered. In the prairies what trees existed were the settler's allies, providing shelter from the winds, and fuel, and the material for building his first primitive shacks and sheds. To break the tough growth of roots and grasses that had been interweaving for centuries was an easier task than felling the forest, and the real enemies of the prairies were the extreme climates and the various parasitic organisms that might destroy the grains which were the only feasible crops.

Much of the prairie consists of dry land, with low rainfalls, which requires special skills to raise a crop, and periods of drought are disastrous; during the dry seasons of the thirties the general effects of the Depression were intensified in Saskatchewan by the winds which stripped the soil from the parched fields, and so denuded the land that thousands of farms were abandoned and have never been brought back into cultivation. At the other extreme, too much rain can be disastrous, as it was in the summer of 1968. At best, the season in which grains can ripen in the prairies is short, and a few days' shortage of sun can greatly diminish the annual crop.

Even in the most favourable conditions, the short growing season means that no wheat bred for use in the Old World can assure a crop. This problem soon became evident when early settlers began to rear their first crops in the prairies during the 1870s and 1880s: in exceptionally good seasons the European strains of wheat would produce excellent crops, but such seasons were rare, and a more reliable strain must be developed if the farming of the prairies were to become economically feasible. The first real step forward was the production by an Ontario amateur named David Fife of a wheat—called Red Fife after its breeder—which was hard and high-yielding, and which matured relatively quickly. Red Fife solved the problems of farmers in the southern prairies. But in the late 1890s the Canadian Northern Railway began a second transcontinental line which moved the region of settlement from the 50th up to the 53rd parallel, and made enough difference in the seasons for Red Fife in its turn to become a precarious crop for the Ukrainians and Doukhobors, English and Germans, who were filling the newly opened regions north of Saskatoon and around Lloydminster and Battleford. This is a region of fertile soils, with short hot summers in which flowers acquire an extraordinary vividness and vegetables fatten to an immense size, and a hardy all-purpose wheat was all that was needed to make it one of the most productive farming areas in North America. At last, after much experimentation, a government biologist, Charles Saunders, developed a wheat called Marquis, which matured ten days earlier than any variety previously used. It was enough of a margin to make wheat growing in the northern prairies a good gamble, and the agricultural frontier moved up the map, and kept moving until, in the Peace River country which spans the borders of Alberta and British Columbia, abundant crops of wheat were being grown at the 56th parallel.

The success of wheat growing in the prairies emphasized a major shift in the character of Canadian farming which began towards the end of the nineteenth century. The earlier farmers in the Maritimes and in Upper and Lower Canada had been concerned firstly with subsistence, and then with selling their surplus in whatever local market existed. This meant that they were mixed farmers in the old European tradition, and the farmhouse, standing in the midst of its pastures and cultivated fields, would be surrounded by an orchard and a vegetable garden, and would rear its pigs, chickens and geese as well as the cattle for meat and dairy products. On such farms, the forms of cultivation were so well balanced that many eastern Canadian families weathered the depression of the 1930s with extremely low cash incomes, living on their own produce and by barter.

The development of this subsistence tradition was due partly to the fact that before 1846—when the British Corn Laws were abolished—the export market for Canadian agricultural products was slight. By the 1890s, with a rising population and a rising standard of living in Europe, the demand for wheat in the industrial countries had become almost insatiable, and the men who settled the prairies were tempted to specialize in cash crops. Some grew wheat and cattle; some grew only wheat. And so the characteristically bleak prairie farmstead sprang up, with a willow or poplar windbreak instead of a productive orchard, with no vegetable garden and few poultry or pigs. The pattern varied, of course; a Russian or Ukrainian farmer was much more likely to aim at subsistence as well as the market than an Englishman or a Scot. In recent years the tendency has been towards centralization and consolidation, so that the old standard homestead of 160 acres (the area given

15. The end of the Day. Chinese market garden workers, Lulu Island, B.C.

16. Japan in Canada. Japanese fishery workers at Steveston, B.C.

17. The Buddhist Temple, Steveston, B.C.

18. The Sikh Temple, Abbotsford, B.C.

19. The Church at Fort Langley. Fort Langley is the oldest settlement in the Fraser Valley and the first capital of British Columbia. Its church is typical of the white clapboard churches of western Canada.

free during the days when the prairies were first populated) is now becoming comparatively rare as farms are consolidated, while the large modern wheat farm, which can be anything from 300 to 2,000 acres, is worked with elaborate machinery. Such farms are as specialized as a factory, and the owners inhabit them only during the growing season, so that even the cows and the few poultry that might once have inhabited a prairie farm have now disappeared along with the obsolete plough horses.

Elsewhere in Canada other forms of specialized farming have appeared. In Prince Edward Island, in parts of New Brunswick, and in the semi-desert region of Ashcroft in central British Columbia there are farmers who grow nothing but potatoes, and in the Peace River country farmers are now tending to specialize in seed growing. A different struggle against the environment to that in the prairies has been waged by other specialist cultivators on the arid sagebrush benches of the Okanagan Valley. In the mid-nineteenth century the Okanagan was still the hunting ground of Indians, among whom, in 1857, the Oblate priest, Father Pandosy, established his mission. Here a small orchard was planted, but it was many years before the potentialities of the region were fully realized. The cattle ranches came first, and then, in the early years of the present century, irrigation systems began to bring water down from the mountains, and orchards spread down the hundred miles of the narrow valley to form the largest fruit-growing area of Canada, with a summer climate that ripens peaches and grapes as well as apples.

All one-crop economies have their weaknesses. Not only do they disturb the natural ecology of a region. They also render the livelihood of its inhabitants highly susceptible to fluctuations in the international market. It is significant that Saskatchewan, the prairie province tied most closely to the production of wheat, has also been the province most susceptible to alternations of prosperity and depression. On the other hand, in the Atlantic provinces, where for many years cash incomes have been considerably lower than in the rest of Canada, the survival of the mixed farm and the tradition of combining farming with other forms of primary exploitation, such as logging or fishing, have kept the wolf of actual destitution away from Nova Scotian and New Brunswick doors even in times of monetary scarcity.

IV

In many parts of Canada logging appeared a natural accompaniment of farming. It had of course existed in primitive forms before the white man came. The Iroquois would cut poles and strip bark to make their longhouses and laboriously fell trees with stone axe and fire to clear their fields; the Pacific Coast Indians were patient and ingenious enough to fell the giant cedars that overhung the inlets of British Columbia; even the prairie Indians at certain seasons would make journeys to cut the thin trees, still bearing the descriptive name of lodge-pole pines, which supported their teepees. Altogether, in the native cultures, a great variety of objects and tools, from houses to fish traps, from canoes to ceremonial images, from birchbark vessels (in which water was boiled by dropping in redhot stones) to woven bark clothing, from the maple syrup tapped by eastern Indians to the soft inner bark of hemlock trees eaten in British Columbia, were provided by trees, and in this sense a forest industry existed long before the Indians escaped from the stone age.

Europeans from the beginning depended upon the forests for their houses and for the stockades which protected them from Indian hostility. And from a very early date they turned the woods to profit, and lumbering became an export industry. Of Leif Ericsson, who found and named Vinland, the saga tells not only that he built his house of the wood he found there, but that he also cut a full cargo and in the following spring sailed it back to Greenland where timber was scarce, and there sold it.

In the pioneering days of New France, as of every other part of Canada, the log cabin was the customary form of building. By the late seventeenth century stone was being used for churches and other public buildings, but in spite of an increasing tendency from the eighteenth century onwards to build masonry houses, wood still remained the principal building material throughout Canada. This alone has always meant a large local market for timber to be used in buildings. In 1606, moreover, the settlers of Port Royal, by building themselves a boat out of native timbers, established a tradition of shipbuilding in the Atlantic provinces which is not even now wholly dead; still, in Lunenburg and other small towns along the coasts of Nova Scotia, one sees a few wooden ships standing in the stocks. In the 1660s an attempt was made to develop a shipbuilding industry on the St. Lawrence; it was hoped that Canadian lumber could be taken to the French islands in the Caribbean in exchange for rum, which could be used as a trade item in buying furs from the Indians. The scheme did not work well, since there were interests in both New France and the mother country which did not favour the colony developing beyond the fur-trading stage, and in later years both the lumber and shipbuilding industries in New France suffered alike from a shortage of labour at home and a lack of markets abroad, though a number of ships of the line for the French navy were built on the St. Lawrence.

The lumber trade took an immediate impetus after the emigration of New Englanders to Acadia in the 1750s and the arrival of British merchants in the towns of the St. Lawrence valley after the conquest. Since the forests of England had long been depleted, there was an immediate demand for dressed timber, particularly for the navy; the Maritimes and Upper and Lower Canada all benefited, and a symbiotic relationship developed between two forms of primary exploitation—farming and logging. This relationship already existed in a rather primitive way in the St. Lawrence valley, where every long strip farm ended in a wood-lot, in which the *habitant* would fell trees for building and fuel and at the end of each winter—when the sap began to rise—would tap his maples for sugar and syrup. The Loyalists and the other American and British farmers who settled in Acadia, in Upper Canada and in the Eastern Townships of Quebec, were more enterprising. It is true that they burned many of the fine stands of oak and other hardwoods along the shores of the Great Lakes merely for potash that would be sold and used in soap making. But the red and white pines were felled, squared with the broadaxe, and sold for export.

The demand for good timbers as masts and spars for sailing ships led timber merchants to explore beyond the areas of settlement, and in 1785 logging operations began on the Saint John river in New Brunswick, followed in 1795 by the first incursions into the great forests of white pines in the Ottawa Valley. When Napoleon closed the Baltic, and cut off supplies of timber from Scandinavia, the demand for Canadian timber at once increased and the loggers spread northward across the Shield, working in areas where the land would never be suitable for farming. Yet even here the link between the farm and the forest persisted, for the loggers were often farmers who would work in the woods during the winter and on their farms after the timber had been floated down river to the ports following the breakup of the ice. Many farming communities weathered their pioneer days in this way, just as later the prairie farmers survived the first cropless years by working on railway construction. Mechanical inventions steadily expanded the lumber industry. The introduction of the steam engine in the 1820s enabled sawmills to be set up in the woods, so that logs need no longer be laboriously squared by hand. In 1866 a process for making newsprint out of ground wood was devised, and the first pulp mill was opened. This meant that forests where the trees were small or of inferior quality could now be exploited, and in large areas of northern Ontario and Quebec, of Newfoundland and of northern British Columbia, cutting wood to satisfy the demands of the world's newspapers has become the principal industry. For many years Canada has been the leading producer of newsprint, and paper and pulp account for two-thirds of the country's exports of wood products.

The eastern Canadian forests whose trees were suitable for constructional purposes were limited in extent, and as the newsprint industry assumed the ascendancy in this region, the rain forests of British Columbia, with their vast firs and cedars, were brought into production. From the beginning logging in the west was a specialist industry. The trees were too large to be handled by farmers with primitive equipment, and once the arable lands of the Fraser Valley and parts of Vancouver Island had been cleared, logging operations receded into infertile and mountainous regions, often far from towns, farms or highways, where a tough breed of professional loggers lived in isolated encampments and dragged the trees out of the woods with elaborate equipment. Here, as elsewhere in Canada, trees were felled extravagantly in the early days, when the stands of ancient, gigantic trees, some of them a thousand years old, seemed inexhaustible, and a wasteful practice of 'slash-and-burn' meant that the smaller trees and the young growth would be destroyed for years to come. By now, much of the vast woodland of Canada is so marred by ill-planned exploitation that it will take generations to recover. This is the field in which man's encounter with the Canadian environment has been most destructive. There are still, indeed, great areas of sub-arctic woodland where the logger has never trod, but the pulp mills are being built farther into the north, and no forest except the stunted growths on the edge of the tundra is now beyond danger.

V

If the soil and the forests and the fishable waters of Canada were being exploited even while the country was still in its fur-dominated infancy, the discovery of the enormous mineral wealth that lay buried in its mountains and under the rocks of the Pre-Cambrian Shield came relatively late. This is all the more surprising, since the sixteenth-century explorers were particularly concerned with the prospect of making easy fortunes from gold and precious stones. Cartier's 'diamonds of Canada', which were mere quartz, we have already encountered. Martin Frobisher became involved in a similar self-deception, for he carried home from Baffin Island many tons of rock under the illusion that it contained valuable ores; it proved to be worthless.

The possibility of mineral wealth interested successive explorers, but until the eighteenth century they failed to realize that the riches which did exist in the earth of Canada would have to be extracted with hard and ingenious toil. Mineral rights were granted by the French kings, and deposits of silver and native copper were discovered as early as Champlain's expeditions in the early seventeenth century, but these were not worked until long afterwards. Fifty years later the visible coal seams in the cliffs of Cape Breton were discovered, but it was only in 1720 that they were first mined to provide fuel for the new fortress of Louisbourg. Shortly afterwards, in 1737, the Compagnie des Forges was founded to smelt bog iron which had been discovered in the valley of the St. Lawrence, but the mercantilist attitude of the French government at this time did not encourage industrial enterprise in the colony, and though other rich deposits of metallic ores were discovered during this period, nothing was done to exploit them effectively.

Even after the conquest, the British who immigrated to Canada were either farmers or merchants who sought quick gains through the fur trade. Interest in mining had not yet reached the levels of mass mania which it attained in the middle years of the nineteenth century with the discovery of the California goldfields. The new inhabitants of both Upper and Lower Canada at the end of the eighteenth century were interested mainly in minerals that could be of immediate use in their pioneering life, and did little more until the 1840s than extend into Upper Canada the excavation of iron ore, which was smelted on the spot, and start the production of plaster-of-Paris and Portland cement from materials locally excavated.

8

At the same time, however, prospectors were roaming over the country beyond the margins of settlement, and in 1842 the government of the Province of Canada established the Geological Survey, which began the first systematic mineralogical exploitation of the Laurentian hills and the rocky regions to the north of the Great Lakes, whose coloured rocks—green and purple and pink—often indicated the presence of mineral ores. In 1847 the first rich deposits of copper ore were discovered on the lonely northern shores of Lake Huron, and the first mining community outside Cape Breton came into existence when the little town of Bruce Mines was built to house the 400 men who dug the ore, which in those early days had to be sent to England for smelting. Eleven years later, in 1858, the first producing oil well was sunk at Enniskillen in Ontario, and the first refinery was built to process the crude petroleum. A boom-town, appropriately named Petrolia, sprang up, and well into the 1880s the oil fields of Ontario were among the most important in North America, but the deposits were relatively limited, and now are virtually exhausted.

The Canadian mining event that made world news in 1858 was not the opening of the Ontario oil fields but the finding of gold in the Fraser Valley, followed by the even more sensational discoveries in the Cariboo mountains. By the mid sixties the Cariboo goldfield had passed its peak of production, and the miners spread northward in a series of small rushes into remote regions like Omineca and the headwaters of the Liard River, which culminated in the most famous rush of all, when George Carmack, a trapper who had gone native in the Yukon region, found gold on the Klondike River, and tens of thousands of men and women hastened there in a *fin-de-siècle* frenzy which provided a fitting climax to the era of the old-fashioned prospector with his pan and his sluice-box.

For the gold rushes of the nineteenth century represented a primitive stage in extracting wealth from the earth—that of the placer miner who takes out of old river beds the dust and nuggets which are the debris from the wearing away of ore-bearing rocks. The great attraction of placer mining was that a man or a small group of men with simple tools and little capital could, if exceptionally fortunate, gain a fortune by digging over and sifting small areas of deposited gravel. It was an occupation admirably suited to the individualistic spirit of the frontier era, which lasted longer in Canada than in the United States and even now is only just expiring in the remotenesses of the Arctic. The classic days of placer mining produced some remarkable self-regulated communities, and, if a proportion of rascals was inevitably attracted to these mushroom towns, most of which sprang up and vanished within a few years, the general standard of morality—surviving until very recently among the northern prospectors—was exemplified in the epitaph which his fellows put over the grave of Twelve-Foot Davis, one of the legendary figures of the Cariboo gold rush: 'He was every man's friend, and he never closed his cabin door.' But the myth of the goldfields is larger than their reality, for the return on the labour which the miners put into searching and digging was comparatively very small. The Klondike Rush was the greatest of them all, but even here during the seven years from 1898 to 1905 the value of the gold mined from the creekbeds around Dawson City was only $111,000,000. Supposing that some of the miners did not report a great deal of the gold they extracted, the total for those seven years of work and privation was probably less than a single year's Canadian output of gold during the 1960s, when relatively few mines are working because of the artificially depressed price of gold; in 1965, the production of gold was a little less than $140,000,000.

The men of the gold rush were most important as pioneers. As a result of their search the highly productive copper and nickel deposits of British Columbia were discovered in the 1890s in the mountains just north of the American border. Some of the mines are there still, seventy years afterwards, providing the lead and zinc concentrates which feed the great smelter at Trail, one of the largest metallurgical complexes in North America. Everywhere in British Columbia, it was the miners who followed the fur traders as the first pioneers, and agriculture and logging developed to suit their needs for food and for mining timber. Hundreds of communities, many still thriving, were founded by them, and it was in the policing of these communities that administration came to the lands of the Far West, British Columbia and the Yukon territory.

The true wealth of the Pre-Cambrian Shield, which is the richest treasury of minerals in Canada, was first revealed when the nickel-copper deposits of Sudbury were discovered as the Canadian Pacific Railway was being built north of Lake Superior. But Sudbury was only the first in a series of sensational discoveries. In 1903 the silver mines of Cobalt were opened, in 1908 the gold mines of Porcupine and in 1911 those of Kirkland Lake. In 1914 great copper-zinc deposits were found at Flin Flon in northern Manitoba, in the 1920s the Noranda mines in Quebec went into production, and in the 1930s mines were opened far north on the edge of the tundra at Great Bear Lake and Great Slave Lake. The Cold War years of the 1950s led to the uranium-mining boom near Lake Huron and in the Northwest Territories at Lake Athapaska.

But the minerals which have shown a sensational and cumulative rise in production since the end of the Second World War are iron ore, petroleum and natural gas. The steel industries which developed in Canada up to 1945 used nothing but foreign ores, largely from American deposits south of Lake Superior. This dependence on external sources led to the successful search for local deposits, and iron ore production, in Ontario, Quebec and above all in Labrador, has increased almost forty times, from a million tons in 1945 to more than 39 million tons in 1965.

The great discoveries in oil and natural gas took place in Alberta, and during the past twenty years have almost completely transformed the economy of that province. Natural gas deposits had been discovered near Calgary in 1913, and the first oil wells in the west went into production in 1924. But it was the discovery of the great Leduc oil field near Edmonton in 1947 that began the phenomenal rise of the Canadian petroleum industry. In 1946, the year before the Leduc strike, the total production of oil was 7 million barrels. By 1965 it had reached 294 million barrels, which placed Canada high among the world's oil producers, and provided not only 80 per cent of Canada's own oil consumption, but also substantial exports to the United States. During the same period of two decades the production of natural gas has increased thirty times and now it supplies about a sixth of Canada's energy requirements.

The rapid expansion in iron ore, petroleum and gas production has revolutionized Canadian transport and even Canadian domestic patterns. Over the railway that now probes through the wilderness of Labrador to the iron mines of Schefferville run automatic driverless trains, while the world's longest pipelines carry Alberta's oil and gas as far east as Montreal and as far south as California. Coal is the one branch of mining that, owing to these developments, has declined. The gigantic steamdriven locomotives of the classic railway days, with their bell-shaped smokestacks, are now extinct in Canada, their place taken by diesel engines, while, with the widespread adoption of oil and gas furnaces, the coal fire is almost a thing of the past. The mines of Cape

o. The Chief's House. Kitwancool, B.C.

21. Ancestral memory. Indian sculpture at Kitwanga, B.C.

2. Fallen splendour. Kitwanga, B.C.

23. Kwakiutl Indian Mask from Coastal British Columbia. (MUSEUM OF PRIMITIVE ART, NEW YORK)

Breton have in any case become so uneconomical to work owing to the exhaustion of the seams that it is planned to let them fall out of production as other industries are brought into Nova Scotia. The Rocky Mountain coal mines of the Crows Nest Pass area have been saved from abandonment only by the opening of an export market in Japan.

Today Canada produces sixty different kinds of minerals. It is the world's leading producer of nickel, zinc, asbestos and platinum, and ranks high among the producers of uranium, gold, lead and other rare and important metals. The production of its mines is almost equal to the production of its farms. Each contributes nearly $4,000,000,000 to the Gross National Product.

VI

Such figures mean that Canadian mines and Canadian farms are in real terms producing far more than they ever did before, in spite of the fact that there are fewer farms and farmers, fewer mines and miners. In both of these two main primary industries concentration and mechanization have released so many men from the toils of the past that in 1968 only one Canadian worker out of ten is involved in the direct exploitation of earth and waters, as against 34 per cent engaged in secondary manufacturing, construction and utilities, and 56 per cent engaged in the tertiary service industries. In terms of cash, the industries involved in the direct exploitation of the land produce in all approximately $10,000,000,000, while the manufacturing industries produce almost $35,000,000,000, more than three times as much.

Yet, to the traveller, Canada does not appear a land dominated by the dark Satanic mills. There are areas around the major cities, and along the shores of the Great Lakes, where the smoke of industry hangs dark in the air; there are rivers where no fish can live and stretches of countryside where the air is foul with the stench of the pulp mills. But the dominant feeling in a traveller's mind is still that of the broad, open country, where the wide cornfields and village elevators, the sawmills on the edge of the forest and the towers of mines standing among the coloured rock outcrops, are still the most characteristic sight. In spite of statistics, the message they convey is not wholly inaccurate. Canada is still nearer to the era of primitive exploitation than the figures suggest. Many of the manufacturing industries, such as the smelting of ore, the refining of petroleum, the preparation of woodpulp, sawmill work, meat and fish packing, fruit and vegetable canning and the preparation of dairy products, are immediately dependent on the primary industries, and these account for at least a quarter of Canadian manufacturing.

The relative unsophistication of Canadian industry is revealed in the foreign trade figures. Canada is still, as at the time of Confederation, predominantly an exporter of the products of the land, in raw or simply processed form, and predominantly an importer of manufactured products. Of the first twelve export commodities listed in 1965, and accounting for well over a half of the total export trade, only one involved elaborate manufacturing processes—'aircraft and parts'—and this was due to a special agreement with the United States whereby the latter exported to Canada the equivalent value of 'aircraft and parts', so that the two items cancelled each other out. Otherwise Canada is largely at the mercy of the tariff policy in the countries to which it exports. It sends out newsprint and paper pulp, but few books and little high-grade paper; wheat and wood, metals and ores, but few metal products and very little machinery. A glance at the list of Canadian imports reveals a very different picture. Except for crude petroleum and fruits from Florida and California, the twelve leading commodities are sophisticated industrial products, with machinery, automobile parts, textiles and farm implements heading the list. Despite the recent shift to urban living, despite the withdrawal of men from occupations which involve a direct confrontation with the land, the economy of Canada is still relatively primitive, and dependent on the American, European and Japanese centres of high industry.

A similar pattern exists internally. Five-sixths of the manufacturing industry of Canada is concentrated in the geographically small region beside the St. Lawrence and along Lakes Ontario and Erie between Quebec City and Windsor, Ontario, and about half the remainder in southern British Columbia. The farther one travels from the three major metropolitan areas of Toronto, Montreal and Vancouver, the more Canadians are dependent on the direct exploitation of the land. Most Albertans still live, in one way or another, from the ranches, the wheatfields and the wasting oil and gas deposits. Saskatchewan, the geographical heart of the country, is still almost as dependent as in pioneer days on the products of its soil. 70 per cent of Saskatchewan's income comes from the products of its farms, and from the mineral resources which have been discovered during the present decade and which are diversifying the traditional one-crop economy. On the other hand, only 10 per cent of Saskatchewan's income comes from manufacturing, as against 70 per cent in the case of Ontario. Paradoxically, though most Canadians now live in cities and evade the direct confrontation with the land and the elements which was the lot of their ancestors two generations ago, most of Canada is still dependent on the exploitation of natural resources. Agriculture, mining and lumbering remain the three pillars on which the Canadian economy is founded, since most manufacturing is based on local raw materials. There is as yet little of the industrial sophistication which one encounters in a country like Switzerland, where specialized skills greatly augment the value of imported raw materials by transforming them into high-grade manufactures. The nearest approach is the aluminium industry; Canada is now the world's second manufacturer of aluminium, using its low-cost hydro-electric power to extract the metal from bauxite imported from Guyana and the Caribbean islands.

Thus the pattern of man's relationship with the land in Canada, though it appears to have changed radically, is fundamentally little altered. Mechanical developments mean that far fewer men are occupied in the fields, woods and mines, and one's impression that the land outside the cities is emptier than before is not erroneous: 1,100,000 men worked on Canada's farms in 1931 as against 650,000 in 1961. But in balance Canada's well-being is still dependent on raw materials rather than on skills, and even in the eyes of its planners the sophistication of its technology is still no more important than the continued confrontation of the wild land that will bring into use its vast untouched resources of water power and find a way to exploit the mineral wealth that lies under the Barren Land of the far north and the icy islands of the Arctic, where Martin Frobisher's instinct was truer than his discoveries led men to assume.

Canada's life is still bound to the land. The difference between the situation now and that a hundred years ago on the morrow of Confederation can be seen in the form of two triangular figures. In 1870 the Canadian economy, like Canadian society, tapered upward from a broad base of people and activities tied to the farmlands, the forests and the troglodyte world of the miners. Through the age of the great pre-1914 emigrations this broad-based pyramid was still the basic form of Canadian collective life.

Today the situation has been reversed, the pyramid has been upended by the miracles of technology, and the primary exploitation on which the Canadian economy still rests has become the narrow end of a triangle that now broadens as it goes upward into the higher realm of the affluent society. This is an achievement, if such it may be called, which is peculiar to the modern cultures of the West, and while many regard this lessening contact with the earth as a step towards the technological paradise, there are those, in Canada as elsewhere, who regard it as the prelude to a new variant on the tale of Babel.

Chapter V

AND HE SHALL HAVE DOMINION

~~~~~~

I

The evolution of government in Canada and the achievement of the country's precarious unity have been based on a peculiar interplay of governmental action and private enterprise which has evolved in a borderland realm between the economic and the political. Those earlier pioneers, Leif Ericsson and Karlsefni, can be regarded as representatives of undiluted private enterprise, since they came and went for their own profit and with no king's blessing. The French and English adventurers who were their nearest successors came also—whichever kingdom sent them—for profit first, under the immediate auspices of companies of merchants who wished, by trading or settlement, to exploit the land. It is true that the names chosen for these regions—New France and Nova Scotia—suggest that from the beginning the minds of monarchs were inspired by visions of setting up, as the Spaniards had done to the southward, miniature replicas of the societies they ruled in Europe. Among the French the enthusiasms of the counter-Reformation ensured that the idea of conversion should also be added to that of conquest. But these were the thoughts of rulers, and it is safe to assume that the merchants who established the first French settlements in Acadia and at Quebec were as deeply concerned with profits as the English companies who came with charters from King James I to Newfoundland and to Nova Scotia.

The disorder of English government during most of the seventeenth century meant that no really serious attempt was made until after the treaty of Utrecht to set up any stable British administration either in Newfoundland or in the parts of Acadia that intermittently fell into British hands. The main British interest until the mid eighteenth century lay in Newfoundland, but here any kind of early political development was inhibited by the failure of the imperial government to mediate successfully the conflict of interests which arose between the wealthy London and Bristol merchants, who wished to set up plantations on the island, and the larger number of less wealthy merchants from Devon and Cornwall who hoped to monopolize the fisheries and were quite willing to commit acts of virtual piracy against the settlers in order to protect their interests. After Sir George Calvert had departed to Maryland in 1629, the fishing interests persuaded Charles I to decree that there should be no settlement within six miles of the coast, but settlements were in fact established, some of them by Royalist supporters who fled from England, and, though attempts to remove them did not succeed, a condition approaching political chaos existed in Newfoundland well into the eighteenth century. It was only in 1699 that the ownership of private property in the island was finally guaranteed by statute, and until that time the sole form of government was that improvised each season by the English fishermen; at each port the captain of the first boat to arrive became 'fishing admiral', and the capricious rule of these annual despots bore down heavily on the settlers who in time became little better than serfs to the merchants. In 1699 the imperial government for the first time intervened directly in the government of a part of what is now Canada by granting a right of appeal from the 'fishing captains' to the commanders of the naval convoy, but this was little improvement, since the sympathies of the officers were with the fishermen, while the general anarchy was compounded by the presence for many decades in the island's interior of bands of outlaws—the Masterless Men—who maintained an egalitarian organization rather like that of the escaped slaves, the maroons, in the highlands of Jamaica. Not until 1729 was a governor appointed, and even he ruled only intermittently, going home to England at the end of each fishing season; he was usually the incumbent commander, and ruled without a council, though a skeleton administration was created through the appointment of justices of the peace in each of the six districts into which the island was divided. Even though a resident governor was appointed in 1817, not until 1825 was he given a council; in the same year the first House of Assembly was elected.

Thus it took Britain's first colony in the region which later became Canada more than 200 years to make even the first step towards democratic self-government. Newfoundland was preceded along this path by Nova Scotia which, after a period of military governorship between the Treaty of Utrecht and the fall of Louisbourg, was granted an elected assembly in 1759. Through the indifference of the settlers in the country districts, the assembly became in practice the preserve of a ruling clique of Halifax merchants. Even so, this oligarchic gathering was the first step towards responsible government and national independence in Canada, and represented a political development far ahead of anything achieved in New France.

II

In terms of purely political organization, the French contributed almost nothing to the founding institutions of Canada. In culture, religion, civil law, the heritage of New France still flourishes in Canada and especially in Quebec, but the political institutions by which the French Canadians have sought since the conquest to defend their rights and extend their independence were given them by the British. The political institutions of New France were consistently authoritarian. For half a century after the foundation of Quebec the colony was ruled by merchants—first of all through viceroys who acted as the agents of merchant syndicates in France, and then, under Richelieu, by the Company of New France, otherwise known as Richelieu's Company, or the Hundred Associates, whose charter committed them to the promotion of colonization. In action, the Company of New France proved unable either to colonize satisfactorily or to carry on a profitable fur trade in face of the active hostility of the Iroquois, and in 1663 the Company's charter was cancelled and the colony came under direct royal administration through the Department of Marine.

Under this administration, power was shared between three high officers. The governor was the titular head and commander-in-chief, responsible directly for military affairs, which in the case of active governors like Frontenac meant a busy life fighting the Iroquois and their English employers and building forts on the steadily deepening frontiers. In general charge of civil affairs—finance, the administration of justice and the internal policing of the colony—was an official called the Intendant, whose office had been established in France during the late middle ages when the kings found it necessary to appoint representatives who would check the power of the baronial magnates. The emphasis placed on conversion as one of the motives of colonization was indicated by the fact that the third great royal officer of New France was the bishop.

The most important of these officers in terms of the welfare of New France was undoubtedly the Intendant, for the most successful military campaigns were pointless if the colony itself was not well administered, and probably the main reason for the failure of New France to resist British invasion successfully in 1759–60 was the fact that in its whole history the colony had only one 'Great Intendant'. This title was given justly to Jean Talon, whose tenure of office extended from 1665 to 1672, and who established industries, imported women to adjust the population balance and induce a steady natural increase, and encouraged immigration and exploration. During the eighteenth century a series of inefficient or corrupt intendants undermined the economy of the colony. The last and the most disastrous of them was François Bigot, who created an intricate system of peculating government funds, and gained a virtual monopoly control of the colony's trade by establishing a Society of Canada—later The Great Company—which exacted its toll from all trade passing in and out of the colony. By the time the fall of Quebec forced Bigot to return to Paris, the colony was in economic ruin. The fact that the British victory relieved them of this kind of imposition was undoubtedly one of the circumstances that reconciled many French Canadians of the time to living under a British administration, which was at least relatively uncorrupt.

The third great officer, the bishop, was more powerful than his ecclesiastical position might suggest, largely through the form which local administration assumed. Having neutralized the power of the aristocrats in the mother country, the French kings had no intention of resurrecting it in the colony. Consequently it was not the seigneury which became the basic unit of rural government, but the parish. The parish corresponded to the local militia district, public meetings were held in the church, and the priest rather than the landowner became the most influential member of the community. The power that derived from this arrangement was used not so much in the interests of France as to the greater glory of the Church. For the Church in Canada was not Gallican; it was ultramontane in outlook. After the Recollets were expelled from Quebec in 1629 (not returning until 1670), the Jesuits and the Sulpicians struggled for ascendancy. The Jesuits won, and the first bishop of New France, François de Laval de Montigny, was a dedicated ultramontanist who set the pattern of French-Canadian Catholicism for

24. Tsimshian ceremonial rattle from the Prince Rupert region. (UNIVERSITY MUSEUM, PHILADELPHIA)

25. The Rocher du Boule, Hazelton, B.C.

26. Late spring in the Bulkeley Valley, northern British Columbia.

200 years, partly by establishing a seminary in which generations of priests were trained according to the doctrines of Bishop Laval. The establishment of obligatory tithes not only gave the Church financial security, but also strengthened its power over the *habitants*.

The varying interests of military and civil authority and of a church that owed its first allegiance to Rome and not to Versailles, resulted in perpetual conflicts between the three great officers, which were reflected in the Sovereign Council, or Superior Council, as it was called after 1702. The Council fulfilled in part the role of a French *parlement*; it was a supreme court which established legal precedents and reinterpreted the Custom of Paris to fit the new colonial conditions. It was also an advisory body whose appointed members, drawn from the various districts, provided information and discussed proposed ordinances, though they did not enact them. Beyond this advisory role, which was restricted to representatives of the seigneurs, the merchants and the professional classes, the *canadiens* had little say in how they were governed; the *habitants* and other people of humble occupations and antecedents had none at all. The disunity that already existed within the administration was projected by the local strife between landowner and priest, and even more by the resentments which were felt by born Canadians towards the civil officials and military commanders sent from France to occupy the most important positions in the colony. Undoubtedly one of the principal reasons why the church retained its prestige in New France while that of the colonial administration steadily declined was the fact that as time went on most of the priests were locally trained *canadiens*, rather than from emigrants from France.

In the end, because it retained this influence among the people, and because it was not Gallican, the church was the one wing of French administration that not only survived the conquest, but continued to gather influence to itself. Owing allegiance to the Pope and not to the French king, the bishops taught acceptance of British rule, and they were granted religious tolerance, embodied in the Quebec Act in 1774 which eliminated the onerous tests that prevented Catholics in Britain from holding public office. The church retained a power over education which became more important with the spread of literacy among the French-Canadian population, and sustained a potent influence in the country districts, where the curés remained arbiters of morals and political advisers. In return, the Church guaranteed loyalty or at least neutrality at a time when British power was threatened throughout

North America. Thus the American invaders, who had expected in both 1775-6 and 1812-14 to win the immediate support of the conquered French, were received with a businesslike caution; the French Canadians sold them produce for cash, but refused to serve in their ranks. Similarly, the republican uprising in the Quebec countryside led by Louis-Joseph Papineau in 1837 was defeated largely because the Church opposed it in favour of continuing the accommodation with the British. Throughout the nineteenth century the Church in Canada acted as a quasi-political power, using its influence to sway elections against *les rouges*, as the liberals were called locally, and it was only when the Papal authorities intervened, and even then with much reluctance, that the Canadian bishops in 1897 finally forbade direct clerical involvement in elections.

Even after 1897 the Church remained powerful in Quebec, through its continuing grip on the educational system and the influence it established in the rising trade-union movement, which in Quebec took on a specifically Catholic orientation. It is true that the overt power of the clergy has declined sharply since the *Révolution tranquille* which began when the liberals gained control of the Quebec provincial government in 1960. On a wave of unprecedented anti-clericalism, the control of schools, trade unions and other Catholic institutions was laicized, with the active consent of the more radical section of the clergy. However, none of these institutions has lost its Catholic orientation, and the Catholic Church in Quebec remains, despite its internal changes and the compromises it has been forced to reach, the one instrument of the *ancien régime* of New France which has survived as a powerful institution throughout the two centuries since the conquest.

III

In political terms the British conquerors were in no haste to impose their own system of government on the newly acquired province of Quebec, as New France now became, and for thirty years they followed an authoritarian pattern not unlike that which they had superseded. From 1760 to 1763 the military ruled. Then, from 1763 to 1792, a civil governor ruled with the advice of an appointed council. The British merchants demanded an elected House of Assembly from which—according to current English practice—Roman Catholics would be debarred. Sensing the explosive consequences of such a move, the imperial government effected a compromise which worked reasonably well. By the Quebec Act, British criminal law and French civil law were adopted, and the idea of an assembly was accepted in principle, but its realization was postponed for a more opportune time. The time came at the end of the American War of Independence, when thousands of men of British descent and traditions, occupying the western regions of the Province of Quebec, began to demand representative institutions. These were finally granted in the Constitutional Act of 1791, by which Quebec was divided into the two provinces of Lower and Upper Canada (the present Quebec and Ontario), each ruled by a lieutenant-governor, with appointed executive and legislative councils and an elected assembly. The assembly had little direct power, except to approve or disapprove the government's budget, and the colonial officials were in no way responsible to it. It was in Lower Canada that the system first showed its weakness, since here the issue of race was added to that of responsibility. The French Canadians quickly realized the value of British parliamentary institutions—even in their colonial form—as a means of exposing grievances and struggles for power. While the British retained a majority in the executive and legislative councils, the French formed the majority in the elected assembly, and very soon the ruling bodies were divided into the conservative 'British' party and the reformist 'French' party; the situation was not so sharply defined as these titles suggest, since there were tame French *bleus* or conservatives in the 'British' party and English-speaking radicals in the 'French' party. Failing to gain control over the way the money they voted was spent, and to establish the right to impeach unpopular judges and other appointed officials, the 'French' party steadily drew nearer the point of rebellion.

Meanwhile a slower evolution in Upper Canada was tending towards the same end. Here power became solidified during the early years of the nineteenth century in the hands of the so-called Family Compact, a clique of merchants and officials who controlled the workings of government and made large profits out of speculation in land grants. Allied with the Family Compact was the Anglican clique led by Bishop Strachan, which used all its power to retain the Clergy Reserves, a whole seventh of the settlement land of Upper Canada which had been put aside for the benefit of the Protestant clergy. The reformers of Upper Canada, if less verbose than their Lower Canadian counterparts, were more inclined to systematize their thoughts on the democratic process, and it was among them that the demand for responsible government was most elaborately worked out. Responsibility was the democratic conclusion of the British system of government, as opposed to the American. The American system divides the executive from the legislative functions; the President and his cabinet stand apart from the law-making assembly and continue to rule even if they do not enjoy majority support within that body. The theory of responsible government holds that ministers must be members of the law-making assembly, must command an effective majority therein, and must be subject to replacement by the opposition as soon as the assembly, which is the voice of the people, expresses its lack of confidence. An implication of responsible government, as applied to a colonial territory or province, is the idea that the imperial government automatically abdicates control over the colony's internal affairs.

In Upper Canada it was the moderate reformers, led by Robert Baldwin, who advocated responsible government through a parliamentary assembly on the British model, while the more extreme party, led by William Lyon Mackenzie, favoured a radical change of government on the American model. The scanty support received by Mackenzie and Papineau in the rebellions of 1837 suggested that Canadians in general did not desire any extreme departure from the British pattern, and this fact was observed by Lord Durham—Radical Jack—when he arrived in 1838 to investigate political conditions in Canada and submit his proposals for constitutional change.

Coming with an apparently open mind, and vague thoughts of Canadian federation derived from the English radical Roebuck, Durham was in turn chilled by the indifference of the Maritime provinces towards the idea of union with the two Canadas; prejudiced against the 'unprogressive' French Canadians by the merchant barons of Montreal; and attracted by the ideas of Robert Baldwin and his moderate reformers. His famous report, one of the historic documents of Canadian political evolution, was consequently a strange hybrid, combining a recommendation for responsible parliamentary government with a proposal for the legislative union of Upper and Lower Canada, based on an extraordinary miscalculation of the future—the assumption that the French Canadians would quickly become absorbed in both language and culture into the Anglo-Saxon world that surrounded them to west, east and south.

Lord Melbourne's government rejected the immediate application of

Durham's more intelligent recommendation, for responsible government, but, by the Act of Union of 1840, gave shape to the less enlightened of his proposals. Within a stormy decade of confrontations between assemblies and governors, responsible government eventually came into being, in 1848, under Durham's son-in-law, Lord Elgin. The voters of the united colony of Canada were now, as far as the democratic process would allow them, masters of their local destinies. In external relations and defence the imperial government still retained full powers, so that, though Canada was now a self-governing colony, it was still far from national status. Nevertheless, as the first British colony to achieve responsible government, it set the pattern that was to be followed in all areas of the Empire where people of European descent were in the majority. The other North American colonies quickly followed suit: Nova Scotia attained responsible government later in 1848, Prince Edward Island in 1851, New Brunswick in 1854 and Newfoundland in 1855, Manitoba immediately on being declared a province of the new Dominion in 1870, and British Columbia when it joined Canada in 1871.

Federalism, the other characteristic principle of Canadian government, took almost another twenty years to establish its inevitability in Canadian minds. The most urgent internal reason for its acceptance was the explosive character of the legislative union of the two Canadas which had followed on Durham's recommendation. Trapped in a unitary system, the divergent interests of the English and the French became more than ever evident. In an attempt to reconcile the divergences, Canadians cabinets contained an equal number of members from each of the two sections; instead of being led by single prime ministers, the administrations were double-headed, each of them having French- and English-speaking leaders of equal status; for a while it was even thought that a government, to remain in office, must command a majority in both Upper and Lower Canada. Vestiges of this system have survived; even today a Canadian cabinet is still delicately planned to ensure proper representation of all provinces and all major racial groups.

But in themselves these cumbersome governmental balances were not sufficient to solve the problems created by the differences between the French and English, and by the rapid demographic changes of the times. In 1830 the population of Upper Canada—almost entirely English-speaking—had been half that of Lower Canada. By 1851, as a

9

result of massive immigration, it numbered 952,000 against 890,000 Lower Canadians, and by 1861 it drew even farther ahead, to 1,396,000 as against 1,112,000. The Upper Canadians inevitably began to rebel against a system by which they had the same number of members of parliament as the far less numerous Lower Canadians; during the 1850s 'rep. by pop.' became the slogan of the liberal followers of the formidable George Brown, editor of the Toronto *Globe*. The French Canadians reacted in the opposite direction; their extremists demanded a dissolution of the union between the two Canadas.

It was in these circumstances that the idea of federation as a possible solution emerged once again. In 1849 it was proposed at the convention of the British American League, a conservative-oriented movement of which John A. Macdonald was a member. During the following years federation in its various forms began to excite the imagination of British North Americans. In the Atlantic provinces there was talk of Maritime Union, either in a federation or under a centralized government. The leader of the *rouges* in Lower Canada, A. A. Dorion, argued for a federation of the two Canadas. Among the conservatives the idea of a general federation of British North America was kept informally in circulation without becoming an avowed party policy.

It was during the years from 1857 to 1859 that, in the words of the Canadian historian Donald Creighton, 'the pattern of Canadian nationality began to appear in its first pale outline. . . .' Already in 1851 the Nova Scotian leader Joseph Howe had seen in a flash of insight the whole of British North America as a 'boundless and prolific region' of which the Maritime provinces were 'but the Atlantic frontage . . . the wharves upon which its business will be transacted and beside which its rich argosies are to lie'. By the end of the decade the concept of a 'northern nationality', as Alexander Morriss put it in 1858, emerged with a portentous clarity in the minds of many Upper Canadians. The best lands of Upper Canada had been taken and cleared, and the farmers' sons as well as the business men of Toronto began to look greedily towards the ancient but crumbling empire of the Hudson's Bay Company in the west. In 1857 the clamour raised by George Brown and the *Globe* led to the sending of a Canadian geographical expedition into the prairies, and in 1858 Canadian interest in the Far West was stimulated by the gold discoveries in British Columbia.

This very urge to the west increased the apprehensions of the French Canadians, who began to fear that to the growing English-speaking population of Upper Canada would be added thousands more flocking into the opened west; with increasing seriousness they began to consider how their culture might be protected from submergence by a racial and linguistic majority whose claims to representation by population could not indefinitely be put aside.

A third element in the situation emerged in the desire of the railway interests, which were developing in mid century, to expand, not only westward out of Upper Canada, but also towards Canada from the Maritime colonies. The Intercolonial Railway, which would unite Halifax and Quebec, had first been mooted in 1836, and the scheme had been revived more seriously in 1850–52. Not only did the Nova Scotians advocate such a railway on commercial grounds, but the military were aware of its strategic value. At this time, however, the recurrent American menace seemed to be dormant, and the Intercolonial collapsed for lack of support in London. It was revived in 1857 and 1858, with the same failure on each occasion, but the very persistence of the Maritimers showed that in their minds the idea of the Intercolonial and the idea of a general union of British North America were closely linked.

Meanwhile the increasing division of interests between the Lower and Upper sections of Canada, and the growing unworkability of the united colony, were leading the Canadians irresistibly towards the view of confederation as the only possible solution to their political difficulties. The first key decision was prompted by Alexander Tilloch Galt, the land and railway promoter, who in 1858 agreed to become conservative minister of finance on the express condition that a confederation of the whole of British North America should be accepted as a party plank. In that year the proposal was carried to a London conference on North American affairs. It was received hostilely by Lytton, then Colonial Secretary, and coldly by the Maritime governments, who regarded railway communication as more urgent than any political arrangement. This rejection of the larger political scheme led Brown and his liberal followers to propose a confederation of the two Canadas, increased by the prairie lands of the Hudson's Bay Company. Clearly it was only a matter of time and the right impulse before the two great Canadian parties would find agreement.

As in 1812, the United States now appeared as the catalyst of Canadian unity. The Civil War broke out, and at the end of 1861 the removal of two Confederate agents from the British mailship *Trent* by the American warship *San Jacinto* brought Britain and the Northern States close to war. Troops were sailed hurriedly to Halifax and, in a brilliant midwinter operation, rushed by sleigh through the forests of New Brunswick to Quebec and Montreal. The need for a united defence and a uniting railway became evident to the British government, and, though the negotiations over the Intercolonial broke down again in 1862 owing to a failure to reach agreement on the financing of the railway, the attitude of London towards the idea of confederation began to change rapidly as the Northern States developed an anti-British feeling kept alive by various interest groups, from land and railway speculators to the Fenian Brotherhood. The victory of the North at Gettysburg in the middle of 1863 and the increasing truculence of the Americans convinced both the imperial government and the Canadians in their new capital of Ottawa that it was time their political house was put in order.

From this point events followed rapidly. George Brown and his liberals shifted their position by accepting the possibility of a federation of British North America, and on the 14th March, 1864, Brown moved in the Assembly that a committee be appointed to consider the question. Three months later Brown's committee reported in favour of confederation, which henceforward ceased to be a party question. Agreement on confederation reconciled, at least for the time being, those dedicated enemies, the dour and righteous Lowlander George Brown and the witty and bibulous Highlander, John A. Macdonald. The two leaders formed a coalition dedicated to the achievement of general confederation of British North America if that were possible, and, if not, a local confederation of the two Canadas.

The opportunity for carrying this decision further was provided by the Maritimers. Conscious of common trade and defence needs, the governments of Nova Scotia and New Brunswick were considering once again a legislative union under a centralized government, which would restore the old French province of Acadia. To explore the idea they called, for September 1864, a conference at Charlottetown of the three mainland Atlantic colonies, Nova Scotia, New Brunswick and Prince Edward Island. As soon as the Canadians heard of it, they asked permission to appear as guests in order to explain their own proposal of a general confederation. Politely, but not enthusiastically, the Maritimers agreed.

On August 29th Macdonald and the seven other Canadian delegates

27. The cult of the pioneers. A reconstructed pioneer village—now a tourist showpiece— in the Okanagan Valley.

28. The end of an era. Derelict gold mine at Wells, B.C.

29. Western Gothic. The miners' church at Barkerville.

30. The heart of the Cariboo. Barkerville's main street, once the centre of a community of 30,000 people, now of a ghost town.

set sail from Quebec to Prince Edward Island. They arrived on the morning of September 1st to find that the discussions had already begun without them. To the Canadians this seemed an unpromising start, but as they had landed they were relieved to hear that the conference, on learning of their arrival, had decided unanimously to put aside its discussions on a union of the Maritime colonies so that the Canadians might present their arguments for a greater union.

George Etienne Cartier was the first to outline the Canadian proposal, followed by George Brown and Alexander Galt. By the time the scheme of confederation, with its remoter suggestions of a great nation spreading shadowily from ocean to ocean, had been fully unfolded, the purpose for which the conference had originally been called—the union of the Atlantic provinces—began to seem meagre even to the Maritimers themselves. Their subsequent regional discussions, from which the Canadians were excluded, bogged down over the insistence of Prince Edward Island—the smallest colony of all—that its own capital of Charlottetown should become the capital of the proposed Maritime union. By September 8th no agreement had been reached on either the Canadian or Maritime plans, and the conference was adjourned to Halifax. There, on September 12th, the Atlantic colonies finally agreed to the Canadian suggestion that a new conference, specifically to discuss British North American confederation, should begin at Quebec on October 10th, and that to complete the colonial roster Newfoundland should be invited.

At first in Quebec all seemed concord and agreement. The general shape of the proposed federation emerged quickly. Each colony would become a province, with the one exception that Canada would be divided once again into two provinces whose boundaries would correspond to those of Upper and Lower Canada before the Union Act of 1841; in this way the French Canadians could feel assured that their culture, their language and their system of civil law would be protected within their own provincial sphere from the increased Anglo-Saxon majority that would come with confederation. Both central and local governments would be responsible, though the question of the limits of provincial sovereignty—destined to plague Canada for a century—was not decided.

It was when the details were discussed that dissension first appeared. It was easily agreed that the central Parliament should be bicameral, and there was no disputing the Canadian proposal that the lower house, later to become the House of Commons, should be elected on the basis of representation by population. The upper house, which eventually became the Senate, was an appointive body, with life membership, so as to remove it from the political storms to which the American Senate was susceptible. It was to be designed so that its membership might tend to counteract the preponderance that the more populous provinces —the two Canadas—would inevitably assume in the lower house. On the method of assuring this, disagreement broke out, expressed most acrimoniously by the truculently independent Prince Edward Islanders. Their delegates demanded equal representation for each province, which was clearly impossible, since it would have put the two large inland provinces at the mercy of a majority from the small Atlantic provinces.

The Canadians countered with a proposal for representation by sections on a geographical basis, the Maritimes counting as one section, and each of the two Canadas as one. Each section would have twenty-four members; those from the Maritimes would be apportioned to the various colonies according to population. Eventually it was worked out that the three Maritime provinces immediately interested in confederation should receive twenty-four seats, ten each for Nova Scotia and New Brunswick and four for Prince Edward Island, with a proviso that there would be four extra seats for Newfoundland should she decide to enter the union, to be balanced later by four for British Columbia and the Northwest. The proposal was carried by all votes but those of the Prince Edward Islanders, who made a bitter stand for five seats instead of four. Thus, at the beginning, the regional strains which partially offset the advantages of any federal system of government were beginning to show.

The Quebec conference was only a partial success. Prince Edward Island was antagonized, and the Newfoundland delegates remained aloof from any commitment. On the other hand, at that moment there seemed no reason to doubt the solid support of New Brunswick and Nova Scotia, and the challenge of absorbing the Northwest seemed more important to the Canadians than the possible defection of the two island colonies.

However, when confederation came up for ratification in New Brunswick and Nova Scotia, the Canadians were shocked to hear that the political leaders who had reached agreement in Quebec did not necessarily speak for their peoples. All the distrust that Maritimers had harboured towards the politically more turbulent populations of the two Canadas reasserted itself and the very idea of a North American confederation was criticized almost as widely as the actual terms which the delegates brought home. The large Acadian and Irish Catholic population of New Brunswick feared that they might not enjoy the same safeguards as confederation would bring their co-religionists in Lower Canada, and the American railway interests, opposed to the Intercolonial Railway that would now be built as part of the terms of union, began to subsidize the enemies of federation. In the general elections held in January 1865, the confederationist government was decisively defeated. Meanwhile, in Nova Scotia, opposition built up among those who would have preferred a closer link—perhaps even a parliamentary one—with Britain, and those whose business interests were directed towards New England rather than the St. Lawrence; economically, Nova Scotia, still a prosperous shipping and shipbuilding colony, looked east and south rather than west. The Nova Scotian confederationists found the tide of opinion running so strongly against them that at first they did not dare to bring the Quebec agreement before their legislature.

Even in Canada there was opposition among the French. 'I say without hesitation,' argued Joseph Perrault in tones which anticipate those of modern Quebec separatists, 'that in the case of a collision, we shall find ourselves at the mercy of a hostile Federal majority, and that it may oppress us, assimilate our laws, suspend our judges, arm the militia against us, and send us to the scaffold or into exile in any way they may think proper, notwithstanding our protestations, and those of the French-Canadian minority in Parliament.' But not many even of the French Canadians agreed with Perrault, and the Quebec terms were ratified in Canada by a large majority.

Canadian steadfastness was justified by events, and, once again, it was the threat from the south that brought the colonies together. By the beginning of 1866 official American belligerency had become muted, but this fact made the Fenian Brotherhood all the more intent on action against the colonies as a means of attacking Britain indirectly. In the spring of 1866, the Fenians in Maine began their preparations for an assault on New Brunswick. The local militia was called out, but this time the Fenians did not come; however, the mere threat of invasion was enough to swing local feeling, and in a new election the confederationists came back to power. At last, on June 1st, the Fenians struck in

Upper Canada, where they captured Fort Erie and, at the battle of Ridgeway, defeated the Canadian militia, only to be driven back over the frontier by the British regulars. If there were any residual doubts among Canadians about confederation, these impetuous Irishmen effectively stilled them.

It was therefore with new confidence that, in November 1866, the delegates from Canada, Nova Scotia and New Brunswick gathered in London to work out the details of union. Lord Carnarvon, the Colonial Secretary, was nominal chairman of the conference, but in practice it was John A. Macdonald who chaired the business sessions, and became, as his French-Canadian colleague Langevin remarked, '*the man* of the conference'. Eight years before, when Canada first officially sponsored confederation, Macdonald had been at best lukewarm; now he took in hand energetically the task of giving it substantial form, and the British North America Act, which was given Royal Assent on 29th March, 1867, was more his work than any other man's.

With the passing of the Act, a new political form came into being within the British Empire, something more than a colony, less than a nation. Its name, everybody agreed, should be Canada, but its title raised a difficulty. Macdonald would have called it The Kingdom of Canada, but Lord Carnarvon, anxious not to offend the Americans by a 'monarchical blister', ruled out the suggestion, as he did that of a Vice-royalty. In the end, Tilley of New Brunswick came up with a text from Psalm 72 which seemed to accord perfectly with the intent of the federation: 'He shall have dominion also from sea to sea. . . .' The Dominion of Canada it became, setting the fashion for the later self-governing countries within the Empire. Only in 1952, with the accession of Elizabeth II, was the intent of the Fathers of Confederation fulfilled. She ascended the throne as specifically Queen of Canada, and the Dominion changed into the Kingdom.

The Canada over which Macdonald—now Sir John A.—ruled as the first Prime Minister consisted only of four provinces: Quebec and Ontario (Lower and Upper Canada renamed), New Brunswick and Nova Scotia. Yet it was already, by the standards of the Old World, an immense country, extending from the Atlantic to Lake Superior in the mid continent, and the first task of its founders was not to expand it, but to keep it together. In 1868, Nova Scotia returned a provincial government dedicated to gaining a repeal of the British North America Act, and a solid contingent of secessionist M.P.'s, led by Joseph Howe, came to the House of Commons at Ottawa. It turned out a less difficult situation than it first appeared. The Imperial government refused to consider any change in the British North America Act, and Howe, faced with annexation by the United States as the only—and dangerous —alternative to confederation, surrendered to an offer from Macdonald of increased federal subsidies for his province.

Sir John was now able to turn his attention to the Northwest, where the decay of the Hudson's Bay Company's dominion was creating a political vacuum which must quickly be filled if the land were not to be lost by default to the Americans. The purchase of the Company's rights, at the price of £300,000 plus a substantial land grant, was completed in 1869. The transfer of the territory to the British government and thence to Canada was fixed for December 1st. In fact, the Red River Rising, led by Louis Riel, delayed the settlement until 1870, when the fifth province—Manitoba—was formed. With the accession of British Columbia in 1871, and Prince Edward Island in 1873, and the cession by Britain of the Arctic Archipelago in 1880, the great design of a land

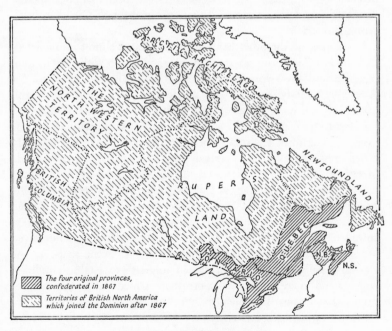

The four original provinces, confederated in 1867

Territories of British North America which joined the Dominion after 1867

3. Canada at Confederation, 1867

from ocean to ocean was complete. Newfoundland, the eastern outpost, still remained aloof, turned towards Europe, and would remain so until long after the death of the men who created the Dominion of Canada.

IV

Canada, when it emerged in 1867, had as its constitution the Act of a parliament far over the Atlantic, and today the sole remaining vestige of imperial rule is that the British North America Act can only be amended in Westminster; no formula has yet been devised by which the constitution can be placed entirely in Canadian hands, though in no case has a Canadian request for amendment been rejected by the Imperial government.

There were other respects in which for a long period Canada remained dependent. In law, for example, the final appeal from Canadian courts was until 1949 to the Judicial Committee of the Privy Council in London. Then, after the Judicial Committee had granted the competence of the Canadian parliament to abolish appeals to it, the Supreme Court of Canada became the ultimate tribunal for all Canadian cases, criminal or civil.

In defence, on the other hand, Canada became almost immediately self-reliant. The British government was anxious to withdraw its own troops as quickly as possible so as to remove all possible reason for American hostility, and the last Canadian campaign in which British units took part was the expedition led by Colonel Garnet Wolseley to the Red River in 1870. This, however, was not technically an expedition into Canadian territory; since the Northwest was not formally ceded until after Wolseley's arrival. The last British forces left Canada in 1871 except for small garrisons guarding the naval bases which the Royal Navy still maintained at Halifax and at Esquimalt on the Pacific coast. The garrisons went in 1905 when the dockyards were handed over to the newly created Royal Canadian Navy, and Britain withdrew completely from the defence of Canada. British officers were borrowed for several decades after Confederation to give some shape to the Canadian militia—an army of citizen soldiers—to establish military colleges and to create the small permanent armed force, with its ceremonial guard units; but when that very typical British blimp, Major-General Middleton, led an army into the west in 1885 to fight the last war on Canadian soil, against the métis sharpshooters led by Louis Riel and Gabriel Dumont, it was an all-Canadian force and consisted mostly of amateur riflemen.

From British wars Canada maintained from Confederation onwards the formal right to remain aloof, though in practice it was difficult for a Canadian government to resist the persuasions applied from without by the British government and the pressures exerted from within by the large proportion of Canadians who still felt that Britain was their homeland. On the first British request, which came in 1884 at the time of Wolseley's Sudan expedition, Macdonald compromised by sending a civilian labour corps and refusing to provide an armed force. During the Boer War Laurier agreed rather reluctantly to send an armed contingent, but when he was urged to provide ships for the British Navy, he preferred to establish a Royal Canadian Navy. Nevertheless, when war broke out between Britain and Germany in 1914, Canada entered without thought of neutrality; the filial link seemed as strong as any treaty could have been. By 1918, however, there were many, particularly among the French Canadians, who had been antagonized by the imposition of conscription, and who developed anti-war and isolationist attitudes which continued into the inter-war period. By this time, too, the Canadian government was more conscious than in 1914 of its dignity as an independent power, and in September 1939 Canada waited a full week after Britain before making its separate declaration of war on Germany. The final stage in this process of withdrawal from automatic commitment to British military ventures was reached in 1956, when Canada refused to support the Franco-British military adventure in the Suez Canal Zone, and instead directed her efforts to finding, in collaboration with India, a way out of a dangerous international situation.

The obligation of self-defence which was implied in Canada's acquisition of dominion status carried as its logical corollary the privilege of an independent control of foreign relations. But what the British North America Act conceded by implication was not quickly gained in practice. Canada's external relations were dominated by past British agreements and the first international accord relating to Canada after Confederation was in fact negotiated between Britain and the United States. This was the Treaty of Washington in formulating which Sir John A. Macdonald served, not as representative of Canada, but as a member of the British delegation; he was forced to agree to a settlement of Anglo-American differences which was distinctly disadvantageous to

Canada. The only thing gained was that provision was made for the Canadian ratification of certain clauses; this implied at least a token recognition by the United States of Canada's national status. But Canada's role as a separate power in a wider international field was slow to develop. Its first representative abroad was the High Commissioner to Britain, appointed in 1880; an agent general was appointed to Paris in 1882. A Department of External Affairs was not founded until 1908, and for long it remained no more than embryonic.

Canada's first real step towards independent status in international affairs came as late as 1917, when its representative was admitted to the Imperial War Cabinet. Later Canada participated in the negotiation of the Settlement at Versailles, signed the treaty as a separate state, and became a full member of the League of Nations. Finally, in 1926, the status of all the Dominions was established by the Balfour Declaration, confirmed by the Statute of Westminster in 1931, according to which they were recognized as equal partners to Great Britain within the Commonwealth. Immediately afterwards, Canada began to establish embassies instead of agencies—in Washington in 1927, Paris in 1928 and Tokyo in 1929. Already, from 1923 onwards, it had been negotiating treaties with the United States. With the final breakup of the Empire after the Second World War Canada took an active role in forming the United Nations, and its liberation from imperial ties was complete. Politically, at least, it stood on its own, and since that period it has tried, so far as its economic and military entanglements with the United States will allow, to play an independent middle-power role in the world community.

Canada's progression towards effective national independence during the century since 1867 has been marred only by the difficulties that always face a middle power living in the shadow of a strong, populous and aggressive country whose people speak the same language and possess a similar culture. But Canadians in this century accept American attempts at domination with as little docility as they did those of the British a hundred years ago. On these complicated questions of continental relations I shall have more to say later on when I deal with Canada's present position in world affairs, and for the moment it is sufficient, as evidence of an essential independence of American moods and movements, to point out that in 1968, when the forces of reaction in America were building up towards a presidential election that would provide a choice of conservative alternatives, Canada in its own parlia-

32. Hoodoos: eroded rock formations in the Rocky Mountain Trench.

31. The ranger. Cowboy at Pavilion, B.C.

33. An ancient land. The face of the Rockies.

34. The National Parks breed trust between animals and man. A mountain sheep on the Banff-Jasper Highway in Alberta.

mentary election exhibited the reverse trend by choosing a personally attractive and politically untried intellectual on a platform in which the liberation of private lives was one of the two promises. The Americans voted for more 'law and order'; the Canadians voted for more freedom.

But they also voted for the unity of the country, since Pierre Elliott Trudeau's other promise was that he would keep Canada together and provide the conditions under which its various peoples could see themselves as men of different languages and traditions indeed, but equal partners nevertheless. He defended the federalism that forms the peculiarly difficult basis of Canadian political life. For, if Canada's journey towards national independence has been relatively plain sailing, her internal political voyage towards the ideal combination of union and diversity has avoided the Niagaras of disaster only by following the rapids of dissension.

V

Ideally, the federal form is doubtless the best of all administrative patterns, particularly for a large country, but there is much truth in the anarchist contention that it will be ultimately successful only when the central government is reduced to a coordinating committee between autonomous regions. All confederations which have attempted to balance strong central power against effective local power have experienced recurrent strife between the different levels of authority. Switzerland has carried the federalist principle as far as it can possibly go without abandoning entirely the element of central power; in theory at least sovereignty rests with the local aggregations, the cantons and the communes. But even Switzerland has never entirely reconciled the desire for unity with the urge to diversity.

In Canada federalism has lent itself to disturbance and dissension, mainly because of the ambiguities and silences of the British North America Act. In governmental terms there exists in Canada a two-tiered structure which diverges from the classic federal pattern. In no sense does the central government derive from the provinces as political units. The parliament in Ottawa is directly elected through a separate machinery from that used in the provinces, the federal cabinet is responsible only to that parliament, and even the Senate, which originally was conceived as a body to protect provincial rights, is in practice appointed by successive central governments who fill its vacancies without ever consulting the provinces. Ottawa appoints the lieutenant-governors of the provinces, who carry out locally the functions of constitutional monarchy, but it has no actual authority over the provincial governments, except to the extent of disallowing provincial legislation as constitutionally *ultra vires*, and even here the final decision in disputes between the central and provincial governments lies with the Supreme Court. There is in fact no effective constitutional link between the two levels of government in Canada. In practice, it has been impossible to do without some machinery of coordination, and in recent years the Dominion-Provincial conferences, in which the Prime Minister of Canada and the provincial Premiers meet to discuss matters of common concern, have assumed quasi-constitutional status. The conferences have no power to legislate or make formal agreements, but they have proved a useful means of dealing with the areas of indefiniteness in the British North America Act so far as central and local rights are concerned.

It would be tedious to list the twenty-nine fields of legislation which the British North America Act reserves exclusively for the Parliament of Canada, and the sixteen reserved exclusively for the provinces. All the matters of obvious common concern in 1867 were accorded to the Dominion, including defence, currency, the postal service, naturalization, etc., while the provinces were specifically authorized to legislate on a series of questions of obviously local concern, such as lands, marriages, public works, etc. There was a curious arrangement regarding criminal law: the central government would legislate and the provincial governments administer it. In agriculture and immigration the two levels of government were granted concurrent powers (providing provincial laws were not 'repugnant to any Act of the Parliament of Canada'). In education the provinces were given general control, but the central government had the right to interfere where the interests of minorities might be imperilled.

These fields where powers were concurrent were to offer ample play for dissension. Furthermore, the legislators of 1867 not only could not foresee the new fields of legislation that might emerge in later generations, but also made no really adequate provision to accommodate them. On the one hand it was stated that the Parliament of Canada should have the right 'to make Laws for the Peace, Order and Good Government of Canada in relation to all Matters not coming within the Classes of Subjects by this Act assigned exclusively to the Legislatures of the Provinces'. On the other hand, there were two catch-all clauses which allowed the provinces to legislate on 'Property and Civil Rights', a vast and totally undefined territory, and 'generally [on] all matters of a merely local or private nature in the Province'. Curiously, there was no specific provision for the conduct of foreign relations (except in the field of ferries).

Inevitably, as the world changed and Canada developed towards nationhood, the specific provisions of 1867 proved inadequate. Under Sir John A. Macdonald, a dedicated centralist who had accepted federalism only as a second best to legislative union, the Dominion government interpreted the clause granting it residuary powers in un-specified areas to mean that, in any new field opened up by technologi-cal development or changing political or social conditions, Ottawa automatically assumed authority. Not merely have the provinces consistently rejected this claim. They have also, at several times during Canada's first century, demanded greater autonomy than the British North America Act contemplated; in other words, they have tried to create a genuine federation.

The first storm over such questions arose during the 1880s. By the middle of that decade the euphoria of Confederation had passed away, and Sir John A. Macdonald, now the Old Chieftain, had aroused, by a peculiar combination of arrogance and calculated inactivity, a deep resentment in many parts of the country. His insistence on the execution of Louis Riel after the Northwest Rebellion incensed the French Canadians, and raised the premier of Quebec, Honoré Mercier of the Parti National, to demogogic leadership of an aggrieved third of the country's population. Earlier in the decade Oliver Mowat, premier of Ontario, had on several occasions successfully extended provincial powers by appealing to the Judicial Committee of the Privy Council under the 'Property and Civil Rights' clause. Mowat found allies in William S. Fielding, the premier of Nova Scotia, who was still flying the banner of secession, and John Norquay, the premier of Manitoba, in arms against the monopoly which Macdonald's government had granted the Canadian Pacific Railway over traffic in the prairies. In 1887 Mercier brought them all together in a 'constitutional conference' and there—with only British Columbia and Prince Edward Island unrepre-sented—the insurgent provincial premiers not merely insisted that the constitution should be interpreted as liberally as possible to accord with their autonomist ambitions, but also demanded constitutional changes that would substantially decentralize authority. Specifically, they asked that the provinces appoint half the members of the Senate, that the federal government relinquish its power to disallow provincial legislation, and that a greater share of the income from taxation be paid to the provinces so as to expand their sphere of activity and—though this was never explicitly stated—of influence. Instead of actively opposing the demands of the provincial premiers, Sir John lived up to his nickname of 'Old Tomorrow' by ignoring them until the wave of regionalist discontent had died away.

But the events of 1887 were only the first of a long series of attacks on the powers of the central government by provincial leaders and alliances of provincial leaders. As Canada has grown more prosperous and socially and technologically more complex, the provinces' governments have inevitably gathered power and influence even without any changes in the constitution. The budget of the smallest Canadian province is considerably larger than the national budgets of many countries which sit in the United Nations, and when the premiers of provinces like Quebec or even British Columbia go abroad to talk culture or trade, they are received with a consideration that would not have been accorded the Dominion Prime Minister in 1867. With their control of great natural resources in a world hungry for raw materials, they are men of considerable economic power. There has in practice been a certain cyclical movement in the relations between federal and provincial authorities. During the two World Wars and the periods following them, provincial influence has waned and the federal government has been able to impose a considerable degree of centralized control. At other times, and especially during the present decade, the tendency has been towards greater provincial autonomy, and the air has been loud with battles over such matters as the ownership of mineral rights below the tideline, the rights of provincial governments to establish banks, and the status of Quebec.

To any neat-minded constitutionalist the perennial disorder of Canada's governmental system must seem lamentable, and there are many Canadians who would like to see this heritage of the 1860s exchanged for a more centralized system devised by a committee of political economists. It can, however, be argued that the British North America Act has served the country remarkably well, since its very ambiguities have provided a flexibility desirable in a rapidly developing and changing country. Perhaps its greatest virtue is in the very fact that it has allowed powerful provincial leaders to stand in some degree as rivals to the federal leaders, which has helped to prevent even the strongest Canadian prime minister—even a Macdonald or a Laurier— from acquiring anything approaching the frightening power enjoyed by the most wretched nonentity among American presidents. Canadian federalism, in other words, tends to be libertarian by the partition of both legislative and executive powers; American federalism, by concentrating power, tends to be authoritarian.

But to talk only of the federal and provincial governments which have replaced the colonial administrations of pre-Confederation days, is to ignore the existence of powerful extra-parliamentary and sometimes extra-governmental bodies which have wielded an enormous influence in Canadian life. They vary greatly in origin and character. The Hudson's Bay Company is a private corporation which for two centuries enjoyed the powers and privileges of a government. The Canadian Pacific Railway, also a private corporation, came into being as the result of government initiative, and government subsidies. The Northwest Mounted Police has been a unique combination of a police force, an occupying army and a pioneer administrative service. And, finally, there are those organizations, of which I have chosen the Canadian Broadcasting Corporation as typical, through which the Canadian government has applied itself to functions which in many other countries have been regarded as the province of private enterprise. Since pre-Confederation days there has been a strong element of unacknowledged socialism in the policies of Canadian governments, and this has come about of necessity, since modern means of transport and communication could hardly have been established in an immense, under-populated and industrially backward country like Canada as late as the 1950s without a high degree of governmental participation.

VI

The Hudson's Bay Company began as a typical trading corporation of the mercantile age. As in the case of the East India Company, the centre of its authority remained in London, and, with all the changes that have befallen the Company since its foundation in 1670, the pattern continues. The title of the Company—though its business is almost wholly Canadian—is still 'The Governor and Company of Adventurers of England trading into Hudson's Bay', and its policies are still determined at the 'Annual General Court' which is held each year at Beaver Hall on Garlick Hill in the City of London. Throughout its long history the Company has never abandoned as its first objective the provision by profitable trading of adequate dividends for its shareholders. Unlike the East India Company, it never reached the stage where territorial domination became its most important function. Except for the brief interlude when Lord Selkirk dominated the Company and founded the Red River colony, it discouraged settlement in the land under its control, mainly because it realized the difficulties this would create in a fur-trading empire. At the height of its power, after its rivalry with the Northwest Company had been terminated by amalgamation in 1821, its total European staff numbered about 2,000 men, scattered over the whole area from the Red River and Hudson's Bay to the Pacific coast of New Caledonia, which stretched from the Russian domain in Alaska down to the southern limit of the present state of Oregon. Compared with the immense establishment of the East India Company, this was negligible, but the Hudson's Bay Company made no attempt to occupy its lands in any intensive way, or to establish any kind of political control over the Indian tribes, though its officers might on occasion use their influence to prevent wars detrimental to trade. It was concerned to protect its trade routes and its forts and posts from attack by the Indians or by rival fur traders, but for this purpose it did not need to recruit a professional army. The voyageurs were capable of carrying out any minor defensive operations that might be necessary.

The general affairs of the Company's domain were ruled by a hierarchy as strict as that of the East India Company. Some Scots and English served all their lives as mariners or artisans and never became part of the hierarchy, but those who did began as assistant clerks recruited—mainly from Scotland as they still are today—to serve for periods of five years, after which they were appointed clerks. A few years later they might ascend to the rank of Chief Trader in charge of a smaller trading post. The final step was to Chief Factor. The managers of all the more important forts held this rank. Above the Chief Factors were the resident Governors of the Northern and Southern Departments, and at the top of the hierarchy the Governor-in-Chief, who supervised all the affairs of the Company in North America. Over the main doorway of the Hudson's Bay Company's store in Vancouver there still stands a mural painting showing the visual attributes of such power. A large birchbark *canot de maître* sweeps over boiling rapids between the almost cubistic crags of the Fraser Canyon; the swarthy voyageurs are paddling feverishly to keep the craft from disaster. And, impassive in the midst of these bituminous shadows and dangers, sits an austere Scottish gentleman, decked out in a beaver hat of the best quality, a black frock coat, a white collar to his ears. He is Sir George Simpson, the most powerful of the Company's Governors-in-Chief, passing in 1828 through his territories beyond the Rockies.

It was only towards the end of its territorial empire that the Hudson's Bay Company began to branch out into ventures other than fur, principally because of the temptations offered by the bland climate and fertile soil of the Pacific coast. Dr. John McLoughlin, the Company's representative in the agriculturally rich valley of the Columbia, started during the 1830s the first large-scale farming project west of the prairies. By 1840 he had created a farm of 3,000 acres, whose grain was ground in mills which provided sufficient flour for the western forts of the Hudson's Bay Company and for export to the Russians in Alaska. McLoughlin also established sawmills in which the great Pacific trees were cut into timbers which found a market in the Sandwich Islands, where the Company set up a post to deal with this trade. But these experiments only justified the older fur traders' apprehensive distrust of the farmer, for they opened American eyes to the agricultural possibilities of the Oregon Territory and encouraged the emigration which allowed the United States to claim the land south of the 49th parallel and brought about the eventual expulsion of the Hudson's Bay Company from this lucrative region.

Meanwhile, in Rupert's Land, there had existed since 1812 an enclave of settlement where an administration concerned with something more than fur trading had to be established. This was Lord Selkirk's Red River colony. The community of Scots, English-speaking halfbreeds and French-speaking métis, which in 1840 numbered more than 4,000, was ruled by a Governor appointed first by the Earl and later, when the land rights were surrendered by his heirs in 1836, by the Company itself. The Governor was assisted by a Council, nominated by the Company, but including Anglican and Catholic clergy and representatives of all sections of the local community, as well as of the Company. This body, called the Council of Assiniboia, was the first political administration of any kind in the West. From the mid 1830s, the Red River Settlement began to develop into a miniature commonwealth. Regulations relating to the good government of the colony were legislated by the Council; customs and postal facilities were established; a Board of

Works and a Committee of Economy were set up. Finally, a judicial hierarchy was created, with local magistrates, a higher court presided over by the Recorder of Rupert's Land, and, as a supreme appellate tribunal, the Quarterly Court of the Governor and Council of Assiniboia. Under Acts of the imperial parliament passed in 1803 and 1821, the courts of Canada had concurrent jurisdiction over offences committed within the territories granted to the Hudson's Bay Company, but there is no record of any cases having reached such courts, and it seems evident that the government embodied in the Council of Assiniboia remained a local instrument of the Hudson's Bay Company designed to give some expression to the wishes of the local inhabitants as well as to the Company's own interests. It remained effective until the disintegration of the old order in 1868–9, when the threat of cession to Canada brought into being the métis Provisional Government led by Louis Riel, which was followed, in 1870, by the establishment of the province of Manitoba.

Meanwhile, in the farther west, a somewhat different experiment in government had been undertaken by the Hudson's Bay Company. After its virtual expulsion from Oregon in 1846, a Pacific headquarters was established at Fort Victoria—on Vancouver Island. Here the Company proposed to create agricultural settlements. The British government granted the island for this purpose, but on this occasion broke precedent by appointing its own governor, Richard Blanshard. Blanshard found himself powerless beside the formidable Company establishment, and left in 1851; he was followed as Governor by the Company's Chief Factor, James Douglas, who represented the Colonial Office and the Company at the same time, to the detriment of effective settlement. It was not until 1867 that the Company's administration of Vancouver Island came to an end.

The early attempts at local government within the territories administered by the Hudson's Bay Company certainly had no influence on the form taken by the Canadian federal government, or even on the provincial governments later set up in the areas where it once ruled. On the other hand, the government of the Northwest Territories, including the regions which later became Saskatchewan and Alberta, was at first modelled on the Company's Council of Assiniboia. In 1870 the lieutenant-governor of Manitoba administered the territories with an appointed Council; in 1876 a separate lieutenant-governor was stationed in the territories, still ruling with an appointed council. It was

35. Edmonton. The new Canadian National Station. (CANADIAN NATIONAL RAILWAYS)

36. The patterns of the Prairies. (CANADIAN NATIONAL RAILWAYS)

not until 1887 that, scared by Louis Riel's second rebellion, Ottawa granted a territorial legislature, and rule by Council ended. However, when Alberta and Saskatchewan were created in 1905, and the present Northwest Territories were formed out of regions north of the 60th parallel, the old pattern of the Council of Assiniboia was revived, and from that time to the present the Canadian north has been governed by a Commissioner and a Territorial Council, with the federal government in Ottawa replacing the Hudson's Bay Company in London as the ultimate source of authority.

The Hudson's Bay Company survives as one of the most powerful commercial organizations in Canada. It has 250 stores of various kinds scattered over Canada, and having successfully absorbed all its competitors it still maintains a virtual monopoly of trade in the North except for the Yukon territory. As well as a vast retail and wholesale trade, amounting to more than $400,000,000 a year, it still controls the major part of Canada's fur trade. Apart from the commercial power which this represents, particularly in the remoter areas of Canada, and apart from creating a form of government for unsettled territories, the most important contribution that the Hudson's Bay Company has made to the present shape of Canadian life is to be found in the patterns of communication and the nuclei of settlement which it established. The exploration of western Canada by the fur traders provided the maps used by the makers of railways and roads, and it was around Hudson's Bay forts that many of the larger cities of Canada first began to form. Winnipeg, Edmonton, Victoria, Brandon, Nanaimo, Prince George and Kamloops all shared this origin in the distant fur-trading past.

VII

As the Hudson's Bay Company receded from power in the prairies, the Northwest Mounted Police and the Canadian Pacific Railway filled the vacuum, one representing power and the other progress—the progress from the hunting economy to an economy of farming and mining. The idea of a railway across the prairies, which had so long haunted the vision of those who foresaw a Canada stretching between the oceans, was the first to emerge, but it did not become a fact until after the prairies had been pacified and the threat of Indian interference had been dispelled by the appearance of the Northwest Mounted Police.

The Mounted Police was the Canadian response to a double threat in the newly acquired Northwest. The end of the Red River Rising and the collapse of Riel's Provisional Government at Fort Garry in 1870 left Canada in firm control of the small area which became the first province of Manitoba. But in the vast spaces of the farther prairies two threats loomed—a general Indian uprising, and an American penetration which was already beginning in the whisky traders' posts, of which Fort Whoop Up was the most notorious example, that were established in Canadian territory. In 1872 Colonel Robertson Ross, one of Wolseley's officers who had been appointed Adjutant General of the Canadian Militia, was sent on a tour of inspection into the plains, and brought back a recommendation that, if peace were to be established and the country to be retained, some kind of armed force must be established in the Northwest. Given the circumstances, it was a realistic assessment. If something of the kind were not done quickly, the Americans would have an excellent case for moving in to deal with fugitive Indians and to establish their own version of order.

Yet, in Macdonald's cautious eyes, there might be a provocation in giving an openly military tone to the Canadian occupation, and, instead of being called the Northwest Mounted Rifles, the new force, established in 1873, became the Northwest Mounted Police. If the Dominion parliament needed any encouragement to pass the necessary legislation, it was provided by the Cypress Hills massacre of the same year. The new force's name accorded with its first tasks, which were precisely those of a frontier police, but in every other respect the NWMP was a quasi-military body. Its original 300 officers and men were almost all recruited from the British regular army or from the small Canadian establishment. The first Commissioner, Captain G. A. French, had held a commission in the Royal Artillery, and he established a strict military discipline. His men, who were forbidden to marry during their early years in the force, lived in barracks, and were subjected to intensive drills and to training in light cavalry guerrilla tactics; they wore the red jackets traditionally associated with the British army, and military pillbox hats.

On 10th June 1874, 275 of the new recruits started on the Great March which was intended to show the Canadian flag in the new west as well as to pacify the country. In the middle of the plains they divided. A small force set off to establish a post at Fort Edmonton in the northern prairies, but the greater number made their way through the vital border country in the direction of the Cypress Hills and the Rockies. Arriving at Fort Whoop Up, they found that the whisky traders had prudently retreated over the border, leaving an American flag defiantly flying over their deserted stockade. They arrested a few straggling traders, and poured to waste a few kegs of the dubious liquor which— well diluted with water and laced with cayenne pepper—was sold to the Indians. Then they proceeded to the foothills, establishing Fort MacLeod as their centre and farther east building another fort which became the nucleus of the present city of Calgary.

With a mixture of boldness and tact, the Mounted Police established good relations with the Indians, who were glad to see the whisky traders and the wolfers expelled, and the American army—notorious for its inhuman methods—kept out of the country. After the Mounties came, there were no further serious conflicts between the Indian tribes; the last great battle had been fought between the Crees and the Blackfoot in 1870 and several hundred braves were killed. The unwonted docility of the Indians was not entirely due to the presence of the Mounted Police. It was partly a result of the decline of the buffalo, and partly also of the fact that the more far-sighted chiefs were beginning to realize that the old order in the prairies had come to an end, and that they had to accommodate themselves to the new. There was undoubt- edly resignation and diplomacy as well as possibly a touch of real gratitude in the famous statement of Crowfoot, the paramount chief of the Blackfoot Confederacy: 'If the Police had not come to the country, where would we all be now? Bad men and whisky were kill- ing us so fast that very few, indeed, of us would have been left today. The Police have protected us as the feathers of the bird protect it from the frosts of the winter.'

Crowfoot made his statement when the treaties were signed to estab- lish peace in the prairies. The first was with the Woods and Plains Crees in 1876; the second with the Blackfoot Confederacy in 1877. Apart from the Indian risings which were incidental to the second Riel rebel- lion in 1885, and in which the Mounted Police showed themselves militarily inept, there were no more Indian wars.

To the role of frontier policemen and tribal diplomats, the Mounted Police quickly added that of administrators. Until the settlers came in large numbers and the Department of the Interior moved in to organize immigration and the allocation of lands, it was their responsibility to see that the government of the land continued. A skeleton force—only

600 men even by 1910—they were scattered over the prairies and represented Canada in a vast region where military authority was non-existent and civil authority rudimentary.

This unique role as all-purpose pioneers of government the Mounted Police carried with them as their responsibilities spread with the expanding frontier. They first appeared in the true North when they were sent to the Yukon in 1898 to assert Canadian sovereignty as well as to impose on the great migration an order which earlier gold rushes had lacked. Their Maxim-gun post at the head of the White Pass not only discouraged American claims; it also kept out of the Yukon the organized crime that dominated the Alaskan port of Skagway where the miners landed to begin their overland trip to the goldfields. Not until 1903 did the Mounted Police establish a first post in the present Northwest Territories, but from 1905, when the Territories were separated from the provinces of Saskatchewan and Alberta, the North came under their direct control, and the NWMP Commissioner doubled as Commissioner of the Territories from 1905 to 1919. This was the period when the Mounted Police assumed in the North the primary task they had followed in the West, that of showing the flag, establishing sovereignty and setting up scattered posts from which long patrols would make their way through the Barren Land. Even after the Department of the Interior took over responsibility for the Northwest Territories in 1919 and appointed a civilian Commissioner, the Mounted Police continued to carry out most of the administrative function in the Arctic, and their ships weaved through the distant channels of the North; one of them, the *Saint Roch*, was the first ship to make its way through the Northwest Passage in a single season. Only when the Department of Northern Affairs was established in 1953 did the Mounted Police give up their all-purpose role in the north and settle down to a comparatively quiet routine of normal police functions, plus the registration of births and deaths, and search and rescue operations.

Elsewhere in Canada the role of the Mounted Police has changed considerably since, in 1920, they were united with the former Dominion Police, a federal security force, and became the Royal Canadian Mounted Police. On a nationwide level, they fulfil a very similar function to the American F.B.I., though they do it with more tact and with at least an outward touch of the good manners which are part of their tradition. What has equally changed the character of the Mounted Police, and has made it a formidable power in Canada, is the custom of contracting to provide police forces for the provinces. The first province to employ the RCMP in this way was Saskatchewan in 1928. The other prairie provinces and the Atlantic provinces followed suit in the 1930s. British Columbia brought in the Mounted Police in 1950, and so, in the same year, did Newfoundland. Ontario and Quebec still retain their provincial police forces. However, the area over which the RCMP now exercises its functions is so large that it has changed completely, from a frontier police and administration force which guarded the advance of settlement, to a monolithic national police force whose role has definite political overtones. Its centralization, its efficiency, even its relative incorruptibility, make it an instrument ready-made for the hands of a dictator.

VIII

It was into a land pacified by the few hundred original members of the Mounted Police that the Canadian Pacific Railway began to make its way after the first prairie sod was cut in 1878. The idea of a transcontinental railway had actually been conceived before that of a frontier police force. Item 4 of the terms of Confederation agreed between British Columbia and Canada in 1870 began with the following words: 'Canada to commence within two years and to complete within ten years, a railway to connect the Pacific seaboard with the railway system of Canada.'

The Canadian Pacific Railway was not in fact either commenced within two years or completed within ten; and the reasons for the delay, which strained the links of the new Dominion almost to breaking point, were partly practical and partly political. This is no place to unravel the tangled skein of disputes between lukewarm liberals and enthusiastic conservatives, or to retell the tale of political corruption which toppled Sir John Macdonald from power in the Pacific Scandal of 1873 and delayed effective work on the railway until his return in 1878. The important point in the present context is the extent of government intervention that was necessary before the grandiose project could be completed of pushing a railway through the mud and rocks of the Shield, across the empty prairies, and over the formidable barriers of the Rockies, to a remote province which in 1871 was inhabited by less than 10,000 people.

The tradition of government involvement in such works, either directly or indirectly, was already well established, partly because roads, canals and railways had so often in Canada been strategically desirable, and partly because no private enterprise would dare the risks a government had to take if it was to open and populate a virgin land. The digging of the Rideau Canal from Ottawa to Lake Ontario had been undertaken in 1832 at the expense of the British government. The opening of Upper Canada was facilitated by roads built largely by the British army, and in the 1860s the Royal Engineers constructed the first Cariboo Road into the interior of British Columbia.

The earliest railways in Canada were horse tramways, and on one of these, which ran for sixteen miles along the St. Lawrence, the first steam locomotive was operated in 1835, setting off a slow railway development which did not get effectively under way until the late 1850s when the first important Canadian line, the Grand Trunk, was built to connect the main centres in the St. Lawrence valley. A great deal of public money went into these early railways, both from the colonial treasuries and from the municipalities who were anxious to be served by railways.

From the beginning railways were part of the politics of Confederation; private interests, concerned mainly with profits, naturally favoured railways that would link the Canadas and New Brunswick with the existing American railroad systems and the markets they served; but if British North America was to be preserved as a separate entity, political and strategic considerations both made communications that would unite its scattered fragments imperative. The dangerous gap between the Atlantic provinces and Lower Canada was revealed dramatically in 1863 when the 15,000 British soldiers sent to Halifax owing to the threat of an American war, had to travel by sleigh over the 370 miles of the Temiscouata Trail between Fredericton and Quebec. Inevitably, the building of the Intercolonial Railway became one of the conditions of Confederation. It was completed in 1874 and became the first national railway of Canada, operated as well as built by the federal government, a precedent that many years later was to be followed on a greater scale.

Having undertaken such a direct obligation in the east, the federal parliament decided that it could not accept total responsibility for the much longer railway to the west, and in 1871 a resolution of the Canadian House of Commons decreed that the Pacific railway 'should be constructed and worked by private enterprise, and not by the

Dominion Government'. Since the undertaking was obviously not financially attractive in any short-term sense, the government decided to follow American precedents and to offer subsidies to any group that would build the railway. The terms fixed provisionally were for a cash grant of $30,000,000 and, in addition, fifty million acres of land along the route which the railway would take.

The accidents of politics prevented the immediate implementation of this decision. Macdonald and his conservative government fell from power in the Pacific Scandal of 1873, and for five years the country was ruled by a liberal ministry under Alexander Mackenzie which was so lukewarm about the railway that it did nothing to establish a company, and made only a token start on the transcontinental railway by laying 160 miles of track over the easier parts of the prairie. This led to the resurgence of secessionism in British Columbia. When Macdonald returned to power in 1878 his first move was to save Confederation by setting the surveyors to work and seeking financiers willing to undertake the risks of the railway. In 1880 a group of Canadian bankers and railway speculators reached an agreement, and in 1881 the Canadian Pacific Railway was incorporated. On 2nd May 1881 the work of construction began.

The difficulties were immense, both physical and financial. Apart from the more spectacular feats of traversing the passes of the Rockies and the Selkirks, the builders had to solve the problems of laying their lines through the terrain of marshes and rock outcrops north of Lake Superior, where the tracks sometimes sank into the quaking muskeg. Construction costs were far higher than had been originally expected; money ran short and sometimes there was not even enough ready cash to pay the labourers. The directors borrowed wherever they could, and sank their own private fortunes in the venture; but, despite all their efforts, a time came in the spring of 1885 when, with construction only a few months from completion, it looked as though the railway would have to go into liquidation. In England and New York the directors sought vainly for loans; and an attempt to obtain a further grant from the Canadian government was coldly rebuffed.

It was at this critical time that Louis Riel appeared again to stage his second rebellion and emphasize the railway's political importance. William Cornelius Van Horne, the Canadian Pacific's general manager, saw the chance Riel had given him; he undertook the transport of government troops to the site of the rising, and did so with such speed and efficiency that the grateful Parliament raised no difficulties about voting in July a loan that made possible the completion of the construction work.

Thus the political necessities that had brought about the beginning of the Canadian Pacific also ensured its completion; and that completion, in turn, made Canadian unity certain by bringing at least a temporary end to secessionist tendencies in British Columbia and making impossible the resurgence of Rielist insurrectionism in the prairies.

But, once in existence, the CPR was to have a deeper influence on Canadian life than can be assessed in merely political terms, and it has always filled a peculiar role in the Canadian imagination—regarded by some as a benign giant, but attacked by populists and urban radicals as a social octopus which has gained more than its share of influence and profit. For many years it was the only link between east and west; and, apart from the federal government itself, it was for long the most important single Canadian institution, multifarious in its activities, providing not only railway transport but also ocean liners and freighters to Europe and the Orient, freighters on the Great Lakes, a nation-wide telegraph service, a series of hotels, and in recent years road and air transport services. Coal mines in the Rockies, metal smelters in British Columbia, irrigation schemes and oil wells in the prairies, real-estate ventures in town and country, in all of these the Canadian Pacific Railway has played a pioneering role, not, of course, without the certainty of profit. It is still the greatest corporation in Canada, with assets worth approximately $3,000,000,000.

Yet more than anything else the CPR's influence on Canadian life can be seen in the general development of the Canadian west. The real exploitation of the wheatlands of Manitoba, Saskatchewan and Alberta began when the Canadian Pacific provided a means of taking the wheat out to the seaports, particularly Montreal and Vancouver, and bringing in immigrants to settle the homestead land which the government was giving away. Many of the large towns of the Canadian west were, by origin, railway towns. Vancouver was a tiny group of shacks and saw-mills called Gastown, with no likely future, until the Canadian Pacific engineers chose it as a western terminus. Regina started as a railway siding, called Pile o'Bones because its first industry was the exporting to eastern glue factories of the buffalo skeletons that were scattered over the prairies. Even Winnipeg, though by origin a fur-trading centre,

37. Travelling birds and a high sky. The typical prairie.

38. The anonymous silhouette. A prairie village.

39. An Ukrainian funeral, Saskatchewan.

40. Assimilated exiles. During the war thousands of Canadian Japanese were deported inland from the Pacific coast. Their children, settled in prairie towns, are still proud of their traditions.

was started on its way to development when the CPR decided to establish its workshops there.

With its line completed and some of the best of the prairie lands for
sale, the Canadian Pacific Railway needed no further government support, and for eighty years it has stood as the archetypal Canadian example of nineteenth-century capitalist enterprise, just as the Hudson's
Bay Company remains as a monument to the mercantile era.

Yet in the end, and unwillingly, the Canadian government found
itself in direct competition with its own creation. The situation arose
because of the need for more railways to open the prairie regions and
the mining areas of the Shield not served by the Canadian Pacific. At
government expense a line was built from Moncton, New Brunswick,
through northern Ontario to Winnipeg. At Winnipeg it joined one of
the oldest Canadian railways, the Grand Trunk, which was re-named
the Grand Trunk Pacific and continued through Edmonton and the
Yellowhead Pass in the Rockies to an almost deserted harbour in
northern British Columbia where the present city of Prince Rupert
eventually grew up. Meanwhile, another group of speculators, after
buying up some small lines around Winnipeg, established the Canadian
Northern, and laid their tracks, also via Edmonton and the Yellowhead
Pass, down to Vancouver through the Thompson Valley. These railways served useful purposes. They enabled the northern prairies and
considerable areas of inland British Columbia to be opened for settlement. They provided work on which homesteaders could survive until
their first crops came in. And when they were completed Canada had
the highest ratio of miles of railway track to population. But, in terms
of private enterprise, the new ventures proved disastrous, partly because
the outbreak of war in 1914 prevented the influx of settlers into the
areas west of the Rockies which the new lines anticipated. By the end of
the war both the Canadian Northern and the Grand Trunk Pacific were
bankrupt, and the Canadian Pacific, which passed through the most
productive terrain, was the only solvent system. In 1923 the Canadian
government took over the Canadian Northern and the Grand Trunk
Pacific, and, adding them to the Intercolonial, created a nationalized
system, which was even larger than the Canadian Pacific, but which
contained all the most uneconomical lines. The consequence has been
that Canada is now in a unique situation of possessing two great
systems, one state-owned, one privately owned, of which the former—
the Canadian National—is constantly in need of subsidies to cover its

deficits, while the latter not only lavishes more service and comfort on its passengers, but also survives as a very viable private company.

IX

The Canadian National Railway is not a government department subject to treasury control or operated by the civil service. It is one of the semi-autonomous Crown corporations through which, during the present century, the Canadian government has entered into many fields which in a classic capitalist society would be provinces of free enterprise. The Central Housing and Mortgage Corporation provides loans for approved housebuilding. Air Canada competes with private airlines in providing domestic and foreign services. Uranium mines and synthetic rubber plants have been worked by federal Crown corporations, and in some of the provinces—particularly Saskatchewan during its socialist era—local Crown corporations were established to provide industries in which private enterprisers saw no immediate profit. Three semi-autonomous bodies of this kind have been playing important parts in the cultural life of Canada, and two of these—the Canada Council and the National Film Board—I shall discuss when I deal with the upsurge of Canadian arts. The other—the Canadian Broadcasting Corporation —has served very much more than a cultural function.

Like the railways and the airlines, radio and television broadcasting are operated in Canada as a 'mixed system', consisting of the publicly owned and operated Canadian Broadcasting Corporation and a fairly large number of privately owned radio and television stations. The first publicly owned radio stations were established in the early 1920s by the Canadian National Railway, and these were taken over in 1932 by the Canadian Radio Broadcasting Commission, which in 1936 became the Canadian Broadcasting Corporation. Though the number of private stations is larger, in terms of revenues and of staff the two sectors are roughly equal. But in terms of achievement, the Canadian Broadcasting Corporation's role has been immeasurably greater.

Though the Canadian radio system as it has been operated since 1936 seems at first sight to be a combination of the British and the American, there are important differences from both these originals. The Canadian private stations are minor operations compared with the great American broadcasting companies, and their influence is usually local rather than national. They offer very little that can be called characteristically

Canadian. The Board of Broadcast Governors—which supervises the whole industry—has struggled long and without notable success to keep these stations from flooding their programmes with American content, which costs less than employing Canadian artists. The most that can be said for such stations—except for a very small minority which provide good recorded music—is that their news programmes and their hotline shows are much more down to the Canadian earth than similar programmes on the national system. On the whole, however, they remain rather pallid imitators of radio programming south of the border.

The Canadian Broadcasting Corporation has sought—in cycles of enthusiasm and defeatism which are visible to anyone who has been closely associated with its work—to promote culture and education as well as providing a great deal of entertainment on a sub-cultural level. Its role in this respect has been quite similar to that of the British Broadcasting Corporation, but there are differences in application and effect. One of the most vital functions of the Canadian Broadcasting Corporation has been to help in knitting together a vast and widely spread country, and in this sense it has been—with the bush airlines—the twentieth-century successor of the Canadian Pacific Railway, keeping in touch with the rest of the country those people in distant and thinly populated areas whom commercial radio stations ignore as unprofitable.

Even more important has been the CBC's patronage of the literary, musical and—since the arrival of television—the visual arts. Until the resurgence of the Canadian theatre during the last decade, the Corporation was almost the only employer of professional actors, and the employment it has given to musicians has helped to keep orchestras together in many places where they would otherwise never have existed. Before the Canada Council was established, and before the universities began to employ resident poets and novelists, the Corporation was also the most reliable source of income to keep writers alive in the meagre world of Canadian publishing. Most Canadian drama during the last thirty years has been written for radio and television, and poets, critics and fiction writers were given steady encouragement during the lean years before the 1960s. For all its faults, which have mostly been imposed on it by philistine parliamentarians, the Canadian Broadcasting Corporation has over the years been the most consistently successful of all the autonomous government corporations, for it has contributed notably—and incalculably—to the shaping of Canadians' view of their world and of themselves. It also provides a link of a peculiar kind between the Crown corporations and the government of Canada, since it is not only a creation of parliament, but a parliament-maker, and in recent years, particularly through television, has played a large but incalculable part in the political and electoral life of the nation.

PART TWO
Canada Today

Chapter VI

PYRAMIDS OF PROSPERITY
AND POWER

I

Canada today is a rich country scarred by poverty, a democracy governed and controlled by élites restricted by class, race and creed. It is a land where legal discrimination does not exist, but where the fact of being a Catholic or an Indian or the child of a poor family may have a considerable and detrimental effect on one's future. It is a land of disparities, regional and human.

In 1966 the 122 richest men in Canada received an average income of $355,245 each. The year before, in 1965, the average family income for the poorest fifth of the population was $2,263, and this did not count farm families, who in parts of the Atlantic provinces and eastern Quebec were too poor to file income-tax returns. The same fifth of the population received one-fifteenth (6·7 per cent) of the national income, while the top fifth of the population in the same year, earning a taxable average of $13,016 per family, received almost two-fifths (38·4 per cent) of the national income. But one can dig deeper than that. In 1961 137,000 families in Canada, and 306,000 people living on their own, had incomes of less than $1,000 a year, at a time when the national average family income was $5,449 a year.

In an attempt to relate the information gathered by census and income-tax data to the realities of present-day life in Canada, the Economic Council of Canada in 1968 established the criterion of poverty as the level at which a family or an individual spent 70 per cent or more of its or his income on the basic necessities of food, clothing and shelter. This criterion would place poverty at the $1,500 level for single persons

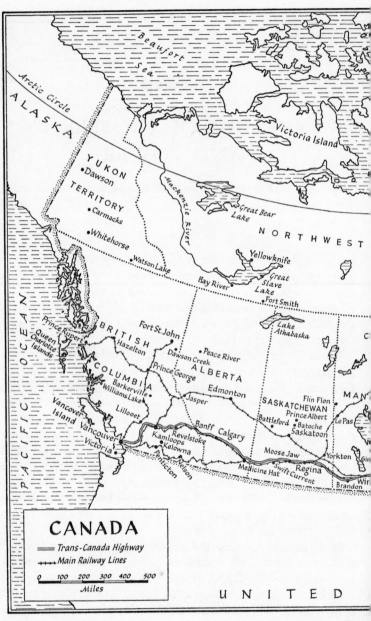

CANADA
— Trans-Canada Highway
+++ Main Railway Lines

0   100   200   300   400   500
            Miles

UNITED

4. Gener

ada

and at the $2,500 level for families of two, and so on, according to the size of the family. The Council calculated that in 1961 914,000 families and 416,000 individuals were living below these levels—not counting the farm population; this meant approximately 4,200,000 people, including 1,700,000 children under sixteen years of age; they comprised some 27 per cent, or rather more than a quarter, of the people of Canada. 1961 was a recessional year of exceptional unemployment, when many people in Canada—particularly newly arrived immigrants —were living meagrely, and the Economic Council estimated that by 1965 the proportion of nonfarm families below this basic poverty line had shrunk to about 20 per cent. In other words, a fifth of the population was not able to live up to the minimal standards of its own society.

Poverty, of course, is relative, and most Asians would be happy if their average income could be raised to that of the poorest fifth of Canadians; there are many parts of India where a family income of $200 a year is exceptional. Even in Europe, particularly in the Mediterranean countries, there are regions where the average income is well below that of people regarded as poor in Canada. But in a nonmechanical society, largely self-subsistent in terms of material goods and cultural activities, it is possible to live a relatively pleasant life on a relatively low income, particularly if the accepted way of life is leisurely and materially simple, as it is in most Buddhist countries, and if the climate is good, so that large amounts do not have to be spent on housing, heating or clothes. It is, as George Orwell remarked, much easier to be poor in a hot country. It is also easier to be poor in a society where only the distant powerful live with less simplicity than oneself and where equality is not part of the dominant myth.

In fact, even the poorest people in Canada take for granted conveniences denied to most Asians. Only one household in a hundred lacks electricity, and only one in fifteen still uses a well. One family in twenty-five is without a mechanical refrigerator; the icebox is almost extinct. Even television sets can be seen in fourteen households out of fifteen. Poverty for the Canadian lies, in material terms, on the borderline between possessing, even if only in secondhand form, these basic household appliances of the North American world, and acquiring those more expensive attributes of average success to which he can only aspire. The poor man's family will probably not be among the three Canadian households out of four who possess their own cars, and will certainly not be among the two Canadian families out of three who own—often at the grace of the mortgage company—the house which they occupy. This means that he is lacking not merely in possessions but also in the prestige of ownership from which an average North American man's self-respect is derived.

What makes this kind of poverty so painful in Canada, as in the United States, is that values and aspirations tend to be uniform. The pioneer culture, which set great store by hard work, endurance, self-reliance, has retreated into the Far North and died there. The peasant cultures which so many immigrants brought as their mental baggage from Europe have ceased to mean anything more than patterns of nostalgia which have little effect on daily life. The *habitant* culture of old Quebec has disintegrated as younger sons and daughters have left the poverty and frustration of the villages to join the industrial proletariat in the towns of the St. Lawrence valley. And nothing has appeared in the cities which resembles the working-class sub-cultures which still exist in Britain and France. In place of these there has arisen a pattern of basically middle-class aspirations. Except for a growing minority of rebels, mainly among the young, Canadians in all levels of society long for the same kind of life, and where social mobility exists it usually takes the forms of individuals or occupational groups rising towards or falling away from the ideal of affluence whose bards and interpreters are the writers and photographers in the glossy consumer magazines. Because material aims are so uniform, Canadian society does not present the same kind of class pattern as exists in England and France. British and French workers still take a pride in the code of manners of their class, and in the very fact of being workers. The successful skilled artisan in Canada will do his best to imitate the life style of the lesser executive or the lawyer, because this is what the cinema, television and the press have conditioned him to envy. Yet class still exists as a fact. I know one part of suburban Vancouver inhabited mostly by foremen and well-paid technicians. The ranch-style houses, with their manicured lawns and gardens in the Pacific coast manner, are almost as large (though more cheaply built) as those of the doctors and professors who live in the University Endowment lands; almost as pretentious as those of the executives who live on the mountainsides above West Vancouver. All three groups in their leisure hours try to carry on the same kind of easy, self-indulgent, gadget-adorned way of life, a life idealized in local snob magazines like *Vancouver Life* and liable to make eastern Canadians imagine that the Pacific coast is a kind of self-indulgent lotus land. Yet—and this is the fact of Canadian life which discredits all the hopeful talk about equality—the workers, no matter how skilled or well paid, no matter how large their houses or their cars, do not mingle with the doctors and the managers and the lawyers, though their children possibly may. Canadian class barriers are not impenetrable, but the kind of money that comes from high wages is not enough to surmount them. The clubs to which professional men belong are not open even to the aristocracy of the working class, to draughtsmen, foremen or printing workers. Yet for all workers the middle-class way of life is still the goal they would like to achieve before retirement and the penury of a pensioned existence makes it impossible.

The real middle class—shading off into the upper class—consists of the eighth of Canadian families who own two cars each; the families in which the wife does not have to work to keep up the mortgage payments on the ranch-style house, the manicured lawns and the station-wagon. These are the people who own dish-washers and employ Japanese jobbing gardeners to tend their lots. They possess or rent a cottage on a lake or seashore where the wife and children spend the summer holidays; if not, they go for relatively expensive holidays, often abroad. Their children attend nursery schools, and often continue through private schools until they go—as is almost universal in this class—to university. The exposure to intellectual and artistic stimuli is likely to be much greater in such families than in those that are fighting their way up out of a lower-class existence.

But the full enjoyment of the middle-class way of life is possible only if one belongs to the more remunerative professions, which range downward from the doctors (who in 1966 averaged incomes of $24,993) through the engineers, architects, lawyers, full professors and dentists, to the accountants with their average incomes of $13,946. The teacher or civil servant, the actor or musician, would normally fall below this ideal condition of middle-class affluence, as would the proprietors of most small businesses, most fishermen, and all farmers except the wealthy cattle rangers of the west and those few prairie farmers who cultivate, with modern machinery, thousands of acres of wheatland instead of the quarter sections of the homesteading past.

II

This is a way of life quite distinct from the upper-class way of life, which few poorer Canadians ever seek to imitate, largely because the Canadian rich are so aloof and unostentatious that it is even hard to tell how numerous they are. An upper-class life can hardly be lived on less than $100,000 a year, but the nature of the Canadian taxation system makes it difficult to determine just how many people have an income of this size. According to tax returns, there were only 935 people in Canada earning this amount of money. But the tax laws have many loopholes for those who live by dividends, while capital gains are not taxed, which allows most of the rich to add considerably to their income by stock-exchange transactions. The number of Canadians whose *actual*—as against *taxable*—income reaches $100,000, is estimated officially to be well over 5,500, and at the top of this Olympian pyramid reside the 600 Canadians who acquire more than $300,000 a year.

Apart from power and security, these great incomes buy a degree of privacy which is beyond the grasp of even the middle class, and a way of life which is aristocratic in pattern if not in tone. The town houses of the rich are not only large; they occupy spacious, well-treed grounds in areas where the land values are high. Each large Canadian city has its suburb where the rich dwell, with their Rolls-Royces, many of them chauffeur-driven, and their English servants or Chinese houseboys. In Westmount, on the edge of Montreal, the English-speaking nabobs of Quebec inhabit their own municipality, distinct from the cosmopolitan and plebeian city beside them. In Toronto the financiers who dominate the business life of Bay Street live clustered in Forest Hill and Rosedale, and in Vancouver the lumber barons and the mining magnates of the west are to be found on Shaughnessy Heights, looking out towards the mountains, or behind the tall hedges of South-west Marine Drive, with a view across the Fraser Delta to the Gulf of Georgia. It is not without significance that these areas where the rich live are, in their respective cities, almost the only districts where the customary grid plan of the North American metropolis is replaced by a European pattern—more pleasing and more secretive—of winding roads and crescents. Guarded by butlers and secretaries in their homes, the rich gather in clubs which are as exclusive as the London clubs on which they have been modelled. They are kept so not only by a rigorous election procedure but also by enormous initial fees which may run as high as $4,000. The 400 members of the Mount Royal Club in Montreal, the 300 of the York Club in Toronto and the somewhat smaller memberships of the Ranchman's Club in Calgary and the Vancouver Club on the West Coast form a directory to the inner circles of wealth and power in Canada. Membership of the clubs not only provides privacy for the meetings of the economic élite. It also confirms acceptance; there are Canadian rich men, self-made and unpolished, who have created their own empires as public works contractors or brewers or sawmill operators, but who have not yet sufficiently adapted themselves to the upper-class ways of the rich to be granted the recognition implied in privileges like club membership and social acceptance.

Apart from his town house and his club, the Canadian rich man will have at least one other haven of privacy—a place in the country, and it will not be a mere lakeside cottage. In the east it will be a farm in rural Ontario or western Quebec, and in the west a ranch, where the American version of landed leisure can be acted out. Often the rich man will have a private plane and a private airfield, or at least a private lake to land on. Almost always he will possess horses, sometimes to race, sometimes for polo, sometimes merely for riding; there are even exclusive Hunt clubs, but these go in merely for riding, since the attempts to introduce English foxes or to chase coyotes in the early years of the century were rather ludicrous failures.

The world of the rich, in other words, is close, but varied. Its members come together in a multitude of intimate contacts and contexts, from the board room to the club, from sports and other leisure activities to the exclusive round of private hospitality. Their children attend private schools which, because of the differing Canadian terminology, are the equivalent of English public schools. (A Canadian public school is one operated by a local school board out of taxes.) All Canadian private schools follow the distant example of Arnold's Rugby, are largely staffed by British masters, insist on school uniforms, impose disciplines of a kind unknown in state-run Canadian schools, and specialize in the creation of 'character' and the fostering of 'leadership'. Like similar establishments in India, they tend to caricature rather than mirror their originals, for there is nothing more absurd than a pattern of behaviour applied out of its proper context. Nevertheless, the private schools have their purposes, to preserve class continuity and to inculcate social skills. They also have their virtues, since academically the best of them are superior to the best of public high schools. It is not by accident that so many of Canada's leading citizens have attended the country's nearest equivalent to Eton, Upper Canada College. Given equal native ability, the Upper Canada College boy is likely to learn more of the ways of seeking, retaining and using power than the boy who has attended a high school in Kapuskasing, Ontario, or Medicine Hat, Alberta. In this, as in many other ways, privilege and privacy go together. Even outside the school, the children of the rich, like their parents, move in closely knit circles, exemplified by the private summer camps which are operated for the well-to-do children and which are sharply distinct from the middle-class camps, or the fundamentalist Bible camps frequented by the under-privileged. And in the years of higher education the rich boy is likely to find his way to patrician establishments like Trinity College or Massey Hall, Toronto, with Harvard, Oxford or the Sorbonne as the termination of his academic career, rather than an English redbrick college or an American state university.

There is, however, one field in which the rich emerge from their privacy in the attempt to create a public image which reflects a desire to perpetuate traditional patrician values. Like the middle class, they become deeply involved in both cultural and charitable philanthropy, but there is a difference in the way of involvement. The middle class provide the workers, the troops of ambitious women filling their vacant hours and furthering their husbands' careers by getting their names and faces into the newspapers in an endless variety of causes. The upper classes are the officers of this great army of do-gooders, giving their prestige as patrons, competing with their friends and rivals in donations, and perpetuating their names on the façades of buildings they have erected with money that would otherwise have gone to the tax collector. They are dense among the governors of universities, on the boards of art galleries and orchestras and festivals. They buy paintings and other objects of art, as they buy jewels, usually with an eye to the eventual investment value, and when they relax the class-bound rigidity of their hospitality, it is usually to admit to their tables intellectuals and artists who combine acceptable manners with conversational daring. There is, of course, a share of Blimpish obtuseness among the upper classes, but there is also a good deal of well-cultivated taste. Taste, after all, is a kind of privilege, and if some possess it innately, others can acquire it with the right mixture of leisure and opportunity.

One sign of the vitality of the Canadian upper class is its great power, whose extent I shall shortly discuss. Another is its ability to throw off brilliant mavericks who succeed in directions other than those usually followed by its members. In two generations, for example, the Massey family has produced distinguished artists: Raymond Massey the actor and Geoffrey Massey the architect. Three outstanding Canadian painters come from élite families: Lawren Harris, John Korner and Sherry Grauer. The same applies in politics as in the arts. Few upper-class Canadians are active in partisan politics, and it is usually assumed that the rich will make the best terms they can with the party that happens to be in power; many of the powerful Canadian corporations habitually divide their contributions towards election funds in the proportion of 60 per cent to the party currently in power and 40 per cent to the opposition, be it conservative or liberal. However, on the rare occasions when the member of a wealthy family does become active in politics, he often rises quickly by *savoir faire* as much as by influence. The outstanding example, of course, has been that of Pierre Elliott Trudeau, whose family fortune (estimated variously at between $2,000,000 and $6,000,000) places him—despite the unorthodoxy of his ways—securely among the upper class.

III

If the Canadian upper class live on high Olympus in comparison with the $25,000 a year doctors and the $13,000 a year accountants, we have to descend to an underworld as grey as the Hades of the ancients to encounter the real Canadian poor. It is a Hades that geographically undermines the whole of Canada. The poor are numerous in the Maritimes, and especially in Newfoundland, which in 1949 brought with it into Confederation a heavy heritage of destitution. The average *family* income in Newfoundland is approximately two-thirds that in British Columbia and Ontario, and this level is kept only because people work longer in Newfoundland and children go to work earlier; the average *per capita* income and the average hourly earnings are about half those of British Columbia. Until May 1969, the minimum wage for men in Newfoundland was still 70 cents an hour for men and 50 cents for women, and many people were being paid that wage. Though slightly less poor than Newfoundland, the other three Maritime provinces and the Gaspé region in eastern Quebec are also well below the national average; in Cape Breton the situation has been aggravated by high chronic unemployment as a result of the gradual exhaustion of the coal mines which once made the region prosperous. Apart from Cape Breton, the worst poverty of the Maritimes is to be found in the depressed rural areas whose shack villages and decaying farm cabins make up a great proportion of the half million Canadian homes of three rooms or less. Agrarian poverty, which is missed out of most statistics, is particularly acute in these provinces, where the farms are largely exhausted and almost always too small for anything but subsistence cultivation; the average income of Maritime farms is less than half the general Canadian average. But even in the towns of these provinces the general earning power is considerably less than in the towns of Ontario and the west. According to Revenue Department statistics for 1966, the sixteen towns with the highest average income per taxpayer were all in British Columbia and Ontario, ranging from Sarnia with $6,185 to New Westminster with $5,572. Fredericton, with $5,229, was the only Maritime city to exceed the $5,000 average, and Fredericton is exceptional, since it is a small provincial capital filled with professors and provincial bureaucrats. The two larger cities of New Brunswick, Moncton and Saint John, hovered at the $4,600 level, and Charlottetown, the most rustic as well as the smallest of Canada's capital cities, showed an average income of only $4,332, about 70 per cent that of Sarnia. It must be noted again that these are figures applying only to *taxpayers*; those too poor to pay taxes (e.g. with an income of $3,100 or less for a man, wife and two children) are not included, and they are far more numerous in the Maritimes than in the central or western provinces.

But if poverty observes in part a regional pattern, this is complicated by an ethnic and a religious pattern which affects all regions. In 1965 John Porter, a Professor of Sociology at Carleton University, published *The Vertical Mosaic*, a remarkable book which since its publication has had a profound effect on social thinking in Canada. Porter's main thesis is that Protestants of British origin—the WASPS of North American racialist jargon—are, with the small Jewish minority, the most prosperous group in Canada, and that, without the Jews, they control all the main organs of power. To illustrate his first point—that of WASP prosperity—Porter discusses income figures from 1951 census tracts (or areas) in a number of Canadian cities with large Catholic minorities, as well as Montreal with its Catholic majority. His concluding paragraphs, dealing with Winnipeg and Montreal, are sufficient to show the nature of his argument.

In Winnipeg (29·9 per cent Catholic) ten out of ninety-one census tracts had median earnings of more than $3,000. All ten were less than 20 per cent Catholic. Ten census tracts had median earnings of less than $2,000. All of these ten were more than 30 per cent Catholic, and seven were more than 50 per cent Catholic.

The fact that the ethnic background is inseparable from religion as a factor influencing income can be seen in Winnipeg. In all ten of the high income census tracts more than 60 per cent of their populations had a British origin. Seven of the ten were more than 75 per cent British and the other three had relatively high proportions of Jews. In the lowest income census tracts, only two had as many as 50 per cent with a British origin. The populations of the other eight lowest income census tracts were each less than 30 per cent British by origin.

A superficial examination was also made of the 309 census tracts in Montreal. With almost 75 per cent of Montreal's population French, it was even more difficult to separate religion and ethnicity. In this city (median earnings $2,224) there were eight census tracts with median earnings of more than $4,000. All of these were less than 35 per cent Catholic. There were 58 census tracts with median earnings of less than $2,000. Forty-one of these were more than 90 per cent Catholic, and only four were less than 70 per cent Catholic. From the considerable work done on Montreal census tracts by Abbé Lacoste it is clear that the French are the group of low median earnings and the English the group of high median earnings. Low median earnings were also associated with large families.

These figures were collected almost twenty years ago, and Canadian incomes have risen considerably since then, but the relative prosperity of the British and the Protestant on the one hand and the non-British and Catholic on the other has not greatly changed. A fair index to prosperity in any social group is a high incidence of professional and financial employment and a low incidence of unskilled employment. With the exception of the minute Jewish and Asian groups (totalling together about 2 per cent of the Canadian population and shaped by special circumstances—such as the fact that for many years Canadian immigration policies favoured the influx of Chinese professional men rather than manual workers), the British according to the 1961 census were in both categories better off than any other group. 10·6 per cent of them were following professional and financial occupations, as against 6·7 per cent of the French (the other founding people), 3·4 per cent of the Italians and 1·1 per cent of the native Indians. On the other hand, only 7·7 per cent of the British were unskilled workers, as against 12·8 per cent of the French, 21·5 per cent of the Italians, and 44·7 per cent of the Indians. In status and income the Italians, most of whom came from the poor regions of the Mezzogiorno, remain in relative terms much where they were in Europe; yet, at the lowest point among immigrant nationalities, they are still a great deal better off than the native races who first populated Canada.

Canadian poverty in the last thirty years has tended to become chronic, squalid and selective. One of the reasons Canadians have been so slow to see it around them is that it is emphasized neither by mass unemployment nor by deaths from starvation, and completely lacks the drama of poverty in the Depression.

Then one Canadian worker in four was unemployed, and the country people were trapped in a subsistence existence on their debt-ridden farms. Millions of people went on relief, and cash largely went out of circulation; those on relief were given vouchers, the farmers obtained what they could not grow largely by barter, and a celebrated example of the improvisations to which the crisis conduced was the Bennett Buggy, named after the incumbent Prime Minister, R. B. Bennett, and consisting of a Model T Ford drawn by a farm horse because petrol had become an unpurchasable luxury. Unemployed single men were not given even food vouchers; they ate in soup kitchens or were herded into labour camps and bossed by military personnel. Thousands of men, old and young, roamed over the country in search of work and bread, riding the rods on the trains and tramping the dusty earth roads of the thirties; the hobo jungles of makeshift hovels where professional transients halted on their way across the country were features of every western city. In the atmosphere of anger and frustration generated by sudden mass poverty, radical politics flourished. The Co-operative Commonwealth Federation, Canada's first socialist party, was founded in 1933. In 1935 Bible Bill Aberhart swept to power in Alberta at the head of a movement of fundamentalist populists who had embraced, of all unlikely gospels, that of Major C. H. Douglas, the prophet of Social Credit. Communists infiltrated movements of discontent among the unemployed as they did at the same period in England. But even without their agitation there would probably have been outbreaks of violence. These were largely provoked by the unimaginative and authoritarian way in which the conservative federal government, as well as most of the provincial governments, treated the unemployed, as if poverty were a crime and almost as if the Depression were the fault of the poor. At one time or another riots occurred in most of the western cities. The worst were the battle in Regina in 1935, when the RCMP and the city police fought with 3,000 men from the work camps who were staging an On-to-Ottawa March, and the later incident in Vancouver when the unemployed occupied the Art Gallery and the General Post office for a month in 1938 and, when the police forced them out, fought back in a riot that scarred the whole centre of the city. The occupation of the Vancouver Post Office went down as a legendary day in Canadian labour history, for the unemployed gained most of what they demanded and at the very end of the depression the government at last began to adopt a positive attitude towards the human problems of the time.

The Depression burnt its impression deeply on the minds of the generation that endured it. Those who suffered remember it with a horror—they never want to see its like again—which is mingled with a feeling of pride at the endurance and resourcefulness their generation displayed. Like war, it was an unwelcome but a salutary and exciting school and a fitting event to celebrate the final passing of the rigorous pioneer days. Those who did not suffer—the fortunate ones who had cash when the prices fell—look back on it as a kind of golden age when money had value and despite occasional riots, the poor were generally docile and deferential. Still, when individual workers show their independence, or strikes drag out too long, one hears the sinister refrain: 'We could do with another good Depression.' For neither group among those who are now fifty or over did the undramatic poverty of the post-war years seem at first worthy of a great deal of attention.

Indeed, it is only during the past three or four years that the statements of economists and political leaders and the pages of newspapers and periodicals have begun to reflect the views of a new generation, for whom the Depression is at most a memory of childhood. These younger Canadians have been brought up on the myth of a new golden age, an age of affluence shared by all, and they are shocked when they realize that this is not the case. Their view of poverty is not that of the people who went through the Depression and thought of it mainly as the lack of three meals a day and a new suit a year. A technological world has brought new styles of living, but also new demands in terms of knowledge on those who would grasp them, and what disturbs the new reformers and radicals most is the continuing restriction of education and hence of opportunity.

41. Prairie metropolis. The empty streets of Winnipeg.

42. The enduring monarch. No ruler has made such an impression on the Canadian consciousness as Queen Victoria. Her bronze statues, like this outside the Parliament buildings in Winnipeg, are to be found in many Canadian cities.

43. The heart of the wilderness. One of the many thousands of lakes that dot the surface of Canada, this water lies in the Shield country of northern Ontario.

Yet in uncovering the circumstances that prevent a great proportion of Canadians from grasping what the future might offer them, a great deal of real poverty of the old-fashioned kind which everyone thought was dying out in the remote corners of Newfoundland has been brought to light even in the most prosperous cities of Canada. I do not propose to relate the case histories from rich metropolises like Vancouver and Toronto which fill many conscience-probing pages of popular magazines like the *Star Weekly* or of journalistic books like Pierre Berton's *The Smug Minority*, which in 1968 brought the conclusions of John Porter's *Vertical Mosaic* to a much wider public. Such cases certainly exist in all western countries, and Canadian concern over them reflects mainly a consciousness that the society they have created is not living up to its own hopes and promises. To the external observer it is not these cases that are especially important, since—however individually pathetic they may be—one can always point to worse cases in other countries. What is more significant is that these instances are not just accidental and isolated, but that they represent the condition of life as it is lived by literally millions of Canadians, not only in the depressed rural areas of the Maritimes and eastern Quebec, but also in Indian reservations throughout the country and especially in city slums from the Atlantic to the Pacific.

Every Canadian city has its skid-row, inhabited by chronic alcoholics, dope addicts and other derelicts, but, though poverty enters deeply into these tableaux of human degeneration, it is not the only or even the main factor. More appalling, because they are forced upon people who have not made a retreat into paralysing addiction, are the conditions under which many thousands of Canadian city dwellers live, mainly because they do not have the means to escape. In the summer of 1967, when millions of visitors were arriving from all parts of the earth to enjoy the bright futurist world of Expo, the walls of certain areas of Montreal were scrawled with exhortations: 'Visitez les slums!' The tourists never found their way into these dejected areas; had they done so, they would have found conditions reminiscent of those George Orwell exposed when he wrote in *The Road to Wigan Pier* of his tour of the English industrial slums in the 1930s. But journalists and university research teams did go there and gathered a great deal of disturbing information on the way in which Montreal's poorest half million lived, crowded together in terraces of old four-storeyed buildings, with the decaying wooden balconies and winding outside staircases which are typical of Montreal and which are built because they cost the landlords less than internal staircases.

The population density of the worst parts of this great slum of central Montreal has been estimated as higher than that of Harlem. Like Harlem, it is something of a racial ghetto; the British do not live there, but many French Canadians do, and thousands of recent immigrants from the Mediterranean countries, particularly Italians and Greeks, the peoples whose lack of skills forces them—when they can get it—to live by labouring. There are parts of the slum where half the men are unemployed, and the family income is likely to vary between $2,500 and $3,000, in a city where the average taxable income is round about $5,500—twice as much. To poverty are added its usual accompaniments of discomfort, ill-health and poor education. Few of the slum dwellings have bathrooms or better heating devices than wood or oil stoves. It is estimated that about 9,000 homes are in need of radical repairs; there are innumerable stories of broken, dangerous staircases and sewage seeping from broken pipes. Many Montreal slum dwellers are undernourished, and the infant death rate is four times as high as that in patrician Westmount. Half the children do not complete high school. The landlords are mostly absentees with unlisted telephone numbers.

Compared with the new commercial Montreal, with its tall skyscrapers and its fascinating underground cities, the adjacent slums offer an almost incredible contrast in decrepitude, yet it was only in November 1967 that the Montreal city authorities created a department to deal with the question of public housing. More surprisingly, it was only recently that the slum dwellers themselves became sensitive to the changing climate of Canadian opinion and began to demand a change in the conditions of their existence. Their former resignation sprang largely from the fact that life in Montreal, meagre as it might be, was no worse than what they had endured in the past. The French Canadians are the half-educated, unskilled rural poor who have left the Quebec starvation farms which earn less than $1,500 a year. The immigrants come from the wretchedness of Calabrian villages and Sicilian slums. Neither has won that dream of golden opportunity which led them to abandon their pasts. And this fact they are beginning to realize. Massed together in the big city slum, the metropolitan poor are gaining a solidarity and a drive which are lacking among the dispersed poor of the rural areas; there are radical priests and social workers to help them.

IV

A similar spirit of revolt against intolerable conditions is finding various forms of expression among the people who inhabit, in terms of prosperity and social recognition, the lowest level of the Canadian pyramid: the native peoples. The Eskimos are a special problem, since they inhabit only one region—the Arctic—and rarely stray from it; their situation I shall discuss in the context of the North. But the Indians are scattered in every province of Canada except Newfoundland (where the native Beothuks were long ago hunted down and killed like the aboriginals of Tasmania).

In some ways, Indian society is a microcosm of that of Canada in general, since standards of living and even degrees of acceptance by other sections of the community vary a great deal from region to region. There are Indian reserves to which geographical accident has brought relative well-being. Some prairie bands benefit from oil royalties, and those who are fortunate enough to possess land on the verges of developing cities have prospered by real-estate transactions. A particular example is that of the Musqueam Indians whose reservation is on the edge of Vancouver, overlooking the Fraser River and the Gulf of Georgia. This band not only received in 1967 an income of $240,000 from real-estate development on its lands; it also made the land transfers conditional on the developers' building new houses for all the band members whose dwellings had to be removed; now it is about to build and operate an apartment block on another part of its land. There are prosperous Indian farmers in Alberta, and prosperous Indian fishermen on the Pacific coast, while many of the Mohawks of Caughnawaga earn high wages as steel-construction workers on bridges and high buildings in eastern Canada and the eastern United States. The best-known citizen of Caughnawaga, and perhaps the best-known Indian in Canada, is a famous and well-paid model named Kahn-tineta Horn, who has devoted herself with missionary vigour to the cause of Indian rights.

The other side of the Indian picture makes it clear that the fight for this cause is necessary and late in coming. The case was boldly put in a recent article in the *Star Weekly*.

As a people [said Walter Stewart] the natives are poorer, sicker, worse housed, less educated and more delinquent than the rest of us. Over 40 per cent of the Indian population is unemployed, and the situation is getting worse, not better. In 1964, 37·4 per cent were on relief; in 1966 the figure was 40 per cent. About 47 per cent of Indian families earn less than $1,000 a year—that is, about half the people have total family earnings of less than $20 a week. Nearly 60 per cent live in houses of three rooms or less, compared with a national average of 11 per cent, and only 9 per cent of these houses have indoor toilets. Their mortality is eight times the white rate for preschool children, three and a half times the white rate for adults. About 24 per cent are functionally illiterate.

In addition, there is the Indian pattern of drunkenness and crime. Because separate national figures of racial origins are not kept for Canadian prisons, it is difficult to assess how much more often in proportion to their numbers Indians break the law than white men do, but estimates given in semi-official reports, like that prepared by the Canadian Corrections Association in 1967, indicate that the ratio varies, according to region, from 3:1 to 5:1. Because of the high incidence of prostitution among Indian girls, the statistics with regard to women are even higher; in Saskatchewan 80 per cent of the inmates of female reform institutions are Indians, though the native peoples comprise only 3 per cent of the population of that province. In all parts of Canada, police and social workers are agreed that 90 per cent of the crimes committed by Indians are due to drinking.

This is partly because Indian drunkenness is a public phenomenon, which takes place when the people of the reserve go into the nearest town on pay day or on the day when they receive their relief cheques. Usually they drink 'fortified' Canadian wines, which make up for their inferior flavour by providing quick and inexpensive intoxication. The Indians frequent taverns in the poorer parts of the towns they visit, mainly because they fear they would be snubbed if they visited the better hotels, and outside such establishments in towns like Kenora, on the Lake of the Woods, or Williams Lake, in the Cariboo region of British Columbia, one often sees Indians—sometimes women—lying dead drunk in the middle of the day. The average non-Indian, seeing such a sight, will repeat the old arguments about Indians being by nature incapable of restraint in drinking. But the problem of Indian drunkenness is not attributable to any physiological or psychological defect that is peculiar to Indians. Its causes are historical and social. The selling of intoxicants to Indians was forbidden in Canada during the 1870s as an understandable reaction to the harm which had been done to the primitive tribes by the peddlers of adulterated liquor. Later this prohibition became to the Indian, not a measure for his protection, but a sign of his inferiority, and once it had been eliminated in the 1950s, it became almost a matter of honour for the Indian to make use of the privilege of drinking. To drink was to show his equality with white men; it was also a means of escaping from his circumstances and his problems.

My experience suggests that in areas where Indians have been able to retain their self-respect, and the respect of other people in the local community, drunkenness is not a problem. I am thinking particularly of the Gitksan people of the Skeena River in northern British Columbia, whose country I have visited often. The region was penetrated late by the white men, and the Indians, who never signed a treaty, retained their independence to such a degree that even in the 1950s the people of the village of Kitwancool policed their boundaries to keep strangers away from their fishing and hunting grounds. For their part, the local white people have shown a respect for Indian traditions and for the arts of the Gitksan; a museum has been built in the local town of Hazelton to house a fine collection of artifacts assembled by the two peoples in co-operation. The relative harmony that characterizes racial relationships in the area extends even to the tavern of the local hotel, where Indians, whites and the local Chinese meet and mingle in perfect cordiality. As a consequence, in Hazelton one saw very little Indian drunkenness.

The situation of poverty and frustration in which so many of the Canadian Indians now find themselves is linked intimately with the system of tutelage under which most of them have lived for the past century. Under the treaties, and under the practice adopted with non-treaty Indians in British Columbia, they were established on reserves so that they would have lands of their own which the settlers could not grab. Some reserves, particularly in the prairies, were large enough to provide for extensive agriculture or cattle raising; others, on the coast, merely gave enough room for the village and a beach for fishing boats. The intent of the treaties was that, apart from the five dollars' bounty which every treaty Indian receives each year to this day, agricultural implements and instruction should be given so that the Indians could be turned into darker counterparts of the white settlers. But to turn primitive hunters into farmers in a generation was impossible, and, in any case, the Indian bands were decimated and demoralized throughout the latter half of the nineteenth century by the white men's diseases, from the smallpox of the 1860s and 1870s to the Spanish influenza of 1918. By the time they began to recover in numbers and morale in the 1930s, the world had gone far beyond the days when the buffalo died and the treaties were signed; it was a world becoming rapidly industrial, to which pre-agrarian men found it almost impossible to adjust, a world which had bypassed the stagnant life of the reserves.

The attitude of Indians towards the reserves in which they are isolated is ambivalent. The reserve has a symbolic importance, since it is the last remaining part of the great lands which were once their patrimony, just as the treaties have a symbolic importance for them as occasions when white men and red men met as equal sovereign identities and made an arrangement which, Indians feel, the white men never respected. The reserve is also a refuge, the womb of tribal life from which the timid need never emerge, and to which the bold can return if they are scarred by life outside.

Yet it is the reserve and the mentality it has created that more than anything else have brought the Indians to the position in which they now find themselves. The old hunting and fishing life is no longer possible; there is not enough game left to feed all the Indians and satisfy all the white hunters, and the markets for furs has been limited by the competition of ranch-grown furs which are usually better in quality than wild furs. This means that Indians living on distant reserves, where no chance of employment exists, must depend on relief payments in order to stay alive. And it is precisely such Indians living in isolation who are the least fitted, because of their inadequate education in Indian schools run mainly by inferior teachers, to enter the urban labour force.

The existence of the reserves is also one of the reasons why the Indians—unlike the Chinese and even the Negroes in Canada—have failed to become integrated into the general life of the community. To live on a reserve marks a man off as different from other men. Until 1962, when they were given the federal vote, the Indians of Canada were legally second-class citizens, and the stigma still holds and is likely to hold while they live in segregation. Against this disadvantage must be put the advantage that the reserve provides a base in which Indian traditions can be preserved and even revived, as the old dances and ritual fraternities are being revived in the reserves of the Pacific coast.

Close to the larger towns, it is possible for an Indian to improve his situation by partaking to some extent of both worlds. The Musqueam Indians of Vancouver, to whom I have already referred, are among the 63 per cent of Canadian Indians whose children no longer attend segregated reservation or residential schools; they enter integrated schools, and as a result a significantly higher proportion attend high school, while Indian students are becoming less of a rarity on university campuses, though even now there are probably no more than two or three to every thousand of the native population; the first Eskimo has entered a university this year. Integrated education is important not merely for the greater range of opportunities it creates, but also because it allows the Indian child to move with a greater savoir faire in the white man's world. Experience seems to suggest that it is acculturation rather than race which is the deciding factor in discrimination against Indians; an uncouth reserve Indian who gets drunk every time he comes to town and has probably been six or seven times in the local gaol will be despised for what is erroneously regarded as 'typical Indian behaviour', an Indian who has received an education and works in a middle-class job will be accepted by all members of the community. This was shown in the 1968 general election when the first Indian to join the federal parliament, Len Marchand, was elected to represent Kamloops, in British Columbia, a preponderantly British constituency in which racial relations have in the past been very unstable. He was a university graduate with a varied civil service record.

Len Marchand is an Indian who has moved off the reserve, and this tendency to get away from the sites of traditional stagnation is likely to be followed by many of the younger people, particularly since the government is now offering housing grants to Indians who wish to move away into the towns. Elsewhere the federal government is setting up pilot projects to move Indians out of the remoter and less economically viable reserves into urban centres where there is a demand for labour. Programmes of this kind have not all gone smoothly. In 1967 the white residents of three Manitoba towns raised objections to Indian families being established among them; they feared it would lower property values. Such situations can become difficult and even dangerous, since they may well turn towards violence the radical movements among the young Indians, like Red Power, an organization intended to mobilize Indians and métis behind a militant policy in gaining not only political and economic equality but also a return of some of the land and wealth which all Indians believe the white men stole from them.

Even more serious, perhaps, is the fact that bringing the Indians to the towns can in itself only shift them one small step up the Canadian social ladder, since if they are not given a better education they will merely add to the ranks of the unskilled workers, who are always the first to be hit by seasonal and technological unemployment.

V

The Indians have a long way to climb towards equality, but so do the other peoples who inhabit Canada's urban and rural slums, and the most important basic reason is the same—an inadequate educational system. In this respect any white man has more chances than a member of one of the native races, yet statistics show that even among white men it is fourteen times easier for a professional man's son to enter university than it is for the son of a labourer, and in the expensive élite faculties, medicine and law, it is rare to find any students who do not belong to the middle class. To put the figures another way, half the students in Canadian universities come from the professional, pro-prietorial and managerial classes, who comprise about an eleventh of the population. The remaining half of the students are the children of the great white-collared, blue-collared and no-collared masses who comprise the remaining 91 per cent of the population. The principal reason for this inequality is the sheer cost of education in Canada, where only about 9 per cent of the total price of a student's education comes from scholarships or grants; the rest he must accumulate by a mixture of loans, parental subsidies and earnings from summer work and even weekend jobs during term-time. The idea that working one's way through university is a laudable and educational experience is part of Canadian folklore, a survival from the pioneer days when exertion was valued for its own sake, but in an age when education is becoming more complex and demanding, there are few students who can learn effectively while their energies and attentions are being diverted by the need to earn a good part of their keep.

The limitations of education and of educational financing have not only resulted in a far greater inequality of opportunity among Canadians than exists among Americans—so that in proportion to the population less than half as many Canadians attend universities as Americans—these limitations have also created a situation in which, for the past twenty years, Canada has failed to train enough professional men and skilled workers to service its developing economy. Indeed, it is no exaggeration to state that the prosperity and technological advancement which Canada now enjoys would have been impossible if it had not followed the example of the United States and imported tens of thousands of men and women trained in Europe and Asia. The intake of professional workers since the last war has been so great that at the present moment about a third of the doctors and engineers practising in Canada, and somewhat more of the architects, are immigrants, and the proportion of skilled workers originating abroad runs to approximately 35 per cent. There are Canadian universities where a minority of the faculty are Canadian by birth; Canadian hospitals where one is more likely to be tended by English, Chinese or Filipino nurses than by Canadians; and some Canadian provinces which are actually chartering planes to bring urgently needed teachers from Australia. One significant factor in this migration is that well over 50 per cent of the immigrant professionals and skilled workers come from the United Kingdom, a considerable number from Australia, and at least 15 per cent from the United States, largely offsetting the steady drain of trained men southward over the border. In other words, present-day immigration is perpetuating the predominance of the British element in the most prosperous and the most influential classes.

VI

By now it will have become clear that in Canada there is a distinct difference between social myths and social realities. French Canada, it is true, has in the past made no great pretence of possessing an egalitarian order. Until recently the learned professions lorded it over the people in the countryside and the small towns, and were not unwilling to share their power in the cities with the British magnates who controlled the industries of Quebec. The Quiet Revolution of the 1960s has disturbed this structure through the emergence of a new class of bureaucrats with strong feelings about French-Canadian autonomy, but, from all one can see at present, the final result will not be the creation of an egalitarian society, but rather the replacement of the frankly acknowledged class system of old Quebec with an unadmitted but no less real hierarchy of power like that which already exists in English-speaking Canada. This kind of assimilation is almost inevitable, while Canada remains united, because the organizational patterns of the

Canadian economy recognize no provincial boundaries and demand a homogeneous structure of power.

Thus, in both English and French Canada, at the end of the 1960s, we have a myth of equality which has no foundation and a myth of affluence which assumes reality for the rich and a small professional and managerial class; the less prosperous strata of society are largely dominated by aspirations towards this affluent style of life, aspirations which mask the existence of a real class division between the skilled and the unskilled, the educated and the uneducated, until, below the Greek or Calabrian labourer striving to leave his Montreal or Toronto slum, one reaches the peoples who in Canada endure a status of special deprivation not unlike that of the harijans in India—the Indians and the métis.

Above, remote, like the citizens of Swift's Laputa, float the five or six thousand families of Canada's upper class, comprising, with wives and children, perhaps a thousandth of the country's population. Some are engaged in the almost passive enjoyment of inherited wealth, but others are actively and potently involved in the shaping of Canada, for it is among them that one must seek the most important of Canada's complex structure of élites.

Here we come to the final aspect of the Canadian social world—its structure of power; and to the second and perhaps the more important conclusion of John Porter's *Vertical Mosaic*—that Canada is ruled, without many Canadians being aware of it, by about 2,000 men, divided into a number of élites, but remarkably homogeneous in ethnic origin, in religious background and in social status. I found *The Vertical Mosaic* impressive, not only for the boldness of Porter's views, but also for the elaborate and telling documentation with which he supported it. If I present his views on status rather than seeking an original analysis, it is because I find them wholly sufficient in terms of the Canada I know.

Porter studied six different Canadian élites—the small groups of men who exercised power at the beginning of the 1960s in economic, political, bureaucratic and academic fields, and in the labour movement and the mass media. Of these the economic élite was by far the most wealthy, and in social terms it constituted the real upper class of Canada. There has been a steady concentration of power in Canadian industry and finance, with a consequent tendency towards the absorption of smaller concerns in ever-larger combinations; Porter began in 1955 by studying the 183 dominant Canadian industrial corporations, and found that by 1960, through amalgamation, they had been reduced to 163. The result is an ever-greater concentration of power, so that in practice 985 men share, through interlocking directorates, the control of all the major Canadian corporations, of all the chartered banks and of the leading insurance companies. Small investors are of little importance in Canadian industry, and the directorates, linked with the higher managerial echelons, represent the centres of economic power. Curiously enough, the question of American domination of a large number of Canadian corporations, which is politically a very sensitive issue, has little effect on the power élite, since Canadians serve on the boards of these American-financed companies and wield genuine power in the framing of policies. Some Canadians, like E. P. Taylor and Lord Thompson, are of course members of the international economic élite.

The North American myth of rags-to-riches is not notably exemplified in the Canadian economic élite. Roughly half its members started high up, as the sons of rich men, most of them with private-school and university training. About a third climbed modestly; sons of the middle class, they found their way to wealth by high professional achievements, mainly as engineers and lawyers. A sixth climbed a long way, from humble origins, but these were men of an older generation, in which the self-made man was still a familiar phenomenon. In recent years the Canadian economic élite has become more than ever a closed upper-class corporation. The only channel through which a man can nowadays make his way upward to the élite without family connections or a professional university degree is that of banking, where the slow climb from the teller's cage to the directorate can still be achieved.

Among the economic élite none are women, none are Indians or Eskimos, none are Asians or Negroes. Less than 7 per cent are French Canadians (as against 30 per cent of the population as a whole). Less than 1 per cent are Jews, who, though numerous in the professions, hold very few of the real positions of power in the Canadian economic world. 20 per cent are foreign-born, most of them in the United Kingdom. Well over 80 per cent of the economic élite of Canada are in fact British in origin, with the Scots particularly numerous among them, and 90 per cent are Protestants.

The members of the economic élite often try to manipulate politics indirectly by their financial power, but for the most part they leave political activity to a separate class of experts. Canadian parties are hierarchical formations, and the real political élite are not the ordinary members of parliament, who may sit a generation in the House of

Commons without assuming office, but the fairly close groups who become federal ministers, provincial premiers, and often end their careers as high court judges. The need for some sort of identification between constituents and leaders means that the political élite can be neither so aloof nor so homogeneous as the economic élite. The French Canadians have to be allowed to share with the English Canadians this particular sector of power, but it is interesting to see how the two founding peoples combine to exclude from high office the quarter of Canadians who are neither British nor French. Out of the élite group of 157 (federal ministers and living former ministers, provincial premiers and former premiers, judges and former judges) which Porter chose, 75 per cent were of British origin and 22 per cent of French origin; only 3 per cent belonged to the other minorities; 70 per cent were Protestant, and 30 per cent were Catholic, as against 43 per cent for the population as a whole, meaning that the non-French Catholics were virtually excluded.

The interlocking of élites is as usual in Canada as the interlocking of directorates. 24 per cent of the political élite came from upper-class families and had close links with the economic élite. Many others, lawyers by profession (64 per cent of the political élite were lawyers), had served in high bureaucratic positions. Lester Pearson, for example, was one of a number of high liberal leaders who were civil servants before they entered active politics, and this interflow between the ministerial offices and the high bureaucracy is one of the peculiar features of the Canadian power structure. Very few men in the senior civil service ranks are lifelong careerists, and a surprisingly large proportion—one in five—are former university teachers. Until the early sixties the preponderance of the British in the bureaucratic élite was extremely high—about 85 per cent. Only 13 per cent were French, and a few others were Jews; none of the other minorities was represented. This, however, has changed greatly in the last few years with the attempt to placate public opinion in Quebec by opening more key positions to French Canadians.

The labour leaders are a group very much to themselves, mainly drawn from the skilled workers and, again, mainly of British origin, but probably dwindling in relative power. The newspapers again are an enclosed power world, the last stronghold—with the exception of some chains of department stores—of the old-fashioned family empire. But the power structure of education shows a most interesting mingling of élites. On the governing boards of universities—appointed by the provincial premiers—the economic élite are strongly entrenched, protecting their interests in the professional schools and research facilities. The professors in their turn have strong links with the world of government. The present prime minister, Pierre Elliott Trudeau, is one of them, and, besides their tendency to enter government departments, academics provide a considerable proportion of the membership of royal commissions, and sometimes, through the engineering and law faculties, actually enter the economic élite. Among the rank and file of professors there are many who are neither British nor French, but it is significant that the key administrative posts usually go to the founder races. The élite fraternity of the academic world is the Royal Society of Canada with about 500 members in the humanities and sciences. Of these, 20 per cent are French, and about 5 per cent belong to other minorities. The remaining 75 per cent are British, and outside the French-speaking institutions they do in fact control the universities, even in the prairie provinces where the British are actually fewer in numbers than other European races. It is significant of power relations within the French-Canadian community that not one of the French-speaking Fellows of the Royal Society is an Acadian; all are natives of Quebec. Interestingly, the academic élite is the only one in Canada which has a place for women; they form a meagre 1 per cent of the Royal Society.

Even this brief sketch of the Canadian power structure will show how unegalitarian Canadian society remains even in the second half of the twentieth century. Rule by élite is in fact much in the Canadian tradition. It existed in New France and early Nova Scotia; it flowered into blatant forms in the early nineteenth century with the Family Compact in Upper Canada and the Château Clique in Lower Canada. The appearance of large corporations, pioneered by the Canadian Pacific Railway, helped to perpetuate it. Early Canadian élites grew rich by grabbing land and exercising political patronage. Their successors acted more unobtrusively and indirectly, but the power they wield is no less real, while the inequalities of economic and social position are as startling as they were at any time in the past, and more scandalous, since the means to prevent poverty are so much greater and so much better understood than in the country's pre-industrial past.

Chapter VII

SUN CITIES AND SATELLITES

I

Through this book has run like a refrain, almost a lament, the paradoxical theme of a vast land where men are deserting the soil, where the urban dweller has become typical and the countryman the increasingly rare exception. Now it is time to pull the scattered references together and decide what Canadian urbanization means in the lives of places and their inhabitants.

Canadians themselves are not always willing to admit the change that has taken place in their way of life over the past half century. Like foreigners and travel agents, they still see themselves as a people of the great outdoors, and their vacation patterns show a desire to recapitulate even if it is only for two or three weeks each summer, the life they believe is truly theirs. They make for the mountains and the lakes; tens of thousands of them endure for a brief period the discomfort which tent-living in the wilderness entails for those no longer accustomed to frontier life. The National Parks, established to preserve fragments of the wilderness and its inhabitants from men who were destroying the natural environment, are now overrun by a later generation seeking a primitive world they have lost. Even those who prefer a more comfortable or exotic vacation for themselves will often seek to implant a feeling for nature in their children by packing them off to the summer camps.

Such deliberate cultivation of a way of life is an almost certain sign of its decline. The pioneer life has become the object of a cult. Now that it has come to an end, the few relics that were not thoughtlessly destroyed are preserved with care and sentiment, and pilgrimages to the kind of places in which their grandfathers or great-grandfathers lived in primitive conditions have become part of the characteristic holiday of Canadians. When the St. Lawrence Seaway was constructed in the 1950s to provide easier access to the Great Lakes for ocean-going freighters, many of the old Loyalist villages were submerged, and their best examples of early nineteenth-century building were carefully re-assembled at a new site, which was called Upper Canada Village. To go there is a curious experience, because one realizes that the Canadians who accompany one identify their own origins with this monument to a long-departed past, even though they may have spent their whole lives away from the ancestral farms. The log buildings, the ox-carts, the women in fancy dress making candles in old clapboard farmhouses, the sound of the sawmill worked by water, and the chatter of geese, the smell of hardwood sawdust, of horse's hooves singeing in the smithy, of bread baking, and steaming dungheaps, become for these visitors part of their worlds of personal reality, which are constructed out of present experience, but out of memory and imagination as well.

If—as they do—Canadians (particularly middle-aged Canadians) still tend to see themselves in this way as a rural, pioneering people, a people of the great wheatfields and the greater forests, it is because most men are always mentally running a decade or more behind the moment in which they are actually living, and so the past can seem more immediate to them than a present which they do not find pleasant and many wish to ignore. But general myths are also important, and in the collective mind of Canada the overbearing fact of the great land, with its appalling climatic extremes (as I write on December 9th I hear on the news that it is already 50 degrees below zero in Dawson City) and its empty north pushing down like a glacier of loneliness on the thin line of human life above the 49th parallel, gives an irresistible and morbid attractiveness to the image of Canadian man pitted, as the pioneers were, against its inhuman rigour. When one considers how many Canadians have lived in towns during the past quarter of a century, it is astonishing that so little of their literature is about the cities, and that so many Canadian writers have echoed the inner longings of their readers and defied the trend of their society, either by refusing, like W. O. Mitchell and Ernest Buckler and Roderick Haig-Brown, to leave the rural setting, or by continuing to write about it while living in the city; Sinclair Ross wrote in Montreal the classic novel on prairie desolation, *As for Me and My House.*

The fact is that, though the land, including the forest and the minerals beneath it, is still the necessary heart of Canadian life, the people who live on the land have ceased to be a power in the country. There is still, indeed, an illusion of the strength of agrarian radicalism in Canada, and particularly in the west, though the farmers are now a dwindling minority of less than a thirteenth of the nation's labour force. That illusion dates back to a time of real agrarian power during the years immediately after the First World War. Then, under the influence of American agrarian populism, the farmers of Canada campaigned against the villainy of the banks and the railways and against the indifference of federal and provincial governments, and formed themselves into political parties which were surprisingly successful. On the federal scene the farmer's movement, the Progressive Party, rose meteorically and in 1921 won sixty-five out of the 235 seats in the House of Commons; for four years it held the balance of power in Ottawa. In some of the provinces the farmers did even better. In 1919 the United Farmers won forty-four seats in the Ontario legislature, the Labour Party eleven, and the two groups formed a coalition majority which ruled until 1923. In Alberta the United Farmers were even more successful; they won the election of 1921 and stayed in power until the Social Credit victory of 1935. Even after the disintegration of the specifically agrarian parties, radical farmers were still important enough to take an equal part with labour groups in the formation of the socialist Co-operative Commonwealth Federation; it was largely their votes that sent the party to power in Saskatchewan as late as 1944. But only in Saskatchewan did the farmers remain for so long an important element in politics, and the termination of CCF rule there in 1964 meant the end of western agrarian radicalism as a significant force and of the farmers as a group able to wield more than marginal influence even in provincial politics. This decline in the farmers' political power from its peak fifty years ago is directly related to the diminishing role of agriculture in the Canadian economy, to the decline in the number of farms and farmers, and to the urbanization which is fundamentally changing the character of Canadian communities, whether villages, towns or cities.

II

At the time of Confederation only one town in Canada—Montreal—had reached the population point of 100,000; its rival, Toronto, was a town of about 50,000 people, and no other community in the new

44. Industrial revolution: Canadian style. Polish workers' houses near the nickel smelters at Sudbury, Ontario.

45. Industrial Gothic. The Abitibi ironworks at Sault Ste, Marie, Ontario.

46. Loyalist Classical. The Barnum House at Grafton, Ontario, built in 1817.

47. Relic of the Wars. Beside the St. Lawrence Seaway at Prescott still stands the windmill now converted into a lighthouse, where the Fenians invading from American soil were defeated in the Battle of the Windmill, 1838.

dominion was larger than a good-sized English market town. Except for Montreal, Toronto and Halifax, then at the height of its prosperity and a centre of international trade, Canada was a country of small towns (some of which served as miniature capitals), villages and isolated farmsteads. There was far more variety among these communities than there is today. Halifax was a handsome stone town which had not yet been defeated by the slums which came with the later nineteenth century and commercial recession. Fredericton was elegantly Georgian, as it still largely remains, and so were Kingston and others of the Upper Canadian towns, including even Toronto, which had not yet entered its industrial age. Some of the lesser Maritime towns resembled those of New England from which their peoples originally came. Berlin—to become Kitchener during the First World War—and Lunenburg perpetuated Germanic urban styles and were surrounded by farms of Germanic neatness. Quebec towered in the mediaeval solidity of its fortifications over the St. Lawrence, and the villages along the river— and towns like Trois Rivières and Sorel—were dominated by the steep-roofed fieldstone houses which Krieghoff immortalized in his paintings of *habitant* life. Sheltered in their rocky coves, and scattered along steep winding paths, the square wooden houses of the Newfoundland outports looked out towards their sea; they glowed a dull red from the foul-smelling mixture of ochre and codfish oil with which they had been painted. Everywhere, as in Europe, the profiles of towns and villages were dominated by the towers and pinnacles of churches.

Beyond civilization, on Hudson's Bay and in the prairies, were the stone and log forts of the traders, and by the Red River straggled the wooden farmhouses of the métis settlers. Over the Rockies, in valleys scarred by the gold hunters, were the makeshift mining towns of roughly sawn plank buildings, a few of them ornately false-fronted. Farther away, in the coastal inlets and on Vancouver Island and the Queen Charlottes, stood the carved and painted longhouses of the Pacific Coast Indians, living examples of the fact that the trend towards urbanization had started before the white men came, not only in the villages of the western sea peoples, but also in those palisaded towns of the Iroquois, Stadacona and Hochelaga, to which Cartier came when he sailed up the St. Lawrence in 1535. Hochelaga was surrounded by a wall of tree-trunks between twenty and thirty feet high, with a gallery for archers. Inside the wall stood fifty bark-covered longhouses, each fifty paces long by twelve paces wide. If one longhouse contained forty

13

people—a fairly conservative estimate—Hochelaga must have been in-habited by at least 2,000 people. It was a larger urban settlement than any place established by the white man until Quebec's population reached 2,000 at the beginning of the eighteenth century.

The cities of modern Canada bear as little resemblance to the towns of the Confederation year as those did to Iroquois Hochelaga. In North America the history of the Old World has been recapitulated with dazzling speed, and in a few generations we have come from the Stone Age to the threshold of the Space Age. An aspect of that accelerated history has been the steady growth of the cities at the expense of the country, a development which began long before Confederation. Even among the earlier immigrant groups there were many who had little or no urge to settle on the land. Most of the Irish Catholics went into the cities to work as casual labourers, the lower level of the first Canadian urban proletariat; its upper level was provided by artisans who emi-grated from England and Scotland and preferred to carry on in their new homes the skills they had brought. Later on there were other groups who were immediately absorbed into the cities: the Jews at the turn of the century and the Italians, Portuguese and Greeks in the last decade are notable examples. As the nineteenth century continued, new kinds of towns appeared and attracted people from the land. The de-mand for agricultural machinery was the forerunner of the factory system, and Canada's industrial revolution began with manufacturing towns like Hamilton, built in the gridiron pattern that was later to dominate western cities, and mining communities like Sydney on Cape Breton where slums worthy of Gustave Doré's pen were built. Only occasionally, as in Sault Ste. Marie, was an industrial town of this period laid out attractively around factories which display the kind of archi-tectural grace that distinguished the best of the early English textile mills.

Even during the decades of Canada's largest land settlements, when the prairies were opened, between 1890 and 1910, the process of urbaniza-tion was steadily maintained, so that, despite the hundreds of thousands of homesteaders who came to break the prairies, the towns absorbed enough people for their proportion of the population to rise from 37·5 per cent in 1901 to 45·4 per cent in 1910. This was the period when the cities began to break out from the sharply defined limits of early Cana-dian towns, largely through the introduction of streetcars—and of steam ferries in the coastal cities—which encouraged the appearance of the first dormitory settlements and the first commuters. This age over-lapped the automobile age. When I first reached Vancouver in the early 1950s the interurban streetcars were still running through half-rural farm and residential areas between Vancouver and the neighbour-ing city of New Westminster, and the ferries were crossing Burrard Inlet to the communities of West Vancouver and North Vancouver in the shadow of the mountains. They are both now departed, and, as in the St. Lawrence valley, the universalization of car-ownership has filled in the empty or thinly populated spaces between the neighbouring communities and created a vast metropolitan area, divided politically into a number of separate and competing municipalities but united by economic interest.

This kind of concentration has brought us to the point where 70 per cent of the people of Canada live urban lives, 50 per cent of them live in the nineteen cities which have a population of more than 100,000, and 28 per cent of them are concentrated in the three metropolitan centres, Montreal, Toronto and Vancouver. It is not only a concentra-tion of people; it is a concentration also of industrial productivity and economic power.

This process, which has involved great physical changes in all the larger cities, has been accompanied by stagnation in many of the smaller towns, and by decline in the villages. Saskatchewan is an example of this process. The one province still more dependent on agriculture than on any other industry, it has been steadily losing a large proportion of its increase in population to the more prosperous western provinces, Alberta and British Columbia. This loss has not affected the main cities of Saskatchewan, Regina, Saskatoon and Moose Jaw, which have shown steady increases in population, but it has become evident in the rural districts; seven out of Saskatchewan's fourteen rural constituencies for federal elections showed an absolute decline in population from 1951 to 1961; the young people had been leaving for the cities. A similar movement of population has taken place between the Maritimes and Ontario, and between eastern rural Quebec and Montreal.

The thousands of prairie villages, which were formerly the cross-roads of trade and communication in the wheat-growing regions, are losing function and population as the farmers decline in numbers, and even the small towns of two or three thousand people which were the district centres are stagnating. The introduction of modern highways has meant a concentration of commerce in larger towns—from 15,000 people upwards—at intervals of 100 to 150 miles across the prairies, which dominate local banking, retail trade, farm equipment and supplies. These towns also form the natural stages on the highway for long-distance passenger and truck traffic, and they derive much of their present prosperity from the gaudy chains of motels, restaurants and garages which they project on to the bypass used by the cross-country travellers. There are about sixteen of such regional centres in the prairie provinces—towns like Swift Current, Medicine Hat, Red Deer, Lloyd-minster, Battleford. They are the only places outside the five major prairie cities—Winnipeg, Regina, Saskatoon, Edmonton and Calgary—that have grown steadily in population and significance, concentrating the farming trade and, in some cases, acting as minor centres in the oil and mining industries that have sprung up in the prairies. Thus one has a peculiar hierarchy of communities, with the five main cities concentrating the financial, administrative and industrial life of the prairies, the sixteen medium-sized centres prospering as their satellites, and the small towns and villages shading out of significance.

Similar satellite patterns exist in the other areas of vital development. Radiating railways and highways make Vancouver the effective centre of British Columbia, the capital of the coastal wood and paper trade and of the western mining industry, the seat of the only stock exchange of any importance outside Toronto and Montreal. It is also the centre where freight is shipped north by sea and rail to the Yukon, where prairie wheat is loaded for Russia and China, the point of arrival and departure for those who travel to and from East Asia and the Pacific. Thus it has a national significance as Canada's western entrepôt, and a local significance as the commercial centre of the Pacific Coast, to which logging centres like Prince George, Port Alberni and Nanaimo, fruit-growing centres like Kelowna and Penticton, farming centres like Kamloops and Dawson Creek, mining centres like Trail and fishing centres like Prince Rupert, are all satellites. Here again, the pattern is one of growing regional centres, and a commercial capital approaching metropolitan stature, while the small mining towns and the villages decline in importance and decay physically. In old coal towns like Cumberland and Natal, in decayed copper-mining centres like Greenwood and Grand Forks, progress came to an end a generation ago, and the same applies to the remote ranching villages with names out of Zane Grey, like Horsefly and Lone Butte, from which life has drained away to the nearest town with ten or fifteen thousand people which the farmer can reach in one or two hours' driving, and where he can get almost as great a variety of consumer goods—and almost as cheaply— as in Vancouver. In British Columbia the elaborate system of paved roads which the Social Credit government has built during its fifteen years in office has accelerated the decay of the lesser communities, except where—like Cranbrook, Revelstoke and the towns of the Okanagan—they lie on the highways which bring the tourists north out of the United States and west from the prairies.

In few of the large western towns, with the possible exception of Victoria, can one form any conception of their appearance even a generation ago. Wood is still the commonest building material, and the process of building and rebuilding is rapid, with little care for the past. Only recently has the newly awakened taste for antiquities led to the belated preservation of the remnants of pioneer mining towns like Barkerville. When I first travelled north on the Cariboo Road from Vancouver in 1950, there was still a feeling of the frontier past in villages like Clinton and Quesnel, where the old log-built stores and hotels remained; the post houses along the highway—the 83 Mile House, the 100 Mile House, the 150 Mile House—were standing and in use, as they had been since the days of the gold rush in the 1860s. Since the paving of the highway, they have all gone, many of the more historic of them pulled down as fire hazards, and in the villages of this area which survive as hunting, fishing and ranching centres there are motor hotels and shopping plazas in no way different from those in California. Even the farmers have deserted their log houses, and this durable and traditional form of building is now used only for barns or for summer homes erected for the wealthy who try sentimentally to recreate the atmosphere of a frontier age their commercial activities have helped to destroy.

As in the prairies, farming west of the Rockies has become more difficult for those who cannot raise capital extensively. In the narrow valleys between the mountains one encounters many deserted and decaying farmhouses, with orchards of unpruned trees and pastures over which the forest is creeping back; one finds them also in Ontario. In the more prosperous provinces this retreat from marginal subsistence farming has been more pronounced than in the Maritimes and Quebec, where there are still many men farming land from which they gain less than $1,500 a year, which places them far down on the poverty scale. It is true that in British Columbia farms vary greatly in size; the ranches of the Chilcotin cattle country are immense—up to a hundred square miles of hayland and open range—and the fruit farms of the Okanagan can be as small as twenty acres and still prove more profitable than a prairie wheat farm ten times as large.

But even the fruit farmers, like the wheat farmers, are faced with the problems created by the shifting labour patterns in Canada. The itinerant casual worker, so familiar in the west at times of harvest, is disappearing in an age of welfare and relatively full employment, and even the summer-working students seek and often find more profitable and less exhausting tasks. Consequently, the farmer and his family have to work even harder than before, and from spring to autumn on the wheat farms and in the orchards a work week of sixty hours is quite customary. This means that the prestige attached to various forms of farming becomes important; in British Columbia, while vegetable farming is declining into a preserve of middle-aged Chinese who are still willing to put in long hours of backbreaking toil, fruit farming and ranching—which carry a certain social prestige—continue to flourish.

The farming villages which seem least affected by the general decline in the agrarian community are those that have some ethnic or religious unity. Dutch, Ukrainians and Mennonites tend to cling to their land, and their settlements retain more life and more individual character than the ordinary villages of the prairies or the British Columbian valleys. There is also, in certain areas, a swing back to the land; this is particularly so in British Columbia, where the Green Revolution movement in the United States has trickled over the borders, and many people, particularly Americans in retreat from the cities, are taking up agrarian lives of almost pioneer hardness.

Far across the country, in the Maritimes, the process of urbanization has been slower than in the west. Even here it has picked up impetus during the past decade, particularly in Newfoundland, where many of the outports have become depopulated since the island entered Confederation, and the process is continuing with government encouragement. But on the whole the changes in this region are not so marked as in the rest of Canada, and have often assumed the form of regression, with fine old shipbuilding towns shrinking into villages. One result of this situation is that in the Maritimes one can still see towns which retain the form they possessed at the time of Confederation; here also one finds villages which have largely escaped the general mobility of Canadian life, and in which traditions and ways of speech and living have been preserved for two and—in the case of Newfoundland—three centuries. But even for the Maritimes the era of change has now arrived, and the draining of population from the small places, far advanced in Newfoundland, has already begun in the other Atlantic provinces. As in the prairies, it is the young who go. In a country where half the population is under twenty-five, one is somewhat astonished to find small towns in Nova Scotia and New Brunswick where the whole working population is middle-aged and old.

The Maritimes and eastern Quebec are the backwaters of Canada, regions still dominated by past glories and disasters, into which the currents of change and growth flow slowly. Their condition is emphasized by the fact that they are bounded on the west by a region in which the process of concentration and urbanization has reached its most advanced stage—the narrow strip to the north of the St. Lawrence and the Great Lakes, running in a roughly south-westerly direction from Quebec to Windsor, which is the heartland of the old provinces of Upper and Lower Canada. This area was once valued for its agricultural wealth, but today its riches come mainly from the highest concentration of industry in the whole of Canada. In its patterns of settlement it resembles Europe rather than other parts of Canada, since, within a sixtieth of the country's area, it contains more than half its people, and the population density for this 50,000 square miles is round about 160, as against less than six for Canada as a whole. The only other part of the country which exceeds it in this respect is the Lower Mainland area of British Columbia, where Vancouver lies trapped between the mountains in the narrow gut of the Fraser valley, and the population crowding the flat lands rises to a height of nearly 1,000 per square mile, with the density falling dramatically as soon as one climbs into the passes at the head of the valley.

III

The St. Lawrence area not only contains Canada's two largest city complexes, those of Montreal and Toronto. It contains in all nine—or almost half—of the Canadian cities with more than 100,000 inhabitants. And it poses on a national level the kind of urban hierarchy which so far we have seen only on a regional level. What, apart from size, distinguishes the major cities of Canada from each other is the function they fulfil in the national life and the degree of metropolitan authority they assume in relation to each other. Here the distinction lies between the cities of national importance, those of mainly regional importance, and those which, despite their size, have only a satellite status. In this way one can create a definite hierarchy of Canadian cities. First stand the two real metropolises, Montreal with a population of almost two and a half million, and Toronto, with well over two million. Vancouver, verging on a million, has already attained the complexity of functions and the national and international links which entitle it to be regarded as the third metropolis, the capital of the West. Considerably smaller, but still enjoying national importance of a kind, is Ottawa, with over 400,000 inhabitants, which is the political capital of the country and an important cultural centre, since it is the site of the National Library, the National Gallery, the new Centre for the Performing Arts, and the Canada Council. It also has a special interest among Canadian cities as the only one that is being developed according to a master plan which has created parks, scenic arterial roads, and a green belt more than sixty square miles in extent in which the new public buildings have been decentralized, so that, taking full advantage of its rivers and canals, Ottawa joins Vancouver and Montreal as one of the three most attractive cities of Canada. Ottawa's influence is, however, purely political and cultural; it has little industry and no financial institutions of importance.

Vancouver lays a more varied claim to metropolitan stature; it is now the most important seaport of Canada, it is the terminus of three railroads, and it possesses one of the three busiest airports in the country. As a headquarters for industrial corporations, as a manufacturing centre and as a centre of stock-market transactions, it is the most important centre outside the St. Lawrence area, and it possesses all the cultural attributes of a metropolis, including Canada's largest university, theatres, art galleries, museums, a symphony orchestra, an active opera and a resident colony of writers and painters, some of whom are among the best in Canada. All it needs is a metropolitan authority which could override its uncoordinated municipalities and bring order into the chaos of unplanning by which the advantages of its splendid setting go largely unexploited.

But at best Vancouver will always be the minor metropolis of Canada in comparison with the great twin-star complex of Montreal and Toronto 2,000 miles away. Canada is unusual among modern countries in not possessing what geographers call a primate city, a city like London or Paris or New York, that is several times larger than its nearest competitor; the ratio between Montreal and Toronto is a mere 1·2 to 1, and it may well become even narrower. That the cities represent the two major ethnic groups of the country is partly responsible for this situation, as is the old political duality of Upper and Lower Canada which has survived into the present, when, in terms of population, the provinces of Ontario and Quebec tower as rival giants over the lesser provinces. But neither of these reasons is quite adequate, especially as the business worlds of Toronto and Montreal are not ethnically divided but are ruled by the same British Protestant élite.

One Canadian geographer, Donald P. Ker, of the University of Toronto, has put forward an imaginative explanation for this situation which derives from the fact that the St. Lawrence area is more easily understood as a single economic region than as a pattern of disparate urban communities. He points to the close interaction between Toronto and Montreal, the heavy transport and communication links and the close interweaving of corporate and financial operations between the two cities, and suggests that they in fact form a 'dispersed city'. The explanation is perhaps too ingenuous. After all, even before Confederation there was a special relationship of rivalry and fraternity between the two cities, just as there is a special relationship of rivalry and fraternity between the provinces they dominate. More than a century of competition to control the trade and industry of the St. Lawrence valley, and by extension of Canada in general, has turned this relationship into a real polarity between the two metropolises which has tended to equalize their power and to bring all the other cities of the region, with the partial exception of Ottawa, into the orbit of their influence. These neighbouring cities could not in fact become anything but satellites, in view of the fact that Montreal and Toronto between them are the centres of 75 per cent of Canada's leading corporations, 85 per cent of its major financial institutions and 93 per cent of its stock-market transactions. Though the two cities are responsible for only 38 per cent of the country's manufacturing activity, they in effect control the 85 per cent of such activity which takes place in the St. Lawrence region. Other towns have limited special importance; Hamilton's steel industry, and the automobile industry in Windsor, are vital to the Canadian economy, and both London and Kitchener, Loyalist sanctuaries where a great deal of inherited wealth lurks under the shadowing trees, are minor centres of financial power because of the insurance corporations located there. But all these places live in the shadow of Toronto, as the industrial centres farther down the St. Lawrence, like Quebec City, Sorel, Trois Rivières and Shawinigan, live in the shadow of Montreal. Quebec City, though it is the political centre of Quebec, resembles Ottawa in being negligible as a centre of corporate or financial power.

In culture and the mass media Montreal and Toronto wield the same power as they do in the industry and finance worlds. They are the centres, respectively, of French and English language radio and television, and of book publishing in the two languages. For obvious geographical reasons, there are no national newspapers in Canada, but the Toronto and Montreal papers are the most prestigious, with the possible exception of the *Winnipeg Free Press* and the *Ottawa Citizen*. All the Canadian mass circulation weeklies and monthlies emanate from these two cities, though, thanks to university and Canada Council subsidies, a number of small-circulation literary journals are published in the west (*Malahat Review* in Victoria, *Canadian Literature* and *Prism* in Vancouver, *Mosaic* in Winnipeg) and in the Maritimes (*Fiddlehead* in Fredericton and *Dalhousie Review* in Halifax). The best municipal and private art galleries, and the most sophisticated speciality shops, are to be found in Montreal, which claims a more cosmopolitan outlook than Toronto. Even the most resolute hermit among Canadian writers and painters finds it impossible to detach himself completely from whichever of these cities speaks his language, since—unless he has international connections—he is dependent on them for most of his income and for the kind of recognition that makes a career in Canada. In the case of performing artists—actors and musicians—it is virtually impossible to get to the head of the profession without spending at least a period in one or other of the eastern centres. Even in the academic world, though this is more decentralized than most fields, and scholars of international standing are to be found in most Canadian universities, the University of Toronto and McGill University in Montreal are still the most venerable institutions of the country, the Oxbridge of Canada.

Outside Vancouver, none of the other Canadian cities even begins to rival Montreal and Toronto as a national centre, though each may have some local function of importance to the country as a whole. There was a time, as the prairies were being settled, when Winnipeg looked like becoming a Canadian Chicago, a metropolis of the central plains. At the height of the western boom, in the 1900s, it became an independent centre of banking, investment and insurance houses, and by the end of the First World War almost a fifth of the bank clearings of Canada were made there. But Winnipeg remained an agrarian centre, with a slowly growing industrial pattern, and failed to establish any links with the mining developments in the Shield country north of Lake Superior, which fell under the control of Toronto corporations. Its basis in the wheat economy was insufficient to support its position as a financial centre, and after 1918 it was eclipsed by Vancouver, whose rapid and varied development allowed it to become the true metropolis of western Canada. Yet Winnipeg, with its half million people, is still no mean city in Canadian terms. Next to Vancouver, it is the most important manufacturing centre outside the St. Lawrence area. It is the capital of that quarter of the Canadian population who are neither French nor British by extraction—the home of their newspapers, of their religious sects and of their cultural activities. But its artistic reputation goes far beyond ethnic songs and dances, for it has a fine theatrical tradition and has gained international recognition for the Royal Winnipeg Ballet, one of the world's best dance companies.

The geographers who have suggested the 'dispersed city' hypothesis to explain the existence in eastern Canada of two almost equally balanced cities, Montreal and Toronto, have been inclined to apply the same hypothesis in Saskatchewan and Alberta, which, unlike British Columbia and Manitoba, are each dominated by paired cities of approximately equal importance, though once again it seems a matter of polarity rather than dispersion. The presence of these rival communities can be explained by the creation of independent railroads to service the southern part and the northern part of the two provinces. Regina in Saskatchewan and Calgary in Alberta developed on the Canadian Pacific; Saskatoon and Edmonton on the northern route which is now the Canadian National. In both provinces the unexpected fertility of the northern prairie lands made it almost imperative—particularly after the discovery of the hardy Marquis wheat—that independent centres should develop, and their growth was given an official impetus when Edmonton became the capital of Alberta and Saskatoon the centre of higher education in Saskatchewan.

In each province the twin cities have, like Montreal and Toronto, shown surprisingly even developments. In 1966, Regina had a population of 130,000, and Saskatoon of 115,000; in the same year, in Alberta, the population of Edmonton was 398,000 and that of Calgary was

328,000. In both cases the ratio was well within that of 1·2:1 which exists in the case of Montreal and Toronto. The difference between the Albertan and Saskatchewan cities—which shows a surprising ratio of 3:1—is due, of course, to the astonishing growth which the former have shown as a result of the oil boom. In the decade between 1951 and 1961 Edmonton's population grew by 91 per cent and Calgary's by 96 per cent, more than twice the average growth of 45 per cent for Canada's major cities. Saskatchewan is only at the beginning of its mineral development, has very little industry (Saskatoon and Regina between them account for only 0·7 per cent of the national total), and is still largely dependent on a one-crop agriculture. Because of the smallness of the two cities in Saskatchewan, and the relatively recent growth of those in Alberta, they are all in some ways still rather primitive in comparison with the five larger Canadian cities—Montreal, Toronto, Vancouver, Winnipeg and Ottawa. Saskatoon was reasonably well planned from the beginning, and is now an attractive provincial city, but the other three are struggling, with varying success, out of the rawness of ill-considered development. Regina has made the least of itself, and no more remains to be said of it than I have already done in an earlier chapter. Edmonton has made the best of itself, particularly during the last five years; having lectured there in 1963 and found it insufferably provincial, I was surprised to discover, when I returned in 1968, that it was marvellously transformed—with a finely architectured civic square, a campus of handsome new buildings, and the great coulée of the North Saskatchewan, which divides the academic area from the business centre of the city, transformed into a splendid wooded park. One cannot say yet—though the arts are developing—that Edmonton is one of the real cultural centres of Canada. Indeed, apart from a still somewhat isolated intellectual minority, centred mostly in the universities, all the four prairie cities I have discussed are distinguished by a demonstrative philistinism, linked with a militant nostalgia for their pioneering past. While Montreal creates an Expo, and a small Ontario city creates the Stratford Shakespearian festival, Calgary chooses to be known by its Stampede, celebrating a muscular cowboy life now followed by only a minority of Albertans, and Edmonton by its Klondike Days, the annual wake for a gold rush seventy years dead. The people of these towns are so new to urban life that their myths are still those of the farm and the frontier.

IV

The unease with which such people regard their new status as city dwellers reflects an inevitable reaction against the rapid urbanization of Canada. It seems—and is—ironical that the people of a land with so much space to spare should in so few years have crowded into the confines of cities which are often younger than their fathers. The results of these movements of people are strange and complex. To the young people, the life of small towns, once full of vitality and interest, is now dull and unattractive in comparison with the dream of city life; the mass media, far from taking everything to every distant man, have only made such people conscious of how much their immediate environments lack. Yet the young who go to the cities find that they are not only cut off from their pasts, but also isolated from the future they have set out to find. Recently a team of reporters combed the West End of Vancouver, where 35,000 people, mostly middle-class apartment dwellers, live in a single square mile of old houses and skyscrapers. The sickness they found most prevalent was loneliness—the loneliness of young people who found it impossible to make meaningful contact with the thousands who shared their predicament. The road from the small towns had, for most of them, reached no destination.

This loneliness creates one of the most persistent patterns in Canadian cities. Canadians—at least in this generation when so many have come from the villages and the small towns of an agrarian past—are not adapted to the life of a great city. They dislike the impersonality of apartment living—significantly it is immigrants who form the hard core of skyscraper dwellers—and soon become nostalgic for the combination of privacy and neighbourliness which comes from owning one's own house in a small town. This is the source of the North American cult of 'togetherness'. To reconstruct that abandoned life of the small town, the young when they marry move out to the suburbs, with the result that the cities spread even farther, consuming the arable land where market gardens used to grow, clambering up the mountainsides, and throwing out tentacles of holiday and weekend colonies so that even in this spacious land the seafronts and lakefronts for many miles away from the cities have been lost to the general public. An early effect of the suburban exodus was a death at the heart of the cities, similar to that which has taken place in many American towns. Their centres became jungles of office buildings and department stores, and

much of the trade departed as the shopping plazas, combining miniature department stores with rows of speciality shops, began to appear
in the suburbs. Only the poor, who could not afford even to mortgage
their next twenty years for an owner-occupied house, continued to live
in the city centres, so that business areas abutted on residential slums.

This trend is changing, and the impetus has probably been given by
the immigrants of the past twenty years, urban dwellers who know
and demand the advantages of city existence, have brought life back
to dying quarters with their restaurants and shops, and have encouraged the erection of apartments to replace the tracts of decaying
wooden houses in the city centres. Now the revivified downtown residential areas are inhabited partly by young people who have not yet
reared families, and partly by older people whose families have moved
into the world. These are largely childless regions. The children, with
their parents, are out in the suburbs, where, while the men neurotically
pursue their urban occupations, the young middle-class matrons attempt
to reconstruct for their families the neighbourly values they remember
from a lost rural past. The people of the small towns hate the cities,
which draw their children away; the people of the cities regret the good
things of rural living at the same time as they hanker after all the advantages of urban existence, and all too often, by seeking the compromise
of suburbia, gain neither. Urbanization is perhaps inevitable, and in the
end its benefits might outweigh its disadvantages, if the cities could be
kept relatively small and develop more evenly across the country. The
decentralization of light industry to areas like the Okanagan valley and
the smaller towns of Ontario has already begun, and this is a healthy
and substantial trend; in 1961 39·9 per cent of Canadian manufacturing
took place outside the nineteen major cities. Suburbanization, which
infinitely extends the boundaries of the city and makes the country even
more distant, is the evil, particularly in areas like the Fraser valley and
southern Ontario, where arable land and recreation spaces are limited.
In the larger cities conservation of space, through the gradual abandonment of individual dwellings, seems inevitable.

These problems are, of course, universal in the civilized world, but
it is strange and disturbing to see them taking on gravity in a land so
spacious and, over most of its area, so little populated.

Chapter VIII

THE NEW POLITICS

Politically, Canada is at the beginning of a new era. The five years of minority government under the liberal prime minister Lester Pearson that lasted from 1963 to 1968 was an interlude of searching in which politicians accustomed to the staid, grey Canada of the past attempted vainly to adapt themselves to a world in which all their values have been challenged. The era to which they belonged began in 1935, when, at the peak of the Depression, the inept conservative government of R. B. Bennett, also incapable of dealing with a changing world, was replaced by the liberals, under that most eccentric of Canadian prime ministers, William Lyon Mackenzie King, descendant of the rebel William Lyon Mackenzie, and an ardent spiritualist who allowed his policy to be governed as much by voices from the other world as by the opinions of his living colleagues. King's contacts among the dead were evidently well versed in political strategy, for they enabled him to forge a liberal rule which lasted for nine years beyond his retirement in 1948, until, in 1957, his successor Louis St. Laurent was finally voted out of office by a country which had become incensed with the arrogance of a party twenty-two years in power.

St. Laurent's evil genius was the most powerful member of his Cabinet, Clarence Decatur Howe, a former American, who had followed a typically Canadian career from university professor of engineering to moghul of the construction business and finally, during the war, to Minister of Munitions and Supply and eventually of Defence Production, an office which he doubled with that of Minister of Trade and Commerce. During the war and the time of post-war reconstruction, Howe became the economic czar of Canada, relying on the

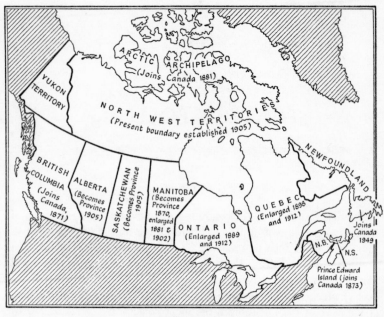

5. The development of Canada

ever-renewed liberal majority to become a law unto himself, an attitude which he strove to encourage among his Cabinet colleagues. Unfortunately for the liberals, Howe was not content merely to govern his actions by such assumptions; he proclaimed them cynically in the House of Commons, and now he is probably remembered less for his genuine qualities as an administrator than for the occasions on which he threw his power in the teeth of his opponents. In 1951 one of the conservative leaders, Howard Green (later Minister for External Affairs), expressed concern that the government might be trying to avoid its commitments. 'If we wanted to get away with it,' Howe replied sharply, 'who would stop us?' And two years later, when another Opposition member questioned the legality of an Order-in-Council, Howe replied, 'If we have overstepped our powers, I make no apology for having done so.'

The height of Howe's arrogance was displayed in the notorious Pipeline Debate, one of the dramatic turning points of Canadian political life, when, in May 1956, Howe introduced a bill to lend the financially embarrassed Trans-Canada Pipe Lines Limited a sum of $70,000,000 in federal funds to meet its obligation to complete the pipe line from Alberta to Winnipeg which would enable natural gas to be exported to the mid-western United States. The request was not out of line with Canadian traditions; one need only remember the timely loan which the archetypal Canadian conservative, John A. Macdonald, provided for the Canadian Pacific Railway at its hour of crisis in 1885. The crucial point was that Howe—without reference to Parliament—had promised Trans-Canada Pipe Lines that the funds would be handed over on June 7th. This required that the bill be passed through all its stages in a maximum of fourteen days of debate. With the connivance of the Speaker, House rules were overridden, the procedure of closure was distorted, and the obedient liberal majority was exploited to get the Bill passed by the required date. Howe won his triumph, and the Liberal Party reaped the result in June, 1957, by a defeat which established the conservatives in power for the first time since 1935.

On the night the Pipeline Debate ended, a western radical tory, John Diefenbaker, remarked to one of his friends: 'At last I understand the meaning of revolution.' Elected leader of the Progressive Conservatives shortly afterwards, Diefenbaker conducted an emotional campaign against corruption and arrogance on the part of a political hierarchy too long in power. He appeared as a populist crusader out of the West— his constituency and homeground was the Saskatchewan town of Prince Albert, on the remote edge of the northern prairie—and he may well have been the last of his kind in a Canada lost to its rural past. As the descendant of a German immigrant, he was the first member of Canada's lesser minorities to break the British-French pattern of leadership which had distinguished the first ninety years of Confederation, and he combined this advantage in the prairies—where the so-called ethnic minorities actually form the majority—with a thunderous eloquence after the manner of William Jennings Bryan and a charismatic presence which suited the boom-conscious style of the 1950s. In 1957 he won a minority victory, carrying Ontario and making deep inroads into the west. In 1958 he went back to the polls and won the greatest political victory in Canadian history; every province returned a majority of conservatives except Newfoundland, where the local liberal chieftain, Joseph Smallwood, was a charismatic politician of the same kind as Diefenbaker. Even Quebec, for the first time since the days of the Old Chieftain, Sir John A. Macdonald, contributed to the conservative landslide by expelling its liberal members, and Diefenbaker ended

14

with 208 conservative seats in a house of 265 members. In six out of
Canada's ten provinces the liberals retained no representation at all.

Diefenbaker proved to be thunder without rain, and his six years of
office, with a clearer mandate from the people than any of his predecessors had ever enjoyed, led the country into a political and economic
chaos unparalleled since the days of the preceding conservative incumbent, R. B. Bennett. Diefenbaker was—and is—a larger figure than any
Canadian Tory leader since Macdonald, and he will stand in history
among the grandiose failures who in Canada are always so much more
appealing than those who succeed; men like Louis Riel and Henri
Bourassa and the attractive but doomed leader of French-Canadian
separatism, René Lévesque. But, for all his oratorical spellbinding and
his talent for political guerilla warfare, Diefenbaker belonged to an age
that was already past in Canada. He was—in spite of his conservative
label—the last of the great prairie radicals, trying to impose the values
of the Deep West on a society that was already urban and industrial,
and his first five years in office revealed that he could do nothing to
please either the rising anger of the young or the demand to be *maîtres
chez nous* of the Québecois who in 1958 had voted him into office with
an enthusiasm which was astonishing at the time and which ten years
later already seems incredible. When he went back to the polls in 1962,
he gained only a minority mandate; the West alone remained solid in
his support.

In the following year, 1963, the situation was reversed: the liberals
won power again, but only as a minority. A further election in 1965
proved hardly more decisive, and Pearson's rule, which began with
promises of decisive action to remedy the deficiencies of the tory interlude, proved far more inept than the Prime Minister's intellectual
powers and the initial enthusiasm of his followers would have led one
to expect. The main reason why in retrospect Pearson's regime gives
one the impression of a hopeless drift on the current of events is that it
coincided with profound changes in Canadian attitudes, some of which
reflected shifts in outlook that affected the whole western world. Few
people except John Diefenbaker and his immediate followers were very
much concerned any more with such standbys of the Canadian political
past as the Empire, the monarchy and the flag. The death of the Empire
had been accompanied, as even some respectable Anglican churchmen
argued, by the death of God. The shift from country to town brought
with it a new morality, no longer dependent on the family as the

foundation of psychological and material stability. Among many technological changes, which affected patterns of work and living, the emergence of television had brought profound changes to political techniques. The new morality might teach—as Pierre Elliott Trudeau remarked—that the government had no business in the nation's bedrooms, but the new technology ensured that its concerns were brought immediately and dramatically into the nation's living rooms. As Peter C. Newman, a leading political news commentator, recently remarked in his record of the Pearson era, *The Distemper of Our Times*:

> Instead of leading the people through this maze of change, the Pearson-Diefenbaker generation of politicians droned on, caught up in the vain hopes of a long-gone epoch, viewing their own peculiar Kiplingesque world through the rear windows of the flag-fluttering limousines in the age of moonflights, mass marches and mod.

II

Canada's second century began on 1st July 1967, and in political terms this date marks an approximate point of change from the politics of the railway age and the imperial heritage to the politics of electronic communications and the pluralist society. Both of the two major parties underwent drastic changes. John Diefenbaker was overthrown by a veritable palace revolution, and Robert Stanfield, the new conservative leader, brought to the succession a dour Nova Scotian assurance which made liberal prospects wilt into apparent insignificance by the end of 1967, only to rise again with completely unexpected vigour when Pierre Elliott Trudeau, the representative of a new generation and a new outlook, came out of obscurity to snatch the leadership of the Liberal Party and to lead it in 1968 to a victory only slightly less astonishing in its magnitude than that of John Diefenbaker a decade before.

These events cannot be thoroughly understood without a consideration of the structure of Canadian politics and of the public preoccupations which have affected it. Of these preoccupations the most urgent and widespread has undoubtedly become, during the 1960s, that of national unity—in terms either of its maintenance or its destruction. Other problems, as we have already seen, have been present and have aroused concern: mass poverty, the relationship between socialization and private enterprise, the inadequacies of Canadian education. Equally passionately felt, as we shall later see, has been the anxiety of Canadians over their relationship with the rest of the world and particularly with the United States. But none of these questions has developed so much intensity as problems which emerge from Canada's particular type of federation, and especially those arising from the deep sense of injustice on the part of virtually the whole French-Canadian population, a mass emotion which mounted in an angry crescendo during the decade of Diefenbaker and Pearson. Astonished, at first indignant, later burdened by a sense of mingled guilt and incomprehension, the English Canadians in turn began to realize by the mid 1960s that geographical and political circumstances had prevented the country, in its whole century of existence, from attaining a true and stable unity, and that the average French-Canadian town and the average English-Canadian town were mutually *terrae incognitae*, whose people not only spoke different languages, but also thought so differently that their only relationship had become one of distant enmity. But the dissension between French and English Canada was only one among many divisions that strained the fabric of Canadian unity, and while it was generally accepted that a true federalism can never be static, it had become evident by the later 1960s that there was a difference between beneficial diversification and change and the kind of shattering confrontations towards which Canada seemed to be bound. Novelists invented fantasies of violent conflicts like those that tore India apart on the departure of the British, and even the most conservative of politicians and political observers began to consider seriously the consequences of a fragmentation of the country that might not end with the secession of Quebec.

Already we have observed the pattern of multiple political jurisdictions on various levels which was the heritage of Confederation—the eleven governments possessing varying degrees of actual sovereignty, in addition to the two less autonomous territorial governments. As well, there are no less than 4,866 municipal governments in Canada, some of them representing as few as 200 inhabitants, but all making their own local by-laws and—in the cases of many small towns— maintaining their individual police forces. If—as I have shown—constitutional links between federal and provincial governments are almost non-existent, those between provincial authorities and municipalities (which are legally their creations) are liable to be marked with bitter hostilities like the perennial feuds which the mayors of cities like Vancouver and Montreal wage against their superior governments,

48. The Minstrel of Cobourb.

49. Remembrance of Time
Past. Upper Canada
Village.

50. The immigrant.

while it is rare to find friendly co-operation between neighbouring municipalities, much less effective coordination. Nowhere in Canada is there a single metropolitan authority with the kind of power wielded by the London County Council; even Metropolitan Toronto, which is the first step in this direction, is a super-municipality which coordinates rather than directs. The devolution of power which this pattern demonstrates is accentuated by the fact that Canadian municipalities are at least in part governed by referendum, which complicates action in areas where co-operation between various authorities is inevitable. To give one example, the Greater Vancouver Water Board serves ten municipalities. When it was recently proposed to fluoridate the water supply, each of these municipalities voted separately on the issue, and the approval of a 60 per cent majority in every municipality was necessary. This kind of local independence, largely proceeding from traditions of autonomy born on the American frontier, has the virtue of offering a measure of decentralization in practice and certain basic democratic safeguards. More important, perhaps, it exemplifies the jealousy regarding local interests which reaches the highest levels of Canadian government, and which can result not only in cultural and constitutional confrontations like that between Quebec and the rest of Canada, but also in actual attempts at territorial aggrandisement, like the obstinate claims of Quebec on Newfoundland's mainland dependency of Labrador, and the recurrent demands of British Columbia that its boundaries be extended to the Arctic so as to include the Yukon and the richer western portion of the Northwest Territories; unlike their European predecessors, these Canadian expansionists are concerned, not with *lebensraum*, but with minerals and water power.

III

Such conflicts and variations of interest have had profound effects on the party structure of Canadian politics. The two larger federal parties, the liberals and the conservatives, resemble the great American parties in being national federations which have to reconcile many widely varied local interests among constituents from Vancouver Island to Newfoundland, and which are generally ruled by compromise and consensus. Strange alliances exist within these parties of the same kind as one finds among democrats and republicans in the USA; the conservatives are generally to the right of the liberals, but the liberals, ever since the 1890s, have contained a strong Quebec contingent which has often been to the right of the more progressive conservatives from the western provinces. Federally, the conservatives are strong in Ontario, the liberals in Quebec, and the West and the Maritimes are the most changeable areas and often therefore the keys to electoral success. Elections where one party carries all provinces, like Diefenbaker's great victory of 1958, are extremely rare, and almost equally so are elections in which Quebec and Ontario have voted in the same way.

Though elections may bring forward a variety of promises and policies, the dominant philosophies of the main parties are not widely different, a fact which is perhaps the inevitable consequence of their having to please so many varied interests. Both support free enterprise, but the liberals are the more inclined to practise state intervention in the working of the economy, though this does not prevent them from being the party favoured by the large corporations. The conservatives, if they favour more free enterprise in business, are less concerned for personal freedom, and, with the Social Credit factions, have provided the main opposition to the amendments by which the liberals have sought to humanize the obsolete Canadian Criminal Code, which still—for example—makes the dissemination of information regarding birth control an offence punishable by imprisonment. However, even in this area the distinction is not sharp; when a free vote was allowed on a suspension of the death penalty for five years, there were Quebec liberals who voted in favour of the retention of hanging, and western conservatives who voted for abolition.

All federal governments up to now have been either conservative or liberal, but since 1917 the system has differed from that in the United States in the constant presence in parliament of representatives of smaller parties, which, though they have never gained power, have often created situations where neither large party could rule with an absolute majority, on which occasions the small parties have wielded a considerable influence over governmental policies and action. The most fortunate time for the minority parties was 1921, when they accounted for 29 per cent of the membership of the House of Commons, and the progressives formed the second party, more numerous than the conservatives. The lowest ebb of the small parties was the year of Diefenbaker's great landslide when they dropped to a tiny 3 per cent. Their present standing, at about 14 per cent of the House's membership, is fairly typical of the post-war trend; except for the low point of 1962, the minority representation since 1945 has hovered between a fifth and a seventh, representing at least a quarter of the popular vote.

Unlike the large parties, the minority groups are parties of principle or restricted interest. From 1917 to the end of the 1920s, the typical minority politicians were farmer radicals, with a few representatives of small local Labour Parties. 1935 brought in both the Co-operative Commonwealth Federation and Social Credit, which surged to the front in Alberta as a federal as well as a provincial party, and secured seventeen seats in Ottawa. These two parties formed the main minority groups from 1935 to 1965, when the Quebec branch of the national Social Credit Party split away to form the Créditistes. In the 1968 election Social Credit was eliminated federally but the Créditistes survived as the fourth federal party.

The CCF began, as we have seen, in the alliance of depression-ridden prairie farmers with the small groups of industrial workers in the cities of Ontario and the West, and a handful of left-wing intellectuals. In the radical thirties it was a rather doctrinaire socialist group, though its proposals for nationalizing the land were soon toned down to suit its large following among the Saskatchewan farmers. In 1935 there were seven CCF members, and in 1945 the party reached its greatest success with twenty-nine members, an eighth of the House, gained with 15·6 per cent of the popular vote. After the débâcle of 1962, when the triumphant conservatives reduced the CCF to a strength of eight, and temporarily eliminated Social Credit, the CCF was reconstructed into a labour party on the British model, receiving official support from the Canadian Labour Congress, the largest trade-union organization of the country, which for the first time abandoned its non-political stance. The reconstructed party—the New Democratic Party—regained some of the former support of the CCF, and climbed back to its present position of the third party with twenty-two seats.

Despite reorganizations, and repeated efforts to reach the mass of the workers, the CCF–NDP has remained a party of Ontario and the West. It has never elected a single member in the Maritime provinces or Quebec, and has always been weak in Alberta, where it has failed to compete effectively with the rival radicalism of Social Credit. Its main strength in elected members has come from the other two prairie provinces and the industrial and mining areas of British Columbia, which have remained its most solid stronghold, faithful even when the prairies were swept by the Diefenbaker tide of 1958. The CCF–NDP has a submerged strength in Ontario, which is too scattered to be effective, with the consequence that in 1957, when there were more CCF votes in Ontario than in the whole of the prairie provinces, the province returned only three CCF M.P.'s as against fifteen from the prairies.

Towards the end of Lester Pearson's incumbency, the popular support of the major parties fell so low that the NDP believed they had at last a real chance of breaking out of their traditional minority situation. In 1966 the opinion polls revealed that 26 per cent of Canadians considered voting NDP in the next election, exactly as many as declared their intention of voting conservative, and a sensational by-election victory at Sudbury over the liberals in 1967 raised the optimism of New Democrats to such heights that they began to consider building a power base even in Quebec, and incorporated in their election platform the demand for a special status for that province. Such was their euphoria that, at the height of the 1968 elections, when great numbers of the young radicals who might have supported them were gripped in Trudeaumania, their leader T. C. Douglas actually declared that 'The miracle could happen and we could at last elect a people's government at Ottawa,' and appeared to believe it. The election saw the NDP back in its usual position of third party.

One reason for the perpetual electoral failure of the CCF–NDP has been, paradoxically, its success in influencing the actions of other parties. The very presence of the NDP has forced both conservatives and liberals into quasi-socialist policies, while the CCF–NDP has produced a number of leaders, from J. S. Woodsworth through M. J. Coldwell to T. C. Douglas, who have won nationwide respect for their integrity and for their constant pressure to bring more humanitarian standards to welfare activities and the treatment of minorities and criminals. If Canada now has at least a moderately serviceable welfare system, and a medicare scheme in the making, if divorce procedures have recently been liberalized, if the Criminal Code is being softened and prison conditions ameliorated, much of the credit for this must go to the dedicated work which the NDP leaders have performed, in and out of season, to reach these ends, on occasion renouncing political advantage in the interests of a humanitarian cause.

It is significant of deeply differing forms of radicalism that, in the vote that temporarily ended the death penalty, the NDP members were unanimously in favour of abolishing hanging, and the Social Credit members and the Créditistes were unanimously in favour of retaining it. Both these latter groups stand to the right of the conservatives. They are in the wider sense ferociously anti-liberal, supporters of censorship, of harsh legal penalties, of the suppression of left-wing opinions; among the social creditors American McCarthyism during the early 1950s found most of its few Canadian supporters and imitators. Generally speaking, they are favourable to private enterprise and, though they started out as partisans of the oppressed little men, the Social Credit leaders of western Canada have not been averse from conducting large deals with foreign corporations over Alberta oil and British Columbian timber, though capitalists who have lost favour with them have on occasion been treated ruthlessly; the most celebrated instance was the expropriation of British Columbia Electric. In the west the original doctrines of Major C. H. Douglas are almost forgotten. During the 1930s, Bible Bill Aberhart attempted to introduce the national dividend on a small scale in Alberta, but was ruled out of order by the federal government and the courts, and since then the nearest thing to a dividend which any Social Credit government has provided is the remission on property taxes—a mere $150 a year—which is given to British Columbians who own the houses they live in.

This abandonment of the pure Douglas doctrine was to become a subject of contention when, in the 1960s, the party suddenly spread from its former western stronghold of British Columbia and Alberta to Quebec. By the 1960s the western supporters of Social Credit, once Depression-desperate farmers, had grown prosperous, and were enjoying the best standard of living in Canada. But when the demagogic car salesman Réal Caouette began to spread the Social Credit doctrine among the farmers—still poverty-stricken and embittered—of the Gaspé and Lac St. Jean regions, it was the pure Douglas doctrine that he preached, demanding the radical reconstruction of the credit system on a nationwide scale, the introduction of the national dividend, and a war against all socialistic elements in the country; Caouette once created a political storm by expressing quite openly his admiration for Hitler and Mussolini. Caouette and his men rode into national prominence on the tide of disillusionment that swept Quebec towards the end of the Diefenbaker era. Quebec had helped materially in the conservative victory of 1958, but neither the patronage nor the legitimate political attention which its people expected had been forthcoming; French Canadians were never prominent in the conservative Cabinet, and

Diefenbaker virtually ignored the Quiet Revolution which in the cities was sweeping away the old Quebec style of life and which was leaving the farmers, who had once seemed the very backbone of the province, in a mood of despairing isolation. The rural districts were won by Caouette's preaching; twenty-six seats—40 per cent of the Quebec representation in Ottawa—went to the Social Credit Party, as against four in the rest of the country.

In the west the Social Credit leaders imagined that this was the beginning of a national trend in favour of the party, but even in British Columbia and Alberta the voters preferred to elect members of other parties to the federal House, and by the 1963 election it was evident that only Caouette in Quebec could maintain a mass following. The populism that inspired the Quebec movement clashed with the conservatism that had overcome the Albertan Social Credit movement, and before 1963 was ended Caouette led his followers out of the Social Credit Party, and founded a new group, the Ralliement des Créditistes, which maintained extreme Douglasism, and demanded associate status for Quebec. The split led to the rapid demise of western Social Credit as a federal party. In 1967 its ranking elder, E. C. Manning, Premier of Alberta and spiritual successor to Bible Bill Aberhart, called for a polarization of Canadian politics into right-wing and left-wing parties, which would mean Social Credit joining the conservatives and the NDP being absorbed into the liberals. The conservatives were cool to his suggestions of a coalition, and in the event the national leader of the Social Credit Party, Robert Thompson, resigned to accept the conservative whip, which meant the end of the English-speaking Social Credit Party in federal politics. In Ottawa, since the 1968 elections, it is only Caouette and his thirteen followers who still represent the doctrines of Major Douglas.

IV

Yet the two far western provinces continue to be governed locally by Social Credit governments, solidly entrenched in Alberta since 1935 and in British Columbia since 1952. This situation exemplifies the deep differences, between provincial and federal politics, which often astonish the visitor who comes to Canada even from the neighbouring United States, where the national division between democrats and republicans is repeated at the state level, and where—since the long distant days of the populists—third parties have been almost non-existent. The monopoly of provincial politics by the two large Canadian parties was broken at the end of the First World War and has never been re-established since that time. Always at least one provincial government has been in the hands of a minority party, and between 1952 and 1960 the four provinces of Quebec, Saskatchewan, Alberta and British Columbia, containing half the population of Canada, were governed by such parties—the Union Nationale in Quebec, the CCF in Saskatchewan and the Social Credit Party in the far western provinces.

Canadians often vote quite differently in provincial than in federal elections. British Columbia, throughout its period of Social Credit rule, has sent mainly liberal and CCF representatives to Ottawa; in Quebec, the federal allies of the Union Nationale are the conservatives, but this has not prevented the province from returning, in every recent election except 1958, a majority of liberals. Furthermore, where the larger parties still govern provinces, there are marked differences between the policies and practices of the federal and the provincial movements. From the early days of Confederation, the liberal prime minister of Ontario, Oliver Mowat, pursued a campaign for provincial rights that often embarrassed his party on a federal level, and in the 1960s the liberal prime ministers of Newfoundland and Saskatchewan, Joseph Smallwood and Ross Thatcher, have both created empires of local influence where they reign with little regard for their party's national policies. But it is in Quebec that the division between local and national liberals has, during the 1960s, been most profound. In the early days nobody was surprised when Maurice Duplessis, the perennial leader of the Union Nationale, fought with Mackenzie King over the extent of self-government he wished to establish in Quebec as a cloak for his deals with American capitalists. After all, the Union Nationale was the provincial equivalent of the Conservative Party. It was more surprising when the same kind of quarrel was continued after the defeat of the Union Nationale in 1960 by a liberal party campaigning under the motto of 'Y faut qui ça change!' The replacement of Diefenbaker by Pearson in Ottawa made little difference to the relationship between the federal and provincial governments, though both ruling parties were liberal. Disputes which were overtly centred on the dividing up of income taxes and succession duties, and on the right of Quebec to 'opt out' of national welfare schemes and start her own social services through an enlarged share of the tax income, were manifestations of a basic difference in attitudes between liberal Quebec and liberal Ottawa on fundamental constitutional questions.

Even if one ignores temporarily the particular question of Quebec, divergences of interests between the provinces and the federal government, and between the Canadian as a provincial and a federal citizen, seem inevitable. Canada came into being as a group of provinces making a compact of unity which was later ratified by the imperial parliament. Therefore the provinces are correct in their argument that they are the 'creators' of federal government; from this point it is not far to the argument—which of course has no constitutional support—that Canada's government is an equal partnership between the provinces and the centre. In terms of interests, it is inevitable that there should be trains and even clashes between the two levels of authority. The federal government seeks to harmonize the needs and demands of the country as a whole, and one of its ways is to keep control of the greater part of the tax receipts, and to distribute portions to the provinces in such a way that the poorer regions receive proportionately more than the larger regions, which have greater local sources of income. This worked reasonably well when the provinces spent little and most of the country's revenue was gained by indirect taxes. Since the last war, however, the provincial governments have grown remarkably in complexity and expensiveness. In 1945 the ratio between federal spending on the one hand and municipal and provincial spending on the other was 3 to 1. By 1952 it had sunk 2 to 1. By 1963 local expenditures were actually greater than federal in the proportion of 1·15 to 1, and a very large part of the revenue covering these costs came from income taxes.

As a consequence of these high public expenditures, a natural division of interests arose between the poor provinces and the rich ones. The poor provinces tended to support a centralist view of Confederation because this would assure the subsidies they badly needed to raise their people from the pit of economic disparity. On the other hand, the larger provinces, faced with ambitious projects of public works and growing educational costs as the post-war and pre-pill generations flooded the schools and universities, felt that they should have more control over income taxes derived in greater proportion from their constituents. Moreover, powerful provincial governments wished to retain complete control—without federal interference—over their natural resources, and to seek out and arrange foreign trade without the supervision of Ottawa. This, of course, would impinge on the right of the federal government

51. The heart of modern
Montreal, centring on
Place Ville Marie.
(CANADIAN NATIONAL
RAILWAYS)

52. Man and his Community. Expo '67. (ARCHITECTS: ERICKSON, MASSEY)

to the exclusive control of external relations, a right which in recent years has been frequently challenged by Quebec, in the cultural as well as the commercial field. Other provinces have not yet gone so far as to claim the right to establish their own networks of foreign relations, but occasions when treaties with other countries affect one province especially are usually extremely delicate, since both levels of government are involved on the Canadian side: the treaty with the United States regarding the development of the Columbia River was concluded only after many hard words between the governments in Ottawa and Victoria over the amount of money that should be extracted from the Americans in payment for power and water.

V

Yet, despite separatist threats from the Social Credit rulers of British Columbia, and periodic tirades against the 'Canadian wolf' from Newfoundland, it has always been between Quebec and Ottawa that the political strains have been greatest, reflected not only in the overtly secessionist movements, but also in the attitudes of provincial parties which do not accept the need for secession. All Quebec parties in the 1960s are nationalist if not separatist, and seek for greater autonomy; this applies to liberals as much as to the Union Nationale, and to the Ralliement des Créditistes as much as to the Parti Socialiste du Québec, the highly doctrinaire provincial equivalent to the New Democratic Party. Moreover, the premiers of Quebec and their governments are traditionally regarded as the custodians of French-Canadian cultural and political rights. In this they are sharply distinguished from the French Canadians who enter the federal Cabinet and towards whom the attitudes of most French Canadians are strangely ambivalent. In one way such national leaders are regarded as lost to Quebec, even as 'vendus', but, on the other hand, they are expected to sustain the interests of the Québecois in Ottawa, and any slight against them, such as dismissal for inefficiency or even for suspected corruption, is regarded as an insult to the French-Canadian 'nation'. The axis of Ottawa-Quebec is in fact a very delicate one, and always when a strong local government is not balanced by a strong Quebec contingent in the federal Cabinet, relations between the French and their fellow Canadians have been difficult. The Diefenbaker–Pearson decade perfectly exemplifies this rule. What happened within Quebec at that time must be seen against the background of an Ottawa scene in which, during the Diefenbaker years, only ignored nonentities represented Quebec in the federal Cabinet, and in which, under Pearson's rule, the French-Canadian federal ministers—until the arrival of Trudeau and his associates in 1967—showed an unfortunate predilection for becoming involved in situations which suggested that they were either corruptible or stupid or both. From 1958 to 1967 the influence of Quebec in Ottawa was lower than it had been at any time in Canadian history, and French-Canadian consciousness of this fact must not be ignored as one of the root causes of the national disunity whose shadow has not yet completely moved away.

Quebec is both essential to Canada and, as its people are endlessly fond of repeating, 'a province not like the others'. Its geographical position, dividing the Maritime provinces from the rest of English-speaking Canada, makes it the true key to the arch of Canada; without it, Canada would become a northern Pakistan, economically if not politically unviable. Even culturally, Quebec is vital to the survival of Canada, if only because it is the region most resistant to American influences. Yet, if secession were to leave Canada broken apart, it would leave Quebec beleaguered, and it is hard to imagine how, without the rest of Canada, the French fragment alone could maintain itself for long against the economic and cultural pressures of a whole continent.

But, granting that in all reason Canada and Quebec need each other, it is impossible to deny the historical and cultural fact of Quebec's difference. It is there not merely in the presence of a people possessing a language, a religion and a tradition different from that of most of their compatriots, but also in the bare prose of the British North America Act, which gives Quebec rights and obligations different from those of the rest of the provinces. Quebec retains its own civil law, based on the ancient Custom of Paris. It is the only province in which French is as yet constitutionally recognized as an official language; it is also the only province in which a minority—the English—has rights which are constitutionally protected. Outside the constitutional pattern, the Québecois sees himself as the member of a French-Canadian 'nation', as opposed to an English-Canadian 'nation', both of these being different from the much more vaguely apprehended pan-Canadian nation. The French-Canadian 'nation' is seen as embracing all those of French descent, wherever they live in Canada, but its territorial manifestation is Quebec, of whose earth the agrarian separatists of a past era used to say: 'Emparons-nous du sol; c'est le meilleur moyen de conserver notre nationalité.' Even today, when classic agrarian Quebec belongs to a quickly receding past, the actual soil of Quebec is for many of its people —like the reserve for the Indian—a place of refuge and a source of strength. Above all, it is the hive where the group swarms. Perhaps the most striking difference between the majority of French Canadians and the majority of English Canadians, is that the former tend to think in terms of the group and—like most minorities—to be concerned principally with group rights, which often means that individuals—and even minorities within the minority—have a rather hard time of it in Quebec. (The notorious Padlock Laws against leftists in Quebec and the persecution of Jehovah's Witnesses under the rule of Maurice Duplessis are still remembered by English Canadians who wonder what kind of totalitarian paradise a separatist Quebec might become.) On the other hand, English Canadians are much more inclined to think in terms of the individual and to stress individual rights. One of the most positive aspects of Trudeau and the French Canadians who follow him is that they have recognized the extent to which nationalism has become a mental prison for the French Canadians, and have deliberately stressed the need to seek for individual as distinct from group rights so that Canada can become a community of free individuals regardless of language.

Yet it is only by the group grievances of the French Canadians being understood that they can be liberated as individuals and Canada be freed from the threats of disunity posed by the disorder of competing nationalisms. Probably the greatest part in educating Canadians in general to this need has been played by the Royal Commission on Bilingualism and Biculturalism whose establishment in 1963 was the most positive single act of the Pearson era.

The Royal Commission is an institution much used and honoured in Canada, since it is an admirable means in a large country of balancing the inevitable centralism of the Ottawa cabinet and bureaucracy. A group of men and women, drawn from various regions and various sections of the community, spends months, sometimes years, wandering over the breadth of the country, even finding their way into the Arctic, listening to thousands of individuals and groups in closed and public meetings, and, with the assistance of secretaries and researchers, studying the available written material on the problem committed to them. The reports of Royal Commissions become classic political documents in a country poor in traditions and precedents, and their conclusions, always received with respect, are very often given the force of law by being translated, almost unchanged, into legislation.

The Commission on Bilingualism and Biculturalism consisted of ten members, forming an admirable balance of the Canadian ethnic groups —with four each representing the British and French and two the Canadians who came later than the founding races; only the native people were unrepresented. An air of intellectual distinction was given to the Commission by the presence as its co-chairman of A. Davidson Dunton, former president of the Canadian Broadcasting Corporation turned university president, and of André Laurendeau, editor of *Le Devoir*, the best Canadian newspaper, and by the inclusion among its members of F. R. Scott, a founder of the CCF who is also one of Canada's finest poets and best constitutional lawyers, and of one of the country's most distinguished academic critics, Paul Wyczynski, while a touch of down-to-earth political realism was given by the presence of Jean Marchand, a Quebec labour leader who later became Minister of Manpower and Immigration and is now—under Pierre Elliott Trudeau —Minister of Forestry and Rural Development. The Commission has cost Canada more than $7,000,000, and even now, more than five years after it was initiated, its definitive report is still appearing, volume by volume. In the end it will contain at least five volumes, and will be the most comprehensive study to date of the relations of the various peoples that form the Canadian nation.

But the B. and B. Commission, as Canadians have come to call it with the familiarity one attaches to something that has been in existence long enough to look like an institution, differed from other Commissions in that its members felt obliged to go beyond their appointed task of investigation, and to educate the people of Canada in a problem which seemed to them more urgent and important the more they studied it. Accordingly, in 1965, they took the unprecedented step of issuing a Preliminary Report in which they declared:

> We believe that there is a crisis, in the sense that Canada has come to a time when decisions must be taken and developments must occur leading either to its break-up, or to a new set of conditions for its future existence. We do not know whether the crisis will be short or long. We are convinced that it is here. The signs of danger are many and serious.

And they added:

53. and 54. A shape for the future. Habitat at Montreal. (54: BARNABY'S PICTURE LIBRARY)

55. The rock of Quebec.

There are those who feel that the problems will lessen and go away with time. This is possible, but in our view, it is more probable that unless there are major changes the situation will worsen with time, and that it could worsen much more quickly than many think.

What the Commission discovered, among many other things, was that not a single French Canadian who talked to them was content with his present situation in Canada or with the partnership of the peoples as it existed a century after Confederation.

This universal sense of discontent, of grievance, which the Commission observed is undoubtedly real; it permeates the literature of modern French Canada. It is the grievance of a people who feel that avoidable circumstances have placed them in the position where, instead of being equal partners in a country, they are an under-privileged minority, always at the mercy of a majority that shares neither their culture nor their traditions.

The French-Canadian discontent is compounded of many factors, accumulated over the two centuries since the Conquest. The Québecois remembers the Conquest itself; he remembers the suppression of the métis on the prairies and the judicial murder of Riel. The recollection of conscription imposed during two British wars still rankles in his mind, and he remembers especially what he regards as the cynical dishonesty of Mackenzie King in the Second World War. King had pledged that there would be no conscription, and then asked the nation to release him from his pledge. In the plebiscite that followed the English-speaking Canadians voted overwhelmingly for conscription, and the French Canadians 9 to 1 against; conscription was enforced in spite of the opposition in Quebec, and ever since then the people of that province have felt that Confederation as it at present exists places them always in the last resort at the mercy of the English-speaking majority, whose power they see constantly increasing because only about one immigrant in fifteen is or becomes French-speaking.

To this sense of political insecurity, must be added the feeling of economic servility which has haunted the people of Quebec since they awakened from the dream of living a withdrawn rural life, blessed by the Church, and found that their commerce and their industry had long passed under the control of British merchants and later of American capitalists. It was not merely that businesses were owned and operated by men who spoke English and rarely by men who spoke French. More insulting was the fact that companies which in South America

15

would have carried on the affairs of their branch plants in Spanish as a tribute to local national feelings, adopted in Quebec a flagrantly coloni- alist attitude by using English as the language of administration not only in cosmopolitan Montreal but even in industrial areas where the people were 100 per cent French-speaking and knew hardly any English. A French Canadian found that in order to succeed in industry or com- merce in his own province he had to learn an alien language and to abandon his own culture. When he journeyed far outside the boundaries of his province he found his language barely understood, so that unless he learnt English, the nine other provinces were like foreign lands in which he could neither travel with comfort nor find employ- ment.

Even sadder was the case of the French-Canadian minorities outside Quebec. Originally, when the generous sentiments of Confederation were still warmly felt, those provinces with large French-speaking majorities—Ontario, New Brunswick and Manitoba—allowed separate schools in which instruction could be given in French. But the turn of the century in Canada was a time when democracy was conceived in its crudest guise, as a condition in which the will of the majority can im- pose uniformity in any minority, however unwilling, and by 1915 any vestige of liberty in education for the French had vanished from all these provinces. The majority decreed that instruction must be in English and there was no effective appeal, since the federal government was reluctant to interfere in what was regarded as a provincial responsibility. In some provinces there was never at any time any provision for the children of French-speaking parents to be instructed in their own lan- guage through the public schools system. I think of my friends in Maillardville, the settlement on the edge of Vancouver whose people came as sawmill-workers from Quebec at the beginning of the present century. In order to get the kind of education they want for their chil- dren, the people of Maillardville have had to maintain their own parochial schools, and in addition to pay the regular taxes for the public schools to which they do not send their children. Even so, they are forced to teach the regular British Columbian curriculum in English, and the hour and a half instruction per day in the French language is given in addition, so that—as well as their parents paying more—the children have to work much harder than those in the regular schools. But the parochial schools provide only elementary education, and if a Maillardville parent wants his child to receive secondary instruction in his own language, he must send him over the mountains to one of the French-speaking boarding schools in Alberta.

In these circumstances, the incentive to retain their language and culture becomes weak among the French of the diaspora, a third of whom have already lost their ancestral tongue. There is little wonder that these French who live outside Quebec see themselves and are seen by their brethren in Quebec as the hostages to White Anglo-Saxon Protestant prejudices, and that their situation breeds the defensive reaction of dreaming of a French 'national state' in Quebec where at least the rights of those who live there will be protected.

French Canadians outside Quebec have little use for separatism, since they realize that this would leave them irremediably at the mercy of the British majority. What they want is a situation in which French-Canadian rights will be so guaranteed that they will feel at home from one end of Canada to the other, and more autonomy for Quebec so that it can flower into the cultural centre of all French Canada and can have political influence to wield on behalf of the French in the outer provinces. Some Québecois want the same; others want a great deal more, but there are many attitudes between Trudeau's revivified federalism and the separatism of the extremists.

Quebec nationalism is a perennial growth, and at intervals in the past it has flowered with an intensity almost matching that of the 1960s. But the years immediately preceding the present upsurge were a period of relatively low intensity, partly because of the presence of a French Canadian, Louis St. Laurent, as the federal prime minister, and partly because the particular kind of conservative nationalism connected with Maurice Duplessis and the Union Nationale of the immediate post-war years had become discredited by monumental corruption within the Quebec administration. In any case, the Union Nationale had made little appeal to the Quebec middle class which, by the mid 1950s, was beginning to become conscious of the need for some change that would give it a greater influence in the economic as well as the political affairs of its own province. It was among this group that neo-nationalism began to appear as a movement whose first duty was the ejection of Duplessis and his government so that the demands of Quebec might command more respect outside the province, and an end might be brought to a situation in which an avowedly nationalist premier not only attracted foreign capital to Quebec with the promise of low-paid labour, but also used all the powers of the state—even in defiance of an aroused Roman Catholic episcopate—to crush those workers who, like the asbestos miners in 1949 and the Murdochville copper workers in 1957, embarked on long and obstinate strikes to win conditions similar to those enjoyed by organized labour in other parts of Canada. The middle class, the radical priests, the Catholic trade unions, the intellectuals began to unite against Duplessis.* A pride in being Québecois, a desire for acceptance at their own valuation, inspired this movement, and the only possible opposition to Duplessis, a revivified Liberal Party under Jean Lesage and Paul Gérin-Lajoie, which stressed the idea of Quebec becoming master of its own house, assumed the leadership.

All the conservative elements in Quebec, the depressed farmers, the small-town business men, the *lumpenproletariat* of the cities, the old-style curés and the representatives of big business, rallied behind Duplessis, and if *le Chef* had not died in 1959 and left a party in chaos, it is possible that Lesage would not have won power in 1960 as the prelude to initiating the Quiet Revolution. As it was, Lesage owed his knife-edge victory to 500 votes spread over five constituencies, so narrow in 1960 was the margin between the new Quebec that looked forward into the twentieth century and the old Quebec that looked back to the days of Bigot and the Great Company.

Lesage's victory set going in Quebec impulses of change that hitherto had been dormant. Two intellectual strains met in combat, emanating from the two great French-language universities of the province. The historians of the Université de Montréal had developed a view of the history of Quebec which blamed all the grievances of French Canada on the British and their heirs; such an approach provided the basis for variations on the doctrine of separatism. The more prestigious Université de Laval in Quebec became the centre of a school of thought which regarded the Québecois and their retarded religious and social attitudes as largely responsible for their own relative backwardness, and suggested that the most urgent task facing the French Canadians throughout Canada was to adjust to the more liberal values of a changing world; both the 'positive autonomism' of Lesage and the neo-federalism of Trudeau derived from currents of thought originating in Laval. Out of Laval developed the desire to preserve 'the French-Canadian fact'

---

* One of the manifestations of the new spirit in Quebec at this time was a left-wing political magazine with a minute circulation, called *Cité Libre*, whose editor, then a socialist, was Pierre Elliott Trudeau.

throughout Canada. Out of Montreal developed the belief that a 'nation' must express itself through the creation of an independent and sovereign state.

The Lesage government was largely dominated by the forces which its election had unleashed. Almost unwillingly, it embarked on a drastic reorganization of the educational system which—with the full approval of many of the clergy—took the schools out of the hands of the Church. And it was pressure of the party's left wing, under René Lévesque, the radical Minister of Resources, that induced the first attack on non-French capitalists through the expropriation in 1962 of the private hydro-electric companies. Inevitably, Lesage found himself fighting the federal government over the same fiscal issues as Maurice Duplessis, and the advent of a liberal administration in Ottawa did nothing to ease the situation, since it would have been politically disastrous for the Quebec liberals to give the impression that they were truckling to the central government. Indeed, it was when he confronted a liberal government, in 1963, that Lesage first began to demand, somewhat stridently, a special status for Quebec, accompanied by 'a genuine decentralization of powers, resources and decision-making in the federal system of government' so that a genuine French-Canadian 'nation' could be developed. The powers of that nation, as Lesage conceived them, extended to external affairs, and it was he who first elaborated the idea that Quebec should be allowed to treat freely and directly with foreign countries, particularly on matters—e.g. education and cultural affairs—which constitutionally were the concern of the provincial authorities.

In his manifestations of nationalism Lesage was urged forward not merely by the radicals within his own cabinet, but by the separatism which during the 1960s seized hold of a great portion of the intellectual world in Quebec and particularly in Montreal. Separatism, like nationalism, is older than Confederation, but its modern revival began just over a decade ago, in 1957, when a group of academics led by Raymond Barbeau founded L'Alliance Laurentienne, which dreamed of the foundation of a Laurentian Republic. The movement aroused little attention, even within Quebec, until 1961, when Marcel Chaput, a former employee of the National Research Council, produced—out of his frustration in an Ottawa institution ruled by English-speaking Canadians—a book entitled *Pourquoi Je Suis Séparatiste*. This resulted in his martyrization by the Diefenbaker government, which dismissed

him from his post, and his sanctification by the educated youth of
Quebec, out of which was recruited most of the membership of the
newly founded Rassemblement pour L'Independence Nationale.
Chaput became President of the RIN, but in 1962 left it to form the
Parti Républicain de Québec. The PRQ was dedicated to political
action, and Chaput tried to give it a touch of Gandhian drama by staging public fasts to raise funds and apply moral pressure to the government. By 1963 the PRQ had run out of impetus, and the RIN regained
the lead among separatists, organizing itself as a political party to pursue
secession by legal and non-violent means. By the end of 1964 a more
conservative party, Le Regroupement National, had emerged to
splinter the separatist ranks.

Meanwhile, in the background, there appeared the clandestine movements dedicated to terrorist violence. If Chaput tried to learn from
Gandhi and dreamed of a great non-violent campaign to expel the
British, the extremists of organizations like the Front de Libération
Québecois (FLQ) and the Armée de Libération Québecoise not merely
admired the Algerian *colons* who had resorted to terrorism but also,
according to some reports, were in touch with them. The actions of the
terrorists were pathetically slight. They blew up a statue of Wolfe on
the Plains of Abraham, put bombs into mail boxes in Westmount,
carried out two or three armed raids, and accidentally killed four people.
They were not representative of the separatists as a whole.

Nor, for that matter, were the separatists representative of more than
a minority of Québecois. An opinion poll in 1963 showed 13 per cent
of those interviewed as sympathetic to the separatists. When the RIN
and the Ralliement National, a newly founded conservative group,
entered the provincial elections in 1966, they polled less than 9 per cent
of the popular vote. These figures suggest that, even at the height of the
separatist movement, it was only one Québecois in every ten who was
willing to commit himself to its objectives. Such supporters were largely
of the middle class, and mostly under thirty-five. The poll I have already
mentioned indicated that in the professional classes one out of every
four was sympathetic to separatism. The proportion was much higher
among the writers, artists, academics, radio and television producers.
I learnt this from direct experience, by establishing in 1959 a bilingual
literary magazine, published from Vancouver. For the first two years I
had excellent co-operation from writers in Quebec, but by 1962 it was
hard to get any contribution from a French Canadian for a magazine

published in English-speaking Canada, and even for my half-yearly reports from Montreal I had to rely on a French-speaking friend of Iraqi origins; only in 1967 did the situation begin to change.

The separatists, like many other movements of extreme nationalism, are characterized by democratic protestations accompanied by an extremity of intolerance which gives their statements and actions a distinctly totalitarian flavour. They see Quebec as a state based on a single culture and a single language. While French Canadians in the other provinces seek freedom to develop their own culture and preserve their own language among those who speak English, the separatists seek to rid the English minority in Quebec of their constitutional privileges, to make the use of French mandatory in all business relations, and to force all immigrants who settle in Quebec to send their children to French-language schools. It is this desire to impose on others the very conditions of which they complain that robs the separatists of the sympathy of those English Canadians who otherwise might be inclined to support them, and which makes the Acadians almost universally anti-separatist.

In the visions of a possible future put forward by nationalists and separatists in Quebec many gradations of autonomy have been envisaged. Those who demand a total break with English-speaking Canada, like that which took place between India and Pakistan, are few in number. Most of those who talk of complete political separation actually envisage economic co-operation through a common market. There are even separatists who argue that a political divorce might be followed by some kind of remarriage, once an equal partnership had been worked out by two mutually independent people. The more moderate nationalists offer many solutions short of separation to assuage the French-Canadian desire for national identity. Some would be content with a special status for Quebec, merely giving it more control over taxation and the right to run its internal affairs without interference from Ottawa. The historian Michel Brunet has suggested a change from a federation of ten provinces to a federation of two national collectivities —French and English. Premier Daniel Johnson, who unexpectedly defeated Jean Lesage and led the Union Nationale back into provincial power in 1966, celebrated his victory by demanding the scrapping of the British North American Act and the substitution of a new constitution recognizing French-Canadian rights and the 'state of Quebec'. Later, at a meeting of the Federal-Provincial Tax Structure Committee in September 1966, Johnson spelt out his version of the demands of Quebec in these terms:

> As the mainstay of a nation, it wants free rein to make its own decisions affecting the growth of its citizens as human beings (i.e. education, social security, and health in all respects), their economic development (i.e. the forging of any economic and financial tool deemed necessary), their cultural fulfilment (which takes in not only arts and literature, but the French language as well), and the presence abroad of the Quebec community (i.e. relations with certain countries and international organizations).

Not far removed from this view is the 'associate state' concept, the idea of a loose confederation of the two national collectivities, with a super-government dealing with such matters as foreign relations, defence, posts and currency, in which each 'nation' would have the right of veto.

In the euphoria of early 1967, when Expo was proving such an excellent example of the kind of achievement which the peoples of Canada might carry out in co-operation, the fevers of separatism seemed to die low, but they burst out again with the visit of General de Gaulle, his cry of 'Vive le Québec libre,' and his departure in angered pride after Lester Pearson had declared that such intervention in the affairs of Canada by the head of another state was 'inadmissible'. Most English Canadians were indignant over de Gaulle's remarks, and most French Canadians were flattered, but it is unlikely that anyone was actually converted to separatism by the General's performance. Yet it served a purpose by drawing attention once again to a serious situation which could not continue. The lesson of the preliminary report of the Commission on Bilingualism and Biculturalism was dramatically underlined, and historians in the future may see the General's intervention as the catalyst provoking a series of events that have already changed the nature of Canadian political life.

VI

The year that followed de Gaulle's arrival saw radical changes in the leaderships of both the major parties, followed by an election in 1968 which returned the liberals to power with a clear mandate to revivify Canadian federalism and restore national unity.

The leadership contests among both conservatives and liberals reflected the necessities of a time of radical change in political objectives.

The Conservatives actually broke a Canadian tradition, by which a political chieftain, once elected, held his position by personal right until he died or retired. All the historically important Canadian premiers—Macdonald, Laurier, Mackenzie King—had been chieftains of this kind and John Diefenbaker seemed at one time destined for such a role. But, with growing political sophistication, the old-time boss had become obsolete; so had the old-fashioned party, powered by patronage and personal loyalty. Diefenbaker, with his incomprehension of French-Canadian aspirations, his love of imperial symbolism, and his gross personal vanity, was unfitted for the political scene of the later 1960s, and, after a series of prodigious intrigues contrived by the president of the Conservative Party, Dalton Camp, and an epic battle at the party convention in September 1967, John Diefenbaker, who less than ten years before had led the conservatives to their greatest victory in Canadian history, was expelled from the leadership. Into his place stepped Robert Stanfield, the former Premier of Nova Scotia, a granite-calm man who impressed Canadians mostly because he was so different in presence and character from his flamboyant and thunderous predecessor. When a Gallup poll was taken two months later, the renewal of the Party's prospects seemed evident. Forty-three per cent of the people interviewed declared they would vote conservative at the next election, as against a mere 34 per cent who were willing to commit themselves to the liberals.

Lester Pearson, a shrewd man if not a great leader, read the signs of the times accurately, and, without waiting for a stormy exit like Diefenbaker's, tendered his resignation in December 1967. His place was taken, not by any of the party stalwarts who had worked for years in cabinets and shadow cabinets in the hope of finally succeeding to the party leadership, but by a dark stranger, almost unknown to Canadians until the early months of 1968, Pierre Elliott Trudeau. Trudeau was a young man in the late forties, a wealthy bachelor who for the last thirty years had combined the existence of a gracious and experimental play-boy with a serious concern for social and political affairs and with firm convictions about the future of Quebec and Canada. He had sat at the feet of Harold Laski, had taught as a university professor, had acted as a labour lawyer and, as the editor of *Cité Libre*, had shown himself a free-wheeling radical, inclined for many years towards the New Democrats rather than either of the larger parties. Yet in the larger sense he was a liberal, with a profound distrust of nationalism, and a belief that federalism—if it worked properly—was the best system of government under which any man could live. He also had strong convictions about the relationship between government and morality; so long as others were not harmed, he believed that men and women should conduct their private lives as they wished, and the puritanical laws of Canada should be changed to allow them to do so. Above all he possessed the very advantages Robert Stanfield lacked: colour, wit, originality.

His rise was meteoric. He did not joint the Liberal Party until, in 1965, he and his friends Jean Marchand and Gérard Pelletier (former editor of *Le Presse*) decided that it was the only party which could save the unity of Canada. He entered parliament in 1966, and his advent, with that of his two associates, meant that, for the first time for a decade, the federal government included a group of French Canadians who were men of brilliant intelligence, strong convictions and forceful personalities, and who were in no way compromised by the errors of the past. Pearson accepted them with gratitude, and promoted them quickly. Trudeau became Minister of Justice in 1967, and set about immediately devising a bill to amend the Criminal Code in a number of radical directions, including the legalization of abortion under certain circumstances, of the dissemination of birth control, and of homosexual behaviour between consenting adults. In explaining his reforms to the press, he used a sentence which caught the imagination of the country: 'There's no place for the state in the bedrooms of the nation.'

In April 1968, when the liberals met to choose their leader, Trudeau had already gathered a following, mostly of intellectuals and young people, with a good many former New Democrats among them; some at least of the more astute elder liberal politicians had sensed his popular appeal. Though Pearson played no overt part in the contest for leadership, he let it be known diplomatically that Trudeau had his confidence. After a convention battle superbly organized by his supporters, Trudeau was elected leader of the liberals and automatically became Prime Minister. In the general election which he called in June 1968, he carried the country as well, winning a clear majority with 155 seats, as against 72 for the conservatives, 22 for the NDP, 14 for the Créditistes and a solitary independent. His great and unexpected triumph was in Quebec, where the separatists had called on the people to practise massive abstention; 55 out of 74 Quebec seats went to the liberals, and 14 of the remainder to the Créditistes, who at least were opposed to separatism. It was an election which broke ground by electing to the Canadian parliament its first Negro and its first Indian member, yet in one respect it showed a retrogression: all the women candidates but one were defeated, which was almost certainly a consequence of the national obsession with Trudeau's slightly off-masculine attractiveness.

Trudeau, in fact, did not impose himself on the people. He provided, as Diefenbaker did in the previous decade, a vehicle for the idea of themselves as a nation stirring among Canadians of all origins. He continued the work begun by Expo in the previous year, the work of self-revelation by which Canadians are beginning to see themselves, no longer as good grey people in a stark grey land, always under some overwhelming shadow of France or Britain or America, but rather as a people capable of originality, adventurous, radical-minded, open to the future. True, the adventurousness is tempered with caution, the radicalism conceals—as with Diefenbaker—a lingering conservatism; Canadians even in their enthusiasms are still eminently sensible. But the image for the moment is one of liberation, and especially of youth.

It was the votes of the young, of the under-forties, which gave the impetus that carried Trudeau up over the weir into power. The election was outstanding for the number of young candidates and younger canvassers. In this constituency of youth, solid Robert Stanfield looked merely stolid, and the socialist pronouncements of the New Democratic leader T. C. Douglas belonged to an antediluvium before the British welfare state fell into disgrace; Trudeau held and captured the contemporary imagination. But the election was not won merely on the battleground of the generations. Older people also supported Trudeau, and among them many who in the past decade had been so distressed by Canadian fractional politics and the inadequacies of minority governments that they had ceased to vote. A great number of the half million extra votes which Trudeau brought to the liberals came from disillusioned Old Leftists.

Trudeau is now in power, and the course of Canadian politics will probably bear his mark for at least a decade. Underneath the youthful charm that wooed flower children and disillusioned idealists alike, he has his strain of arrogance, and he is already running a tightly disciplined Cabinet. The civil servants have less power than they enjoyed under a minority government, and Ottawa may become rather more efficient. But how much will actual policy change? Here Trudeau still remains very much the untried and enigmatic stranger. He was cautious in evading the kind of pre-election commitments which had dogged

Pearson through his years of office, and he may well reveal himself a calculating pragmatist rather than the adventurous radical many people imagined him.

Undoubtedly he will see that the Criminal Code is drastically revised. He will also finally introduce medicare, but has declared emphatically that this will be the last step in social welfare for a long time ahead. He does not favour tax changes aimed at squeezing the rich, or measures to curb foreign ownership of Canadian corporations. Regarding the rest of his policy he has not only been personally uncommunicative, but has also imposed rules of silence on his Cabinet. Whether he will turn out to be a sphinx without a secret is a question that is now troubling some of those who worked for his victory. Above all, there hangs in the air the great query of whether he will succeed in keeping Quebec in confederation.

Here the signs seem more hopeful than they have done for the past six years. Trudeau's electoral success in Quebec showed that most French Canadians were willing to accept, from a prime minister of their own people, the tough line, according to which special status for Quebec will be rejected in favour of a revision of the constitution and of existing laws to make Canada truly bilingual and bicultural. The first steps in this direction have already been made. Pearson had begun as early as 1963 the process of creating a bilingual civil service. The provinces of Ontario, Manitoba and New Brunswick, in which live three-quarters of the dispersed French Canadians, have in the past two years amended their laws to provide for public schools in which French is the language of instruction. The reports of the Commission on Bilingualism and Biculturalism are being taken seriously as a basis for legislation in the autumn of 1969.

It is true that the separatists received an accession of strength when René Lévesque finally left the Liberal Party to found the Mouvement Souverainité Association (now the Parti Québecois), aimed at a federation between two sovereign states so loose as to be virtually separatism. On the other hand, recent months have shown that the people of Quebec are well aware of the economic difficulties which secession from Canada would create and are unwilling to make the sacrifice, at least while there seems a chance that Trudeau may be able to reform Canadian federalism in such a way as to rid them of their grievances, some of which are already vanishing as industry moves into the province, and wages rise towards the general Canadian level.

My view is that the advent of Trudeau, like that of Laurier in the 1890s, will bring a steady decline of nationalism in Quebec. I believe, in fact, that the turn of the tide came with the rapid series of events in 1967—Expo, followed by General de Gaulle's catalytic intervention, and the departure of the old political leaders—and that now Canada stands a very good chance of surviving its second century. Of the spirit that will guide that future Canada we may perhaps catch a glimpse in a statement made by an earlier Quebec nationalist, wiser than most of his successors. In 1904 Henri Bourassa declared:

> The fatherland, for us, is the whole of Canada, that is to say, a federation of distinct races and autonomous provinces. The nation that we wish to see developed is the Canadian nation, composed of French Canadians and English Canadians, that is to say, two elements separated by language and religion, and by the legal arrangements necessary for the conservation of their respective traditions, but united in an attachment of brotherhood, in a common attachment to a common fatherland.

Chapter IX

CULTURE AND THE DEATH OF COLONIALISM

I

There is a Lost World quality about colonial cultures. They preserve, in remoteness and isolation, forms of expression that have often died away in the places of their origin. To read a piece of colonial literature is rather like listening to an Indian talking in Kipling's slang. The forms it uses, even the sentiments, have no longer any meaning in that distant land called the Old Country, and they have never had any real meaning in the land into which they have been imported. In Canada, for whole generations, the arts presented nothing but such antique forms blossoming nostalgically in isolation. Or, rather, the arts then recognized presented nothing else. For in the very nineteenth century when Canadian poets were producing attenuated imitations of Keats and Rossetti, and painters, at their most daring, were portraying gold miners in the style of the pre-Raphaelites, two great native traditions were moving towards their peak. Until the present generation the works of sculptors on the Pacific coast and in the Arctic North were regarded only as ethnological curiosities. Their originality was recognized at the moment, fifty years ago, when the arts of English and French Canada began to move out of colonialism into maturity.

I have already mentioned the character of social life among the Indians of the Pacific coast—a life based on physical abundance and on the elaboration of status and ceremonial, and flooding over the language barriers which divided the five peoples that formed the cultural complex associated with the potlatch feast and the totem pole.

The principal arts practised by these peoples were wood carving, horn carving, painting and weaving. As among many primitive peoples, these arts were divided along sexual lines, and there were differences not merely between what men and women made, but also between the styles which custom allowed them to use. Carving and painting were practised by men, who used a symbolic style based on radically adapted natural forms; this style was heraldic in intention, and quasi-religious in origin, for even the patterns that decorated wooden utensils for every-day use were based on ancestral myths. The women, who wove, used for the most part geometrical designs which appear to be older than the symbolic forms of the male artists. There was only one connection in which women could use the symbolic style; this was in the weaving of the beautiful ceremonial mantles of mountain goat's wool worn by the chiefs, but even then the heraldic design which the weaver followed was drawn by a male artist on a large pattern-board from which it was copied faithfully.

It is the male symbolic style that particularly distinguishes the art of the Pacific coast. But here again, in this richest of primitive traditions, a distinction arises between the public art associated with rituals of personal and clan aggrandizement and the esoteric art linked with the elaborate winter ceremonials of secret societies.

The rituals of aggrandizement centred on the potlatch, and were manifested most durably in the massive sculptures—the largest ever carved by primitive man—known generally and erroneously as 'totem poles'; in all the intricate symbolism of their carving, these were the lasting records of a chief's identity and standing. They varied considerably in intention and character. Some were the supporting timbers of house structures, carved with appropriate animal emblems; others—the mortuary poles—commemorated past chiefs whose ashes or bones were often enclosed within them; the heraldic poles—the tallest and most spectacular of all—had as their sole function to tell the ancestral legends and spiritual histories of the chiefs who raised them. Like all the symbolic art of the Northwest, they did so by means of highly stylized representations of animals, of mythological beings, like the Thunder Bird and the Lightning Snake, and of human forms; plants forms were never used, and what appear to be geometrical shapes are usually stylized natural forms, like the rectangles with rounded corners which some-times represent eyes and at other times joints. Each animal had its recognized attributes, and need not be represented by more than one of them—the beaver, for example, by his broad tail (or merely some cross hatching to suggest it), the killer-whale by his dorsal fin, the raven by his straight bill. Such economical suggestions often make the poles difficult to interpret; this obscurity was sometimes deliberately sought to mask the meaning of a jealously guarded legend.

While the sculpture of the Pacific Indians had a common symbolism, and shared techniques, there were variations in style between the different peoples—variations which may be suggested by using with caution the analogies of European movements. The work of the Tsimshian and their Gitksan cousins seems the most naturalistic and also the most classical, often attaining a remarkable restraint of mood; that of the Haida, who carved the largest poles from the great cedars of the Queen Charlottes, mingled with its massiveness a kind of baroque conventionality of spirit; that of the Kwakiutl and the Bella Coola, the most mystically inclined of the tribes, was the most original in feeling and showed a grotesqueness of invention which tempts one to describe it as Gothic-romantic.

The carving of heraldic poles was the most spectacular, but also the youngest of Pacific Indian arts. It is true that when the white men first arrived simple carvings were already being worked on house poles; in the late eighteenth century Captain Cook saw them among the Nootka on Vancouver Island and Alexander Mackenzie among the Bella Coola on the mainland. But the task of sculpting massive logs with blades and adzes of stone and jadeite was difficult, and few chiefs could afford to employ artists frequently for such protracted works. The arrival of the European fur traders at the beginning of the nineteenth century changed the situation dramatically. They brought metal tools, and they provided trade goods in exchange for furs, which enabled the clan chiefs to spend extravagantly on elaborate poles, carved in more intricate detail and coloured more vividly with store paint.

The peak age of pole carving, and of the potlatch culture, was between 1870 and 1900, when the stimulation from the invasive white culture was at its height; the celebrated 'groves' of poles at Skidegate (Haida) and Alert Bay (Kwakiutl) were carved at this period. After 1900 the decline, due to worsening economic conditions, depopulating epidemics, and a missionary-inspired law forbidding potlatches, was relatively rapid. On the coast itself no poles of significance were raised after the early 1920s, though the Gitksan on the fairly remote reaches of the Skeena River were erecting poles as late as the 1940s. In recent years there has been a revival of the craft, encouraged partly by museums

. A village church beside the St. Lawrence.

57. Pilgrims ascend the Sacred Staircase at Ste. Anne de Beaupré.

58. A farmstead near Quebec.

59. A wayside oven.

60. A clue to crisis. The English in Quebec.

wishing to reproduce decaying poles and partly by commercial entre-
preneurs anxious to meet the demand for primitive art, but even the
best of this recent work is no better than correct imitation.

This applies even more to the esoteric art of the winter ceremonials,
which lost most of its meaning with the decay of the tradition. The
Indians themselves recognized a clear distinction between the two forms
of carving. The carver of poles was an artist who worked on commission, using a limited range of recognized symbolic forms and following
closely the requirements of his chiefly patron. The carver of masks and
ritual objects, on the other hand, was expected to display originality
and ingenuity, which seem to have been regarded as the sign of spiritual
inspiration, of contact with the supernatural beings. The Tsimshian
divided their carvers into two classes, the *ukgilyae*, who made only
secular objects, and who worked quite openly, and the revered and
exclusive *gitsontk*, who carved the masks and contrived the illusionist
devices for the societies' initiation ceremonies; to come upon him at his
sacred task was said to mean death to the beholder.

The most spectacular of the esoteric artifacts were those of the
Kwakiutl, whose masks were distinguished by extreme stylization, by
the caricaturing of human faces, by the simplification and boldening of
natural forms. Fantasy, mechanical ingenuity and even a touch of
comedy are to be found in the more ambitious Kwakiutl masks. They
were worn indoors during the long nights of the winter initiation ceremonies, and their shapes were deliberately calculated to arouse the awe
and terror of the uninitiated as they watched the dancers performing
their rituals to the tune of drums and spirit whistles in the shadow-
deepening light of the fires that burned in the long house. Some of the
most striking were used in the dances of the Hamatsa Society, the ritual
cannibals whose members stood at the head of the spiritual hierarchy.
Hamatsa initiates proved themselves by eating fragments of corpses,
and while they whirled in their macabre rituals they were accompanied
by mythical birds whose masks extended into articulated beaks five feet
long that clacked menacingly during the ceremony. Other masks,
operated by strings invisible in the dim light, were intended to astonish
or even perhaps to amuse; from some of them long red tongues would
suddenly shoot out at the onlookers or telescoped noses would grow
rapidly to four feet in length. Some of these trick masks were used to
emphasize the complex symbolism of the ceremonials. A hawk or eagle
mask, for example, might open out at a critical point in the dance to

reveal within it the human manifestation of the spirit represented. The best of the Pacific Coast masks and rattles were not in fact these over-elaborated Kwakiutl constructions, but rather those of the Tsimshian, restrained and sensitive in their recordings of human features, and of the Bella Coola, grotesque but not marred by excessive straining after effect.

It is to this more intimate art of the Pacific Coast Indians that one turns for the full expression of their culture after the first emphatic effect of the great pole sculptures has subsided. For such objects, with their great individuality, demonstrate the variety of attitudes which gives its richness to this civilization of fisher-craftsmen. In their contrasts one realizes how many different ways of perception can evolve even within a tribal culture with strong social patterns and a largely uniform material existence.

II

Yet, however individual in creation and feeling these artifacts from the forested fjords of British Columbia may have been, they still had their reason for existence in a very elaborate social setting—as elaborate in its own way as that which produced the great ecclesiastical art of the European middle ages. The art of the Eskimo was far more personal, far more the act and expression of an individual. The world of the barrens and the frozen seas produced no such year-round abundance as that enjoyed even by Stone Age men in British Columbia, and in conse-quence the most elaborate social unit was the extended family. The Eskimos had no organization beyond the family, though they did have a shared corpus of shamanistic beliefs, and on the west and south coasts of Alaska, where life was more temperate and fish and game more abundant, it was the custom to gather for elaborate winter festivals of a kind rarely seen among the Eskimos of the Canadian Arctic. These Alaskan Eskimos, probably influenced by the Pacific Coast Indians who roved the same seas, carved and constructed, out of driftwood, masks which were distinguished by an extraordinary surrealistic fantasy. The Canadian Eskimos never carved masks, and one looks vainly among their sculptures for the light-hearted grotesquerie practised by their western cousins.

Among North American and even European connoisseurs, the art of the Canadian Eskimos has recently become celebrated, but most of the work on which judgments are based is very new indeed, carved since—about 1949—the Eskimos were encouraged by missionaries, traders and government arts officers to make works for the market as a means of shoring up financially their collapsing way of life. Except where it has resulted in mass production by men of little talent, under the impression that any Eskimo artifact will sell outside the Arctic, this stimulation has not necessarily been a bad thing. It has in fact served the same purpose as the arrival of the traders with steel tools on the Pacific coast, since it has taught the Eskimos to carve on a larger and more elaborate scale and has encouraged them to give rein to an imagination kept tense and active by perpetual confrontation with the demanding world of the North.

But the intricate and often very sophisticated works which Eskimo sculptors make in the 1960s are very different from the small and simple carvings which their predecessors had been producing for at least a thousand years before their traditional way of life began to disintegrate during the 1940s. The primitive Eskimo would take a walrus tooth, or a fragment of soft soapstone or whalebone, and whittle away until the form it suggested emerged, usually an animal, or more rarely a human figure or some curious blending of man and animal emerging out of the stories told in the winter igloos. Long before western sculptors thought of it, the Eskimos learnt to coax the right form out of each material, and the carvings they produced were appropriate not only to the stone or bone out of which they emerged but also to the hand that made them, for they were shaped to be held and carried until the grease of the palm gave them its soft patina. Yet the primitive Eskimo sculptures were not merely playthings. They often served as ornaments (little bone seals and walruses of this kind have been found in Thule graves a thousand years old) but more important in the case of the animal carvings was their magical intent, which explains their compelling naturalism. They were evocative—catching the tension as well as the form of the living animal —because they were intended literally to evoke, to call the animal whom the hunter desired to kill, or to propitiate him when he had been killed. As in the paintings of Lascaux and Altamira, one senses in this early Eskimo carving, and in the best of the modern animal sculptures, carved by older men with long experience of the hunt, that peculiar symbiotic attraction which in primitive hunting societies exists between man and his quarry.

The Eskimo was not merely a carver. His imagination, dominated by his magical view of the world, found expression in songs and drum dances, meant also to call the animals to him, and in many poems and stories. This was so with the Indians as well. The stories and songs of the various peoples from the Atlantic to the Pacific are even now not fully collected, and it is probably too late to complete the recording of the dramatic ceremonials with their appropriate songs, choruses and orations, which formed the substance of the winter ceremonials of the Coast peoples. Yet, though there is such an abundant oral literature among the native peoples of Canada, it was above all in sculpture, whether the gigantic works of the Pacific Indians or the miniature creations of the Eskimos, that their cultures found most complete expression and still speak most eloquently to men of other worlds.

If I have spent so much time on the arts of these native peoples, it is because I regard them as forming the most interesting and certainly the most authentic of Canada's early traditions, while I dismiss most of the literary and artistic productions of Canadians before the twentieth century as of no more than antiquarian interest.

III

Pioneers are people whose creativity goes into the reshaping of the land. They have neither the time nor the energy to turn their minds to original thought or artistic creation, and they are usually so engrossed in the idea of reproducing in a strange land the world from which they came that the thought of giving a novel expression to what they see is remote from their minds. It is only later generations which perceive that what the pioneers have actually built is a new and different society, in a new and different land, and which then try to find appropriate ways of expressing this newness and difference.

Peasant art most hardily survives the transplantation involved in colonialization, since the preoccupations of an *habitant* in Canada are very similar to those of farmers left behind in Brittany or Normandy, and the peasant art of New France, and of Quebec for at least a generation after the Conquest, retains a vitality which still makes it the most interesting European work of Canada's first two centuries. Many fine primitive paintings, religious sculptures and examples of rural architecture have survived from that age, and they are complemented by a rich and varied tradition of folk song not only nostalgically recalling the lost homeland, but also celebrating the lives in Canada of the *habitant*, the

61. The quiet revolution. Old Quebec is discarded.

62. Pop Art—Quebec style.

63. Lagoons and sea: the coast of Nova Scotia.

64. The shipyards of Lunenburg.

voyageur, and their nineteenth-century successors, the lumbermen and raftmen. In comparison, the folk traditions of the Maritimes are rich in songs and stories, but—thanks to the Puritan tradition imported from New England—poor in the visual arts, as was the case in Upper Canada. In the west, the peasant peoples of eastern Europe had hardly settled before they were engulfed in the tide of modernization brought with the railways, with the consequence that their cultures have provided very little in Canada of any artistic significance.

There are some times and lands in which a vigorous folk tradition will have a vitalizing influence on the high arts; this was certainly so in nineteenth-century Russia, and in the case of jazz it has been so in twentieth-century America. But in Canada this did not happen. The peasant tradition remained isolated and was despised by those who attempted to reconstitute in the tiny cities of the new land the high arts of the old. All such arts were handicapped by the fact that professional writers and painters, musicians and actors, were not then among the classes which readily emigrated, mainly because there was little scope for them to make a living by the practice of their arts. The consequence was that amateurs took over and competent or incompetent imitation was substituted for imagination or originality. As the poet Louis Dudek has remarked, English-Canadian literature 'begins with decadent romantic lyric and with the lees of late eighteenth-century sentimental poetry imported from Europe'. Much the same could be said of French-Canadian literature, except that there the pattern of low-grade imitation begins in the seventeenth century. Almost all writers in the two Canadas before about 1880 used styles, sentiments and situations appropriate to European rather than North American circumstances, but always just a little out of date, like colonial slang. The result is that usually one has to go to the historians and their contemporary documents in order to get the true period flavour which the novels and the poems do not give.

There are a few exceptions, created by peculiar circumstances, among them the indefatigable Strickland sisters, Susanna Moodie and Catherine Parr Traill, who wrote out of a bitter experience of trying to combine gentility with pioneering and, later, of attempting to establish literary journalism in early Upper Canada. Susanna's *Roughing it in the Bush* and *Life in the Clearings*, and Catherine's *The Backwoods of Canada*, are memoirs which together provide an excellent if somewhat idiosyncratic picture of life during the 1830s in the rural areas and small towns

of Upper Canada, a picture far more convincing than one will get from
any Canadian novel before the end of the century. The fiction that had
a true relation to the life of Canada was that of the Nova Scotian
humorists, who flourished at the same period, Thomas Chandler
Haliburton and, less-known but even more interesting, his predecessor,
Thomas McCulloch. Both McCulloch and Haliburton were at heart
frustrated social reformers, concerned with the political ineptitudes and
personal follies of their contemporaries, and they turned to satirical
fiction in the hope of driving out folly with laughter. They did not
succeed in this aim, but they were the first Canadian writers to make an
effective use of vernacular and to take the undiluted daily life around
them as both material and frame of reference for their writing.

IV

Most of the Victorian age was a desert in Canada so far as writing and
painting are concerned. The anthologists still dutifully present the effete
neo-Augustan verses of Oliver Goldsmith the Younger (who capped
his great-uncle's *Deserted Village* with his own *Rising Village*), and the
ponderous Spenserianisms of a poet and closet dramatist called Charles
Heavysege, while art historians record the clumsy genre paintings of
Cornelius Krieghoff and Paul Kane and the undistinguished works in
which the members of the Royal Canadian Academy, founded by
Viscount Lorne in 1879, applied to the Canadian scene a convention-
alized perception indistinguishable from that of Royal Academicians in
London. There were amateurs trained in topography, like Thomas
Davies, who saw the magnificence of the setting with a fresher eye than
their professional contemporaries, and it is to these and a few *plein air*
enthusiasts like William J. R. Hind that we owe the first real attempts to
interpret the landscape, which was later to become so much the abiding
preoccupation—one might almost say obsession—of writers and painters
in Canada.

In literature the consciousness of setting first began to appear with
the group of writers generally known as the Confederation Poets, a
somewhat misleading title in view of the fact that only one of them,
Charles G. D. Roberts, began to write even as early as the 1880s. The
other three, Bliss Carman, Archibald Lampman and Duncan Campbell
Scott, were men of the 1890s, and in many ways they were typical of
their decade, with its neo-romanticism and its sentimental rebellion

against the Victorian conventions. Their models were Keats, Rossetti and Matthew Arnold, whom they followed skilfully, but all of them occasionally rose above mere derivativeness, and Duncan Campbell Scott did so frequently. It is to them—in poems like Carman's 'Low Tide at Grand Pré' and Roberts's 'Tantramar Revisited'—that we owe the first effective evocation in literature of the forms and moods of the Canadian countryside, while Scott, who worked for many years as deputy superintendent of Indian Affairs, expressed in verse that was often very moving his observations of the native peoples at this time of their greatest decline.

This was also the period when the influences of Baudelaire and the poets who followed him in France first became evident in Quebec with the work of the group of poets known as the Montreal School, whose members absorbed rather eclectically the rapidly changing French fashions of the 1890s, from the Parnassian to the symbolist. Among them was the first Canadian poet who might conceivably be regarded as great: the golden boy Emile Nelligan, who produced his whole work in his teens, lost his reason at the age of twenty, and survived for more than forty years, unproductive, insane and unrivalled almost to his belated death.

From France also came the influences that helped to mould the perceptions of the first two major Canadian painters, Ozias Leduc and James Wilson Morrice. Leduc, a self-taught Quebec church decorator, was probably the best of the painters who received the impulse given by the Impressionists, and used it to produce—in an obscure Laurentian village—paintings of illuminist authenticity, still lifes as glowing and splendid as those of Chardin, and landscapes where the Impressionist light gains an otherworldly limpidity. Morrice, son of a rich family of Montreal merchants, became a truly cosmopolitan painter, passing from the orbit of the Impressionists into that of the Fauves; he was the only Canadian painter until the 1940s who moved as an equal among the cosmopolitan painters of the School of Paris.

V

Canadian art—like Canadian writing—seems to swing, once it has passed out of colonialism, in great oscillations between subjection to cosmopolitan influences and assertion of identity with the overpowering local environment. Even today the great talents of Leduc and

Morrice, and the extraordinary proto-surrealist visions of their contemporary, the Sulpician priest Arthur Guindon, are obscured by the vast and not entirely justified reputation of the nationalist painters known as the Group of Seven, who succeeded them. Though they first came together on the eve of the First World War, the Group of Seven did not really begin to make an impact on the Canadian consciousness until after 1918. Their great preoccupation was the artistic exploration of the Canadian landscape, which, adapting styles and techniques borrowed from the Impressionists, Cézanne, van Gogh, Art Nouveau and British painters like Walter Sickert, they translated into evocative if not always great painting. Arthur Lismer, Frederick Varley, Lawren Harris, A. Y. Jackson and J. E. H. Macdonald were the members of the Group of Seven whose work still seems alive and valuable; the Group, in other words, had a high average ability, yet probably the best works associated with the movement were by a man who died too soon to belong to it, but who opened the eyes of its members to the means by which the Canadian environment might be tamed into art. This was Tom Thomson, whose expeditions into the wild country to the north of Lake Huron first led his friends of the Group of Seven to grapple with the reality of the Canadian landscape instead of remaining imperceptive of its distinctive aesthetic possibilities, which had been the case with most Canadian painters before them. The shapes of the Laurentian mountains, the tortured forms and strange colours of the pre-Cambrian rocks of the Shield, the incredible shifting blues, greens and purples of the Ontario lakes, the vibrating tints of Canadian trees at autumn and the strange forms and colourings of Arctic ice, the scapes of Canadian towns under snow, at thaw, in high, dusty summer: all these formed for the first time an empire for the Canadian painter to plunder at will. The Group of Seven has a position in the history of Canadian art out of all proportion to the talents of any of its members (thought not to the talents of its drowned precursor, Thomson) because it liberated artists from their dependence on foreign masters and influences. Canadian painters were no longer transplanted British academicians or French impressionists; they were men diligently exploring the formal inspirations of their own environment and using—rather than being used by —the means developed in the European tradition.

The impact of the Group of Seven, coming at a time—the 1920s— when Canada was developing a great deal of national self-consciousness, also had its negative effects. The members of the Group themselves tended to find a nationalist rationale for their painting; they saw their work, in the words of J. E. H. Macdonald, as 'a real stirring of Canadian ideals', and there is no doubt that if—after a period of resentment on the part of a public used to academic sentimentality—they became universally accepted as the classic Canadian painters, this was far more because they appealed to patriotic sentiments than because of their artistic merits. Throughout the past fifty years this tendency to see all Canadian art and literature in nationalist terms has tended to bedevil critical judgments. As Robert Fulford, the editor of *Saturday Night*, has pointedly remarked, 'It is a process which makes culture into an artificial historical event, a part of an unending quest for Canadian identity.'

The other negative result of the success of the Group of Seven was that they implanted a style of perceiving the environment which imprisoned most of the generation of painters that followed them. It was a Wildeian situation. Perhaps Canadian nature did not literally imitate the art of the Group of Seven, but certainly the way the Group of Seven presented nature affected the way Canadians saw it. It needed another swing of the pendulum, twenty years afterwards, to send Canadian painters back across the Atlantic to receive the inspirations that would enable them to look at their environment and their own inner visions in a new way.

VI

In some respects the development of a literature which could be called Canadian and not merely colonial resembled that of Canadian painting. A touch of national if not always nationalist sentiment, and a feeling of discovering the land newly and directly, were characteristic of the writers who carried the work of the Confederation poets on to the elaboration not only of a Canadian content in literature but also of a Canadian idiom and a Canadian tone. As in the early days, it was a humorist, Stephen Leacock, who (in such books as *Sunshine Sketches of a Little Town* and *Arcadian Adventures with the Idle Rich*) pioneered in presenting aspects of Canadian life which were not merely observed with a satirical eye, but also portrayed with local authenticity.

But it was out of the travail of immigrants in the prairies that a fiction which really grappled with the conflict of man and the Canadian environment first emerged. The prairie novelists were not major literary artists, with the dubious exception of Frederick Philip Grove, a kind of clumsy giant who wrote a series of flawed and powerful novels— *Settlers in the Marsh, The Master of the Mill*—which still haunt the imagination with half-articulate narratives of man at odds with nature and his own passions. Writers like Grove, and Robert Stead and Martha Ostenso, who really had something original to say, did so with a harsh heaviness which was not entirely inappropriate to the setting and which matched the lack of skill with which so many of the immigrant farmers had approached a new calling in a frightening land. The skill, the professional touch which they lacked, was in fact beginning to appear in Canada at this time, but it was in the hands of writers who sought to portray Canada romantically in order to please the circulating library publics of the age; the most successful of them—and the best in their particular manner—were Mazo de la Roche and Ralph Connor, both of whom became international best-sellers by presenting a view of Canada which was neither contemporary nor obsolete for the simple reason that it had never been true.

The marriage of skill and local authenticity which marks the beginning of a national literature first emerged among Canadian writers with the poets of the twenties and the thirties, heirs of English and American modernist influences, but nevertheless vitally concerned to find a way of speech that would express accurately the world they knew. E. J. Pratt, the Newfoundlander who settled in Toronto for an academic lifetime, but never forgot the epic nature of life in his island birthplace, is now regarded by most Canadian poets and critics as the pioneer of a genuine native poetry. In some ways Pratt—writing from the 1920s to the 1950s—was a curiously archaic figure, adapting Hudibrastic forms to describe the myths and epic stories of a frontier society—tales of the Jesuit martyrs, of laying the Canadian Pacific Railway; but though his forms were derivative, his manner was not, and he developed a vigour in dealing with native themes that was to be imitated by many later Canadian poets. Giving an artistic form to Canadian geography, he was probably as near as a Canadian writer ever got to the Group of Seven.

It was a younger and more sophisticated group—in the 1960s the deans of Canadian poetry—who followed Pratt in establishing the first cohesive movement since the Confederation poets. They were writers largely centred on McGill University; the names that come through the haze of thirty years with the emphasis of continuing reputations are F. R. Scott, one of Canada's best satiric poets, A. J. M. Smith, a lyrical perfectionist who is also his country's classic anthologist, A. M. Klein, a Jewish poet of great emotional power and symbolic diversity, and Dorothy Livesay, who parlayed the influence of the British thirties poets into a style of great individuality. At the same time there emerged the first Canadian novelist who combined literary skill with the authentic voice of the country; Morley Callaghan is still writing today but his best books are three novels he wrote a generation ago, *They Shall Inherit the Earth*, *More Joy in Heaven* and *Such in My Beloved*.

In Klein and in Callaghan a new voice began to speak in Canadian writing, that of the urban man. The consciousness of urbanization has undoubtedly played a great part in the development of a sophisticated Canadian literature during the quarter of a century since the final years of the Second World War. It is not merely the physical fact of more people living in cities that has wrought the qualitative change in Canadian literature. It is rather the shift in the national tone from the bucolic to the urbane. The influx of educated European immigrants helped to change the intellectual standards of the cities, besides contributing many writers, not all of British origin. At the same time the ease of travel to the United States and the exchange of students and academic personnel led to a south-north movement of influences, from San Francisco to Vancouver, from New York to Toronto, while between Montreal and Paris the interplay in all the arts became more active than ever before. Complementing these foreign influences over the past two decades has been a strong countervailing force of national feeling, not always political. Canadians, having got rid of the idea that they are British or French in the European sense, are certainly not willing to consider themselves Americans. They recognize but resist the outside influences that impinge upon them, and it is from this dialogue between influence and resistance that much of the vigour and variety and sophistication of recent Canadian writing have emerged.

In addition, the growth of the three Canadian metropolises has helped to create at last the skeleton of a local literary world. It is true that most Canadian writers still feel the need to live some part of their lives— which may vary from a year to a decade—in the traditional centres of literary activity; there are always small colonies of Canadian novelists and poets—and painters and actors as well—in London, Paris, San Francisco and New York. But now Canada is beginning to offer them more than it did in the past. Though the specialist writer may have to seek acceptance abroad, very few good poems or novels go begging for Canadian publishers, and—while twenty years ago I found two very thin Canadian literary reviews in existence—now at least a dozen reasonably thick ones are published in centres across the country from Fredericton to Vancouver Island. In addition, there is a whole underground of private presses and little magazines which did not exist even ten years ago, and which make it difficult even for the worst poem to escape print. In Montreal and Toronto—and even to a less extent in Vancouver—there are developing those little literary societies, with established elders and rebellious young, which most writers need at least at some stage in their lives. Yet Canada is also a good place for the writer who temperamentally is in need of solitude. Malcolm Lowry, living in his solitary cabin on the shores of Burrard Inlet, isolated even from the local literati of Vancouver, was one of these. I could name a dozen more who follow his example today, living in remotenesses far more distant than Lawrence's Cornwall or even Orwell's Hebrides.

But now it is necessary to talk of the work of the writers who represent this new literary Canada; the names are many, and I must neglect those with only half-established achievements and the very young who tend to move like fry in mutually imitative schools and show their individuality—even in this age of youth rampant—only when maturity begins to stabilize their turbulences. In poetry over the past twenty years Canada has been rich in new trends and new poets, and here there is some significance to local traditions. Montreal has been a strong centre of English as well as French poets since the 1930s, and this is undoubtedly to a great degree due to the relationships—which tended to break down during the separatist phase of the 1960s—between poets working in the two languages. The English Montrealers have always tended in one direction towards a social realism linked with a politically radical tendency (represented in the 1930s by F. R. Scott), and in the other direction, towards metaphysical goals, sometimes combined with left-wing politics and varying from the Jewish mysticism of Klein to the Lawrencian vitalism of Irving Layton. Klein, the best of this group of poets, has published nothing since *The Rocking Chair* in 1948, and during most of the sixties the centre of the Montreal stage was occupied by Layton, a prolific, chaotic and combative poet who has published a score of volumes and brochures since his first book, *Here and Now*, came out in 1945. Layton's chief fault is an almost total absence of self-criticism; his best poems, which have a true lyric fire, have always to be dug out from between thick layers of rhetorical rubbish. But when

65. Germanic style; houses in Lunenburg, N.S.

66. The mackerel fishers, Rustico, Prince Edward Island.

67. The potato pickers, Prince Edward Island.

he succeeds in his exuberant game of hit-and-miss he can present, as no other Canadian poet does, a joy in the glory of life or a devastating contempt for life's enemies. Leonard Cohen, a younger Montreal poet, has solved more effectively than most other Canadian poets the problem of writing a verse that is speakable and even singable (he has gained a great popular repute among the young for his poems chanted to guitar) while still standing up to the test of the printed page. Other important Montreal poets have been Louis Dudek, also active as an editor of poetry magazines and a publisher of younger poets, and Patrick Anderson, an immigrant from Britain who played an important role in the Canadian poetic renaissance during the 1940s, but has long since returned to Britain and the Greek islands.

Generally speaking, Toronto poets have been less inclined to 'social significance' than the Montreal group, though here an exception must be made for Raymond Souster, as near to a genuine populist poet as one can find in Canada, not in the sense of a writer of songs for the masses, but of a man who has sought to identify himself with the lives and passions of ordinary people, to write in the rhythms of the vernacular, and to build on the lessons of Imagism a sparse, laconic, North American way of writing stripped of the literary devices of the European tradition. He has fulfilled this difficult task extremely well, and, after a quarter of a century of writing, is still trusted and accepted by the very young as a kind of poetic guru. The other leading Toronto poets (by no means all of whom originated in that city) have been more metaphysical in their approach and more concerned with traditional poetic craftsmanship than the Montreal group. These qualities were already evident in the work of the writers who carried over from the Second World War period, such as Anne Wilkinson, Douglas le Pan and P. K. Page, but they developed during the 1950s among the mythopoeic group of poets, centring on the little magazine *Alphabet*, who arose under the influence of the critic Northrop Frye. These poets not only created mythological structures to illuminate their personal messages; they were also adept at a kind of wit which depended on the astonishing marriage of the ridiculous and the sublime. The best of them, Jay Macpherson, Eli Mandel and James Reaney, are among the most sophisticated and the finest poets writing in Canada today, though at times even their discrimination is dulled by an intoxication with their own wit. This applies particularly to James Reaney, who has experimented in many forms, and just as many moods, varying from the clotted Gothic melodrama of his early lyrics in *The Red Heart* to the allusive clowning of *A Suit of Nettles* and the strange mixtures of farce and pathos, inanity and depth, that emerge when he turns—with a versatility rare among Canadian poets—to play, opera and masque.

Among the other poets active in the post-war period in Canada, it is hard to find such clearly marked groups as have existed in Montreal and Toronto. Even among the Toronto poets Margaret Avison stands apart in metaphysical isolation, one of the most self-critical of Canadian writers and one of the few religious poets of real stature in the country, while Alfred Purdy, who comes out of small-town Ontario and calls himself a 'degenerate Loyalist', is entirely *sui generis* and extremely adept in his blending of Canadian locutions and traditional lyrical devices into a kind of incantation on the borderland between poetry and prose. And, though there are a number of very distinguished British Columbian poets, it is hard to find among them a uniting thread. Earle Birney, an indefatigable experimenter, writes a vigorous free verse, often satirical and richly allusive, celebrative of landscapes and townscapes native and foreign; Roy Daniells is a fine traditional sonneteer who handles spiritual subtleties with great wit and technical mastery; while Phyllis Webb writes with a honed-down intellectuality that is at times excessively chilling. Among the younger poets, international styles—the beat, the hip, the Black Mountain, the concrete—have acquired great influence in the inevitable pendulum swing against the nativist trends of the forties and fifties. One is often depressed by the power of fashion to hamper individuality, but a number of talents stand out among the young, and I would mention particularly Margaret Atwood, Gwendolyn MacEwen, George Bowering and John Newlove.

With rare exceptions, Canadian fiction has not shown the experimental tendency of Canadian verse, nor has it shown the same kaleidoscopic variety of approach. Significantly, the two most prestigious novelists in contemporary Canada—Hugh MacLennan and Morley Callaghan—are both rather conservative in philosophy and in technique. Morley Callaghan, an excellent short-story writer and at his best a good novelist, has written nothing since 1945 that approaches his achievements of the thirties, with the sole exception of a fascinating literary memoir, *That Summer in Paris*, which tells with the vigour, directness and naïveté characteristic of earlier days, the story of his literary youth and his association with Hemingway and Fitzgerald.

Hugh MacLennan, who published his first novel, *Barometer Rising*, in

1941, is a classical scholar with a sense of mission towards Canadian nationalism. He is preoccupied to the point of obsession with the fact of living in a country where a sense of separate identity as a nation has become during his lifetime an emergent force; he is equally preoccupied with the danger to the new nation which he expounded in his novel *Two Solitudes*, presented by the division of Canadians into two mutually unassimilated groups—English-speaking and French-speaking. Almost every novel MacLennan has written is marred by the didacticism which such preoccupations force upon him, and by the distortion of both character and action when they are bent to serve prevailing arguments. The exception, *Each Man's Son*, is his best novel. It concerns a Cape Breton mining settlement shadowed by the distortions of a puritanical attitude towards life, and in its record of the downfall of a boxing professional brought up in this environment, the fatalism which MacLennan derived from his study of Greek drama serves well to render the Calvinist view of existence. MacLennan writes admirably on action (there is a marvellous record of the famous Halifax explosion in *Barometer Rising*), but with a fatal embarrassment on anything remotely erotic; his most ambitious novel, *The Watch That Ends the Night*, is ruined by the sentimental implausibilities of the central sexual triangle between a doctor who returns after having long been given up for dead in the Nazi concentration camps, his former wife, and the thin-blooded political commentator who has since married her and who narrates the novel.

Some of the most vital Canadian fiction of the post-war period has been written by people who for various geographical or ethnic reasons belong outside the main stream of ordinary Canadian life which writers like MacLennan and Callaghan seek to represent. There are, first the immigrants. Probably the best of all novels ever to come out of Canada is Malcolm Lowry's *Under the Volcano*, completed when Lowry was living in his British Columbian solitude. But *Under the Volcano* was conceived in Mexico and its first versions were written there. More truly Canadian were the short stories which Lowry wrote on the basis of his fifteen years of life on the Pacific coast of Canada, from 1939 to 1954. Published after his death in 1957, as a volume entitled *Hear Us O Lord from Heaven Thy Dwelling Place*, these stories showed clearly that Lowry had lived his way into the Canadian environment and could render its spirit as admirably and with as much wayward originality as he rendered that of the Mexican plateau in *Under the Volcano*. His premature death has raised acutely the question of whether a potentially great career was cut short; possibly not, for in his last years Lowry found it almost impossible to finish a work of major dimensions. One of the three unfinished novels on which he was working in Canada, *Dark as the Grave Wherein my Friend Was Laid*, has appeared recently; it is no more than a gloss—and a most prolix one—on *Under the Volcano*.

Brian Moore fits just as elusively into the pattern of Canadian writing as Malcolm Lowry. He is Belfast-born and, like Joyce, has carried his Ireland with him. The Irish lonely in their own land of his early novel, *Judith Hearne*, become the Irish lonely as aliens in *The Luck of Ginger Coffey*, a tragic-comic tale of the misadventures of an Irish bounder in Montreal, which is easily the best of the many novels that have attempted to give expression to the predicament of the immigrant in Canada. Moore has since left for the United States, and his most recent novel, *I am Mary Dunne*, rejects his Canadian experience in an emphatic way which suggests that Moore still belongs to Ireland rather than to either of the lands where he has settled as a bird of passage.

Life abroad of a different kind from that which shapes the attitude of the immigrant has shaped the work of Margaret Laurence, who is a birthright Canadian. Margaret Laurence lived for fairly long periods in Somaliland and West Africa, and out of her experiences in these places she wrote a group of fine short stories, a first novel of West Africa, *This Side Jordan*, and one of the few good travel books written by a Canadian, *The Prophet's Camel Bell*. She has now reversed her earlier process, by going abroad—to England—in order to write novels about the Canada of her pre-African youth: *The Stone Angel* and *A Jest of God*.

One of the most interesting literary phenomena in post-war Canada has been the emergence of a body of excellent writers from a Jewish community miniscule in proportion to the whole English-speaking population of the country. These writers, who include poets like Layton and Cohen and Klein, as well as novelists, would object to being lumped together in a 'Jewish school', for they are all militantly individualist in approach, but they write from a common background and they are all concerned in one way or another with the generation-by-generation progress through which a Jew in North America steps from his narrower traditional community into the wider community of the world; indeed, for many of them the Jewish youth at odds with his family or his neighbours is merely the aspect they know best of the general problem of the individual at odds with society. The best of Canadian-Jewish novelists are the poet A. M. Klein, who has written a single very moving allegorical novel of Zionist flavour, *The Second Scroll*, and Mordecai Richler. Richler is an iconoclastic novelist, much concerned with the individual's self-liberation from his own as well as his world's hypocrisies. In such novels as *Son of a Smaller Hero* and *The Apprenticeship of Duddy Kravitz* he mounts a nihilistic attack on current moralities, using a prose that at best is brutally alive and direct, and at worst as flat-footed as a policeman's walk. Other Jewish novelists who rank high among Canadian writers are Adele Wiseman, Jack Ludwig and Leonard Cohen.

Regional novels that rise above sentimental pseudo-history or amiable rusticity have continued to be rare in Canada. Of the recent novelists who have tried to encompass the life of the prairies, only Sinclair Ross has really succeeded; his *As For Me and My House*, published in 1941, achieved the aesthetic completeness in describing the physical ardours and mental destructiveness of prairie life which earlier writers like Grove had sought in vain.

Since the war Vancouver has become a literary centre only less important than Montreal and Toronto. Apart from its poets, and apart from the unhappy shadow of Lowry, which still haunts many local memories, it is the home of at least one major Canadian novelist, Ethel Wilson, who has woven the données of her environment into a series of highly sophisticated, ironical and dry-humoured *récits*. Ethel Wilson began to write short stories in her forties; she did not start with novels until her fifties, and published her first, *Hetty Dorval*, in 1947 at the age of fifty-six. Well into her seventies she continued to write with wry wisdom and an acute and careful sense of style. Her best novels, *The Innocent Traveller*, *Swamp Angel* and *Love and Salt Water*, are all set in the Vancouver region where she had lived since she came from England in her childhood and the childhood of the city, but they are as universal in their intent as good nature poems.

Other fields of literature have been less generously represented in Canada than poetry or the novel. Much drama has been written, but mostly for radio and television, the greater part of it buried unpublished in the files of the Canadian Broadcasting Corporation, so that its value is for the present impossible to assess. Those dramatists wishing to write for the stage have been frustrated until recently by the absence of theatres in Canada that might perform their plays, so that there are only two writers of any consequence in this genre. One, Robertson Davies, is the author of somewhat heavily satirical novels and of stage farces characterized by a donnish skittishness; the other is the poet James Reaney, whose plays, theatrically rather disoriented, are so filled with fantastic business that they hold one's attention tightly enough to appreciate the passages of magnificent verse with which they are studded; Reaney's best pieces are *The Killdeer* and *Night Blooming Cereus*, the latter first conceived as the libretto for an opera.

The appearance, during the last twenty years, of a strong native school of criticism is the sign of a maturing and self-conscious literature, and it is significant that only in the last fifteen years have Canadians turned with any seriousness or depth to the critical consideration of their own literature. Much that passes for criticism is still mere appreciation, for the Canadian literary world is small and overrates the virtue of mutual kindliness. But the general situation has changed considerably since 1945, partly through the example of Northrop Frye as a theoretical critic, partly through the iconoclastic views on literature disseminated from Toronto by Marshall McLuhan, and partly through the appearance of a number of critics trained in the more rigorous standards of the British literary world, such as Paul West and George Woodcock. With such younger Canadian critics as Milton Wilson, F. W. Watt and Hugo McPherson, these writers have helped to create a more mature view of literary criticism—an attitude crystallized by the appearance in 1959 of the first Canadian critical quarterly, *Canadian Literature*.

VII

In comparison with English-Canadian writing, that of French Canada is today as rich in fiction and poetry, and richer in criticism and the occasional philosophical essay. During the past decade there has been a wide acceptance of Quebec writers in France, not out of any Gaullist desire to re-establish a political relationship between Paris and Quebec, but from a genuine appreciation of interesting works emerging from a fresh and youthful tradition. A whole issue of *Les Lettres Nouvelles* was devoted to Canadian writing; significantly it included translations from English-Canadian writers as well as original pieces by French Canadians, as if to deny a political implication in the interest which the editors had shown in Canada.

Like the English Canadians, the French had their generation of the

thirties and forties which moved the literature of Quebec forward out
of a colonial dependence on French trends and influences into the
maturity of independence. In poetry, the initiator of the new movement was Saint-Denys Garneau, who published his two books of verse
in the late thirties and died young. His contemporaries and friends,
Alain Grandbois, Rina Lasnier and Anne Hébert, continued his work of
developing a poetry that stood in the light of its own originality and
excellence, and they are, today, the elders of the renaissance in French-
Canadian writing. Anne Hébert's *Le Tombeau des rois* is possibly the
best volume of poems ever published in Canada, French or English.

The effort to find an authentic French-Canadian style has been carried on by a whole succession of younger poets, among whom the most
interesting have been Gilles Hénault, Roland Giguère, Fernand
Ouellette, Jean-Guy Pilon and Pierre Trottier. Recent political and
social trends in Quebec—the revolt against English-Canadian domination and the rejection of the standards of conservative Quebec implied
in the Quiet Revolution and its aftermath—have led many of the
youngest generation of Quebec poets into a course which combines
separatist radicalism with literary iconoclasm. These writers, gathered
around a magazine entitled *Parti pris*, carry the search for a Canadian
idiom to a rigorously logical conclusion by finding it, not in correct
literary French, but in an adaptation of *joual*—the slang of Montreal
which is virtually incomprehensible not only to English Canadians but
also to visitors from France. Paul Chamberland, André Major, and
Claude Jasmin have all practised with varying degrees of success this
form of writing which has some affinities with the anti-art of Dada;
Chamberland is actually on record as having said that he writes best
when he is writing badly.

In fiction, French Canada carried for thirty years the burden of its
most famous novel, *Maria Chapdelaine*, written by the Frenchman Louis
Hémon who spent some years as a drifter in Quebec. Hémon projected
the view of rural, peasant Canada which remained a literary convention
long after his novel appeared in 1914. It was not until Ringuet published *Trente Arpentes* in 1938 and described the decadence of agrarian
Quebec, that fiction in French Canada began to liberate itself from the
dominance of the stereotypes it had helped to create.

The change from a rural to an urban Quebec, and the shift in values
which this involved, were first transmuted into fiction by Gabrielle
Roy, who remains the most considerable of French-Canadian novelists,

translated and acclaimed in English Canada. Her *Bonheur d'occasion* (*The Tin Flute*), published in 1945, and her later *Alexandre Chenevert* (*The Cashier*) described poignantly the social malaise which the trend to the cities created in Quebec, and established a completely new attitude in fiction, which abandoned the sanctification and sentimentalization of the values of Old Quebec, and, long before the Quiet Revolution, led an honest search for the truth of the human condition. This does not mean that the French-Canadian novel became necessarily naturalistic. On the contrary, it probably developed a greater tendency towards fantasy and surrealism than its English-Canadian counterpart. But the search was still for an idiom related to present reality rather than to the dreams of the past. In the succession of novelists that have followed Gabrielle Roy, one must give special mention to Yves Thériault, Claire Martin, Gérard Bessette, Hubert Aquin, Marie-Claire Blais, Réjean Ducharme and Jacques Godbout, who in the 1960s have presented a body of work that would have done credit to any literature. Canada, in fact, has awakened everywhere during the past quarter of a century as a land of good writers, and the divisions between English and French have resulted in generative and productive tensions, so that in literature, as in the other arts, the two 'nations' have moved forward together, a fact which gives some hope that the present political disagreements may in their turn and in the end have good rather than negative results.

VIII

In painting the 1940s were equally important as an era when Canadian artists everywhere moved out from under a shadow—in this case the shadow of their own nationalism represented by the Group of Seven. During the 1930s there had already been painters who had moved away from the influence of the Group of Seven on strongly individual courses—Emily Carr, for example, and David Milne, who led a life as dedicated as Cézanne's to the pursuit of meaning in form and colour. In many ways Milne was the perfect complement to the Seven, but he was well before his time, and remained a solitary figure. Perhaps the most important catalytic event in the development of contemporary Canadian painting was the exhibition, *Art in Our Day*, organized in 1939 by the Contemporary Art Society, which belatedly brought to Montreal the works of the great painters of the School of Paris and of miscellaneous Mexicans, Russians and Englishmen who were then internationally accepted as part of the modern movement that had sprung from Post-Impressionism. Shortly afterwards two young French-Canadian painters, Alfred Pellan and Paul-Emile Borduas, the disciple of Ozias Leduc, found their way to Paris, and by the late 1940s Montreal and soon the whole of Canada were beginning to feel the effect of their return. Not only were Pellan and Borduas remarkable and explosively experimental painters who did not shrink at the eventual abandonment of all the past presumptions of figurative art; they were also influential teachers, some of whose disciples became major painters, like Jacques de Tonnancour and Jean-Paul Riopelle.

The new spirit which Pellan and Borduas evoked very quickly disseminated over Canada, and contemporary schools of painting began to emerge in Toronto and Vancouver as well as Montreal; for the past twenty years, in fact, the history of the visual arts in Canada could very well be charted in terms of the rivalry between these three cities. All of them, as the fifties progressed, fell under the influence of trends in New York, which at that time was rivalling Paris as a world art centre, but there were many variations in the way in which American influences were received and transmuted into local painting. New York style was probably least diluted in Toronto. In Montreal the links with Paris have always remained strong, and American influences are absorbed through a French filter. In Vancouver, there have usually been a number of filters—British, Oriental, San Franciscan; many of the leading Vancouver painters have been British by origin and several of them Japanese or Chinese.

Two factors prevented Canadian painters between the late 1940s and the mid 1960s from falling completely under the spell of international fashion. One was the better heritage of the Group of Seven—the knowledge of the Canadian landscape as a source of images and forms which continued to influence even those who regarded themselves as recruits to non-figurative abstractionism. The other was the presence of many artists of strong individuality, like Harold Town, Tony Urquhart and Graham Coughtry in Toronto, Jack Shadbolt and Gordon Smith in Vancouver, Bruno Bobak in Fredericton, who had the ability to absorb influences coming from outside and yet to forge their own styles.

Today, in the rapid turnover of schools which is a characteristic of modern art movements, these painters, who were at the height of their popularity only a few years ago, have already become inhabitants of history, as Pop Art, Op Art, Psychedelic Art, neo-Dada and all the other new movements have swept over an art world which has in recent years acquired the structure of similar milieux in New York, Paris and London: dealers anxious for profitable novelties, collectors anxious to display complete contemporaneity in taste, critics dependent on new themes, and a host of young men and women, mass-produced by the art schools and conditioned to respond quickly to the demands of the market. As a consequence, the Canadian art centres have become so sensitive to what is taking place internationally that it takes only six months after a new fad has been launched in New York for its effect to be seen in the galleries of Vancouver. Even the museums and public galleries are falling into the hands of an art establishment dependent on novelty, and the result is a situation in which change is cultivated for its own sake, the instant effect is sought and immediately discarded, and the productions of the newer artists become anonymous and interchangeable, their differences depending on the market rather than the maker. The total result is the same as that of periods of academic domination; the true artist works in isolation, barely recognized, waiting for the swing of fashion, and the regional schools which flourished in Canada during the 1950s and the early 1960s are languishing because of the international emphasis, though—if one can judge from past developments in Canadian painting—this may well be a passing phase.

IX

In the civic arts there have been changes in the Canadian scene fully as dramatic as those in literature and painting, and much more direct in their effect on the lives of the majority. Changes in architecture, for example, have transformed the appearance of Canadian cities during the past quarter of a century. Sudden and dramatic reconstructions, like those of central Montreal and Edmonton, have been rare indeed, though most Canadian cities are discussing the replanning of their obsolescent downtown areas. But there has been a steady replacement by attrition of nineteenth-century buildings, and the newer towns, as well as the vast suburbs of existing cities, are built mostly in contemporary styles. The sham-Tudor mansion, the fake-Spanish colonial villa, may still appear in nouveau riche areas, but they are no longer typical.

The changes have not always been for the better. It is true that the designers of government buildings no longer feel impelled to follow

Westminster neo-Gothic or Washington neo-classical. It is true also that in the west it is now rare to find a city whose most impressive buildings are the sham chateau of the railway hotel and the vertical barns of the grain elevator. In architecture too, Canada has passed out of the colonial stage, but there are times when one feels that it has done so merely to assume—as in recent painting—a characterless internationalism. The brick or clapboard villas of the colonial age, with their touch of New England classicism or their flavour of turreted Gothic, have given way to a genus of flat-roofed and ranch-style houses, with great unprivate picture windows, which are less interesting because they are even more uniform in appearance; travelling in the mazes of suburban streets, it is often hard to find a house distinctive enough to serve one's memory as a landmark. Among public buildings, a kind of dead functionalism too often prevails. Most schools, for example, are low-elevation rectangular blocks built to uniform patterns and looking like enlightened prisons; the same applies to the chimneyless factories of the electrical age, and to most apartment blocks, while the flat-faced, glass-fronted office building—bend sinister in Le Corbusier's lineage—is still the customary fashion in the business areas of the cities.

Yet there are moments of excitement and peaks of inspiration in Canadian architecture, as those who travelled to Expo in 1967 realized, both on the site itself and in the city of Montreal. There are architects who create splendid patterns of light and shadow, void and solid, while fulfilling the practical demands of their patrons, and with a little trouble one can see beautiful buildings serving many different purposes. There are churches like the gigantic stylized conch of Our Lady of Fatima, built in 1963 at Jacquerie in Quebec. There are buildings for the performing arts like the Place des Arts in Montreal, the O'Keefe Centre in Montreal, the Queen Elizabeth Theatre in Vancouver, the festival theatre at Stratford with its imaginative adaptation of the Elizabethan form, and the delightful miniature theatre for the summer seminars of Jeunesses Musicales at Mount Orford, Quebec. Among municipal buildings the most striking is the Toronto City Hall, whose two great half-cylinders, confronting each other over a low connecting building, provide the focus for the renewal of the city's centre. The new international airports created by the Ministry of Transport on the outskirts of the main Canadian cities, not only offer scope for some of the boldest of Canadian planning, but also provide settings for sculpture and mural painting as elements in architecture. Jack Shadbolt's vast mural, 'The

Bush Pilot in the Northern Sky', painted for the Edmonton International Airport in 1963, is not only the most remarkable Canadian work in that genre, but equal in grandeur—though opposed in idiom—to the finest of Mexican murals; it is an admirable example of the imaginative combination of abstract expressionist techniques with a profound feeling for the grandeur of the Canadian landscape.

I can name many fine Canadian architects—John Parkin, Ronald Thom (who designed the modernized collegiate Gothic of Massey College in Toronto), Robert Fairfield, Raymond Affleck, George Eber —but if I had to pick out the great Canadian architect, of this or any other time, I would unhesitatingly name Arthur Erickson. Erickson's work is varied, audacious and far-scattered; it includes private houses in Vancouver, university buildings in many parts of Canada, the Man in Community pavilion at Expo and—still only in the design stage—a Canadian Pavilion for the Osaka International Exhibition of 1970.

Erickson has liberated his buildings from the long thraldom to function; he sees in houses not only places to live but also places to stimulate the imagination, and—like Japanese dwellings—those he designs may sacrifice total comfort to aesthetic interest. He is most concerned with what architecture does to the mind, and deliberately designed Simon Fraser University (sited on the top of a small mountain overlooking Vancouver Harbour and offering a view up Indian Arm into the heart of the Coast Mountains) to give the students and faculty the maximum of sheltered walking, since, as he said, 'walking is good for talking'; he also provided massive buildings with soaring stairways and a great agora to encourage the clash of opinions. Whether Erickson wished it or not, Simon Fraser has been the most turbulent university in Canada, and anyone who stands at the head of its most grandiose vista will understand why; one is impelled to respond to this disturbing vastness or to react against it.

In architecture Erickson represents most emphatically the Canadian artist's immersion in the Canadian landscape; he has learnt lessons from Japan, where he has travelled often, but he has applied them to the Canadian landscape, both in his integration of building and setting and his use of evocative materials. The characteristic Erickson houses are airy light-filled structures of glass on slender columns of wood or brick, with winglike roofs, so built that, as in a Japanese pavilion, house and garden and view seem to exist in a natural continuity. Erickson's exhibition buildings are probably those that have given him the most

pleasure to design, because in them he has been able to indulge the
poetic fantasy which is part of this man who loves deserts and the
extremities of natural environment. In his Man in Community building
at Expo he constructed a sky-probing occidental pagoda out of hexa-
gonal frames of Douglas fir; a building which may have seemed a little
out of place on an island in the St. Lawrence, but which would have
merged as perfectly into the forests of his native British Columbia as a
Japanese temple into its grove of cryptomeria trees. Erickson's models
for the Canadian pavilion at Osaka show a building of tilted mirrors so
constructed that its outer walls by reflection seem to merge into the sky.
As Erickson observes, Canadians are always conscious of the sky, and a
mirror building evokes much more of their land—its lakes and rivers,
its icy north, its very vastness. During the last five years Erickson has
advanced into the position of an architect of world importance, but of
all Canada's builders he has probably the purest and the most evocative
vision of his country's character.

X

The performing arts of Canada tell more of the changing tastes of
Canadians than of Canadian creativity, since it is rarely that a Canadian
opera company or a Canadian orchestra performs a work by a native
composer, or a Canadian theatre company presents a play by a local
dramatist.

Twenty years ago in Canada it was low tide for the performing arts.
The cinema had killed off the old theatres and opera houses, and, except
to Montreal and Toronto, touring companies of actors came rarely,
and then were usually of the lowest quality. Most theatrical performances were amateur and devastating. Those who lived in western
Canada or the Maritimes either relied on the radio, or waited for the
next trip to San Francisco or New York or Europe in order to see good
plays or hear good music.

Today all that is completely changed. Since 1957 the attendances at
concerts and theatrical and operatic performances have increased from
1,500,000 to 4,000,000 per annum, and this increase has been due to the
existence of vastly expanded opportunities. Twenty years ago, when I
returned to Canada, there were two symphony orchestras in the country; now there are twelve. One could hear opera only in Toronto and
Montreal; now one can also hear it from local companies in Vancouver,

Edmonton, Quebec and Stratford. There was a single excellent ballet—the Royal Winnipeg; now there are notable ballet companies in Montreal and Toronto as well, and a National Ballet School. And during the past two decades an amazing number of professional theatrical enterprises have come into being, starting with the Stratford Shakespearian Festival in 1953, and including Le Théâtre du Nouveau Monde, Le Rideau Vert, and La Comédie Canadienne in Montreal, the Crest Theatre in Toronto, the Manitoba Theatre Centre under John Hirsch in Winnipeg, the Neptune Theatre under Leon Major in Halifax, the Playhouse Theatre under Malcolm Black in Vancouver, the Citadel Theatre in Edmonton and the Circle in the Centre at Calgary, as well as a number of seasonal events, like the Charlottetown Festival and the annual Shaw Festival at Niagara-on-the-Lake.

The only field in which Canada has not entirely lived up to the hopes placed on it is that of the cinema. This is not due to lack of talent, for in recent years the National Film Board and private film-makers have produced some of the world's best documentaries, but a tradition of Canadian feature films has never developed, and this is probably the direction in which the proximity of the United States has most adversely affected the growth of a native Canadian culture. Certainly the competition of Hollywood seems to have intimidated those Canadian producers who have not fled there, for the few feature films that have appeared from Canadian studios have been artistic and financial failures, and even the amateur films of the Bohemian underworld have been pallid reflections of their American models.

The upsurge that has occurred in most of the performing arts has been due largely—like so much else in Canada of the 1960s—to the sophisticated immigrants who arrived from Europe during the 1950s. They provided not only audiences, but also producers and performers who enabled new theatrical and musical ventures to develop where in the past there had been too few either active or passive participants to support them. But the consciousness of other Canadians that a local culture could not be created without effort was also important. Already in 1949 it inspired the creation of Vincent Massey's Royal Commission on National Development in the Arts, Letters and Sciences, which in 1951 submitted a report recommending the foundation of a Canada Council to encourage the arts and humanities. In 1957, after two multi-millionaires had died and left the Canadian government with an unexpected heirloom in the form of massive succession duties, the Canada

Council was actually founded. At the time it was thought that the Canada Council might well become an instrument of nationalist policy and state intervention, which would turn the arts into the handmaidens of politics. In fact, this autonomous but state-financed foundation has given its help to individual creative artists, and to performing groups, with an extraordinary tact and without the least pressure to glorify the nation or to carry out anything but the project submitted. In material terms the Canada Council has given many artists periods of freedom from economic compulsion, has enabled many theatrical companies, orchestras, little magazines, etc., to expand and develop, and even has helped publishers to bring out commercially unfeasible books. What the Council itself has given is not everything, since its presence has encouraged others to give. Nowadays about 50 per cent of the income of the performing arts comes from actual ticket sales, about 20 per cent from the Canada Council, but almost 30 per cent from other patrons—individual and corporate—who have been moved to emulation. It is a result of the new mass interest in the arts that so many new ventures in theatre and music and literature have started up during the past ten years, but it is the financial help and moral encouragement of the Canada Council that has made the difference between inception and survival. The Canada Council, in fact, is probably the best example of Canada's characteristic pluralism, by which the state provides the means for independent artists to follow their vocations in just the same way as, with subsidized railways and gifts of lands, it provided the means for independent farmers to populate the prairies.

Chapter X

BACKS TO THE WALL OF ICE

I

To men in the North, the rest of Canada is 'Outside', and to Canadians who live Outside, the North is almost, but not quite, an alien land. Few Canadians ever travel north of 60°, and those who do, go in the same spirit as the British visiting those colonies which, however strange their way of life, were never quite foreign so long as the Union Jack flew over them. The North, in fact if not in name, is Canada's empire, and the attitudes which most Canadians except its native Eskimos and Indians adopt towards it are strictly colonial.

Rather than attempting at the outset to describe in nature and spirit the million and a half square miles of taiga and tundra and ice that form Canada's Arctic and sub-Arctic regions, let me begin by evoking a community which in memory holds for me the essence of the North. Up the narrow channels of Chesterfield Inlet from Hudson's Bay the sea probes into the Barren Land, and during the short months between breakup and freezeup the small vermilion ships of the Department of Transport sail there and ride at the offshore booms in Baker Lake, where the fresh water meets the salt and the great Thélon and Kazan Rivers flow down out of the deserted tundra. Today the settlement that bears the lake's name is, by Arctic standards, a large and active community. All summer long, Baker Lake is dusty with construction work, busy with the coming and going of government men, and the beach is noisy with float planes and outboard motors and brilliant with the walls of stridently coloured oil drums that mark the shore of every northern outpost. Behind, in the rows of wooden houses that line the dirt roads on the tundra, live more than 600 people. Of these, 550 are Eskimos; the other eighty or ninety are white, which in Arctic terms includes the Chinese nurse from Hong Kong and the Trinidadian head mechanic of Pakistani extraction. In summer the number of whites is likely to double, and every bunk in the Department of Transport hostel and the Oblate mission compound is occupied by transients.

There are, of course, degrees of transience, and all the white men in the North are in one sense transients, temporary residents in a land where even birds and mammals are mostly creatures of passage. Walk into the hills behind Baker Lake, over the springy mat of the tundra, avoiding the marshes flagged by cotton grass, and you eventually reach a bare rock platform, stripped by the glaciers and painted green and gold with map lichen. On this outcrop, in rough wooden boxes, lie the dead of Baker Lake, buried Arctic-style under long piles of rocks, with wooden crosses at their heads on which their names are recorded in English and in Eskimo syllabics. They are divided in death as in life, Catholics from Anglicans, with a bare-rock no man's land between in which lie the two solitary uncrossed graves of obstinate pagans. Those whom the rock piles preserve from the wolverine and the wolf are all Eskimos, though there is a monument to one missionary lost in the Back River when his sleigh plunged through soft ice—and that, too, is significant. Few white men have ever died in the far North except by accident, starvation or unexpected sickness; few have stayed there willingly to live their lives to the end.

Yet there is a difference between now, when white men come for a few months or, at most, a few years, and the past, which in places like Baker Lake ended little more than a decade ago. Then life was very different. The Eskimos did not live in the village. They roamed west, summer after summer, on their traditional hunts after the caribou which migrated over the Barren Land; in the fall, when the air grew crisp, they would cache meat for the winter of trapping; at long intervals they would come in to trade at the Hudson's Bay store at Baker Lake.

Their life had already changed, yet not enough—even by the middle of the 1940s—for them to have any feeling that the continuity with their long nomadic past had come to an end. They were people who had come—no one knows how long ago—over the landbridge from Asia into an environment, the treeless Arctic, which for sheer inhospitality is rivalled only by the desert of Arabia and North Africa. Like the Bedouin of the desert, they learnt how to live in the Barren Land, and invented the techniques to master it. Snow became the material to build defences against itself, and the Eskimos constructed that pioneer geodesic dome, the igloo. The kayak was a perfectly devised craft for hunting the marine mammals on which most Eskimos lived. Methods of fishing and hunting under conditions of deep winter were highly elaborated.

Even with such elaborate skills, the Eskimo's life was hard and uncertain, and once again one compares it with that of the Bedouin. The Eskimos were always on the move in search of the food with which the northland is so capricious. I have heard old men with long memories singing the songs that celebrated the hungry camps of the seasons when game was scarce, and Eskimo lore is full of grim tales of unwanted children killed and old people abandoned so that the young might live.

Feast-and-famine is a pattern of life among all hunting peoples, and the highly social organization of the Eskimos was conditioned by it. Rarely—and only at seasons when food was especially abundant—did they come together in large numbers. 'That government is best which governs not at all,' the American wise man Thoreau once said, and the Eskimos were near to such an anarchic state. The head of the family wielded a benevolent kind of authority, and the shaman exercised a certain influence because men feared his powers, but formal authority did not exist. Crime was rare, and usually the result of sudden anger, since few Eskimos owned more than they needed to travel, and to kill and sometimes cook the game which fed and clothed them. The accumulation of wealth in such a precarious economy was virtually impossible. One would have to be an arrant romantic actively to envy the Eskimos their extreme existence, and a great deal of nonsense has been talked about the innocence of these children of a winter land. But at least, as races go, the Eskimos were pacific; their relations with each other always struck outsiders as gentle, and more than gentle where children were concerned; and, compared with their Indian neighbours and their white invaders, they were a people given to laughter.

The people who came in the past to trade at Baker Lake were hunters of the caribou. Eskimos speak one language, though they have a number of dialects and the basic division between them in Canada was between those who inhabited the coasts and islands and lived mainly by killing marine mammals, such as seal, walrus, narwhal and white whale, and those who inhabited the tundra and lived by hunting the caribou which came each year on vast migrations from the forests that lay to the south of the thin forest, or taiga, which formed a deep barrier be-

tween the Barren Land and the prairies. For so long that these Eskimos
had no tradition of any preceding way of life, the tundra had been populated by wandering bands of hunters, following the great deer as the
Indians followed the bison on the plains, wintering in igloos, summer-
ing in tents of caribou skin, and so skilled in the ways of the wild that
their language was immensely rich in technical terms relating to the
hunt and the weather.

The Eskimos possessed no rich farmlands, and the mineral wealth of
the Arctic was long unprospected, so that the civilization of the white
men came upon them slowly. The first contacts were fleeting; with the
great influx of explorers who plunged through the Arctic in the 1850s
in search of the ill-fated Franklin, and later with the whalers who roved
the Arctic seas for a generation until paraffin replaced whale oil in the
lamps of Europe and metal stays replaced whalebone in ladies' corsets.
The Arctic mainland became Canadian when the Hudson's Bay territories were acquired in 1870, and the Arctic Archipelago was ceded by
Britain in 1880, but Canada was too busy settling the prairies to pay
much attention to the North, and when interest became active in the
first decade of the present century it was mainly a matter of claiming
sovereignty over vast areas of tundra and permanent ice in which other
people—Americans, Russians, even Norwegians—were inexplicably
interested. The fur traders came first, then the missionaries, and finally
government, initially in the form of the all-purpose Mounted Police.
The slowness of this development can be seen by the example of
Aklavik, on the Arctic Ocean at the mouth of the Mackenzie River.
The Hudson's Bay Company arrived in 1912, the missionaries put in a
first appearance in 1919 and the Mounties established the rudiments of
government there in 1922. Later, in the twenties and the early thirties,
a few mines were opened on the edge of the Northwest Territories, but
the penetration from the south remained relatively unimportant until
the Second World War, when strategic needs led to the establishment
of airstrips and military bases, and brought into the region military and
technical personnel, who trained many Eskimos in western ways and
then, at the end of the war, left them on their own, the first of their
people alienated from the traditional pattern of life.

Baker Lake did not experience this wartime intrusion and at the end
of the 1940s it was still a part of the pre-war North. Down the beach
from the store stood the other buildings which symbolized the white
man's light and almost reluctant domination: the RCMP post, the

missions of the Anglicans and the Oblate Fathers. The six or seven
policemen, missionaries and traders were the only white men for thousands of square miles. The police tried to maintain a semblance of white
men's law; the missionaries undermined the power of the shamans and
established Christian routines rather than Christian faith; the traders
detached the hunters from their Stone Age tools and weapons, and
made them dependent on steel traps and modern rifles. In all these ways
the old Eskimo life, which had been evolved over millennia, was
slowly worn away, but until starvation brought it to a forcible end in
the early 1950s there were few people who envisaged any radical
interference with traditional Arctic ways of existence.

   This was because the white men themselves had accepted the North
as a way of life, with all the hardships attendant on it in the age before
bush planes and ski-doos. They knew, before they ever saw the tundra
of Keewatin or the mountains of Baffin Island, that the yearly boat,
with its cargo of supplies and mail, would be their only link with the
rest of the world, and that if one season's ice happened to be heavy they
might have to wait two years, or even three years, before they would be
back in communication with Outside. Before the technological developments of the twentieth century, the only way to survive physically
and to maintain the alertness that preserves sanity was to imitate the
experts in marginal living, the Eskimos. Explorers who learnt this
lesson had been successful, like the great Vilhjalmur Steffanson; those
who failed to learn it perished, like Franklin. Later white men remembered Franklin's fate and adopted the methods of travel, hunting and
fishing used by the people of the land; they wore Eskimo clothing and
often ate Eskimo food. In this way they became largely assimilated into
the native life, and instead of wishing to replace it by an imitation of the
life they had lived Outside, which most of them despised, they tried
merely to ameliorate it with a little law, a little religion, a trade carried
on, like shopkeeping played by children, with token coins, bearing the
Hudson's Bay Company's emblem of the beaver.

   Such men often found that Outside they were as unhappy as a primitive Eskimo in Piccadilly. The North, like the land of Yeats's 'Byzan-
tium' is 'no country for old men', nor is the south if you have lived
away from it all your prime years, and one meets these Old Arctic
Hands still, lingering in the embryo towns that have sprung up on the
rim of the North—men like Brother Volant of the Eskimo Museum in
Churchill, who came forty-four years ago as an Oblate missionary at

the end of his French military service in Syria, and Peter Baker, the octogenarian Lebanese trader of Yellowknife, whose Arab name no one remembers, and whom the Indians call Orange because he sailed into the Great Slave Lake fifty years ago in a scow loaded with golden fruit that they had never seen before. Such men are already living legends in a land where few of the growing thousands of more recently arrived white men choose to imitate them. When they remain in the remoter settlements they become, like Father Choque of Baker Lake, links between old and new ways. Father Choque has been in the North a quarter of a century, and remembers with regret the days when he would spend his winters driving behind a dog team across the Barren Land from one igloo encampment to the next. Now he is the only man among the eighty or ninety whites of Baker Lake who speaks Eskimo fluently, and that in itself is a measure of the difference between the old order in the North and the new. Bilingualism is no part of the world which the new type of Arctic white man is shaping today.

II

The influx of white men into the north—so that today there are ninety at Baker Lake as against six or seven twenty years ago—was precipitated by the collapse of the traditional Eskimo life in the Barren Land when the caribou migrations failed at the end of the 1940s and the early 1950s. This failure had been brought on by the change in Eskimo methods of hunting. While the Eskimos hunted with the spear, they killed just enough caribou to preserve the natural balance; that changed quickly when they acquired firearms, and old hunters still tell of the massacres of whole herds when the Eskimos killed without need or thought, intoxicated by the power of destruction which modern weapons had given them. It was this destruction, and the consequent changing by the caribou of their migration routes, that brought, in famine and despair, the end of the old way of life in the Barren Land. Appalled by the deaths in the starvation camps of Ennadai and Padlei, the RCMP herded the survivors to Baker Lake and the coast of Hudson's Bay, where they formed the nuclei of new settlements at Rankin Inlet and Eskimo Point.

Living first on hurriedly despatched supplies, provided later with welfare allowances, and finally given at least partial employment, the Eskimos of the Barren Land began their painful progress from Stone

18

Age culture to Space Age civilization. When the mine was opened at Rankin Inlet in 1956 they surprised everyone by taking to the work with enthusiasm and a will to learn; for people accustomed to the long night of the northern winter and used to adapting themselves to extreme situations, the mine held no claustrophobic terrors. But after a few years it closed down, as the wartime military camps had done, and with it the only real industry in the region. The Eskimos became a people between two worlds, following the ancient ways by doing a little fishing and hunting when that was possible, but surviving mainly on what the government in its benevolence might give them or arrange for them.

A radical change had in fact taken place in the Eskimo pattern of life. For the wandering way, dependent on complex inherited skills, was substituted a static existence; for the small camps of the past was substituted the large permanent village. In 1953, by setting up the Department of Northern Affairs, the government of Louis St. Laurent finally and belatedly assumed responsibility for the people of the North, took the administration out of the hands of the scattered Mounted Police and began to create a new Northern bureaucracy. The reorganization of the Arctic way of life has since been carried out mainly by the Department of Northern Affairs and by its successor, the Department of Indian Affairs and Northern Development.

During the fifteen years since the people of the North became an all-Canadian commitment, the pattern of paternalism initiated by the removal of the Eskimos from their hunting grounds has continued, and the whole shape of Northern existence has changed. The Barren Land is empty of human activity for the first time since the Eskimos arrived many centuries ago. The Eskimos continue to live in the settlements, in houses provided by the government, and so do the white men, in rather better houses. It has been decided as part of official policy that the legal differences between whites, Eskimos and Indians in the North shall be eliminated, and that the Eskimos shall be brought as rapidly as possible into the white man's world.

No doubt this is excellent in theory, but in practice it means that everything traditionally important in Eskimo life is thrust aside with a firm benevolent hand. Education is compulsory, and is conducted in English. While the missionaries in the past used the Eskimo language and taught the syllabic alphabet, the new integrated educational system has abandoned them both. Already, the old men tell one, the language is being lost; the young people speak a kind of basic Eskimo and have lost all the rich vocabulary of the hunt. And, indeed, the hunt is going with the language that it created. The education in the ways of the Barren Land which the Eskimo boy traditionally acquired from his father is now impossible. During the vital winter months the boy is kept at school, and many Eskimo children finish their education with two years in a residential school hundreds of miles away from their country at the very time when they could be learning the most useful things about life on the land. As a result, few of the younger Eskimos are skilful hunters, or have learnt the lore of topography and weather and animals which their fathers knew so richly. Last summer when I was at Baker Lake only five families were out in the hunting camps out of 600 Eskimos. The kayak has already vanished, except for specimens kept in museums. The other characteristic Eskimo invention, the igloo, is on its way. For the first time, during the winter of 1968–9, all the people of Baker Lake were provided with some kind of wooden house or hut, and no igloos were put up by the people who beforehand had camped with their dog teams on the edge of the settlement. In the smaller and more isolated colonies of the northern Arctic the old ways survive a little longer, and igloos are still built, but the art of constructing snow houses will disappear with men who are now middle-aged, and, because of the nature of their material, there will not even be a specimen left to stand beside the kayak in the museum! Even the dog teams, which so recently provided the winter transport for everyone, white or Eskimo, in the Arctic, are also dwindling quickly. Out of more than a hundred families at Baker Lake, only twenty still possessed teams; the rest had abandoned their traditional mode of transport for the clattering ski-doo. The more intangible elements of the old culture are departing with the language and the way of life. When I asked to hear the songs of the hunters, it was only the old men who would sing them. At a drum dance in the community hall at Baker Lake, the chants were sung by a trio of aged women, and middle-aged men beat the great caribou skin drum and danced the stamping, shambling dance. The young do not know the songs, and are disinclined to perform the dances, since they know that most white men despise them; in any case, they themselves prefer the Beatles, in whose honour many of them wear the long hair that formerly was the mark of the shaman.

Many of the inland Eskimos, even among the guitar-playing young, are still so conditioned by the old pattern of living by feast and famine that they cannot adjust to the new rhythm of work all the year round, or to the new economics which provides for the morrow. Many of them earn good wages on construction—the principal means of employment—during the summer, and a week after the work ends during November they are destitute, asking for welfare payments. Most of them—young and old—dislike the crowding together in the new villages; they are used to the vast spaces of the tundra, the magnificent skies and the open spaces filled with the wind. The old people think nostalgically about the old days of hunting, and find western habits and western food insipid. The young aspire to the white man's world, but do not really belong to it; the most Canadianized among them are the bitterest and the most unhappy. The less sophisticated still present the smiling Eskimo face, but their deeper feelings are shown in their art. I am not thinking of the slick, over-polished walruses and the sentimental mothers and children sold in gift shops Outside as Eskimo art. I am thinking of the sculptures my wife and I brought back from Baker Lake. They face me now, dark human figures with a strange earth-weighted heaviness, and sombre, lost faces—the faces of alienation. They tell that a unique culture has died; civilization has been its executioner.

III

What is emerging in the North is no longer a world in which white men follow the ways of the Eskimos in order to survive; it is a world where technology and bureaucracy are ensuring that in the future people of all races will follow the ways of the white men. And, inevitably, the kind of white men who work in the North is changing. The missionaries remain, their influence diminishing, though the Eskimos still pack the little wooden churches on a Sunday as part of the routine of Arctic life. The Hudson's Bay men also remain, their trade increasing. Now it is a different kind of trade. Fur represents less than an eighth of the present-day business of the Arctic stores; the rest is carried on with the Eskimos in exchange for welfare vouchers or for cash earned from handcrafts or construction work, and the old-fashioned trading post is being replaced by the miniature department store, selling the same goods as the stores Outside at greatly increased prices. The one feature of the old northern routine that still continues, apart from the diminishing fur trade, is the annual ship which delivers the year's stock after the ice breaks up in summer. The Company still holds almost a

68. The shores of Hudson's Bay.

9. The Indian canoe harbour
at Churchill.

70. The Arctic plane arrives on the airstrip at Rankin Inlet.

71. Instead of a dog-team. Arctic transport today.

monopoly of private enterprise; it has ruined or absorbed all its competitors except for a few recently established co-operatives, which are kept going largely with Government assistance. Occasionally a mine will open and close down after a few years, but other unofficial ventures are so rare that the cannery for Arctic char and muktuk★ operated by a German immigrant in Rankin Inlet is famous throughout the North as an example of what others might do but don't.

The great industry in all the new settlements of the North is, in fact, Government. Most of the money that passes into Eskimo hands comes through local officials, either in payment for art objects or for construction work or in welfare maintenance during the months of deep winter. And at least 90 per cent of the white men and many of the white women in Arctic settlements like Baker Lake, Rankin Inlet, Frobisher Bay and Inuvik are employed by the government, as area administrators, resettlement officers, co-operative officers, art officers, as nurses and teachers, as policemen, meteorologists and radio technicians, as engineers looking after power plants and utilidors, as clerks and maintenance men. The summer transients expand the spectrum even wider. They include the doctors (none of whom live in the settlements so that people who are seriously ill may have to be flown out under bad weather conditions) and paediatricians, the dentists and radiologists, the aerial photographers and geological surveyors, the wild-life men and bush pilots, together with the carpenters and plumbers and mechanics and electricians and telephone linesmen who come to earn phenomenally high wages on summer and autumn construction work.† Except for a few prospectors and a few men spying out possibilities for foreign investors, almost all of them are, once again, employed by the government.

These white men are the servants of a system of administration that is firmly rooted in the colonial past. There is a myth of 'The True North, Strong and Free'. But in no political sense has the North ever been free. At most, a handful of individuals have found in its vastnesses a personal independence they would never have enjoyed elsewhere. But politically the North has always been a dependency, first of Britain,

---

★ Arctic char, I should say in parenthesis, is the most delicious of all Canadian fishes, like a particularly delicate salmon, while muktuk, a noted delicacy among Eskimos, is the skin of the beluga, the beautiful little white whale of the Arctic.

† As I was recording the drum dance at Baker Lake, a French-Canadian carpenter sat beside me. He pointed to my tape recorder. 'How much does it cost?' 'Six hundred dollars.' A shrug. 'Just two weeks' wages!' The same man bought an expensive Arctic falcon, carried it around on his shoulder for two days, and then set it free.

later of Canada. In the handing over, an amazing continuity in the traditions of domination has been preserved, and even today there is a great deal in the way the North is governed that reminds one of the British Raj in India.

The parallels are numerous and obvious. In the days of the Raj, government was shared between Westminster and Delhi. In Westminster the centre of power was the India Office. In Delhi it was the government of India, headed by the Viceroy and his Council. A Civil Service, consisting mainly of white British subjects, administered India with paternal benevolence and probably with a great deal more justice than it had enjoyed in the past. A few British-educated Indians served in the ranks of the Civil Service, and an even smaller number among the Viceroy's advisers. In the last years before the British departed, the elective principle was being applied with monumental gradualness to the legislative aspects of government, but executive power and the final veto rested with the Viceroy and ultimately with Westminster.

To anyone who has travelled in the Canadian Arctic, the resemblances to what he has seen will be obvious. Say Ottawa instead of Westminster, and the Department of Indian Affairs and Northern Development springs into focus as the equivalent of the India Office, holding ultimate control over everything that happens in the North. Say Yellowknife instead of Delhi, and on a minor scale, without the pomp and circumstance of the Raj, the Commissioner for the Northwest Territories, with his Executive Council and his Territorial Council, bears a surprising resemblance to the departed Viceroys. As in India, there has been a gradual substitution of elected for appointed councillors. Until 1966 the Council of the Northwest Territories still had an appointed majority, and even now the elected majority is a precarious seven to five. Moreover, two of the most vital functions—land and natural resources—are regarded as outside the Council's competence. Ottawa, like Westminster, keeps its hand on the real fulcrum of power, in the case of the North its possibilities of development. Finally, as in India, some representatives of the native peoples serve on the Council or in Civil Service positions, but once again they are a small minority.

When I have pointed out this parallel to Canadians, I have encountered two objections. I am told that the Canadian government acts to help the native peoples and to encourage them on their way to self-help and self-government. But the British in India had—after all—a phrase about 'the white man's burden', and the best Indian administrators saw their function as that of preparing the Indians for independence in the future. The other objection is that my argument makes the white man in the Canadian north the equivalent of the sahib in India. This is precisely my intention. The way in which Canada has used its North has led to the establishment of a caste of rulers who in many ways do resemble the sahibs. The resemblance arises largely from the fact that Canadian policy in the North has, since 1953, become markedly ambivalent. It is directed at fostering the welfare of the native peoples. It is directed also to exploiting the riches of the North for the benefit of the rest of Canada.

I shall return to these mutually contradictory aims, but first there is something to say of the peculiar society of these sahibs of the North. As a class they have little of the staying power of their predecessors, and even the 'permanent' members of the new hierarchy seldom remain long in the settlements. There is no need now to await the yearly boat; the plane, as a means of quick escape, is frequently taken long before a year is up. Missionaries and traders still stay longest in the Arctic. Most Oblate fathers have several years' experience behind them, and most Hudson's Bay men stay at a store for at least two or three years. But the new bureaucrats of the North are even more volatile than the ordinary nomadic Canadian worker.

Robert Williamson, Head of the University of Saskatchewan's Institute for Arctic Training and Research, is one of the few relative newcomers to the Arctic to show real staying power and devotion to the North, perhaps because his interest is basically scientific. An elected member—mainly by Eskimo votes—of the Territorial Council, he has lived for eight years at Rankin Inlet on Hudson's Bay (where there are about 500 Eskimos and fifty white people), and has acquired a knowledge of the local language unrivalled among the Government men. During Williamson's eight years, the key post at Rankin Inlet, that of Area Administrator, has been held by no less than eight different officials. At Baker Lake the situation has been even more fluid; there have been eleven Administrators in seven years. Yet the tasks of an Administrator, who is responsible for the welfare of all the people in his area, are so complex that officials in the Territorial government offices at Yellowknife admitted to me that they could not be learnt in less than a year and that for the local people to reap any benefit from an official's experience he must serve at least three years.

The Eskimos agree. 'We spend months talking to a new administrator about our problems,' I was told by Michael Amarook, the chairman of the Eskimo Community Council at Baker Lake. 'He begins to understand. Then he goes away, and we start all over again with a new man.' The turnover is just as rapid with teachers, and even more so with nurses. At Eskimo Point, the most insanitary and sickness-ridden of all the Central Arctic settlements, there have been sixteen nurses in fourteen months.

There are many reasons for the malaise that underlies this volatility. One is the fact that native Canadians have rarely taken to the real North. Traditionally, it has been the stamping ground of adventurous Europeans. The English and the Scandinavians were its best explorers. Hudson's Bay men have always been recruited mainly from Scotland and Northern Ireland, and still are. Anglican missionaries are English, and the Oblate Fathers are French and Belgian. But, though there are notable exceptions, the majority of recently imported government employees have been Canadian, and, on the whole, they have not taken to the life of the North, even in its new form.

But it is not merely a matter of climate or topography. It is even more, I believe, the question of a government policy which is breeding feelings of alienation among both the Eskimos and the white men at present in the North. The arrival of the memsahibs is now recognized by social historians as a significant turning point in the history of the British in India, and, in Canada, the arrival of appreciable numbers of white women and children in the Northern settlements during the 1960s is meaningful because it shows the kind of society which is being officially nurtured. The presence of families is encouraged by monetary allowances, and special supplies of year-round rations shipped in at reduced prices, in the hope that the families will form the nucleus of something resembling normal southern Canadian communities, into which the Eskimos will eventually be absorbed. In self-defence against the environment, the families themselves try to reproduce the image and substance of Outside suburban living. The hi-fis, the indoor planters with their evergreen creepers, the little plastic greenhouses where parsley and lettuce are grown in the cold summers of the Central Arctic, the curling clubs and the minuscule social gatherings where the same people meet: the effort is gallant, and one feels a kind of pioneer genuineness about the ingenuity with which people make their own amusements. But it all wears thin during the long winter night of the

North, when the supply of fresh visitors from Outside has dried up and
the snow piles over the windows, and over the roofs, and people scuttle
down snow tunnels into their front doors like groundhogs into their
burrows.

The new white men of the Arctic have not succeeded in facing the
North as it is; they are trying always to reproduce the life of the south,
and that life, of course, is lived successfully only in the south. There is,
even about their ways of combating the old climatic enemies, a curious
precariousness. Some of the new communities, like Rankin Inlet and
Inuvik, have developed a kind of artificial environment dependent on
the power station and the utilidor. The utilidor is a lifeline connecting
the various buildings and houses, and consisting of a conduit in which
the water pipes and the sewers are perpetually thawed by a constant
stream of hot water which circulates from the great boilers in the power
house. The power house also supplies all the electricity for lighting,
cooking and other purposes, for the telephone system, for radio communication. As I stood in the power house at Rankin Inlet, listening to
the chief engineer explaining its functions, I felt I had stepped into the
world of E. M. Forster's story 'The Machine Stops'. For if the power
house ever broke down at midwinter in Rankin Inlet or in Inuvik, it
would mean the death of the community.

One of the reasons why these artificial little communities were
created and the importation of white families was encouraged, is that
it was hoped this might further the official programme of integrating
the three races of the North. In practice, the hope that white and Eskimo
women would mingle freely has not worked out; it is difficult to mix
when housing conditions and incomes are so far apart. But children
have to go to school, and there they cannot do other than mingle. This
would be excellent if integration in the schools, as elsewhere in the
Arctic, were not handled as if it were intended to turn all Eskimos
overnight into imitation white men. No teacher in the government
schools of the Arctic knows Eskimo, and there is no official instruction
in the native language. I was astonished on going through the expensive
new school at Baker Lake to see not a single Eskimo word or a single
syllabic sign in evidence, though there were alphabet charts with 'B for
bull' and 'C for cat' in a land of bears and caribou where bulls are
mythical creatures and cats so rare that the Anglican missionary's Tom
was an object of awe and terror to the Eskimo children. The teacher in
a school of this kind has no direct contact with the younger children;

he has to instruct them through a 'classroom assistant', a teenage Eskimo who knows a little English and acts as interpreter.

A similar situation exists in government offices in the Arctic, where the Administrator must talk through an interpreter with the people he is trying to usher into the twentieth century. There are rudimentary orientation courses for teachers, though they do not include effective language training; but there are no real orientation courses for officials, so that the government man arriving in the North all too often feels forced into a position rather like that of a benevolent sahib ruling a strange and incomprehensible tribe. His situation is made all the more difficult because, however genuine his desire to create a real co-operation between whites and Eskimos, he is condemned to be a member of a paternalistic élite, while the rigid directives laid down by Ottawa leave little room for individual initiative or imaginative planning. Nor is there any real way of release from the frustrations of such a situation except by escape, since the fact that the white people in the settlements are almost all government employees means that local criticism of official policies and practices can rarely be openly developed.

IV

For most of this chapter I have been talking of the true Arctic, which is not a matter of latitude so much as isotherms; the line of climate determines not only the treeline but also the population. On the western side of Canada, in the northern Yukon and the Mackenzie River delta, the treeline almost reaches the Arctic Ocean and extends well above the Arctic Circle. But it runs down on a diagonal from the Mackenzie delta to the southern end of Hudson's Bay, well below the 60th parallel, so that the port of Churchill, actually in Manitoba, is on the edge of the treeline—so much so that its tiny spruces grow branches only on the side facing away from the windy Bay. The area within the treeline, regardless of latitude, has warmer summers than the bare tundra, though the winters in the Yukon are the coldest in Canada. Where there are trees, there are Indians instead of Eskimos.

This area, the true sub-Arctic, includes the whole of the Yukon Territory, and a large south-western triangle of the Northwest Territories, dipping down into northern Saskatchewan and Manitoba. It is here—and in Labrador—that most of the northern discoveries of minerals accessible enough to be exploited have been made, and it has therefore been subject to intrusion from the south for much longer than the true Arctic. There were prospectors in the Mackenzie and Yukon valleys as early as the 1870s, and in 1898 the Klondike Gold Rush brought such hordes of people into the North that a community of 30,000 people—Dawson City—flourished briefly near to the Arctic Circle.

The sub-Arctic in fact is a zone of social as well as climatic and bio-logical transition, for here are situated the few places of the North which can be considered towns in the southern sense. Apart from Dawson, there are only three of them: Whitehorse in the Yukon, Yellowknife in the Northwest Territories, and Churchill, which is the focal point of activity on Hudson's Bay and in the Barren Land of Keewatin.

These four towns of the North are still frontier communities, the last in Canada, and they present to the visitor a peculiar combination of isolation, rawness and uncoordinated vigour. They are worth visiting, since they represent a transitional and dying type of community; Dawson, in fact, is already a ghost town, and Whitehorse, at the other end of the spectrum, is on the verge of becoming a modern community like any town Outside.

Churchill, geographically the nearest to Outside, is the place through which anyone visiting the Eskimo communities of the Central Arctic must travel, since the planes leave from there, and the provision ships are loaded at the wharves which are open less than three months every summer along the Churchill River. There is a railway which snakes to Churchill through the deserted taiga of northern Manitoba, but most people come in by air, since the town is unconnected by road with the rest of Canada, though it has five miles of asphalt highway of its own, a fleet of taxis and buses, and even a motel. More unexpectedly, this town in the northern wilderness has a rough plank hotel whose Hungarian cook is one of the best in Canada, and a first-rate Eskimo Museum run by the Oblate Fathers. It also has a handsome coastline on Hudson's Bay: glacier-smoothed Henry Moore rocks, with little pools white in summer with water flowers, and dwarf gooseberries with tart little berries flattening themselves into the crevices to escape the wind from the bay which is really an inland sea, its farther shores lost deep below the horizon. Standing on the tallest boulder of these rocks, I looked over the Churchill River to the grey star-shaped ruin of Prince of Wales Fort, the oldest building in western Canada, which the

Hudson's Bay Company started to construct in 1732; Churchill had a
fur-trading history of two and a half centuries before it expanded into a
large military camp and airbase in the Second World War. As I lingered
there, the little beluga whales were coming up the river in a great shoal,
their white backs rising brilliantly above the clear blue of the water.
There are moments of pleasure like this everywhere in the Arctic—the
tern hovering and swooping along a lakeshore, the small brilliant
blossoms of the millefiori tundra—flashes of natural beauty which
remind one how minute and unmetropolitan even the largest town in
the North is. The total population of Churchill is about 6,000, but an
Eskimo girl at Rankin Inlet said to me: 'What a big town Churchill is!
I got lost there!' And in a way she was right, for in these regions there
is endless space, and the temptation is to use it. Churchill's few people
live scattered in no less than five little communities dotted over as
many miles along the shore of the Bay.

There is Churchill Townsite, dominated by the railway sidings and
the great elevators where the grain ships load in summer. The Hudson's
Bay route is the shortest way to Europe from the prairies, provides
Churchill's main industry and supports the little town of gravel streets
bordered by weathered wooden houses and dominated by the inevitable Hudson's Bay Store, the two hotels, the Anglican and Oblate
missions. Nothing here looks prosperous or comfortable; the northern
weather wears everything down to a uniform drabness. But the Townsite is high in civilization compared with what one encounters on walking across the railway tracks.

This is the district known as the Flats, one of those dreadful northern
slums where the local métis live in wretched one and two-room hovels
of plank and tarpaper, impregnated by the stench of the local plant for
processing the beluga whales, which the Indians hunt from their canoes
with harpoons and rifles. The métis, who signed no treaties and to whom
the government therefore owes no obligation, are far worse off than
the Indians of Churchill, who have their own village a mile or so away,
in which the Department of Indian Affairs has been building the so-
called 'three-bedroom houses' now being allocated to native peoples in
the North. The name is useful in the deliberately deceptive press releases
issued by government departments; what it actually means is a house
with a living room and three cubicles large enough for bunks to be
squeezed in, and without either running water or sewer connections.
It is today's instalment of civilization so far as the Indians and Eskimos

72. Changing lives. An Eskimo family shops in the Hudson's Bay store.

73. The stone carver.

74. A caribou hunter finds a new career.

75. Eskimo ceramic sculpture.

are concerned, and, meagre as it is, much better than what exists in the no man's lands of neglect inhabited by the métis. At Churchill both métis and Indians live largely on welfare payments; their only certain employment comes during the quick weeks of summer when the harbour is open and they can work on loading the grain ships. The racial ghettoes of Churchill are completed by another isolated village, Akudlik, where a few Eskimos live; since this is Indian country, they are expatriates from the north, most of whom came down originally to be cured of tuberculosis. The last part of Churchill—Fort Churchill, five miles away from the docks and the Townsite—is also, in its own way, a ghetto. It is the old military establishment, whose white clapboard buildings, linked by the great pipes of the utilidor, house the government offices and the dwellings of the bureaucrats who control operations along the shores of Hudson's Bay and in Keewatin.

Churchill is not unique among the northern towns in its sprawling chaos. Yellowknife on Great Slave Lake spreads its 5,000 people over a very considerable area, particularly if one includes the two large gold mines whose wooden shaft towers rise white above the low forest of the lakeshore and dominate little company villages of dormitories and messhalls. From the air Yellowknife reminds one—rather incongruously—of Syracuse in Sicily, since, like the first Syracuse, the original Yellowknife was built on a rocky peninsula projecting into the lake, and there the old-timers of the gold rush in the 1930s still live along the winding hilly roads, in gardens filled with the vividly coloured flowers and enormous vegetables that grow in the short, hot summer of this region. The local Indians also live on the headland, with their canoes and dog-teams, and its coves form natural bases for the North's largest fleet of water planes and its largest population of bush pilots.

But the focus of life in Yellowknife has now moved up to the new town on the mainland, to which the government of the Northwest Territories was transferred in January 1968, when three plane loads of officials were flown in from Ottawa and set up their desks in the local bowling alley. Since this influx, a sophistication of the old mining town has begun. Residential subdivisions are being laid out among the mud and rock outcrops, and apartment blocks are going up on the road to the airport, hastily constructed in the long almost nightless days of the short northern summer when time is so precious that neither Sundays nor holidays interrupt the pace of work. Yellowknife has an excellent school system, open alike to Indians and whites, and it even provides adult courses in the arts. Yet in its tough frontier hotels one enters a different kind of modern North from that of the new villas in their flowery gardens. Here is a note from my diary describing the clientèle of the Yellowknife Hotel, the best in town.

Even the Yellowknife is largely a workingman's hotel, used particularly by young workers with higher standards than their elders; the high wages of the North allow them to satisfy the bourgeois taste of the modern Canadian proletarian. While in the past most people who came to northern mining camps were labourers, now the great majority are technicians, artisans and operators of sophisticated machinery. In the Yellowknife's dining room all northern types come together: the Canadians, and the immigrants who have made the North their own; the coarse old sweats, rotted by alcohol, and the other old men whom Arctic life has given a look of almost Gidean spareness and intensity; the young toughs, with tight-arsed strut and chewed toothpicks, and the bearded young intellectuals of survey or photography teams, some very mod, with Dundreary whiskers under broad Stetsons; the Indians from the reserve at Rae, drunken women, sober, self-possessed young men, occasional children like the girl I saw this afternoon, who, with demonstrative delight, ate apple pie with ice cream, *followed* by chips well soused in ketchup. The girls at the desk affect an outdated flashiness that goes with the myth of mining camps; they wear high-piled hair, vivid makeup, sequined gowns, high-heeled silver or red lacquer shoes; a suggestion of sin that in this age of the sexual revolution has lost its meaning.

Another note, culled from the hotel menu, reflects the expansive northern style:

PROSPECTOR'S SPECIAL, $4·75
JUICE
BUTTERED TOAST
SIX EGGS AND SIX SLICES OF BACON
20 OZ. CLUB STEAK
SIX CUPS OF COFFEE

Even so, Yellowknife has not quite the boastful, philistine hustle one encounters in Whitehorse. The two cities are rivals, since Whitehorse is also a capital, of the Yukon Territory, and Yellowknifers admit grudgingly that their city is neither so large nor so modern. Whitehorse, with nearly 8,000 people, is the most populous place in the

Canadian north, and it no longer has much of the look of a sub-Arctic settlement. Its main streets are much like those of a medium-sized British Columbian town—say Prince George—and the ranch-style houses its nouveaux riches are building ($75,000 homes, as one is boast-fully assured) resemble those in the showier districts of West Vancouver. A few log cabins in the back streets, an Indian slum on the water's edge, and the great corpses of the Yukon paddle-wheelers rotting on dry land beside the railway yards are all that remind one of the old gold-bound past. Whitehorse has been much influenced by proximity to Alaska; its manners and values are, as I suppose those of the Yukon always were, American rather than Canadian, and one has to accept a certain brash-ness among its people, a loud dedication to gargantuan drinking, eating and money-making. Still, it is a town that can at times generate live-liness, which is more than one can say for Dawson City, isolated and decaying at the end of 300 miles of lonely road to the north. This is a long way to travel for so little, to see a valley ruined by the gold dredges, and a town ruined by time, with a few buildings expensively and un-convincingly reconstructed, and the rest sinking under the grey pall of a summer's dust. I have seldom seen a historic site so badly neglected, or come to a destination so romantically misrepresented by propaganda, which draws thousands of Americans every year to a certain but perhaps deserved disappointment.

V

All the towns that I have been describing have one thing in common with the new settlements of the true Arctic. They may have other means of living—the mines at Yellowknife, the Alaska Highway at White-horse, the harbour at Churchill—but the real stabilizing element in their existence is the fact that they too are government towns, Whitehorse and Yellowknife territorial capitals, and Churchill the administrative centre of a large Arctic region. Only Dawson City is not a government town, and in a dramatic way this fact proves the rule that at the present time no city in the North can be sure of survival unless it is involved in the great northern industry. What finally killed Dawson City was not the exhaustion of the gold mines. It was the shifting of the Territorial government from there to Whitehorse in 1953.

All these places share another characteristic—that they live on expec-tation—and, indeed, the North is the one region which Canadians always think of, when they remember it, in terms of the future. Since it is a vast, almost unscarred region with great reserves of metal ores and mineral fuels, its future is not only interesting, but also economically important to Canada and the world in general, particularly at a time when scientists are warning us to expect an eventual world shortage of almost every useful mineral except aluminium. Clearly the conservation as well as the exploitation of the wealth of the North demands attention, and so far, in spite of the great call to open the North which helped carry Diefenbaker to power in the 1950s, little has really been done to tap its resources, which is a good thing in view of the fact that little also seems to have been done to create a comprehensive plan not only for using the North but also for ensuring its people a just and meaningful life.

It is inevitable that the very magnitude of the problems created by northern development should have called into being some strange futuristic visions. One hears prophecies that the Arctic seas will become the Mediterranean of the late twentieth century. One reads of schemes to keep Hudson's Bay open to shipping all the year round by the use of nuclear-powered thermal devices; of fleets of underwater barges dragged by nuclear submarines that will transport the minerals of the North under the winter ice; of dams across the Bering strait and great pumping stations that will use the waters of the Japanese Current to melt the Arctic icecap; of new northern cities under vast domes that will protect them from the rigours of the Arctic winter. Such schemes are not impossible. Already, revolutionary changes have taken place in the North. A variety of tracked vehicles has completely changed the nature of winter transport. There are planes specially adapted for landing on the uneven tundra, and the development of ground-effect vehicles and vertical takeoff planes will further change Arctic travel, while the utilidor and other improvements along the same line have gone a long way towards creating an artificial environment. Life in the Arctic has changed radically in the past fifteen years, and it is likely to do so at an accelerating pace.

But these are changes in means rather than aims, and what chiefly concerns those comparatively few Canadians who are interested in the North is the economic and social direction which development in the Arctic should take. Should it follow the course of events in Greenland, in Alaska, in the Soviet Arctic, all of which appear in various ways more advanced? None of them in fact seems the model that would fit Canadian circumstances. There is much worth imitating in Greenland's ushering of the Eskimos into the modern world, but little to learn from its control of very limited natural riches. The frenetic activity of Alaska is based almost entirely on its function as the great north-western fortress of the United States; most of its people are employees in the vast defence system. Russia, north of the 60th parallel, has a population running into millions and a number of cities far larger than any in the equivalent region of Canada, but their existence is based largely on resources which Canada north of 60° hardly possesses at all. The glaciers did not strip the soil cover from northern Siberia as they did from the Barren Land of Canada, and though Siberian winters are savage, the summers are hot enough to grow thick forests, so that in the Soviet north both lumbering and agriculture can flourish; in the Canadian north they will always be negligible.

Much more profitable than considering the examples of other countries may be the effort to project one's thoughts forward from what is already being done in the Canadian Arctic. There are several marked trends. One, as we have seen, is the special kind of urbanization, by which centres of between 500 and 1,000 people are being established, to which the native hunters and fishermen are drawn in order to modernize their lives. Many people with long experience of the North have condemned this policy, and have suggested ways in which instruction in the more useful modern skills might have been imparted to Eskimos who continued to live on the land until such time as they showed a voluntary inclination to change their lives. However, much as I sympathize with these alternatives, it is now too late to apply them. The link with the past has been broken, and the attempt to resurrect the traditional way of life would in any case be contrary to the other dominant trend, which aims at integrating all the peoples of the Arctic on the level of white civilization.

All one can hope is that, even if materially they become assimilated, the Eskimos will preserve and adapt at least enough of their traditional culture to enable them to recover a proper pride in their past. This can happen only if the stifling pressure of unimaginative official paternalism is immediately relaxed. Here one may consider what is happening to Eskimo sculpture. The reasons for the disturbing decline in quality in the work of most Eskimo artists is at once evident if one visits the government-controlled art centres and observes the unimaginatively regimented conditions under which the native sculptors are expected to

19

work, following a regular eight-hour day, using what are very near to mass-production methods, and intimidated into selling their works through a mercilessly exploitative series of official middlemen. A white artist, selling through a private gallery, will get $66 for a painting that sells at $100. An Eskimo artist, selling through his local government arts centre and through the officially approved wholesalers is lucky if he gets $20 or $25 for a sculpture which sells at $100 in an art gallery or a crafts shop. I met well-known Eskimo artists, and found they were poor men who earned from their carvings barely enough to pay for the necessities of life at the high northern prices.

There are more positive aspects to the situation, and if these dominate the future of the native peoples in the North this may not turn out to be so bleak as it now seems. Undoubtedly the battle against ill health will be won; already the situation in which 95 out of 1,000 Eskimos die in infancy, and the average life expectancy is twenty-one years, is changing radically. Education, even if it ignores the Eskimos' language, will at least enable them to take the skilled jobs which are now done by imported white men, and there will be more Eskimos in administrative posts, and even Eskimo teachers. But the most hopeful tendency for the future of the Eskimos is the active interest they are showing in the co-operative movement, which presents a viable alternative to the present almost universal governmental interference in northern life.

The co-operatives have significantly been most successful in smaller and remoter Arctic communities where there is no governmental administrator and no bureaucratic apparatus; the presence of the Oblate Fathers, on the other hand, is usually beneficial to such enterprises. The shining example is a little community of thirty-odd Eskimo families called Pelly Bay, where an effective co-operative has almost eliminated the need for welfare allowances. The Pelly Bay Association is a multi-purpose co-operative which carries on almost all the operations of the community, social as well as economic. It runs a general store and a fur-trading post, a fish-marketing service and a handcrafts-marketing service, a bakery, a laundry, a garbage-collection service, a fuel-oil service, and even those rare facilities in an Arctic community, a coffee shop and a tourist lodge. Up to the present the most ambitious of the co-operative's undertakings has been its contract to erect thirty-two houses under the Eskimo Housing Plan. These houses were put up in a record thirty-two days, in the summer of 1967, at a great deal less than the cost of similar houses built by imported white carpenters in the other Eskimo settlements. The co-operative's special task for the summer of 1968 was the completion of an air strip 5,000 feet long. The men of Pelly Bay are seacoast Eskimos who are coming into the modern world of their own free will and on their own terms, and their achievement is all the more extraordinary when one adds that they have done it all on very small government loans, with slight overhead costs, and no paid officials. Such a community shows how effective co-operation can help to wean the northern peoples from state tutelage.

The affairs of the peoples of the Northwest Territories are the responsibility of the new Territorial government, and its strengthening as a locally based administration may lead to the encouragement of decentralism and of local initiatives like the Pelly Bay co-operative. But the development of northern resources, as distinct from northern communities, remains the responsibility of the federal government, and is not necessarily carried out according to the wishes of the local inhabitants. There is obviously justice in regarding such resources in a wider than local context. But it is disturbing that there is no evidence of an overall plan of development and exploitation linked to sound conservationist principles, and equally disturbing is the extent and nature of government participation in starting new northern enterprises. It is true that under existing conditions, with the high cost of transport in the North, private enterprisers are unwilling to venture there without considerable government support. Without considering the situation thoroughly, the government in Yukon and elsewhere has followed the easy line by offering large subsidies merely to get mines in operation.

The two questions of conservation and government participation in northern enterprises are closely interlinked. In the shrinking world of today it would seem obvious that the non-renewable resources of the Arctic should be kept as a world reserve of minerals, to be used only when justified in relation to global requirements. There are many experts who consider that the minerals of the North are not at present needed, since enough exist—and are more easily accessible—south of the 60th parallel. A research paper for the Carrothers Commission on Northern Affairs as recently as 1965 stated categorically that the principal obstacle to the development of mining in the Northwest Territories was 'the apparent lack of any scarcity in southern markets of the known mineral resources of the Territories'. It is obviously pointless to open distant and at present unnecessary mines, particularly as this often causes a disruption of local communities by attracting Eskimos and

Indians with the promise of work and then leaving them stranded when the mine is played out, as happened with the nickel mine at Rankin Inlet in 1962.

Rather than spending money on opening mines at present unnecessary, the government should concentrate on exploration, so that non-renewable resources can be mapped, assessed and catalogued, and on providing a transport network, so that existing communities in the North are linked by railways, roads or at least winter roads, bringing down the present cost of living and of moving equipment and mine products. It would then be possible to select intelligently those areas where the minerals of the North might be tapped without unwise depletion, and the actual work could be done by private enterprisers willing to take the risk on the assurance of efficient and inexpensive transport. In the meantime there are many ways in which renewable resources might be used to provide employment for the Indians and Eskimos. Tourism and sport fishing are almost completely undeveloped. There are profitable commercial fisheries on Great Slave Lake, but elsewhere there is much room for development, particularly in the case of fish like the Arctic char which might find a large international gourmet market. There is also Farley Mowat's interesting suggestion that the Canadian tundra, like the Russian, could provide grazing for large reindeer herds and domesticated muskox to help meet the world shortage of protein. The North is indeed a treasure house, which should be used for the benefit of the whole world, but, like most wealth, its contents have to be husbanded with foresight and care.

Chapter XI

THE FACES OF JANUS

'It is perhaps in her external relations that the greatest opportunities lie,' Barbara Ward said recently of Canada. 'Of all the middle powers, Canada has the greatest resources, the most central position, the finest web of contacts and influence and, relatively speaking, the highest proportion of experts both bilingual and in each language, of any nation of the world. If all these advantages were used not to affirm Canada as a state but to develop Canada as a model-builder, then with the hindsight of history, the latter-day Solons, the creative institution-makers, the citizens who help recreate the world's image of itself might be recognized to have been citizens of Canada and Canada itself an "Athenian" variation on an Atlantic theme.' (*The Canadian Forum*, October, 1968.)

A paragraph later Barbara Ward admits that this is only 'vision', but still argues that Canada might be the first 'international nation' in history, and as such might not only have an unpredictable impact on other states, but might also in the process transform her own political life. I am unaware that her article raised any great response among Canadians, yet it struck, with the child's accuracy that is possible only to a stranger, at the heart of Canada's problems regarding foreign relations. As an independent country Canada might indeed use its advantages to wield an immense influence in the modern world. But at this point two questions immediately rise in one's mind. With the shedding of colonial dependence, did Canada ever become truly independent? If not, is such independence within its power to win?

These are questions that today torment Canadians as much as the problem of national unity, and which throw in doubt this country's claims to strength and influence. Indeed, if one looks at its position by all the normal criteria, Canada stands satisfyingly high among the 120 nations of the world. It is one of the great trading nations, fifth in terms of total foreign commerce, and—in terms of per capita trading—three times as active as the United States. It is sixth among the world's manufacturing nations, and among the top three—below the United States and equal to Sweden—in per capita Gross National Product. At the end of the Second World War it was ranked fourth in influence among the world powers by the pundits of foreign relations; today, with the revival of Western Europe and Japan, it has slipped to ninth place, but, considering that it was regarded as holding fifty-sixth place as recently as 1940, this represents a satisfying progression.

It is also to Canada's advantage that it always has been a hybrid nation in which so many foreign strains and traditions have come together that it is difficult to determine what is distinctively Canadian, until one realizes that the synthesis, after all, is the point of originality. Few nations have been subject to more foreign intrusions in their distant, formative years. Over eastern Canada the French, the British and the people who later arrogated to themselves the name of Americans met in armed conflict from the earliest days of settlement to the end of the war of 1812. There was a time, at the end of the eighteenth century, when four different powers—Spain, Russia, Britain and the United States—sustained conflicting claims over the land that became British Columbia.

Out of this tangle of imperial demands Canada rose as a loosely united nation, but a nation on which the outside world exercised strong centrifugal pulls. Up to Confederation, the colonies which later became Canada were more closely linked economically with Britain and the United States than they were with each other, and Newfoundland retained until the 1940s its European orientation. If the circumstances of the Conquest weakened the connections between the original Canadians and their French motherland, there developed during the nineteenth century a strong triangle of relationships between British North America, Britain and the United States. Politically this was partly due to the fact that after 1812 it became a cardinal point of British foreign policy to avoid the exhausting experience of a war with the United States, but it can equally well be attributed to the economic realities which dictated that as early as the 1850s most Canadian exports went to the United States, even if most Canadian imports still came from Britain.

In spite of the lingering presence of France, to grow brighter on occasion in later years, and in spite of the links that were created through immigration (that with Holland remains especially strong), it has always been within the 'North Atlantic Triangle', as John Bartlet Brebner called it, that Canada has faced the world. Sometimes it has appeared a triangle of hostility, sometimes of friendship (but not without reservation), yet there has never been any escaping the triple relationship. The relative importance of its partners may have changed, with the United States taking over the position of dominance which Britain once assumed by right of power and tradition, but the triangle has persisted and Canada, up to the present, has always been the least of its partners.

The possibility that one day the great triangle may be broken has become during the last decade a matter of urgent discussion among Canadians, for to many of them it is only outside the boundaries of the traditional relationship that real independence can be achieved. And when in the 1960s Canadians talk of independence, what they mean is not independence from Britain, which all regard as long won, but independence from the United States, which many regard as almost lost. This feeling is particularly strong among French Canadians, and—elsewhere—among the intellectuals and the young. When forty-nine Canadian writers, including many of the best, recently put together a volume on the United States entitled *The New Romans*, the majority viewed present American political trends with such disapproval that the demand for disengagement was implied or explicit in about 80 per cent of the contributions. Undoubtedly, during the next decade, the United States will be Canada's great external problem, perhaps even more persistently than Quebec will be its great internal problem.

II

To understand this situation, which conditions Canada's relationship with the rest of the world, we must look back over past relations between Canada and Britain, and Canada and the United States. At a superficial glance, Britain appears as the dominant influence in almost all aspects of Canadian affairs for many years after Confederation. A succession of whiskered Victorian noblemen act as Governors General and create around them little replicas of British court life amid the rigours of Ottawa. Canadian troops go off to British wars, Sir Wilfred

Laurier rides at the head of the colonial prime ministers in the Diamond
Jubilee Parade of 1897, the green bronze statues of Queen Victoria take
up their permanent positions across the land, the shiftless younger sons
of hall and rectory find refuge in the West, the Hudson's Bay Company
continues to rule the North, British capital builds the canals and the
great railways, and in 1914 75 per cent of the foreign investment in
Canada is still British. In 1914, and again in 1939, hundreds of thousands
of Canadians went to fight and often to die on what can only be described as a crusade of loyalty, since on neither occasion did their
country have any immediate reason to fear German aggression.

Yet in reality throughout this period the ties between Britain and
Canada were steadily loosening. As we have already seen, this was due
in part to Canada's evolution towards nationhood. But it was equally
attributable to the fact that there were times during the nineteenth
century when Britain was in an unimperialist mood, and anxious to
shed its dangerous obligations on the North American continent. This
consideration made Britain less intent than Canadians felt it should have
been on defending the territorial margins of British North America.
After the war of 1812, when boundaries might well have been adjusted
to provide easier communication between New Brunswick and Quebec,
Britain accepted the *status quo ante bellum*, and in 1842, under the
Webster-Ashburton Treaty, drew a boundary as far west as the Rockies
which suffered from the fact that the British negotiators never matched
the Americans in obstinacy. The most resented betrayal of Canadian
interests came long after Confederation. In 1903 an international commission met to settle the boundaries of the Alaska Panhandle, the
narrow strip of coastal territory which separates northern British
Columbia from the ocean. Since the original Alaska boundary treaty
had been negotiated between Russia and Britain in 1825, there was a
British representative, Lord Alverstone, on the commission, together
with three Americans and two Canadians. By voting with the Americans, Lord Alverstone deprived Canada of access to the sea, but assured
British friendship with the belligerent regime of Theodore Roosevelt.
This lesson that the senior members of the North Atlantic Triangle
were always willing to sacrifice Canadian interests was not lost on the
Canadians themselves. It increased their desire for a foreign policy
separate from that of Britain, a desire which bore fruit during the 1920s
in a series of crucial decisions by which Canada proclaimed that she was
assuming a separate course in foreign affairs. In 1922, at the time of the

Chanak incident, Canada refused to support Lloyd George's threats to Turkey; in 1924 it independently gave official recognition to the Soviet government in Russia; in 1925 it refused to accept the obligations of the Locarno treaty. Such deliberate manifestations of an independent foreign policy were the prelude to Canada's setting up a full diplomatic service and conducting her own treaties without the intervention of British diplomats.* Long before this, Canada had begun to speak with an independent voice within the Empire, as when, in 1887, despite the traditional Canadian hatred of the Fenians, the federal parliament, with a conservative majority, passed a resolution recommending Home Rule for Ireland.

Yet the progressive shedding of the political and diplomatic vestiges of colonialism, accelerated by Mackenzie King after 1935, did not lead to real independence. It resulted merely in a shift within the North Atlantic Triangle, so that Canada passed from one kind of dependence on Britain to another kind of dependence on the United States. The year of 1940, when King and Roosevelt signed the Odgensburg Agreement of a Permanent Joint Board of Defence, forms as clear a mark as one can find of the final transition from British dominance to American influence. It was the astonishing end of more than a century of Canadian-American relations that had varied between hostility and cool correctness, but had rarely achieved anything that might reasonably be described as cordiality.

III

The confrontation between Canada and the United States, as a phenomenon distinct from the confrontation between Britain and the United States, really began with the War of 1812. During the American War of Independence, there had been an invasion of Canada, but the French Canadians had remained mainly neutral, as had most of the American settlers in Nova Scotia, and it was the British who fought the war on Canadian soil. There was as yet not even the seed of a national spirit in Canada, but this was implanted, ironically enough, by the success of the American rebels, which resulted in the flight of the Loyalists to the Maritimes and Upper Canada. The Loyalists bore an enduring grudge

* Vestiges of British domination remain in the élite structure of the Canadian Ministry of External Affairs, modelled on the British Foreign Office, and in the practice by which, in places where no Canadian representatives are stationed, British consular officials still act in their stead.

for the persecutions they had endured at the hands of their political enemies, and Canadian self-consciousness was born in the first stirrings of anti-Americanism. When the Americans invaded again in 1812 they found that the Canadians—English and French alike—were mostly united against them. It is true that once again the major fighting was done by British regulars, and that the war might have gone very differently if it had not been for the resourcefulness of that gallant and chivalrous officer, Sir Isaac Brock, yet the final defeat of the American invaders was due largely to the steady support given to the British cause by the Canadian militia and by the Indians, led by the great Tecumseh. The war of 1812 left Canadians with a pride at having repelled a numerically superior foe, but also with a bitterness towards the Americans that was not quickly dissolved. To the English the war of 1812 seems a small incident in the great Napoleonic conflict; to Canadians it is one of the major events in their history, and at least one historian has described it as 'our war of independence, because it made Canadians aware of a reason to fight'.

Throughout the nineteenth century a widespread and persistent animosity was nurtured among Americans towards Britain and anything British, including Canada. There is a streak of aggressive arrogance in the American national character which in our generation has been directed beyond North America, with such results as the Vietnam war and the invasion of the Dominican Republic. In the nineteenth century it was concentrated in the sub-continent, and assumed such alarming forms as the wars against Mexico, conducted with no other purpose than to grab as much land as a weak and divided country could be bullied into surrendering. Spectators of these events, most Canadians agreed with the opinion expressed by the *Quebec Gazette* in 1845, that 'no country can be safe in the vicinity of the United States'. Canada was preserved from actual invasion by a display of firmness on the part of the British which persuaded the Americans that a full-scale war might follow if brinksman diplomacy were carried too far, but there were at least six occasions between 1814 and 1867 when war seemed a possibility. In 1838 the sympathizers of the Canadian rebels, Mackenzie and Papineau, tried to create trouble by mounting invasions from American territory. In 1839 militia from Maine and New Brunswick clashed on a disputed borderland in 'the war of Pork and Beans', which fortunately ended in comedy and compromise. In 1846 hostilities seemed very near when Britain and the United States clashed over Oregon, and President

Polk, intoxicated with dreams of Manifest Destiny, issued the warcry 'Fifty-four forty or fight' in support of his claim to the whole of the Pacific coast as far as the southern boundary of Alaska at $54°40^1$. In 1859 there was again an uncomfortable season in the west, over the disputed San Juan Islands in the Gulf of Georgia, while on at least two occasions in the 1860s the resentment of the northern states over Britain's recognition of the Confederacy as a belligerent brought the shadow of war over the Canadas and the Maritimes.

Throughout the nineteenth century all military preparations in Canada—except for those directed against local rebellions—were planned in anticipation that the United States would be the enemy. Such precautions were provoked by the fact that many Americans in important positions openly advocated the seizure of Canadian territory, and, though in the latter part of the nineteenth century the emphasis shifted to peaceful means, annexationist sentiment remained strong well into the twentieth century. Canadians reacted accordingly. As late as 1933, according to the military historian James Eayrs, Defence Scheme No. 1 of the Canadian general staff was 'a war plan the general assumption of which was that there existed a clear and present danger of attack upon the Dominion of Canada by the armed forces of the United States'. (*Contemporary Canada*, ed. Richard H. Leach, 1968.)

But the combination of fear and hatred engendered among Canadians by American aggressiveness was only one aspect of the relationship between the two countries that began to develop during the mid nineteenth century. There was also the example wielded by a dynamic society which was ruthlessly taming the wilderness and building great industrial resources, and whose citizens displayed both destructive fanaticism and self-sacrificing idealism in a fratricidal war that deployed the largest armies since the days of Darius in the most savage conflict since the Thirty Years' War. To some Canadians the vigour which these gigantesque activities exemplified was irresistibly attractive, and they emigrated in tens of thousands to play their part in the American epic. Others dreamed of somehow extending the benefits of American progress to their own country, where development, at least until after the completion of the Canadian Pacific Railway, was markedly slower.

The proposals which early Americanophiles elaborated varied all the way from tariff treaties to annexation. In 1849, at a time of commercial depression, a group of Montreal merchants issued a manifesto calling for annexation, and there were similar movements at the time in the

Maritime provinces, and in the 1860s in British Columbia. American agents were certainly at work on the Red River in 1870 under Riel's provisional government, trying to prepare a seizure of the Northwest. Later, in the 1880s, one of Canada's leading intellectuals, the scholarly journalist Goldwin Smith, former Regius Professor of History at Oxford, became a strong advocate of annexation, though his influence was most evident in the less extreme Commercial Union movement of the same period, which advocated a *zollverein* without political union. More popular with the liberals of the later nineteenth century was the idea of a Reciprocity Treaty, which would allow the duty-free interchange of goods without a formal customs union. A limited treaty of this kind had in fact been signed in 1854, covering the exchange of a wide range of raw materials between the United States and the Province of Canada, but this was eventually revoked by the Americans, and United States tariff policies after the Civil War were opposed to concessions to the new Dominion; it was widely believed in Canada during the 1870s that this rigidity on the part of the Americans was aimed at forcing Canada into the Union by restricting its markets for raw materials. The whole question of tariffs was complicated by the need for a system of protection for Canada's emerging manufacturing industries, and this became the basis of Macdonald's National Policy, which the majority of Canadians supported.

Yet, despite such protectionist policies, and despite the political, sentimental and financial links that remained between Canada and Britain, it was evident, as the nineteenth century drew towards its close, that the two societies north and south of the border were developing strong affinities. Canadians and Americans in that age moved even more freely in and out of each other's countries than they do today; there were no restrictions on residence or work for North Americans on either side of the border, until the 1920s, and this constant interchange led to the emergence of characteristics which Americans and Canadians shared and British did not. A practised ear can tell Canadian from American accents, just as a lexicographer can assemble impressive lists of words which are peculiarly Canadian, but the similarities between the way Americans and English Canadians speak are more impressive than the differences, and speech patterns are evidence of patterns of thought. Despite differences of political structure, there was also a social democratization which both Americans and native-born Canadians shared. Though this was a question of manners rather than of substantial equality, it made for freer and franker forms of intercourse, so that on both sides of the border English formality and English speech, shaped by the most rigid caste structure outside India, were widely resented; by the end of the century immigrants in western Canada began to encounter those celebrated notices—'Englishmen need not apply'—and even today, when Englishmen who have lived twenty or thirty years in Canada come together for a grumbling evening, the refrain one hears is still 'Of course, they hate us.' There were also many material ways in which Canadian and American life tended to approximate. The currencies—both in dollars—were interchangeable, railway equipment and farming methods were similar, newspapers looked alike, American touring companies played in Canadian theatres, architectural styles moved south to north over the border, and the Canadian standard of living moved upward—or slumped downward—in response to the American, though there was always a respectable gap between the two, so that Canada entered the automobile and the telephone eras a little later than its southern neighbour. Even a Canadian's leisure hours were likely to be taken up with sports he shared with his neighbours—baseball, ice-hockey and that ritual mayhem which in North America goes by the name of football—and he read the same books as they did, for by the 1870s competition between English publishers and American publishers who pirated their books had become acute. 'It is idle to suppose that American reprints can be kept out of Canada . . .' commented the editor of the *Toronto Mail* in 1872. 'Costly English editions are unsuited to Canada where everybody reads and every reader owns the books he reads. *Lothair* at £1. 16. stg. may find its way into English circulating libraries and the mansions of the aristocracy; but a dollar edition is what is wanted for Canada.'

It was inevitable that, as Americans became accustomed to the permanence of Canada as a nation on their northern border, as the fervours of Manifest Destiny died down and the resentments bred in 1812 were less bitterly felt, the two countries should grow together in feeling, and one can certainly say with confidence that few ordinary Canadians by the 1930s agreed with the General Staff in regarding the United States as Enemy No. 1. America and Canada turned isolationist at the same period and moved into the Depression together, an experience whose common problems created a great deal of fellow feeling between the two countries. At the end of the 1930s, as Mackenzie King steadily moved Canada out of the British orbit, it seemed natural that a political cordiality should develop between him and Franklin D. Roosevelt of a kind which had never before existed between a Canadian Prime Minister and an American President. The change in the image of the United States from the potential aggressor to the protective friend was signalled by Roosevelt's oral statement in 1938 that the United States would automatically come to the assistance of Canada in the event of aggression.

Roosevelt saw Canada not only as a northern neighbour, but also as a link between Britain, increasingly committed to action in Europe, and his own country, most of whose people were still lost in the dream of isolation. It is significant that the first American move towards involvement in the Second World War should have taken the form of an agreement with the Canadian government—the Ogdensburg Agreement on Common defence—and that the Lease-Lend Agreement with Britain of March 1941 should have been followed immediately, in April, by the Hyde Park Agreement with Canada which, for the rest of the war period, merged the economies of the two countries in the defence effort on 'the general principle that in mobilizing the resources of the continent each country should provide the other with the defense articles which it is best able to produce . . . and production programs should be co-ordinated to this end'. This agreement was reached several months before the United States entered the war; there are many Canadians who believe that it set the seal of their country's vassalage to its gigantic neighbour.★

IV

For if Canada's most acute internal problem is the resentment which French Canadians feel at what they fervently believe is the excessive and unfair domination of their economic and political life by English Canadians, its most acute external problem is the growing consciousness among Canadians of all origins that their country is wealthy and populous enough to be playing an independent role in the world, and that it is prevented from doing so by its peculiar relationship with the

★ Despite the intimacy of contact which began to develop at this point between the two North American countries, Canada, still an international nonentity, was very much the third partner of the North Atlantic Triangle, a situation stressed by the fact that when Churchill and Roosevelt met at Quebec City in 1943 and again in 1944 to discuss the progress of the war, Mackenzie King was allowed to be their host, smiling in photographs, but was not allowed to take part in their meetings.

United States. Conservative nationalists, New Democratic socialists, the descendants of the nineteenth-century Canada First movement who now edit the rabidly chauvinistic journal, *Canadian Dimensions*, and even libertarian internationalists like the writer of these lines are moved to indignation, rebellion and a sense of the urgent need for change when they realize (a) that the most vital sections of Canadian industry have long passed into American control, (b) that Canadian military policies are largely the result of American pressures, (c) that the positive role in foreign relations which Canada began to frame in the 1950s has been completely frustrated by the stigma of association with American adventurism, and (d) that the worst rather than the best of American cultural influences are those which have in recent years become most powerful north of the border. If, during the next few years, Canada's internal divisions are diminished, passions involved in the confrontation between English and French will turn outward, as such passions did in the United States themselves after the Civil War, and the resistance to American influences will give rise to a mass upsurge of nationalist sentiment, an undesirable but perhaps inevitable result of the present situation.

Of this situation most Americans are totally unaware, because of a patronizing attitude towards Canada which merely increases the resentment of their neighbours. To them, as the Canadian poet Douglas le Pan once remarked, Canada is 'a hinterland rather than a country'. While most Canadians live near to the American border, and thus are acutely aware of the proximity of their vast and disturbing neighbour, most Americans live far away from Canada and are hardly aware of its existence as a distinct identity. This, as Canadians are becoming aware, is the reward for having been for thirty years the compliant friend. Americans ignore their friends and pay attention to their enemies. Cuba and Vietnam attract far more attention among the mass of Americans than Canada.

Canada might have been more independent had this indifference among Americans been universal. But there is a minority which has not shared it and these are Americans who count in terms of power—the industrialists and financiers, the generals and the political leaders. The American economic élite has accepted Canada as the most convenient field of business opportunities beyond its own borders. The governing élite has regarded it as a territorial shield against its enemies and a useful adjunct to its diplomatic activities. In the process Canada has lost in terms of freedom but benefited materially. The New Rome, like the Old, rewards those who acquiesce.

In the economic field, up to 1914, American investments in Canada were relatively small—less than a fifth of the British. During the First World War, when British resources were strained to meet military needs, American financiers began to move in, and by the mid 1920s enough capital had flowed north of the border for the United States to usurp the first place among foreign investors which Britain had formerly held. When the Depression called a temporary halt to expansion, Americans were already in control of 20 per cent of Canadian manufacturing industry, either through purchasing native enterprises or through establishing branch plants or subsidiary companies. During and after the Second World War the process was accelerated, and today Americans control well over 50 per cent of Canadian manufacturing industry, and are especially well entrenched in the key sectors. In the automobile industry their control is as high as 97 per cent, in rubber products 91 per cent, in the electrical apparatus industry 67 per cent, in petroleum and natural gas more than 60 per cent, in chemicals 54 per cent, in mining and smelting 52 per cent, in agricultural machinery 52 per cent, and in pulp and paper 35 per cent.

One of the strongest reasons for this proliferation of American control of industries in Canada is the existence of high Canadian tariffs. American firms find it more profitable to open branch plants or to take over Canadian firms than to export goods to Canada, and so, ironically, the protective measures which were intended to foster Canadian industries have merely laid them open to foreign control within their own country. One of the results has been the phenomenon of low productivity in many fields of Canadian industry; branch plants are not expected to compete on the export market with their parent American companies, and so they produce merely for the Canadian market and, with relatively small manufacturing runs, pay lower wages and charge much higher prices than those current in the United States.

But the magnitude of foreign investment is only one aspect of Canadian economic dependence on the United States. As we have seen, trading is three times as important to Canadians as it is to Americans, and a fifth of Canada's Gross National Product is exported. About two-thirds of Canada's international trade is with the United States. 60 per cent of its exports go there (as against less than 20 per cent to Britain) and nearly 70 per cent of its imports come from there (as against less

76. The shoreline at Baker Lake.

77. The meteorologist, Baker Lake.

78. The old town at Yellowknife.

79. Arctic cemetery.

than 10 per cent from Britain). In this arrangement Canada is the more vulnerable partner, since the same figures, read in a different way, amount to 20 per cent of America's exports and about 22 per cent of its imports. The United States would not be profoundly affected by the loss of trade with Canada, though it would find it more difficult to obtain certain essential raw materials. Canada, on the other hand, would suffer drastically from such an eventuality. A demonstration of its vulnerability and the possible consequences was given when the uranium boom came to an end in 1959. From 1942 onwards the mining of uranium was an increasingly active industry in the North, encouraged by the vast purchases of the United States Atomic Energy Commission in Canada, which amounted in 1958 alone to more than $260,000,000. In 1955 the United States had undertaken to continue the existing contracts 'in full force and effect except as modified or revised by mutual agreement', and in the expectations raised by this agreement prospecting went ahead, new mines were opened, and at Elliott Lake in Ontario more than $50,000,000 was invested in the building of a new town, which in 1959 was inhabited by 25,000 people and promised to be the centre of a revival of the old Algoma mining region to the north of Lake Huron. In that year the United States declared unilaterally that it would buy no more Canadian uranium after 1962. Within a year 7,600 out of Elliott Lake's 10,500 miners had left the mushroom city, where expensive houses had become worthless, and today, less than a decade after the peak of its prosperity, Elliott Lake is almost a ghost town, quietly killed by Canadian economic dependence on the United States.

This situation presents Canadians with an intolerable dilemma. Since Canadians themselves are not ready investors in manufacturing industries, it is the flow of American capital over the past twenty years that has kept the economy growing and has steadily raised the Canadian standard of living. Can the necessary flow of capital be maintained without essential control passing out of Canadian hands? Can Canadian control be re-established without American retaliation, which many Canadians fear? There is obviously some justification for this fear; when the Canadian government considered imposing a discriminatory taxation on American magazines which published special Canadian editions—specifically *Time* and *Reader's Digest*—Kennedy's government immediately threatened reprisals, and the Canadian authorities hastily abandoned their proposal.

It is true that other neighbours of the United States have taken decisive action to repossess their economic destinies. Mexico and Cuba immediately come to mind. But these very examples create alarm among Canadians, for it is obvious that Mexicans and Cubans have signally failed to make the same progress in living standards as Canadians have achieved through a subservient economic policy. But are Mexico and Cuba—countries which began in poverty—true examples? Perhaps it might be better to take Sweden and Switzerland, both of which have been able to create healthy economies and high living standards while retaining their independence. At the present stage of Canada's industrial development it should be possible, with a little sacrifice, to re-establish control of the economy. The United States could hardly do more than apply economic sanctions, and these would be largely negated by the fact that Japan and the western European countries are anxious to expand their trade with Canada.

Linked with the present fact of American economic domination is the fear of domination in other fields essential to any nation's free development. Because the economies of the two countries flow together, because Canadian and American businessmen have at least complementary interests, American social organizations have spread widely north of the border. The great fraternities of the middle class—the Shriners, the Kiwanis, the Lions, and all the other inhabitants of the ark of male juvenility—are indistinguishable whether they live north or south of the border, and the Canadian Clubs which channel patriotic sentiment in the larger cities are pale wraiths in comparison with these robust, hearty and inane movements of euphoric backslappers which know no continental frontier. Among women—and I have never been able to discover the reason for it—the boundaries are more sharply etched, and the Imperial Order of the Daughters of the Empire stands in determined confrontation to the Daughters of the American Revolution. I am not prepared to argue that it does a Canadian any harm to make an ass of himself in an American way by parading in a Shriner fez or performing the puerile weekly rituals that embarrass the visiting speaker when he addresses a gathering of Lions or Kiwanis. Internationalism, no matter how naively manifested, is a good thing, provided it does not result in international domination.

Unfortunately, the attempt has in more than one instance been made to use Canadian organizations with international affiliations to establish American domination. In 1967, for example, it was revealed that the

CIA had been subsidizing the Canadian Union of Students. Even more disturbing is the phenomenon of international trade unionism. If this really meant a true internationalism of working men, striving to further their common interests, it would be admirable. In fact, the word 'international' in this context merely means common to Canada and the United States, and implies the domination of the majority of Canadian unions by American officials with little knowledge of the situation of their Canadian members and equally little awareness of their interests. The parallel here between unionists and industrialists is disturbingly close, the freedom of the branch union being no greater than that of the branch factory. The fact that they emerged under the aegis of the Church saved the Quebec unions from American domination; even so 75 per cent of Canadian organized labour belongs to 'international' unions.

Cultural penetration across the border also has its economic aspects, particularly in the field of literature. Most of the paperbacks in Canadian bookstalls and drugstores are American in origin, and so are at least 80 per cent of the periodicals which appear on the magazine racks. This is not due to any deliberate American attempt to dominate Canadian cultural patterns. It is, again, an aspect of the pattern of economic domination. American press runs are immense, and Canadian small; a locally published magazine finds it hard to compete with a foreign magazine whose Canadian sales are a mere fraction of its general circulation, and the same applies to paperback books. Again, even if one ignores the fact that about 40 per cent of Canadians regularly view television shows or hear radio programmes from south of the border, an amazingly large proportion of the time of Canadian broadcasting stations is taken up with programmes originating in the United States, for the simple reason that it is cheaper to rent foreign programmes than to create original ones. French Canadians are largely preserved by language from this intrusion of the highly organized American kitsch industry.

V

But the most serious effect of Canadian economic dependence on the United States is that it encourages the feeling that Canadian and American world interests are identical, and thus contributes to a similar dependence in defence and foreign affairs. Canada is not only committed to the concept of a common continental military policy, embodied in NORAD (North American Air Defence); it is also committed to a common policy of involvement in Europe through NATO (North Atlantic Treaty Organisation). This double alliance with the United States obviously inhibits Canada's independence in foreign affairs, and in practice makes Ottawa subservient to Washington even in areas which are not covered by the provisions of the NORAD and NATO pacts.

It is significant that Canada became a formal ally of the United States in only 1949 with the signing of the NATO pact. The wartime agreement established a coalition against a common enemy, but in the case of both Canada and the United States Germany represented only a possible future threat. It was under the impression that Russia was an immediate threat that Canada became involved as an ally first in NATO and then, in 1957, in the more intimate NORAD pact.

In its whole history, Canada has been aware of only two concrete military threats, from the United States and from Russia, and the threat from Russia has been entirely the product of modern military technology. A hundred years ago, before Canada became a nation or had any interests in the west, Russia had presented a minor threat on the Pacific coast because of its possession of Alaska, but during the Crimean War the British and Russian authorities in this region maintained a gentlemen's agreement of mutual non-aggression, and the Russian presence vanished in 1867 when Alaska was sold to the United States. In 1914 and again in 1941 Russia appeared as a distant ally, and in the years between the two World Wars Canada demonstrated its lack of hostility by recognizing the Soviet regime a decade before the United States.

It was therefore with astonishment and dread that Canadians heard the revelations made in 1945 by Igor Gouzenko, the cipher clerk from the Russian embassy in Ottawa who bought his right to asylum with documents which proved that the Russians had throughout the war been directing a local spy ring in which many Canadians were involved. This was the first of the Russian espionage scandals of the post-war years, and it made Canadians aware of the threat which existed on the other side of the Arctic seas and which year by year grew more urgent with the development of Russian atomic power, of intercontinental aircraft and, eventually, of ballistic missiles. The display of Russian aggressiveness in Europe which culminated in the Czechoslovakian *coup d'état* in 1948 led Canada to seek, in the words of Louis St. Laurent, 'to associate ourselves with other free states in any appropriate collective security arrangement'. Largely through Canadian efforts, the NATO pact was signed in Brussels in 1949 between the North American and West European powers, with the United States, now that Britain's decline was well advanced, as the principal partner. From this alliance, it was a natural course that Canada and the United States should enter into a series of arrangements for the mutual defence of the North American continent against long-distance bombers, and radar warning installations paid for by the American government were established on Canadian soil from 1955 onwards. A natural further conclusion was the NORAD agreement which led to coordination in depth between the air forces of Canada and the United States.

In the beginning few Canadians, except for a tiny minority of pacifists and Communist sympathizers, were disturbed by such arrangements. Russia was a threat in any case, and Canada would stand in the way of any Russian-American war, so that it seemed sensible to have maximum mutual protection. But in twenty years conditions have changed. Canadians have been more aware than Americans of the modifications in the communist world which have diminished the likelihood of Russian aggression; they have also become aware, particularly since the beginning of the war in Vietnam, that American adventures can be as great a danger to world peace as Russian threats. They realize that they have been deceived—perhaps unintentionally—by politicans like Lester Pearson and Paul Martin who have claimed to be able to influence American policy by 'quiet diplomacy'. Furthermore, there has been a growing doubt of the meaningfulness of military defence in the age of ballistic missiles, as well as an increasing desire to explore the possibilities of peace-making by other methods than deterrent alliances. But in seeking a new role Canadians find themselves frustrated by their peculiar relationship with the United States, and here the Canadian mind shows itself strongly divided. Caution still suggests doing nothing to disturb the North American alliance; but there is a deep under-current of feeling that for years has been drawing Canada towards the Third World of military neutrality, international pacification and worldwide economic co-operation.

At this point one must emphasize that Canada has never accepted complete subservience to American policies. Particularly in relations with the Communist nations there have always been token points of difference. Canada and Mexico alone in the Americas have persisted in keeping open the channels of trade with Cuba, using the argument that isolation in the western world will merely strengthen Cuba's Communist tendencies. As a trading nation Canada has also, despite American disapproval, sold large quantities of wheat to a Chinese government which, ironically, she does not yet recognize de jure. It is the failure, up to now, to give this final recognition that shows how limited Canadian diplomatic independence really is. For almost a decade, Canadians of all parties have recognized the realities of the Chinese situation and have regarded recognition of the Peking government as necessary and timely, but none—up to the writing of this book—has taken a step which would deeply disturb Canadian-American relations. In the case of Vietnam, though great numbers of Canadians (probably at least half the population) are by now thoroughly opposed to American action in that country, Canada has officially done nothing more than recommend a cessation of the bombing of the North. Though she is a member of the International Control Commission under the Geneva Agreement, which forbids foreign interference in Vietnamese affairs, her political leaders have never objected to the American presence in South Vietnam. Worse, under an agreement for the exchange of defence materials which was clearly not intended to cover adventures in south-east Asia, Canada has supplied the Americans with military supplies, including large quantities of napalm. Those who advocate a withdrawal from military alliances with the United States use the ambiguity of Canada's role in Vietnam as an example of the moral difficulties which subservience to a major power can involve.

VI

The pattern of Canada's relations outside the American alliance can be lightly sketched. Canada has never joined the Organization of American States, and the only countries of the Americas with whom she has a special relationship outside the United States are the small states of the Caribbean islands. This relationship dates from the days of Nova Scotia's maritime greatness, when one of the regular runs of Bluenose ships was to the Caribbean with timber and dried cod which would be exchanged for sugar, molasses and rum. When these minute nations broke away from the British Empire some of their leaders actually suggested the possibility of becoming politically integrated into the Canadian Confederation, and, though this idea was never extensively explored, Canadians retain an interest in the distant islands and in recent years have actively assisted in their development, through voluntary organizations and through governmental aid.

Foreign aid in general has until recently been more praised than practised in Canada; though Canada in proportion to its population is one of the three most prosperous countries in the world, its foreign-aid contribution, in relation to Gross National Product, stands only four-teenth among the donor nations at 0·59 per cent (1967), and is exceeded by many less prosperous countries, including France at 1·64 per cent, Germany at 1·26 per cent, Britain at 1·10 per cent and Belgium at 1·01 per cent.

The way in which Canada's aid has been given reflects its natural foreign ties. It has been given mainly to the Commonwealth countries of Asia and Africa, with India and Pakistan taking the major share, while a much smaller proportion has been spent, in deference to bicul-tural ideals, in aiding some of the former French colonies in Africa. Canada is a senior member of the Commonwealth, and the great majority of Canadians, even when they are not sentimentally attached to the organization, regard it as of considerable non-military impor-tance, as an alternative grouping to NATO and a means of sustaining contact with the Third World. In the councils of the Commonwealth, Canada has maintained good relations with the African and Asian members, not only because of her aid to them, but also because of the decisive way in which Canada rejected the racialist policies of South Africa.

Canada's relationship with France is at the moment dramatic, but whether it is in reality much deeper than it has been for the past two centuries is still uncertain. For French Canadians in the generation after 1760, France was the motherland that had abandoned them; in 1789, Catholic Quebec, holding on to its traditions to preserve its identity, rejected the Revolution, and for long any loyalties that persisted were to a departed France, still symbolized by the fleurs-de-lis which to this day appear on the provincial flag of Quebec. Nineteenth-century events in France aroused little interest in Quebec. The revolutions of 1830 and 1848 were virtually ignored, and though the people of Quebec City made a holiday in 1856 out of the visit of a warship of the French imperial navy, it was Irishmen and not French Canadians who flocked to the French recruiting office in Montreal when Napoleon III's rule was in peril during the Franco-Prussian war. The deeper loyalties of Quebec were at this time to the Papacy, and several hundred young

French Canadians took part as Papal zouaves in the defence of Rome against the armies of United Italy. The plight of France in two World Wars did not arouse among French Canadians the same sympathies as the plight of England raised among those of British extraction, as was shown by the determined resistance to military service in Quebec, and many of those who in the Second World War had strong feelings about France were inclined to be Pétainist.

The resurgence of French-Canadian nationalist feeling over the past decade, with its emphasis on the unity of French culture, has aroused a genuine interest in re-creating links with France on the cultural and even the political levels. Yet the rapprochement between the Gaullists and successive provincial governments of Quebec may be less close than public statements suggest; there is reason to believe that each side is rather cynically using the other to further its own particular aims. De Gaulle had for long been trying to buy uranium unconditionally from Canada, and had been irked by Ottawa's insistence on a guarantee that it shall not be used for military purposes, so that his support of Quebec independentism may well have been a form of political pressure on the federal government. In exactly the same way, the rulers of Quebec used de Gaulle's calculated indiscretions to promote their own demands for financial arrangements and constitutional changes. Up to the present this situation has had very little effect on Canadian diplomacy, though it is possible that a Canadian decision to move out of NATO and NORAD and adopt a neutralist policy might lead to a degree of reconciliation with France, particularly if Trudeau remains and the present strength of the French-Canadian element in the federal cabinet is maintained.

VII

Outside the Commonwealth and the American alliance, Canada's strongest commitments are to the Unit d Nations, to whose ideals her leaders have always declared an unqualified loyalty. Canada has been an exemplary member of the organization, pay ng its dues and serving extensively in the appropriate agencies and commissions. Its early connection with the development of the atomic bomb made it the only middle power with permanent membership of the United Nations Atomic Energy Commission, and it has enjoyed a special position in subsequent bodies concerned with disarmament. The United Nations role in which Canada has taken most pride is that of peace-broker and peace-keeper. By its role in the Suez crisis of 1956, in which it dissociated itself from the imperialist adventurism of Britain and France, and joined with India in seeking and securing the cessation of hostilities, Canada gained international gratitude and Lester Pearson diplomatic prestige, both of which dimmed considerably in the decade that followed, largely because there were no further occasions on which a middle power could intervene so dramatically and so successfully. Canada went on a large scale into the business of peace-keeping, assuming a leading role in United Nations forces in the Near East and Cyprus, and taking part in United Nations Commissions in Kashmir, Lebanon, West Irian, Yemen, Congo and other crisis spots in a troubled world.

In the end, Canadians have found that it is more difficult to ride two horses in the international arena than in the Calgary Stampede. The role of peace-broker and that of loyal ally of the United States have often seemed contradictory, and in recent years, despite sincere efforts to contain small wars, Canada has found her aid progressively less welcome and her sincerity less accepted. There came a particularly disillusioning moment in May 1967, when Nasser not only asked the United Nations Emergency Force to leave Egyptian territory, but, when Pearson protested, accused him of 'plotting, with the United States, active aggression against all Arabs'. The accusation was patently unjust, and yet in a way it was earned by Canada's inability to understand that the special role it has chosen to play in world affairs could only be carried out effectively by a country of impeccable neutrality. Apart from such wounding blows, Canada has also to learn the equally painful lesson that peace-keeping and peace-making are not the same thing, and that a decade of watching the borders may end merely in the renewal of war if the fundamental issues dividing nations are not settled.

Canada, at the present moment, is faced by difficult choices in foreign policy. Even conservative leaders like Dalton Camp, the doughty king-maker who deposed Diefenbaker and raised Stanfield in his place, have called for a radical decrease in the military establishment so as to provide funds which could be directed towards pacification through economic aid. Prime Minister Trudeau has indicated that Canada's commitments under NATO and NORAD are under review, and the New Democratic Party, which wields a great deal of concealed influence, is already on record as favouring withdrawal from both pacts. The choice, baldly expressed, is between independence and the American alliance, between the positions of India and Britain. There is no doubt that in the past the unwillingness of Britain to evolve a more independent foreign policy has narrowed the alternatives for Canada, but, as the Suez situation showed, there is no reason why Canada should indefinitely continue to follow the same foreign policy as the United Kingdom. India does not, and remains within the Commonwealth. If, as I anticipate, the French Canadians take a wider interest in federal affairs in coming years, they will undoubtedly wield a great influence in the direction of independence. A United States now tending towards the right politically would probably do its best to hinder the transition by economic means, but there are signs that Canadians may be willing to make sacrifices in order to escape from a relationship which they are finding yearly more humiliating. Whether, as some people hope, Canada can assume the leadership of the Third World, is doubtful; it is still, after all, a 'have' country which has shown no great inclination to open its wide spaces to Asian immigrants or to devote a high proportion of its income to helping Asians at home. However, any substantial gesture of independence on Canada's part, such as forthrightly denouncing American actions in Vietnam, would not only hearten other nations which are seeking to rid the world of domination by the great power blocs, but would have a profound effect in encouraging the genuinely liberal elements within the United States. Perhaps the most neighbourly action Canada could perform to America would be to help it to rediscover its own better self, the America of ideals, dreams and fulfilments that has been lost in the jungles of Indo-China.

Chapter XII

AN EYE TO THE FUTURE

~~~~~~

Autumn has passed into winter and the year has turned on its solstice since I began to write this book. It is one of the rare snowy nights of Vancouver, a white night like those one imagines from Dostoevsky's St. Petersburg, with the skeletons of trees which I know to be half a mile away etched clearly against the sky in the light of the whiteness contained between clouds and earth. Yesterday the vast cherry tree that overshadows my house was populated with birds which come there rarely: the varied thrush with his rosy chest and velvety black torque, and the flicker, a semi-woodpecker, whose splendour is revealed only when he flies away to the flash of back and underwings the colour of dying salmon. It will not be long to the sound of geese returning, and the sight of snow retreating up the mountains over the harbour as the streams of spring run down towards the Pacific. But for the moment, with the process of the seasons, the landscape is transformed, and in the same way my own views of Canada and the Canadians have undergone a transformation in the writing of this book. It is not that they have fundamentally changed, any more than the garden which glimmers below me in the snow-light has fundamentally changed. It is rather that in considering the land and the people and their relationship, and the influences that have pressed upon both of them from far and near, I have become more aware than in twenty years of previous living here of the complexities of existence in a land so large and varied. I am conscious of much that has still not been said, of notes unused and ideas unexplored. I am conscious also that I have made many remarks that may annoy and unintentionally wound, but I make them with the privilege of one who stays by choice in the country he at times finds it necessary to criticize.

Now that I draw the threads together, and return to the land and the people at this point of time, with the last third of the century already well on its way, I try to create an image of Canada that will give the quintessence of its changing present, or rather, since the land remains fundamentally the same, of Canadian Everyman, as he exists, if he exists, in the later twentieth century, and of the future that may carry him to the end of the earth's most terrible and most splendid millennium.

Wilfred Laurier once declared, in a burst of politician's optimism, that, if the nineteenth century had been America's century, the twentieth would be Canada's. As his words have commonly been interpreted, they seem absurd; there is no chance—and there was none when Laurier spoke—that Canada will become a great power of the calibre of the United States or Russia, or of Britain at its prime, though it is certainly possible that in a generation it will have become more important than most of the old imperial powers of Western Europe. In another sense, however, this indeed may be Canada's century; her society—shaken as it is—and her people—divided as they are—may approximate more than any other to the kind of people and society which the world must evolve if man is not to leave a globe fit only for the adaptive and resistant legions of the insect world.

In a brilliant and barely recognized essay which appeared in the *Star Weekly* during the centennial year, the novelist Hugh Hood analysed the way in which Canada's peculiar history led it out of the main currents of life in nineteenth-century Europe and America, so that it avoided both romanticism and its political equivalents, Bonapartism—the cult of the hero—and the complementary cult of the masses. 'This country', he declares, 'offers an alternative life style to people who do not want to share in the benefits and deficiencies of mass society.'

The case which Hood puts forward gives point to the differences between Canadians and Americans which I have already observed. The Americans may have imposed their pattern on Canadian industry, they may have dominated its popular culture,* they may have bedevilled its attempts to act as an independent foreign power, but they have not been able to change the fact that during the generations which created

---

* Though in recent years Canada has been throwing up its own charismatic pop singers like Gordon Lightfoot and Leonard Cohen.

in the cities of the west the monolithic and totalitarian elements of modern society, Canada was a country of villages and small towns, where the simplistic values of the Enlightenment, tempered by Jansenist and Calvinist puritanism, still prevailed. Canada has always shown itself impatient of ideologies; even its socialists have been singularly Orwellian in their tendency to prefer decency to dogma; and to this day, when the more negative aspects of its puritan tradition are wearing away, it retains, personified in its political leaders, the emphasis on reason (Pierre Trudeau the rational man), rectitude (Robert Stanfield the upright man) and conscience (Tommy Douglas the justly angry man).

I am embroidering on Hood's argument, but I slip back into his essay to pick up the idea that Canadians are no myth-makers and 'have no concern with the cult of the hero . . .'. One can go farther than that. Canadians do not like heroes, and so they do not have them. They do not even have great men in the accepted sense of the word. There are no Canadian world conquerors, no splendid Canadian corsairs, no Canadian political geniuses, and not a single writer or artist or musician whose name could be mentioned in the same breath as those of Proust, Picasso and Stravinsky. Even those Canadians who have somehow broken into wider skies than their own have left singularly feeble trails; who now thinks of Beaverbrook or Bonar Law as a political genius, or Mary Pickford and Raymond Massey as among the great names in the history of acting? And outside politics and the films, where have Canadians become even temporary world heroes? Marshall McLuhan? A heroic jester! Pierre Elliott Trudeau? A nine days' wonder!

Canadians do not only lack heroes. They lack a really heroic history. Consider what has taken place on Canadian soil. A few minor wars; even the Franco-British conflicts so grandiosely described by Parkman were forest campaigns involving a few thousands of Europeans in impractical parade ground uniforms and of Indians stripped for the battlefield! A few wretched rebellions, with a few hundred participants! A political revolution that was no revolution, created by generations of pragmatists through the endless compromises that have made and are still making the fabric of Confederation!

Canada has its epics, indeed—the great journeys of the fur traders, the building of the Canadian Pacific, the sailing of the *Saint Roch* through the Northwest Passage—but they are epics of endurance, epics of imagination, not in any true sense epics of heroism, and the few recent attempts that have been made to fabricate heroes out of the men who made Canada have usually had the opposite effect; Alexander Mackenzie and Simon Fraser and their kind stand revealed as a set of capable anti-heroes who would endure anything to pave the way for trade but risk nothing at all for the sake of glory. Counting out Wolfe and Brock as born and bred outside the local tradition, there are probably only two men in Canadian history who might fit the pattern of the hero in the high romantic vein. One is Norman Bethune; but it is in China that Bethune is venerated as a hero, not in Canada. The other is the métis military leader in the Northwest Rebellion of 1885, Gabriel Dumont; but it is about Riel the martyr, not Dumont the hero, that plays have recently been proliferating on the stage, television and radio.

This is in the true Canadian vein. Heroes impose on others, and Canadians do not like to be imposed on, but they think they are, and hence they are inclined to identify with martyrs, particularly as martyr-dom is the kind of fate into which even a moral, rational man can be trapped. What most attracts modern Canadians about Louis Riel is not his micro-patriotism as leader of a few thousand people who called themselves a nation, nor his frenzied chiliasm, but the fact that at his trial he preferred condemnation as a man who acted from reasoned motives to acquittal as an inspired lunatic.

The sense of being imposed on is not necessarily a sign of paranoia. It is the natural consequence of the Canadian's universal sense of being one of a minority. If he is a French Canadian or a Mennonite, a Douk-hobor or an Indian, he lives in a state of lifelong vigilance to avoid being absorbed into the English-speaking majority within Canada. And if he is an English-speaking Canadian, he sees himself in a similar state of perpetual vigilance against being absorbed by the even greater majority of Americans among those who speak English in North America. Such attitudes have the virtue that they preclude not only uniformity, but also the fevers of aggressive patriotism. The national voice in Canada is muted. To quote Hugh Hood for a last time, there can never be an Uncanadian Activities Committee because 'Uncanadianism is almost the very definition of Canadianism.'

So the Canadian, bred in a world withdrawn from the nineteenth century but tempered by the twentieth, sees himself as unheroic, but as rational and decent and at times willing to endure and suffer for reason or decency. He is prudent, and therefore he distrusts men of genius as much as heroes and breeds none of these either, but he can also show the daring which comes from the belief that there are few tasks which men of talent and patience cannot accomplish once they try, and so he some-times embarks on tasks at which other men might quail (such as 3,000,000 people setting out to conquer the second biggest country in the world with a single-line railway) and succeeds in them. He is liable to value honesty to the point of dullness, and to distrust European deviousness even in its benevolent forms, which is why Canadian politics lacks finesse and Canadian criminals are uninteresting. Modern Canadians are, on the whole, a gentle people, with more savagery in their institutions—the Criminal Code, the law courts, the police and the penitentiaries—than in their natures; most of Canada's violent crimes are committed by men who have graduated from its prisons. Even the passion of opinions rarely burns high enough to be lethal; the number of Canadians killed in political conflicts is remarkably small. A final virtue which Canadians prize—with a great deal of nostalgia for the past of small towns and pioneer farms—is that of wholesomeness, which is associated with clean-cut physical health; the popularity of Nancy Greene, the open-faced, genial small-town girl from British Columbia who became world skiing champion, exemplifies this parti-cular cult. What pleases most Canadians about Nancy Greene is the fact that she is at once exceptional and ordinary, the champion who is also Canadian Everygirl.

Of course, Canadian Everygirl can also be a teenybopper in a mini-skirt, for implicit in the Canadian resistance to mass-cult is the stress on individualism, always provided it is not too strident. And when we seek for a personification of Canadian Everyman we have to bear this in mind, and also that, while Canada has its minorities which keep to themselves, and its regions which shout their independence, it is a land of increasing mobility, whose young people love to spill over national as well as regional borders, a land where intermarriage is always blur-ring the shifting outlines of majorities and minorities. In 1961 there were 100,000 English Canadians with wives of French origin, and an equal number of French Canadians with wives of British origin. One of the delightfully ironic situations in Canadian ethnic politics was that which obtained just after Trudeau became Prime Minister; half French and half Scottish, he confronted a fervently Francophone Premier of Quebec who carried the name of Daniel Johnson and was of Irish descent.

The Canadian combination of prudence and intelligent daring helps to explain the dramatic events of the past two or three years. Expo '67, revealing aspects of the Canadian mind of which neither Canadians nor outsiders were very much aware, was a combination of imaginative audacity and careful organization, the creation of many men and women of talent whose achievement reached the level of collective genius. The dramatic shifts in the political scene during 1967 and 1968 were essentially similar. Diefenbaker was not deposed, nor was Trudeau elected, merely on an upsurge of feeling. Both events were carefully planned by the groups which carried them out, and they succeeded because they presented to the ordinary Canadians who were delegates at the Party congresses new leaders who fitted the popular idea of what was necessary at the time. In the end Trudeau won, and this was not—as newspaper reporters loved to explain—because he was 'a swinger'. It was rather because, like most modern Canadians, he possessed prudence and a very shrewd sense of the practicable, and combined them with imagination and style. Like most Canadians of the 1960s, he wished to break the shackles on behaviour which belonged to a past when prudence was equated with puritanism, and he did so in his own eccentric but fastidiously correct behaviour as a private citizen and in his efforts to liberate other people from restraints which in our age have become intolerable. Linguistically and racially, he belonged to both founding peoples, and—a rich man—he travelled the world as an impecunious wandering student. He showed his practical abilities as a labour lawyer, demonstrated his powers as an intellectual while masquerading as a playboy, and combined an inner toughness with moods of apparent diffidence; he showed himself an execrable orator, and won his audiences with the charm of a man young after his time and able to make the best of a deceptively vulnerable appearance; he glittered with talents, but the stamp of the heroic, the stigma of genius, were reassuringly absent. Women could see him as a possible partner, men as a cleverer self. More than anything else the reason for Trudeau's success was that he was nearer than other politicians to Canadian Everyman as Canadians saw him in the beginning of their second century.

The unique outlook of the Canadian people, and the shape it imposes on their aspirations and actions, give Canada during the coming generation a great potential role in the world, not as a leader so much as an exemplar, a country conditioned to politics as a process of cooling and reconciliation. On a larger and more positive scale Canada might become what Switzerland failed to be in the past through its negative

80. Voyages ended. Grounded paddlesteamers at Whitehorse.

81. The Palace Grand Theatre at Dawson City.

82. The Indian slum, Whitehorse.

83. High-rise cabins in Whitehorse.

interpretation of neutrality. It is here, perhaps, that Trudeau most exemplifies the collective genius of Canada, in his re-assertion of the perils of nationalism and the importance of federalism, not merely as a method for the internal organization of countries, but also as a principle for the re-structuring of global politics. In the end, we must federalize or perish, just as we must perish if we do not succeed in bridging the gap—not between Communist and non-Communist nations, which is artificial—but between poor and rich nations, which is real. Canada, if it survives the next generation as a united nation, will have done so only through acquiring unique experience in federalism and in political reconciliation. With a foreign policy independent but not withdrawn into isolation, it might conceivably, as Barbara Ward has hinted, lead the world into the era of cool politics that is indispensable to the nuclear age.

Whether many Canadians are aware of such a potential international role is quite another matter. The habitual tendency of the mass of Canadians is to leave foreign affairs in the hands of their government and to pay as little attention as possible—except during international crises—to what is happening beyond their own borders; they feel powerless in a world dominated by great powers, and are not yet convinced that there is an alternative way to settle its problems. Even those who appear to be in rebellion are inclined to view foreign affairs through a narrow-angle lens which sees only Vietnam. A few politicians, a few newspaper editors, a few intellectuals are seriously and vocally concerned over the constructive role Canada might be playing in the world, and a few hundred young people go out each year under schemes like Canadian University Service Overseas to give practical expression to their concern by working in underdeveloped countries. But only a minority in the general population follows them, and this is the real reason why Canada's financial commitment to foreign aid is so shamefully small; there has yet been insufficient pressure to convince successive governments that an ambitious programme of assistance is politically necessary.

Even the argument that foreign aid is a form of peace-making does not convince a generation that has come to dread only the great atomic war unleashed by the super-powers, and depressingly often one hears the neo-isolationist argument: 'Enough problems to take care of at home!' It is an absurd cry in the context where it is most used, for nobody in the world's third wealthiest country—not even the most depressed Indian or métis—is as badly off as hundreds of millions of people in the other half of the world.

Yet those who make this argument are right in the other context of Canada itself. Trudeau and his liberal government, adapting the Kennedy tradition, have set as their aim the Just Society. What I have said already about the differences in wealth and opportunity, and about the links between poverty, ethnic origin and religion, will have shown how far from this ideal Canada still is. And in the narrowest sense of justice, that of the law courts, Canada is still haunted by the ghosts of Dickensian barbarism.

The Canadian Criminal Code, in terms of its penalties, is still one of the most severe in the world, loaded with heavy mandatory sentences; for example, a magistrate cannot give a sentence of less than six months for the mere possession of marijuana. There are provincial laws, outside the Code, which are positively mediaeval in their effects; in Nova Scotia debtors can still be imprisoned, and only recently a Negro was kept in gaol there for five months for not being able to pay a small poll tax levied by the town in which he lived. To the law's severity are added the law's delays. A Toronto man recently spent six weeks in prison, at the end of which the case against him was dropped for lack of evidence. A man in Vancouver was held for four and a half months without any charge ever being laid; he was a material witness in a murder case. An eighteen-year-old youth who could not raise bail of $5,000 was kept in gaol for four months before his trial came up; he was sentenced to two years imprisonment and appealed; his appeal came up seven months later and had to be postponed because the court clerks had not yet prepared a transcript of the original trial; if he is eventually acquitted by the superior court he will have spent at least a year in prison without justification.

There is no provision built into the Canadian Criminal Code for the treatment of first offenders, and the probation system in most Canadian provinces is rudimentary. One of the worst features of the system is the frequency with which offenders—especially Indians—are sent to prison because they cannot pay fines; such a period in jail is often the beginning of a lifetime's career of petty crime. In addition to these injustices, there are some Canadian court procedures which always shock the new-comer. I remember, the first time I attended a magistrate's court, being astonished to see the witnesses sitting in the room throughout the trial and hearing everything that was said before they gave testimony.

Unlike American courts, Canadian courts can and do convict on evidence obtained illegally by the police, while nowhere in Canada are the police obliged—as they are in the United States—to allow a prisoner to consult his lawyer before interrogation.

Canada, in other words, treats its criminals and even those who are wrongly accused of being criminals, according to the harsh rules of a frontier society that has long passed away. Similarly, even when the federal laws on homosexuality, abortion and birth control have been civilized, there will remain a great number of provincial Blue Laws which belong to a past age of puritanism. A man who buys liquor in Saskatchewan must take it home immediately; if he stops on the way, he commits an offence and can be fined or imprisoned. In British Columbia's beer parlours, it is illegal to drink standing up, and one's beer is brought by waiters who must be male and who are known euphemistically as 'beverage dispensers'. It will take a long time and much effort before all these injustices and plain absurdities are worked out of a system designed for a lost past.

Apart from poverty and legal tyranny, which complement each other because it is mainly the poor who run foul of the law, Canada is still faced with vast areas of discontent where its powers of reconciliation will be sorely tried in the generation to come. The French Canadians, the native peoples, the ethnic groups terrified that a rapprochement between those of French and British descent will leave them even farther out in the cold: their problems have been with us long enough for at least a beginning to have been made in solving them. The areas of discrimination against French Canadians are lessening, and the Indian Act is due for changes which will free the treaty tribes from many of the paternalistic restrictions that have prevented their furthur progress. The problems linked with such minorities are fairly tangible and concrete. But there are two areas of discontent which may well prove more intractable precisely because the issues are less easily defined. One is the revolt of the young. The other is the discontent of women which another Royal Commission—that on the Status of Women—has already revealed to be a bubbling crater of grievances.

It is extremely hard and very dangerous to generalize about the rebellion of modern youth, or even to describe as a rebellion what actively involves only a minority, and mainly a middle-class minority at that. Even among the rebels there are those who revolt against authority, and those whose insurrection, more than half consciously, is against the particular kind of sentimental permissiveness which since the days of John Dewey has permeated the educational system and even the homes of North America. There is even a kind of rebellion appearing which turns back into conservatism. The seventeen-year-old son of one of my radical friends defied the family code by joining the Canadian army because he felt his father had failed to teach him the discipline necessary for coping with life. This is still an exceptional kind of stance, and in general youth rebellion in Canada follows lines familiar elsewhere in the western world—the soft line of the flower children and the hard line of the New Leftist militants, still mostly confined to the academic enclaves of universities and colleges.

In almost every large Canadian city there is a hippy district, with its attendant dance-halls, shops and cafés by which the world makes a respectable profit out of those who so self-consciously forsake it, but Vancouver, with its mild climate and its traditional reputation as a lotus-land, is the true Mecca for hippies, as it was for hobos during the Depression. My impression is that the philosophically dedicated hippies, who two years ago waged a notable civil liberties battle against the police over the right to linger in the city's open squares, are retreating into work of various unorthodox kinds, and that the visible part of the movement has now become a fraying fringe of alienated and unhappy adolescents; in other words, the hippy movement, for all its gentleness, has not been able to keep its promise of a paradise for those who abandon social norms. It is for this reason that the hard-liner political rebels among the young, who two years ago seemed submerged by the hippy cult, have regained their influence.

This hard-lining element is most evident among the student activists, inspiring a minority of militants who give extreme expression to the discontent of students in general with the faults that appear in education when universities grow into multiversities. Several Canadian universities have been subjected to demonstrations of non-violent student power, led mainly by members of a militant organization called Students for a Democratic University. If it has as yet achieved few positive results, the movement has at least directed attention to the extent to which the universities in Canada as in the United States have subordinated the interests of true learning to those of industry and the state. So far the student radicals have had little effect on the general political situation in Canada, and they find few supporters off the campuses for their iconoclastic social philosophies, so that their activities seem at times as remote from the real world as other happenings in ivory towers. Even on the campuses most students are still mainly concerned to get degrees which will equip them for the professions, and the majority of the rebels are to be found in the arts faculties where the futures of the students are most unsure. Yet the present limitations of the movement do not mean that it can be dismissed lightly. Many of the criticisms the student activists bring against the Canadian educational system and against the existence of privilege in Canadian society are just, and in putting them the militants speak for vast numbers of less vocal and less openly iconoclastic members of their generation. Even the vote for the Trudeau government, like the movement supporting Eugene McCarthy in the United States, was a manifestation of mingled hope and discontent on the part of youth, and if their wishes are not heeded, in the educational and other fields, this may result in general radicalization of the young which need not necessarily take on a libertarian direction, though I suspect that the natural Canadian tendency to compromise will in fact prevent the emergence of neo-Fascism or neo-Maoism in any serious way. Up to now student insurrections in Canada have taken on neither the magnitude nor the violence they assumed at Berkeley and Columbia, and university authorities have moved in the direction of reforms which might lead to a long-needed revivification of Canadian education.

For there is no doubt that Canada is not yet equipped either academically or technologically or organizationally for the future which the young demand, which is prefigured in the hippy urge towards a leisure society, and which alone can meet the complaints of that battalion of women who came to lay pleas before their Royal Commission, and who revealed, with a unanimity that reached from prostitutes to professors, the hollowness of the myth that Canadian society is a working matriarchy. With a system of higher education only half as effective as that in the United States, with a satellite industry which keeps down the standard of living and perpetuates the great islands of poverty, and with a vassalized foreign policy which demands uneconomic expenditures on useless military establishments, Canada is still far off realizing in material terms the full extent of its independence. It is still a lonely land, waiting the people to repopulate its half-deserted vastnesses; it is still a nation finding its way towards self-recognition. And, if destiny—manifest or otherwise—is a concept that does not fit the Canadian's ironic view of himself and his country, let us say that his is a land which has a task waiting for it in the world and the means to perform it.

As for the will, one may have faith in the rising generation which has given so many forms to its challenges and its quests; in the volunteers who found service and often sickness and sometimes death in the poor lands of the earth; in the creative hippies who have challenged the puritan ethic in the name of joy and love; in the student rebels who are not afraid to risk their middle-class security in taking up as their own the cause of the neglected and forgotten in their own country; in those of the young who seek no extreme way but who have come in their legions to a desire for honesty in life and meaning in work that will not be denied. In their hands Canada will not become a great country, which no Canadian wants, but it may become a humane country; its future not safe or splendid, but as free and audacious as any future can be in this world and time.

CANADIANA—A BOOK LIST

This is not an exhaustive bibliography of Canadiana, or even anything approaching a complete list of the books on Canada I have consulted in preparing this book. It is a selective list aimed at giving the reader an initial insight into the Canadian past and—even more—the Canadian present. For the most part I have chosen recently published books as likely to be available more easily, but there are exceptions. I have listed more books on Canada today than on Canada yesterday, and in dealing with the past I have tried to balance general histories with illuminating accounts of special periods or of particular geographical areas. Finally, I have included a few books on Canadian arts and letters, and some rather personal narratives, like Wallace Stegner's *Wolf Willow* and George Whalley's *The Legend of John Hornby*, which present much of the reality of Canada in the microcosm of one unpublic man's experience.

In addition to the books I have listed, there are Canadian periodicals which anyone interested in the country will find useful, and sometimes more than useful. In literature and the arts these include *Tamarack Review*, *Malahat Review*, *Canadian Literature*, *Artscanada*, *La Vie des Arts* and *Liberté*; in affairs, *Saturday Night* and *Canadian Forum*; for a flavour of popular life, the *Star Weekly* and *Maclean's*. Finally, covering almost every area of Canadian life, there is the *Canadian Annual Review*, edited by John Saywell and published each year by the University of Toronto Press.

BERTON, PIERRE. *Klondike*. Toronto, 1958. *The Smug Minority*. Toronto, 1968.
Book of Canada, A. Ed. William Toye. Toronto, 1962.

BREBNER, JOHN BARTLET. *North Atlantic Triangle.* New York, 1945. *The Explorers of North America.* New York, 1933.

BROWN, J. J. *Ideas in Exile: A History of Canadian Inventors.* Toronto, 1967.

Canada. Ed. Earle Toppings. Berne, 1967.

Canada, a geographical interpretation. Ed. John Warkentin. Toronto, 1968.

Canadian Dualism: La Dualité Canadienne. Ed. Mason Wade. Toronto, 1960.

Canadians, 1867–1967, The. Ed. J. M. S. Careless and R. Craig Brown. Toronto, 1967.

CARELESS, J. M. S. *Canada: a story of Challenge.* Revised edn. Toronto, 1963.

CHADWICK, ST. JOHN. *Newfoundland: Island into Province.* Cambridge, 1967.

Changing Perspectives in Canadian History. Ed. K. A. MacKirdy, Y. F. Zoltvany, John S. Moir. Notre Dame, Indiana, 1967.

CLARK, GERALD. *Canada: The Uneasy Neighbour.* Toronto, 1965.

CLOUTIER, EUGÈNE. *No Passport: A Discovery of Canada.* Toronto, 1968.

Contemporary Canada. Ed. Richard H. Leach. Toronto, 1968.

COOK, RAMSAY. *Canada and the French Canadian Question.* Toronto, 1966.

COOK, RAMSAY, JOHN T. SAYWELL and JOHN C. RICHER. *Canada: A Modern Study.* Toronto, 1963.

CREIGHTON, DONALD. *Dominion of the North.* Revised edn. Toronto, 1967. *John A. Macdonald, the Young Politician.* Toronto, 1952. *John A. Macdonald, the Old Chieftain.* Toronto, 1955. *The Empire of the St. Lawrence.* Toronto, 1956.

DESBARATS, PETER. *The State of Quebec.* Toronto, 1965.

Dominion Bureau of Statistics. *Canada One Hundred, 1876–1967.* Ottawa, 1967.

DRUCKER, PETER. *Indians of the Northwest Coast.* New York, 1955.

DUFF, WILSON. *Arts of the Raven.* Vancouver, 1967.

Early Travellers in Canada. Ed. Gerald Craig. Toronto, 1955.

EAYRS, JAMES. *In Defence of Canada.* 2 vols. Toronto, 1965.

ECCLES, W. J. *Canada under Louis XIV, 1663–1701.* Toronto, 1964. *Frontenac, the Courtier Governor.* Toronto, 1959.

Economic Council of Canada. *The Challenge of Growth and Change.* Ottawa, 1968.

FREUCHEN, PETER. *Book of the Eskimos.* New York, 1961.

FULFORD, ROBERT. *This was Expo.* Toronto, 1968.

GLAZEBROOK, G. P. DE T. *A History of Canadian External Relations,* 2 vols. Revised edn. Toronto, 1966. *A History of Transportation in Canada.* Toronto, 1938.

GOWANS, ALAN. *Building Canada: An Architectural History of Canadian Life.* Toronto, 1966

GRANT, GEORGE. *Lament for a Nation: The Defeat of Canadian Nationalism.* Toronto, 1965.

GRAY, JAMES H. *The Winter Years: The Depression in the Prairies.* Toronto, 1966.

GUILLET, EDWIN C. *The Story of Canadian Roads.* Toronto, 1967.

GWYN, RICHARD. *Smallwood, the Unlikely Revolutionary.* Toronto, 1968.

HARPER, J. RUSSELL. *Painting in Canada: A History.* Toronto, 1966.

HITSMAN, J. MACKAY. *The Incredible War of 1812.* Toronto, 1965.

HOPKINS, E. RUSSELL. *Confederation at the Crossroads: The Canadian Constitution.* Toronto, 1968.

Independent Foreign Policy for Canada, An. Ed. Stephen Clarkson. Toronto, 1968.

INNIS, HAROLD A. *The Fur Trade in Canada.* Revised edn. Toronto, 1956.

JENKINS, KATHLEEN. *Montreal.* New York, 1966.

JULIEN, CLAUDE. *Canada: Europe's Last Chance.* Toronto, 1968.

KESTERTON, W. H. *A History of Journalism in Canada.* Toronto, 1967.

KIERANS, ERIC W. *Challenge of Confidence.* Toronto, 1967.

KROETSCH, ROBERT. *Alberta.* Toronto, 1968.

LÉVESQUE, RENÉ. *An Option for Quebec.* Toronto, 1968.

Literary History of Canada. Ed. Carl F. Klinck. Toronto, 1965.

LOWER, ARTHUR M. *Canadians in the Making.* Toronto, 1958.

MCCOURT, EDWARD. *Saskatchewan.* Toronto, 1968. *The Road Across Canada.* Toronto, 1965.

MACLENNAN, HUGH. *The Colour of Canada.* Toronto, 1967.

MCNAUGHT, KENNETH. *A Prophet in Politics: A Biography of J. S. Woodsworth.* Toronto, 1959.

MCNUTT, W. S. *The Atlantic Provinces: The Emergence of Colonial Society.* Toronto, 1965.

MANNING, E. C. *Political Realignment.* Toronto, 1967.

MOORE, BRIAN. *Canada.* New York, 1967.

MORTON, W. L. *The Critical Years: The Union of British North America, 1857–1873*. Toronto, 1964. *The Kingdom of Canada*. Toronto, 1963. *The Progressive Party in Canada*. Toronto, 1950.

MOWAT, FARLEY. *Canada North*. Toronto, 1967. *Ordeal by Ice*. Toronto, 1960. *People of the Deer*. Toronto, 1967. *The Desperate People*. Toronto, 1959. *The Polar Passion*. Toronto, 1967. *West-Viking*. Toronto, 1965.

MOWATT, FARLEY, and JOHN DE VISSER. *This Rock within the Sea: A Heritage Lost*. Toronto, 1968.

NEATBY, HILDA. *Quebec, the Revolutionary Age: 1760–1791*. Toronto, 1966. *So Little for the Mind: An Indictment of Canadian Education*. Toronto, 1953.

NEWMAN, PETER C. *Renegade in Power: The Diefenbaker Years*. Toronto, 1963. *The Distemper of Our Times: Canadian Politics in Transition, 1963–1968*. Toronto, 1968.

OLESON, TRYGGVI I. *Early Voyages and Northern Approaches, 1000–1632*. Toronto, 1963.

ORMSBY, MARGARET A. *British Columbia: A History*. Toronto, 1958.

PACEY, DESMOND. *Creative Writing in Canada*. Revised edn. Toronto, 1961.

PATMORE, DEREK, and WHITELAW MARJORIE. *Canada*. Toronto, 1967.

Patterns of Canada. Ed. William J. Megill. Toronto, 1967.

Peace River Chronicles. Ed. G. E. Bowes. Vancouver, 1963.

PEACOCK, DONALD. *Journey to Power: The Story of a Canadian Election*. Toronto, 1968.

PHILLIPS, R. A. J. *Canada's North*. Toronto, 1967.

PORTER, JOHN. *Canadian Social Structure: A Statistical Profile*. Toronto, 1967. *The Vertical Mosaic*. Toronto, 1965.

RABY, PETER. *The Stratford Scene, 1958–68*. Toronto, 1968.

RASKY, FRANK. *The Taming of Canada West*. Toronto, 1967.

ROLAND, SOLANGE CHAPUT. *My Country, Canada or Quebec?* Toronto, 1966.

Royal Commission on Bilingualism and Biculturalism. *Preliminary Report*. Ottawa, 1965. *Report. Book I: The Official Languages*. Ottawa, 1967.

SCHULL, JOSEPH. *Laurier*. Toronto, 1965.

SCHWARTZ, MILDRED A. *Public Opinion and Canadian Identity*. Toronto, 1967.

SIEGFRIED, ANDRÉ. *Le Canada: Puissance Internationale*. Paris, 1937. *The Race Question in Canada*. London, 1907.

SLOAN, THOMAS. *Quebec, the Not-So-Quiet Revolution.* Toronto, 1965.

SMITH, A. J. M. *Modern Canadian Verse, in English and French.* Toronto, 1967.

Social Purpose for Canada. Ed. Michael Oliver. Toronto, 1961.

STANLEY, GEORGE F. G. *Louis Riel.* Toronto, 1963. *The Birth of Western Canada.* Toronto, 1936.

STEGNER, WALLACE. *Wolf Willow.* New York, 1962.

STORY, NORAH. *The Oxford Companion to Canadian History and Literature.* Toronto, 1968.

TOUGAS, GÉRARD. *Histoire de la Litterature Canadienne-Française.* Paris, 1960.

TOYE, WILLIAM. *The St. Lawrence.* Toronto, 1959.

TRUDEAU, PIERRE ELLIOTT. *Le Féderalisme et la Société Canadienne-Française.* Montreal, 1967.

TURNER, JOHN N. *Politics of Purpose.* Toronto, 1968.

UNDERHILL, FRANK K. *In Search of Canadian Liberalism.* Toronto, 1960.

WADE, MASON. *The French-Canadian Outlook.* New York, 1946. *The French Canadians, 1760–1967.* 2 vols. Toronto, 1968.

WALLACE, M. STEWART. *The Macmillan Dictionary of Canadian Biography.* Revised edn. 1963.

WARKENTIN, JOHN. *The Western Interior of Canada: A Record of Geographical Discovery.* Toronto, 1964.

WEIR, E. AUSTEN. *The Struggle for National Broadcasting in Canada.* Toronto, 1965.

WHALLEY, GEORGE. *The Legend of John Hornby.* Toronto, 1962.

WILSON, EDMUND. *O Canada.* New York, 1965.

WOODCOCK, GEORGE. *Ravens and Prophets.* London, 1952.

WOODCOCK, GEORGE and IVAN AVAKUMOVIC. *The Doukhobors.* Toronto, 1968. London, 1969.

INDEX